PROVOCATIONS TO READING

Provocations to Reading

J. Hillis Miller and the
Democracy to Come

Edited by

Barbara Cohen and Dragan Kujundžić

FORDHAM UNIVERSITY PRESS

New York 2005

J. Hillis Miller's essay "Three Literary Theorists in Search
of o" is a revised version of a section of his *Zero plus One*
(València: Universitat de València, Biblioteca Javier Coy
d'Estudis nord-americans, 2003). An earlier version of the
de Man section has been published in *Glossalalia*, ed. Julian
Wolfreys (Edinburgh: Edinburgh University Press, 2003).
Copyrights of both belong to J. Hillis Miller.

Jacques Derrida's essay appears here with permission as a
reprint from *Critical Inquiry* in its Spring 2005 volume.

Library of Congress Cataloging-in-Publication Data

Provocations to reading : J. Hillis Miller and the democracy
to come / edited by Barbara Cohen and
Dragan Kujundzic. — 1st ed.
p. cm.
"The essays in this collection grow out of a conference titled
" 'J': Around the work of J. Hillis Miller," held at the
University of California, Irvine, on April 18 and 19 of
2003"—Pref. Includes bibliographical references and index.
ISBN 0-8232-2431-7 (hardcover) — ISBN 0-8232-2432-5
(pbk.) 1. Miller, J. Hillis (Joseph Hillis), 1928– .
2. American literature—History and criticism—Theory, etc.
3. English literature—History and criticism Theory, etc.
4. Criticism—United States—History—20th century.
I. Cohen, Barbara L., 1945– . II. Kujundzic, Dragan,
1959– . III. University of California, Irvine.
PS29.M55P76 2005
810.9—dc22
2005018153

Printed in the United States of America
07 06 05   5 4 3 2 1
First edition

We dedicate this volume with profound gratitude to
J. Hillis Miller: colleague, mentor, and friend.

CONTENTS

Contributors   ix
Preface   xiii
BARBARA COHEN
Introduction
DRAGAN KUJUNDŽIĆ   xv

Part One   THE ETHICS OF READING

1. "J" Is for *Jouissance*
    JULIET FLOWER MACCANNELL   3
2. Broadening the Horizon: On J. Hillis Miller's
    Ananarratology
    DAN SHEN   14
3. Finding the Zumbah: An Analysis of Infelicity in *Speech Acts
    in Literature*
    GLENN ODOM   30
4. Between "the Cup and the Lip": Retroactive Constructions
    of Inheritance in *Our Mutual Friend*
    LARISA TOKMAKOFF CASTILLO   43
5. Hillis's Charity
    JENNIFER H. WILLIAMS   64

Part Two   THE POLITICS OF FORM

6. "J"; or, Hillis *le mal*
    TOM COHEN   83
7. The Afterlife of Judaism: The Zohar, Benjamin, Miller
    HENRY SUSSMAN   95
8. On the Line
    ALEXANDER GELLEY   117
9. War on Terror
    MARC REDFIELD   128

10. American Literary Studies and American Cultural Studies in
the Times of the National Emergency: J's Paradoxes
DONALD PEASE 159

Part Three JUSTICES

11. "J" Is for Just a Minute: It's Miller Time When It Shimmers
PEGGY KAMUF 197

12. Three Literary Theorists in Search of o
J. HILLIS MILLER 210

13. Justices
JACQUES DERRIDA 228

Notes 263

Index 311

LARISA TOKMAKOFF CASTILLO is a PhD candidate in the Department of English at the University of California, Irvine.

BARBARA COHEN is Director of HumaniTech in the School of Humanities at the University of California, Irvine. Her most recent publications include "J. Hillis Miller: In Print and On-line" in *The J. Hillis Miller Reader* (Edinburgh: Edinburgh University Press, 2005) and *Material Events: Paul de Man and the Afterlife of Theory* (Minneapolis: University of Minnesota Press, 2001), which she co-edited.

TOM COHEN is Professor of English at the University at Albany, State University of New York. Among his latest books are: *Hitchcock's Cryptonymies, Vol. 1: Secret Agents*; *Vol. 2: War Machines* (Minneapolis: University of Minnesota Press, 2005); and *Ideology and Inscription: "Cultural Studies": After Benjamin, de Man, and Bakhtin* (Cambridge: Cambridge University Press, 1998).

JACQUES DERRIDA was Director of Studies at the Ecole des hautes études en sciences sociales, Visiting Professor at New York University, and Professor of Humanities at the University of California, Irvine. The most recent of his many publications include: *Béliers* (a translation of this and all his writings on Célan is forthcoming from Fordham University Press); *Le "concept" du 11 septembre*, with Jürgen Habermas and Giovanna Borradori (Paris: Galilée, 2003); in English, *Philosophy in a Time of Terror* (Chicago: University of Chicago Press, 2003); *Chaque fois unique, la fin du monde* (Paris: Galilée, 2003); and in English, *The Work of Mourning* (Chicago: University of Chicago Press, 2001).

ALEXANDER GELLEY is Professor of Comparative Literature at the University of California, Irvine. He was most recently editor of *Unruly Examples: On the Rhetoric of Exemplarity* (Stanford, Calif.: Stanford University Press, 1995).

PEGGY KAMUF is the Marion Frances Chevalier Professor of French and Comparative Literature at the University of Southern California. She is the author of *Book of Addresses* (Stanford, Calif.: Stanford University Press, 2005) and was editor and translator of *Without Alibi*, a collection of Derrida's essays (Stanford, Calif.: Stanford University Press, 2002).

DRAGAN KUJUNDŽIĆ is Associate Professor of Comparative Literature and Director of Russian Studies at the University of California, Irvine. His most recent works are *The Returns of History: Russian Nietzscheans after Modernity* (New York: State University of New York Press, 1997) and *Vospalennyi iazyk* (Language/tongue in heat) (Moscow: Ad Marginem, 2003).

JULIET FLOWER MACCANNELL is Professor Emerita in the Departments of Comparative Literature and English at the University of California, Irvine. She is most recently the author of *The Hysteric's Guide to the Future Female Subject* (Minneapolis: University of Minnesota Press, 2000).

J. HILLIS MILLER is UCI Distinguished Research Professor in the Departments of English and Comparative Literature at the University of California, Irvine. His latest books are *Others* (Princeton, N.J.: Princeton University Press, 2001), *Speech Acts in Literature* (Stanford, Calif.: Stanford University Press, 2002), *On Literature* (New York: Routledge, 2002), and *Zero Plus One* (València: Universitat de València, Biblioteca Javier Coy d'estudis nord-americans, 2003). *Literature as Conduct: Speech Acts in Henry James* is forthcoming from Fordham University Press.

GLENN ODOM is a Ph.D. candidate in the Department of Comparative Literature at the University of California, Irvine.

DONALD PEASE, Professor of English, is Avalon Foundation Chair of the Humanities and Chair of the Liberal Studies Program at Dartmouth College. He is general editor of the Duke University Press series "The New Americanists" and is most recently co-editor of *The Futures of American Studies* (Durham: Duke University Press, 2002).

MARC REDFIELD is Professor of English and holds the John D. and Lillian Maguire Distinguished Chair in the Humanities at Claremont Graduate University. He is the author of *Phantom Formations: Aesthetic Ideology and the Bildungsroman* (Ithaca, NY: Cornell University Press, 1996) and *The Politics of Aesthetics: Nationalism, Gender, Romanticism* (Stanford, Calif.: Stanford University Press, 2003). Most recently he edited a special issue of the on-line journal *Romantic Circles Praxis Series* (*RCPS*), "Legacies of Paul de Man," http://www.rc.umd.edu/praxis/ (forthcoming).

DAN SHEN is Professor of English and Director of the Center for European and American Literatures at Peking [Beijing] University. Her most recent books are *Anglo-American Narrative Theory* (first author) and *Narratology and the Stylistics of Fiction: Literary Stylistics and Fictional Translation*, both published in China.

HENRY SUSSMAN is Julian Park Professor of Comparative Literature at the University at Buffalo, State University of New York and Visiting Professor of German at Yale University. His forthcoming book is *The Task of the Critic: Poetics, Philosophy, and Religion* (New York: Fordham University Press, 2005). He previously co-edited, with Carol Jacobs, *Acts of Narrative* (Stanford, Calif.: Stanford University Press, 2003) and authored *The Aesthetic Contract* (Stanford, Calif.: Stanford University Press, 1997).

JENNIFER H. WILLIAMS received her PhD in English from the University of California, Irvine in 2004. She is Assistant Professor of English at Calvin College.

PREFACE

The essays in this collection grow out of a conference titled "'J': Around the Work of J. Hillis Miller," held at the University of California, Irvine, on April 18 and 19 of 2003. A group of literary scholars and critics assembled to deliver papers on their latest work, running the gamut of study from Victorian literature, to film, to speech acts, to psychoanalysis. Represented among the group were several generations of scholars, spanning graduate students and academics at the beginning, middle, and advanced stages of their careers. What they had in common was that they all were either J. Hillis Miller's students—former and present—most of whom had been formally taught or advised by Miller at Johns Hopkins, Yale, and UC Irvine, or colleagues for whom Hillis Miller has served as friend or mentor. While the essays each have a unique voice in their respective fields, the work of Miller (or "J") resonates in all.

This collection owes a debt of gratitude to many for both the conference and the volume. Dragan Kujundžić and I thank the generous conference cosponsorship by the following at UC Irvine: the Department of English and Comparative Literature; the Humanities Center; Dean Karen Lawrence and the School of Humanities; the UCI Libraries, the Office of Research and Graduate Studies; the University of California Humanities Research Institute; the Program in Russian; and the Critical Theory Institute. We extend our double thanks to Ngũgĩ wa Thiong'o and Colette Atkinson of the International Center for Writing and Translation for their support of the conference and publication. We extend our appreciation to the "J" Graduate Student Steering Committee for their steadfast commitment of time and creative energy. They are John Barton, Jessica Haile, Rachel Meyer, Glenn Odom, Brendan Quigley, Larisa Tokmakoff Castillo, Jennifer Williams, R. John Williams, Catherine Winiarski, and James Zeigler. We would also like to thank Jeffrey Atteberry, John Barton, Megan Becker-Leckrone, Paul Gordon, Sara Guyer, James Kincaid, Carol Jacobs, Steve Miller, W. J. T. Mitchell, Andrzej Warminski, Fengzhen Wang, and James Zeigler for their provocative conference papers and participation. Finally, our thanks go to Larisa Tokmakoff Castillo and to Gina Anzivino, each of whom has played a critical role from the beginning in the realization of this volume.

Our indebtedness to the conference's first keynote speaker, Jacques Derrida, who died too soon and not long after his generous contribution to this volume, is manifold. It is from the core of his paper, built on a reading of a reading (Miller on Gerard Manley Hopkins) and on his deep friendship with J. Hillis Miller, that we derive the core of this collection. It is from the reading, writing, and teaching of J. Hillis Miller that the essays herein find a beginning. It is from his justice that they find their substance.

Barbara Cohen
University of California, Irvine

Dragan Kujundžić

This volume is inspired by the work of J. Hillis Miller (b. 1928). Miller's career and work span more than five decades, some fifty edited volumes and monographs (not counting translations and frequent reprints and editions of his works), and honorary doctorates and teaching positions in dozens of universities in the United States and abroad. Miller's students and colleagues are numerous and form an ever-growing group of outstanding scholars of every generation, as this volume and several others currently in progress amply testify.[1]

From J . . .

The keynote presentations by J. Hillis Miller and Jacques Derrida at the "J" conference mentioned in the Preface serve as the concluding essays in this volume. The last two contributions are a testimony to friendship and mutual recognition and admiration between these two leading American and French critics, longtime friends and colleagues.

The contributors were asked to reflect, at their discretion or choosing, on any aspect related to "J." A number of essays in this volume have taken up explicitly the topic of "J" and made it a theme of their analysis. The inventiveness and humor of " 'J' Is for *Jouissance*" (Juliet Flower MacCannell) or " 'J' Is for Just a Minute: It's Miller Time When It Shimmers" (Peggy Kamuf) are hard to miss. The volume and the papers that were transformed into essays exceeded the occasion and required rethinking and recontextualizing the material, presented here in three different parts. Given the conference's time limitations, the first occasion attempted, something of a sketchy outline, improvised variations on the "J" string. This volume includes new, solicited work and substantially expanded contributions, each opening onto a new line of inquiry, taking as a point of departure or being drawn to, as to a black hole, the work of J. Hillis Miller.

Thus, while Miller's work serves as the gravitational point for the essays included in this volume, co-edited with Barbara Cohen, they also offer

original reflections on numerous topics and disciplines affected or transformed by Miller's work: Lacanian psychoanalysis (Juliet Flower MacCannell), speech-act theory (Glen Odom, Marc Redfield), American Studies
(Donald Pease), film, technical and digital reproducibility (Tom Cohen),
religion and justice (Henry Sussman, Jacques Derrida), "ananarratology"
and theories of narrative (Dan Shen and Alexander Gelley), and literature
(Peggy Kamuf). A number of essays, as will be discussed below, take inspiration from Miller's recent work (particularly the essay on zero that he
presented at the conference and that serves as the penultimate paper in
this volume), but transform it, or are transformed by it, into hybrid investigations that zero in on, among other things, the burning political issue of
the "war on terror" (Donald Pease, Marc Redfield, Tom Cohen).

The work of J. Hillis Miller has its beginnings in studies of Charles
Dickens,[2] but has since grown into an opus that includes Victorian Studies,[3] the "disappearance of God" in English literature (essays on Browning, de Quincy, Emily Brontë, Matthew Arnold, and Gerard Manley
Hopkins),[4] and the ethics of reading (which, as Jacques Derrida points out
in "Justices," should stand metonymically for the entire opus of J. Hillis
Miller's work).[5] Miller has been increasingly (but in fact from the very
beginning) concerned with others and alterity,[6] whether explicitly thema-
tizing that concern, as in *Others*, or exploring the internal differences of
literary texts from themselves, their otherness, as investigated by Miller
under the various titles of ananarratology, Ariadne's thread, the anacolu-
thonic lie, speech acts, prosopopoeia, the performative, fractal mosaics,
and the excess or ethics of reading.

The differences at play in any text or in the act of reading are most
succinctly formulated in the seminal text "The Critic as Host," which, it
could be said, also inaugurated Miller's programmatic contribution to
what has become known as "deconstruction."[7] In "The Critic as Host,"
Miller formulated a far-reaching and productive definition of what the
project of "deconstruction" might entail: "Deconstruction attempts to resist the totalizing and totalitarian tendencies of criticism. It attempts to
resist its own tendencies to come to rest in some sense of mastery over the
work. It resists these in the name of an uneasy joy of interpretation, beyond nihilism, always in movement, a going beyond which remains in
place, as the parasite is outside the door but also always already within,
uncanniest of guests."[8]

Miller has been a "parasite" of deconstruction from the very beginning
of his career: "Contrary to the persistent rumor," writes Derrida in this
volume, "Miller did not convert, one fine day, to deconstruction. The

latter is already at work beginning with his first book. One has just to read." This affinity led him to a more thematic engagement with "theory" in works such as *Speech Acts in Literature*.[9] In *Topographies*, on the other hand, Miller takes up explicitly the question of nationalism in literature and philosophy and announces his ever-increasing interventions in the ways in which ideology underpins a reflection of philosophy. (Miller's criticism of Heidegger's nationalist landscape mythology in *Topographies* is, more than any other I know of, just merciless: both just and merciless.)

Attention to such questions also directs Miller's thinking toward the ways in which various national or other boundaries traverse religious texts in modernity. (See, for example, "Border Crossings, Translating Theory: Ruth.")[10] Miller's interest in modern Jewish philosophy and literature (evident with regard to Walter Benjamin in *The Ethics of Literature*, for example, or in his numerous references to and interpretations of Kafka) and in the transformation of rabbinic literature into one of the sites of European modernism prompted this reflection from Henry Sussman:

> The senior scholars at this colloquium, which . . . I fancifully imagine as a Talmudic conference, were J. Hillis Miller, of course, and Jacques Derrida, the latter of whom came from Paris to deliver a remarkably comprehensive, moving, and realistic overview of and tribute to J. Hillis's contributions. . . . Miller figures as Rabbi Yose and Derrida as Rabbi Eliyahu or Eli.

As for Jacques Derrida, the "J" conference was a context that, apart from an investigation of two "Js," Joseph H. and Kafka's Joseph K., inspired the following reflection: "In the filiation of Joseph the ancient, the Egyptian Jew, the political sage, the interpreter of the dreams and phantasms of sovereigns, I would be tempted to inscribe, so as to pay him the most admiring tribute, all the political, politico-institutional, geopolitical, technopolitical vigilance of Joseph Hillis Miller. This is not talked about enough as I see it" ("Justices").

Some of Miller's latest works return to his early childhood reading (*Swiss Family Robinson*, discussed in *On Literature*),[11] but now assess it through the experience of his own subsequent scholarship, attuned to issues of violence in *Swiss Family Robinson*. (A rare occasion where violence finds its way into a title of J. Hillis Miller's work is in the analysis of this childhood reading). In *On Literature*, Miller rereads *Swiss Family Robinson* (*Alice in Wonderland* as a deconstruction of that text) by turning to issues of imperialism and performs a deconstructive or postcolonial reading of *Robinson Crusoe* and its imperial mythology.

. . . to Z

Miller has lately turned, as he does in this volume, to the problems that zero poses to literature and literary theory. His work, as well, has been said in this volume to have the properties of the "zero" or the properties of the "black hole," both recent titles in Miller's oeuvre and the objects of his reflection. Wherefrom this affinity for zero, black holes, and the perceptiveness with which some of the readers in this volume likened Hillis Miller's own work to the object of his recent studies? What could that mean? Is it possible that Miller's entire body of work, which is celebrated by many and taken as a point of departure and orientation in this volume, amounts to zero? Which is not to say that it amounts to nothing, since zero is more than nothing. But still, for an opus that spans more than five decades and that features numerous books that have taught generations how to read literature, it seems like a provocation on my part, to say the least, to qualify it as amounting to, well, just about zero. There is zero ground, it seems, for that assessment.

A provocation is not necessarily bad. It may be that what teases out words (pro-*vocatio*), is indeed a speech that may be seen in favor of or for, *pro domo*, the object of elocution (*pro*-vocatio). Miller is no doubt the author who has done most to establish, as rigorously as possible, an ethic of reading to which Jacques Derrida, in his "'Le Parjure,' *Perhaps*," declares full allegiance: his "profound agreement about what Hillis Miller calls 'the ethics of reading' and perhaps, if I dare to say it, 'ethics' period."[12]

In the essay included in this volume, Derrida calls Hillis "the Just," and Jennifer H. Williams, justly so, in "Hillis's Charity," declares that "J. Hillis Miller has loved well as a writer, critic, and theorist." In themselves, these admirable statements would seem to contradict profoundly the groundless and irresponsible calculus of zero.

Let me therefore say at once: If this seems like a provocation, it is only to tease out, by way of an impossible introduction to an infinite opus and essays about it, a latent trait in Miller's work noticed by a number of readers in this volume, a trait that may, at this historical conjuncture, prove the most promising. Zero, apart from being the problematic zero degree of all numbers, also stands for multiplication when positioned to the right of any number (that the zero also by that fact obscures and covers), by ten, hundred, thousand, ad infinitum. And it is this capacity to multiply, fractally (to use J. Hillis Miller's term from his "Fractal Proust,"), it is this multiplication toward the infinite, that has to be avowed by anyone who ventures an attempt to "introduce" J. Hillis Miller and his work, as well as the essays presented here, that take Hillis's work as their zero degree of writing.

So, why, out of all rich aspects and venues of Hillis's work, many of them touched upon in this volume, zero in on zero? And, we may also ask ourselves, why a sudden but explicit turn, as in his contribution to this volume, toward the zero by Miller himself? (This turn, in only slightly different context, Donald Pease calls in his essay a "J-turn.") If the opus by J. Hillis Miller does not amount to zero (an opus of which you have seen nothing, yet, for it is a growing body of work demanding to be read, and opening toward the future), it is certainly justifiable to say that, at this point in his career, the author himself zeroes in on zero. It is a zero, in "Three Literary Theorists in Search of o," that crowns, here, J. Hillis Miller's writing.

Let us turn toward Miller's essay (and we do so briefly and without doing justice to it, leaving to the reader to decipher it—"cipher," by the way, is another word for zero—and its innumerable secrets). The three theorists are read by J. Hillis Miller in their own relation to literary language and zero. In Wolfgang Iser's work, literature tends without success to move from zero to one; for Maurice Blanchot, literature is what tends, impossibly, from one toward zero; and for Paul de Man, literature is a trope of zero: a name of the unnamable. In the essay about the three theorists in search of zero we find all the seemingly familiar topoi of Miller's writing: the ethics and allegories of reading, justice, so-called "deconstruction," rhetoric, and a rigorous reflection on the nature of literary language.

But all these concepts invoked by Miller in his essay have undergone a tropological shift, as they do in numerous other contexts, when we feel, as in literature, that in fact they "mean" something slightly different, unnamable, something for which the names of "justice" or "rhetoric" are only catachreses, false names. After these concepts have made a J-turn, they have become unreadable in a manner of referential completion, allegories with ever-incomplete meanings, always under the ethico-political imperative to be read, incessantly, for the future to come, always provocations to reading. Which is another way to say that, after J. Hillis Miller has gone through or is "finished" with zero, no concept, no cultural, theoretical, or political name as we know it and that we take for granted, will ever be the same again.

Miller thematizes this capacity not in relation to his own work, but in relation to allegory, one "version or another of the unknowable: zero, irony, death. . . . These names are all posited pseudonames for that unrepresentable blankness or radical otherness." At this point, where, in the words of Jacques Derrida in "Justices," Hillis's writing traverses "the constative knowledge, the ontotheology, the theology, or the epistemology that serves as presupposition or foundation of the performative stratum of the poetic act," it does so to reveal that they rest only on a foundation in appearance, what Peggy Kamuf focuses on as "shimmering." Below the ground of metaphysics or ontology, there is an abyss, what Derrida calls "a more originary engagement, an initial performative, the preperformative of a pre-event that prepares everything." As he says, Miller's work brings "to light this still more profound foundation," one where everything, as it were, starts from zero. Miller's work prepares all grounded concepts for their not yet read, not yet understood, wholly other future, for which all names have yet to be invented and in which all inaugural events have yet to be performed. In that sense, the aftershocks of Miller's work reorganize everything, while at the same time, nothing has yet happened. Hence, what Jennifer H. Williams identifies as Miller's "tireless seeking to hear again the call of the other and to respond afresh once more." Miller's work, in other words, prepares a democracy to come.

The consequences of these aftershocks are assessed in Donald Pease's essay about American literary studies in light of the state of national emergency that followed the events that are known under the name of "9/ 11"—another catachresis. Pease's argument assesses Miller's intervention in *Black Holes*, in the chapter entitled "Literary Study in the Transnational University," concerning the move from theory to cultural studies and beyond that marked recent decades in the humanities. The insistence on reading, on the always "liminal event presupposed by Miller's reading at every step," as Peggy Kamuf puts it, allows Miller, in Pease's assessment, to remain forever open to what is "other" to the tradition and therefore not reducible to any disciplinary appropriation. Miller's work thus forms its own ground of resistance to all forms of national mythologies, American Studies, or cultural studies.

Because Miller's intervention is always open to the democracy and the other to come, it unsettles the stability of any disciplinary concept while safeguarding the need to intervene, politically, at every moment, on behalf of the other and every other other. After that intervention, academic disciplines and, by the same token, the ruling nationalist ideology, will be not able to sustain their ideological stratagems. It is a testimony to the political urgency of Miller's work that it can be used to unsettle the dominant ideological premises of the disciplines of the humanities. At the same time, by its insistence on the "democracy to come," according to Pease, it "inaugurates a performative praxis, exposes the emergency state as itself the cause of the traumas it has purported to oppose."

In another essay that deals with Miller's *Speech Acts in Literature*, Marc Redfield claims to see a more profound, double ground that unsettles dominant ideological and political formations. Miller's work allows us to see how and why "sovereignty simultaneously exploits and evades the revolutionary force of performative language, casting responsibility for itself onto the terrorist."

The radical capacity of Miller's work to function like a zero or a black hole and to transform the discourses with which it comes into contact finds its apogee and apology in Tom Cohen's " 'J'; or, Hillis *le mal*." Cohen ascribes to the work and figure of Miller the function of a black hole. Behind the benign, avuncular appearance of Hillis "the Just," so well known and beloved by many who have had a chance to be touched by it, lies a capacity to absorb and swallow any discourse that approaches it and to transform it into something radically other. The patient explications for which Miller is justly famous, his minute readings and subtle irony, are only a foil covering a capacity to draw in, irreversibly, a reader or a writer coming into contact with them or within their gravitational pull. Concepts, cultural practices, philosophies, the concept of literature, ethics, justice, as well as attempts to sum up or write *about* this work, are transformed in the encounter with Hillis *le mal* "otherwise": "You will come out otherwise," Cohen says, "you may not even recognize or be recognized."

In her essay, Peggy Kamuf performs the "ethics of reading" called for by J. Hillis Miller. The experience of reading, both her reading of "Bartleby, the Scrivener" and the experience brought about by reading Miller's own work, leads through, if not a zero, then through a "paralysis." This paralysis requires a "leap over the threshold of decision, an event that the narrative economy can never account for." This liminal event forms the (im)possibility of ethics, says Kamuf, and "is presupposed by Miller's reading at every step."

This is also the liminal point of departure for this volume—indeed, its ultimate provocation to reading. It is the point where we would like to trail off and leave to the reader the enjoyment, what J. Hillis Miller might call "the uneasy joy," of reading these essays.

PART ONE

The Ethics of Reading

CHAPTER I

"J" Is for *Jouissance*

Juliet Flower MacCannell

For me, the most valuable aspect of J. Hillis Miller's work is his persistent questioning of literary language in the context of a widely ranging philosophical inquiry into the human (and lately the inhuman) conditions in which literature emerges. From his first to his most recent books, we find Miller courageously confronting whatever the mind has thought unfathomable. Indeed, Hillis Miller is one of the few great critics of our time to underscore precisely the *provocative* element in literature as he unfailingly highlights how literature stirs the mental labor necessary to face whatever threatens to flood the mind and ruin our powers of articulate thought.

In a very early book, *The Disappearance of God*,[1] Miller grapples with the situation of literature in an atheistic world where language has lost its theocratic, theotautological raison d'être. He initially undertook the book, he says, with the "presupposition . . . that all an author's writings form a living unity. . . . Though literature is a form of consciousness, consciousness is always of something. A work of literature is the act whereby a mind takes possession of space, time, nature or other minds. . . . Literature may also express a relation of the self to God" (viii).

With astonishing economy, Miller thus quickly aligns his book with the Husserlian/Pouletian criticism then being embraced in literary studies, with his phenomenological inspiration plain to see in the series of claims being made: that a writer's work is a "living unity," an extension of his or her cogito; that "consciousness is always of"; and that consciousness is a form of world making. Hillis Miller sets these fundamental assumptions down with exemplary grace, violating neither philosophical rigorousness nor refined literary sensibility—nor, for that matter, the profound convictions of faith.

Yet, truth be told, this is not what the book turns out to be about. In it, Miller dauntlessly enters scenes of writing and of art that strongly deny phenomenology's basic claims. He works with texts like Thackeray's *Vanity Fair* to explore "a set of people living without God in their world" (7), and alludes to eras like the Baroque—whose central artistic anxiety is indeed the disappearance of God. The book, that is, develops a profound inquiry less into writing's "living unity" with its author's phenomenological cogito than into the "self" of man minus God. It becomes a much larger exploration of how so lacking a "self" can possibly express itself within such a void.

"Theory," Miller's method thus seems to say, is useful only where it can be tested *against* the strongest demonstrable counterclaims. He of course never "says" this directly: You must read the books he writes, and read them very well, to infer this to be his "method." Yet, it is one of the reasons why reading him gives you an immediate sense of his importance, well beyond the diverse topical concerns he addresses. Miller's books push on to the very heart of whatever at its deepest motivates the *work* of literature: the desire to take artistic command of the power of language.

It is no accident, therefore, that the overriding characteristic of Hillis Miller's oeuvre remains his obvious delight in literary language. Nonetheless, it is also true that Miller has repeatedly elected to read literature through complex philosophies of language that trouble easy assumptions about the stuff—language—of which literature is made. In book after book, he has (quite systematically) analyzed how thinkers like Ludwig Wittgenstein, Jacques Derrida, J. L. Austin, and Paul de Man (to name only the most prominent) confront language. And he has fully and genially accepted the logic of their philosophical conclusions, however much they go against his original grain.

In Paul de Man's case, for example, Miller writes that an "encounter, through rational analysis of the non-rationalizable, the unintelligible, is the main movement of de Man's work throughout."[2] He describes as the one continuous thread tying de Man's earliest to his latest work the sense that "language itself, in its aboriginal and then endlessly iterated appearance, [is] the product of senseless self-positing that is entirely independent of human consciousness."³ If we recall the originating hypothesis of *The Disappearance of God*, we must note that its fundamental assumptions lie here in ruins. Yet in his essay on de Man, Hillis meets, grants recognition to, and, yes, fully concedes the correctness of de Man's challenge to language as a mode of consciousness and as a palliative for the stark abandonment that characterizes the human condition.

Has Hillis simply changed his mind in favor of a new and better "theory"? But asking whether or not he ultimately agrees with de Man is in any case beside the point. The point is rather that Paul de Man evokes in Hillis something he feels he *must respond to*. And by virtue of the deep honesty of his response, Miller will quietly manage to challenge de Man's challenge—and do so in a way that could take place only within *literary* language, the language Miller equates (in an entirely novel way) with its performative power.

Language, de Man had said, was an initially "violent positing" that is "half erased by a device of language that never ceases to partake of the very violence against which it is directed."⁴ Miller carefully restates de Man's theory of the origin of language this way:

> The initial violence, though it engenders history and has material force, is outside of time, punctual, instantaneous. . . . The first violent positing is immediately covered over by the second act of positing that confers meaning on what is a senseless act of power. . . . De Man comes by way of his own special investigation of speech acts as senseless positing back up once more to the borders of unknowability. . . .
>
> I ask now a question that is not at all innocent. Much hangs on the answer. Does de Man's own work have a performative component? At first it would seem not. . . . Nevertheless, it is easy to show that de Man's work, like any text, but in this case in particular ways, has a crucial performative component. One way is in a characteristic locution that appears many times in different forms in de Man's writings. This is the phrase "what we call." (*Speech Acts*, 149)

It turns out then that de Man, too, can be read "literarily" (or "performatively"), as well as "theoretically." Miller's response causes de Man's neutral-seeming position to reenter the *literary* and even *passional* domain. Beyond the elegant exposition of de Man's thought, then, something more is actualized in Hillis Miller's writing here: a truthful and hard-hitting questioning of that thought, produced entirely by setting it squarely into the literary. The relay Hillis engages here strikes me as reading (and our profession) at its finest.

A true critic, for Hillis, is one who answers a "call from the other" with a special sense of critical "responsibility"—a compelling responsibility apparently, because Miller says such calls "impassion me" (ibid., 215), moving him to his own kind of "responsible" writing. What makes his impassioned writing consequential for literature is that the "call" to which Miller passionately responds is a call that often most strongly contradicts his original sense of literature's essence and ethics. This is not to say that theoretical provocation inspires captiousness in him. Rather, it simply stirs him to *respond responsibly*. It urges his *literary* imagination (like Pascal's) beyond the limits of the already imagined, beyond the limits of the imaginable.

I find equally exemplary the way Miller positions his "response" as an ideal "demand from the other," offering it as a *literary* provocation in turn identical in force and appeal to the *theoretical* one posed by the questioner of literature. His critical move effectively "saves" literature from the dustbin of history—to which philosophers and other theorists often readily consign it. The poised prose of Hillis Miller's response removes all the sting of unanswerability that automatically resides in powerful theoretical assertions. By taking on even the most dire philosophical prognostications with such aplomb, Hillis's own critical performance suggests that after each and every apocalypse, "the literary" will still be standing—if only in the form of such responsible questioning.

One such literary moment occurs in *Speech Acts in Literature*, where Hillis makes an observation regarding the ever-looming technological eclipse of literature. He is looking into Proust's image of his grandmother, whom "Marcel" sees as eerily split in two by the invention of the telephone. Hillis writes:

> The introduction of a new technology, while it still overlaps with the old, provides inadvertently, by allowing Marcel to juxtapose the two grandmothers [one telephonically near, the other real and far away], a striking confirmation of Marcel's assertion that we superimpose upon or project into the dark and forever impenetrable shadow that is another person this or that set of assumptions about what is really there. . . . It also provides a way to understand what Derrida means when he says that the new regime of telecommunications will put an end to literature, philosophy, psycho-analysis, and love letters. (*Speech Acts*, 193)

Miller's response to Derrida's pronouncement on the impending "end of literature" heralded by humanity-altering technologies (here the lowly telephone) actually occurs well ahead of the Proust passage. It is the following:

The comment Derrida makes through his protagonist in *The Post Card* [on the end of literature, etc.] . . . is truly frightening, at least to a lover of literature like me . . . the comment arouses in me (by an efficacious performative effect) the passions of anxiety, fear, disgust, disbelief, and perhaps a little secret desire to see what it would be like to live beyond the end of literature, love letters, philosophy, and psychoanalysis. It would be like living beyond the end of the world. (*Speech Acts*, 155–56)

The response evoked in Hillis by Derrida's thesis is not mere conventional anxiety. Anxiety is avowedly part of it, but it is supplemented with a surprising *jubilation*, an unexpected anticipation of incalculably new things to come. It is also supplemented with a remarkable "little secret desire" to know what cannot, according to the current logical arrangement of things, actually be known. The anticipation Hillis articulates here is no shallow, casual or even rational reaction. What Derrida prompts Hillis to desire is no less than to witness strange new events and to do so from the point where the literary writer always stands: at a point "beyond the end of literature." This, I think, is what Hillis means by his sense of being moved (beyond) to respond as a critic when he coins the curious phrase "they impassion me."

A clue to the nature of such a passion appears in his following comment: "In hiding an impenetrable secret, a work of literature is strictly parallel to a love affair: my sense that my beloved hides an unrevealable secret, that she is unfathomably mysterious, arouses in me the passions of love and desire for the beloved" (*Speech Acts*, 160).

It is no accident that this sentence, so close to Plato's *agalma* in spirit, follows almost immediately upon Miller's citation of "one Nicholas White," who visited Mary Queen of Scots and found that meeting her face-to-face stirred in him a feeling of "joy, a lively impetuous passion, and carrieth persuasions to the heart, which moveth all the rest" (159).

A passion, then, even a love for what is unfathomable in an undeniably *other* being. Yet, stubbornly enough, Hillis Miller's passion remains ethical: it "takes the form of a wholly unfulfillable sense of obligation" (*Speech Acts*, 159). What is this obligation that Hillis feels so keenly, and so vainly, toward the other? And what is the precise nature of the other toward whom it is felt? I believe that Hillis senses a duty to respond to a fundamental demand from the other, a demand to participate fully in the astonishingly *joyous* element that secretly sustains all subjects of language—and all literature, as well. I am convinced of this because the one irrepressible element in all of Hillis Miller's work, the one afterimage that marks the traces of each and every passage he delights in, is something that could only be called joy: *jouissance*—the "secret" heart of literature and of its subjects alike.

In Miller's writing, one must agree, any hint that the labor of criticism is dull, tortuous, or humorless mental drudgery is fully banished. His works are characterized by a relish taken in every critical encounter. (Can anyone who has read his essay on J. L. Austin deny that it is a most lively and amusing read?)[5] Even when faced with the darkest implications—of, say, de Man's view of the sheer mechanical random application of power in language, or of Derrida's telecommunicational vision of a future where all familiar discourses disappear—Miller's response is neither dystopian nor utopian: it is simply full of wonder. And what he primarily seems to wonder is how (and not just if) a person (and literature) can find their sea legs in the terrifying eddies and abysses of such darkly profound critical reflections.

I think the very fact that Hillis can engage in such wonder, however muted, however oblique, is essential to the central task of literature, which is to *respond* to the problematic situation in which language has always put the speaking being. Don't philosophical speculations and the critical topoi of our time all seem to be seeking a "final solution" to our problematic relation to language? "Might we at last find a way out of the perplexed situation language has always created for languaged beings?": At the base of contemporary thought from Nietzsche to Heidegger to Derrida and Lacan there lies this radical concern. Hillis Miller's unique way of responding to it suggests the possibility that literary language, because it conveys and deals with *enjoyment*, provokes the very question to which it alone constitutes the only adequate or even possible "responsible response."

There is an important theoretical and not merely experiential reason why I say that the sense of enjoyment (and Hillis's attunement to it) is of paramount importance in literary studies. Consider the history of the conceptual fine-tuning that the term *jouissance*—so eighteenth century, so Kantian—has critically undergone in modern times. Kant and Nietzsche, following Rousseau, knew the secret passion of which Hillis speaks—the not fully fathomable, the not fully bearable experience of *jouissance*. They came to terms with it in one way by means of art. So did Freud and Lacan. A brief look into the vicissitudes of *jouissance* as an increasingly important supplement to human understanding now seems to be in order. Here, again, Hillis Miller's work will take on the virtue of exemplarity.

Jouissance, *or: Enjoy-meant*

The word *jouir* is derived from the Latin *gaudere*: to rejoice, be glad, be joyful, take pleasure, be pleased, delight, to give joy and to receive it; to be in a joyous state, to have free use of for one's lot, to have one's will of a woman, gratification, pleasure, use of something that affords pleasure or advantage, profit, delight, pleasure, sensuality, voluptuousness, usufruct. The French has stronger overtones than the original Latin: an intense sensation, an extraordinary pleasure, a strong delight imparted to another. The medieval French verb *enjoier* was both intransitive and transitive (to enjoy and to give enjoyment to). *Jouissance* today means all these, but it also conveys extreme sexual pleasure.

Enjoyment: a delight in/of/imparted by—by/in/to—one's lover; by/to/ in art. For Kant, subjective delight in art, independent of all purposiveness, is essentially defined the same way the French Enlightenment first thought about *jouissance*: as a good that could be conceived of independently of either possession or of useful purpose. "*Jouir de*" also implied the legal right and the legitimate power to profit from a good, whether one possessed it or not.

Because it also means *usufruct*, or the surplus value of goods, revolutionaries from the eighteenth century onward took up the cause of *jouissance*, the ban on which they believed needed to be lifted. Consider the graffiti on the walls of Paris in May '68: "*Défendu de défendre.*" Capitalism rallied around *jouissance* in the guise of unlimited profit (which is another of its meanings). That both revolution and capitalism rarely failed to take their *jouissance* to excess is also part of the history of the term[6] into which the concept of the excessive is built.

Yet, there is another twist to the significance of *jouissance*, which eventually becomes critically important. *Jouissance* (after Sade, Freud, and Lacan) came to be identified with its apparent opposite: *pain*. A perverse pleasure is to be had it seems, in simply suffering. To suffer is the root meaning of the word *passion*.

Although it is so obviously subjective, by the end of the twentieth century, *jouissance* achieved wide currency in critical literary, psychoanalytic, and philosophical circles. The later twentieth century, like other anticlassical eras, was one that, as Frost put it, did not "like a wall." It rejected the division of the communal from the subjective, of the physical from the psychical, of the intimate from—well, the "extimate." It was therefore quite logical for *jouissance*, which came to prominence in the wake of eighteenth-century revolutions, secularizations, and liberalizations, to make itself once again seen and heard. It was a material concept that could contest fundamentally the distinctions of logic and language: for it is their indivisible remainder (Žižek), their dangerous supplement (Derrida), their accursed share (Bataille). Today, *jouissance* and attendant fantasies have steadily emerged from the unconscious depths to which they were once consigned to claim their place in the heart of the most rational of deliberations. *Jouissance* is completely subjective and individual and it is also something everyone holds in common. As such, it offers a unique vantage point on communal structures that misrecognize, repress, or ban *jouissance*. It provides a much-needed perspective, too, on those ("individualists") who deny its commonality, its shared quality.

In the eighteenth century, *jouissance* began to appear as the horizon that lay beyond every logical distinction. It became a mythical, sublime substance that everyone wanted very much to keep undivided, but in which each nevertheless demanded a fair share. *Jouissance* became the obscure, but true, objective of every intersubjective struggle: Whoever appeared to possess an outsized portion of "it" became a target of envy, although everyone secretly knew that no human subject could ever *really* have "it." Ever since, a transcendental utopia of enjoyment has haunted Western culture as a regulative ideal set over against an increasingly restrictive socioeconomic order. Peoples have rebelled and even murdered in its name. Fredric Jameson, who does not himself use the term much, tells a plausible tale of sensual enjoyments ruined by the accelerated rationalizations of capitalist culture.[7] Yet it is conceptually incorrect (though understandable) to regard *jouissance* nostalgically, as a lost utopia of undivided, Edenic enjoyment in which everyone "once" had a place and a share. *Jouissance* really only represents what each subject deeply feels to be his or her true birthright, something to which each one feels he or she has a fundamental and incontestable right, and yet something of which each has nevertheless been deprived. Neo-Blakean historicist narratives ("binding with briars my joys and desires") of a pure *jouissance* that rational, oedipal, industrial, or capitalist society has exiled fall short of capturing the more enduring flavor of *jouissance*, its permanent subjective allure.

But the story of *jouissance* in the critical/philosophical field today stems from its subjective side, not from the history of its social and economic recognition. That is, from a strictly theoretical as opposed to a historicist viewpoint, *jouissance* is to be defined this way: It is how the subject represents its "real," "true" substance[8] to itself, unconsciously. It is the secret "stuff" that seems to belong uniquely to oneself and to be coextensive with one's being. It is the "essence" of which language, reason, and social constraints all seem to have deprived one. Identified thus with one's being, *jouissance* contrasts starkly with one's meaning, which language alone is capable of promising.

Language makes meaning the chief (and really the sole) recompense for depriving its subjects of being. What's more, language reshapes the original organic logic of life to suit its own, necessarily social bias, for there is no language without society, and there is no society without language, the common coin of social intercourse and exchange. But it does not appear this way to the subject, for whom *jouissance* seems precisely what language can never capture. The logical, social bias of the linguistic signifier is in fact always already subverted, for, in the very act of closing off the avenues for *jouissance*, it inevitably produces an opening for its return. That *jouissance* comes back to the subject (in the unconscious) is, in effect, the return of the native, a resurgence of the antisocial element in the subject, who in practice cannot actually do without a society of his or her fellows (whom, as Kant astutely remarked, the subject cannot bear, but cannot bear to be without). Indeed, all of the more interesting complications and mysteries of human existence are aftereffects of civilization or culture's efforts to contain or expel *jouissance*. *Jouissance* is the remainder of (and over) language (Derrida's *reste*) that makes the subjectively credible claim that it is indeed the very stuff of life itself. *Jouissance* the subjective concept is therefore eminently suited to a postclassical art that defies measured divisions and strict distinctions and favors dissonance and chaos over harmony and balance.

What constitutes perhaps *jouissance's* most pungent enigma for critical thinking in our time is its claim to be able to dispense with language—when it is in fact a creature of the operations of language itself. This is because language (and its correlate, society) must of necessity energize the excess (*jouissance*) they expel, calling it back from the outer darkness and rendering it far stronger and more productive than "natural" satisfaction could ever be. If theorists like Alain Badiou, currently, as Gilles Deleuze formerly, have devoted themselves to trying to occupy the field of *jouissance* (which only ever really opens in poetic space),[9] the fact remains that, however much they or we might wish to banish the linguistic problematic, language alone can convey the hint of so much secret bliss. Language alone can point toward the fulfillment that everywhere else remains beyond our grasp. It does so in an act of promising that becomes itself an other sort of *jouissance*.[10]

Consider for a moment what it would really mean for art to refuse all the dictates designed to create social harmony and instead for it to trespass fundamentally on the distance we place between ourselves and others. Limits are useful for our mental balance and our emotional and social aplomb, limits we should—indeed must—honor. But must art do the same? No. When these limits keep us too safely away from the "forever impenetrable shadow that is another person," they permit us to justify *not responding* to what is moving mysteriously, painfully, and joyfully in that other: *jouissance*, passion, suffering, and fulfillment—even a suffering through fulfillment.

While the sociocultural implications of the enigma of *jouissance*[11] might seem broader then than the strictly "aesthetic" study of works of art and literature allows, scholars should not forget that art first enunciated its emancipation, its autonomy from the utilitarian in Kant's aesthetic delight, which was to be without practical, economic, or moral purposiveness. If we are to grasp why Kantian aesthetics is now being constantly replayed through the modern lens of *jouissance*, we must follow some further twists in the story of its conception. Even now, the image of unalloyed, unfettered, unrestricted *jouissance* is held as a distant prize to compensate for the accelerating fractionalizations of modernity, mythified as a unique substance capable of resuturing everything that has been fragmented. But these pure hypotheses, rooted in unattainable fantasies of wholeness are redoubled (and undone) by the articulated work of art, which has had to grapple with *jouissance*, especially since Kant.

Freud attributed an intensification of what Lacan later called *jouissance* to the work of art. In his essay " 'Civilized' Sexual Morality and Modern Nervousness,"[12] Freud noted that art mysteriously engineers things to permit a certain measure of "direct satisfaction" (enjoyment, *jouissance*) to be experienced through it—a direct satisfaction he judged to be necessary to human life (at least from time to time). Art, he says, is a sublimation that arranges things so that *jouissance* escapes conscious moral censure and unconscious repression alike. This in turn makes art socially valued: It offers a roundabout satisfaction in sublime or sublimated form. Art stages an otherwise unattainable *jouissance*—but the very act of its articulation defuses its socially painful power.[13]

Look back to Kant who, following Rousseau, broke the founding distinction made by Augustine (*De doctrina christiana*) between the *uti* and the *frui*, between the things that are to be used and the things that are to be enjoyed for their own sake (although only, of course, because they bring us nearer to perfect, divine joy). Kant refused the distinction and left us, and especially art, swimming in *jouissance*.

Calling the "intensity of gratification" by the term "enjoyment" in book 1 of *The Analytic of the Beautiful: First Moment*, § 3:30, Kant systematically refused the fulfillment of *jouissance* to beautiful and moral works in which the subject takes pleasure. But in reading Kant, one also has to acknowledge that, quite apart from reasonable subjective pleasure, something else, the *jouissance* that reason and judgment make every effort to set aside, continues to insist—beyond his strenuous division of aesthetic pleasure from "enjoyment." It is as if erecting a wall between them produced the very opposite of the desired result.

Indeed, at more than one point in his writing, Hillis Miller refers to Paul de Man's judgment that Kant's third *Critique* was "an occurrence, something happened there, something occurred—[but] in the whole reception of Kant from then until now, nothing has happened, only regression, nothing has happened at all."[14] What failed to happen is the responsible response Miller calls for: thinkers have failed to respond to (and/or failed to understand the necessity of resisting) the unappeasable appeal or "call" of *jouissance*.

Nevertheless, this very confrontation with *jouissance* is key to truly critical activity, particular in its contemporary instance, with our acute awareness of accelerating linguistic collapse in the face of the *jouissance*'s extravagations. Ardent and arduous efforts to swim that tide characterize the work of J. Hillis Miller. He opens himself to *jouissance* and nurtures the literary language that both harbors it and finds a unique way to deal with it. That he chooses to engage literature's "secret" by offering himself as a model respondent to the call of *jouissance* puts all other sorts of efforts at damage control—such as the policing of language by the politically correct—to shame.

J is for *jouissance*.

CHAPTER 2

Broadening the Horizon:
On J. Hillis Miller's Ananarratology

Dan Shen

Of the influential deconstructive theorists and critics, J. Hillis Miller distinguishes himself by his serious engagement with structuralist narratology. About two decades ago, Miller carried out an influential dialogue with the narratologist Shlomith Rimmon-Kenan in *Poetics Today*,[1] and quite recently, in his *Reading Narrative*, which he calls "a work of ananarratology,"[2] Miller gives a forceful challenge to structuralist narratology in terms of both plot structure and discourse presentation. The present essay argues that ananarratology and narratology, although holding opposite and irreconcilable views on narrative, are to a certain extent complementary to each other. Miller's ananarratology functions to broaden the horizon of narratological investigation by deconstructing, primarily in a philosophical or intertextual way, various conventional or textual boundaries.

The Beginning and Ending of the Narrative Line

The image of the line figures prominently in Miller's narrative theory, constituting the foundation of four of his books: *Ariadne's Thread, Illustration, Topographies,* and *Reading Narrative*. In the ananarratological book

Reading Narrative, Miller conducts an insightful investigation of the beginning and ending of the narrative line by way of deconstructing Aristotle's assumptions of the completeness of action or plot structure. Aristotle, who pioneered the rational investigation of narrative structure, is regarded as the ancient ancestor of structuralist narratology. According to Aristotle,

> Tragedy is an imitation (mimesis) of an action that is complete, and whole, and of a certain magnitude; for there may be a whole that is wanting in magnitude. A whole is that which has a beginning, a middle, and an end. A beginning is that which does not itself follow anything by causal necessity, but after which something naturally is or comes to be. An end, on the contrary, is that which naturally follows some other thing, either by necessity or as a rule, but has nothing following it. A middle is that which follows something as some other thing follows it. A well-constructed plot, therefore, must neither begin nor end at haphazard, but conform to these principles.[3]

Most modern narratives deviate in various ways from this classic conception of a complete, well-constructed plot. Yet it is widely assumed that conventional plots "are unified, moving from a stable beginning through complications to another point of equilibrium at the end."[4] Structuralist investigations of certain kinds of narratives lend support to this view. The thirty-one functions of Russian folktales as identified by Vladimir Propp, a pioneer of structuralist narratology, start with the preparatory function *one of the members of a family absents himself from home*, follow a logical sequence of development, finally end with the resolution *the hero is married and ascends the throne*.[5] But, of course, many narratologists are more interested in investigating "anachrony," that is, the discordance between the two orderings of story and discourse. The most influential investigation on anachrony is offered by Gerard Genette,[6] who discusses narrative beginnings and endings on two different levels: the macrostructural (the whole story) and the microstructural (an episode). In terms of the former, Genette comments on the beginning of the *Iliad* as follows:

> In the eighth line of the *Iliad*, the narrator, having evoked the quarrel between Achilles and Agamemnon that he proclaims as the starting point of his narrative (*ex hou de ta prota*), goes back about ten days to reveal the cause of the quarrel in some 140 retrospective lines (affront to Chryses—Apollo's anger—plague). We know that this beginning *in medias res*, followed by an expository return to an earlier period of time, will become one of the formal topoi of epic.[7]

That cause of the quarrel in an earlier period of time is apparently treated as the stable beginning of the narrative. Discussing the anachrony in "a micronarrative" taken from *Jean Santeuil*, Genette says, "If we take section *A* as the narrative starting point, and therefore as being in an autonomous position, we can obviously define section *B* as retrospective."[8] Significantly, with this conception of the narrative starting point as "autonomous," structuralist narratologists' view of the ontological status of narrative beginnings is essentially the same as that of Aristotle.

This "autonomy" is a mere illusion to Hillis Miller, who points out that:

> [t]he paradox of beginning is that one must have something solidly present and preexistent, some generative source or authority, on which the development of a new story may be based. That antecedent foundation needs in its turn some prior foundation, in an infinite regress. . . . Any beginning in narrative cunningly covers a gap, an absence at the origin. This gap is both outside the textual line as its lack of foundation and visible within it as loose threads of incomplete information raveling out towards the unpresented past. [9]

Miller's deconstruction of the stable beginning is based on philosophical reasoning, which can be backed up by the mimetic tracing of the "unpresented past." The beginning of the action of the play *Oedipus the King* is usually taken to be that Oedipus as a baby is abandoned on Mount Cithaeron as a result of the Delphi oracle, but given the mimetic function of the story, we can trace it back to the marriage of Oedipus's parents, to the growing up of Oedipus's parents, and to the respective marriages of Oedipus's parents' parents, in infinite regress. After all, without his grandparents' giving birth to his parents, Oedipus would not have come into being. Now, suppose that Sophocles had made the characters talk about those events or had made the performance start with those events. Then those "unpresented" past happenings would explicitly become part of the play, and the causal connection would be made manifest. In this light, the beginning of a narrative is merely a joint function of the writer's arbitrary choice (often associated with conventional and social forces) and the artificial boundary of the text, which cannot withstand philosophical reasoning, intertextual linkage, or readers' mimetic inferences.

According to Miller, *Oedipus the King* by no means exemplifies Aristotle's stipulations. For one thing, the play "has no plot in the ordinary sense of the word."[10] "The 'action' the *Oedipus* 'imitates' is made up almost exclusively of people standing around talking or chanting. . . . The play begins long after the real action has taken place."[11] "[T]he real action" of a classical tragedy usually consists of three major parts: the crimes, the discovery, and the reversal of fortune. The play *Oedipus* begins in the middle (after Oedipus has killed his father and slept with his mother), then gradually moves to the discovery of the crimes through Oedipus's own investigative interrogation and other characters' words. This is followed by Jocasta's suicide and Oedipus's self-blinding, which are also revealed by words, rather than performed on the stage. As we know, in drama, there is no mediating narrator, and the real action is either directly performed on the stage or indirectly presented through characters' dialogue and chanting. Characters' words, that is to say, take on a "narrating" function. When watching the performance of *Oedipus*, although the audience members have direct access only to characters' talking or chanting, they are constantly trying to reconstruct from characters' words what Miller calls "the real action" or the "decisive physical occurrences" (*Reading Narrative*, 10) that the play imitates. In terms of the reading of the play text, it may be true that any careful reader will soon get "caught up in the complicated integument of recurrent complex words and figures, puns, double meanings, ironies" (ibid., 12), but most, if not all, readers, when telling the story or plot of *Oedipus the King*, will focus on "the real action," rather than on the words or the language itself.

As regards the end of the play, *Oedipus*, Miller points out that it is not really the end.

> It cannot be said that nothing follows causally from it. Oedipus is left at the end of the play uncertain about what Creon will do with him, whether or not he will allow him to go into exile. We know that something will follow next, as Creon consolidates his new power as king. Moreover, as the audience well knows, the events of this day are only an episode in a story that leads to Oedipus's own death and transfiguration at Colonus, and to the brother battle of his two sons leading to the death of Antigone. (ibid., 11)

This extension of the ending of the narrative line is based on mimetic inference and intertextual relationship. The audience's knowledge of what follows comes from another two tragedies by Sophocles, *Oedipus at Colonus* and *Antigone*. In deconstructing the stability of narrative endings, Miller refers extensively to intertexual relations. Many novels with apparently closed endings are reopened by later creations. For instance, Virginia Woolf's seemingly definitive treatment of the Dalloways in *The Voyage Out* is reopened much later to produce *Mrs. Dalloway*, and Anthony Trollope in the Barset series and in the parliamentary series "reintroduces in later novels characters whose lives have seemingly been entirely closed in earlier novels" (ibid., 53). From this wider perspective, an individual work is "not a self-sufficient whole but an arbitrarily excised segment of a larger action" (ibid., 11).

From Miller's argument we can see that the boundaries of single narratives and various relevant distinctions are merely conventional and rest on nothing solid, that is, on anything that can be considered an origin or foundation. The difference between structuralist narratology and Miller's ananarratology is essentially between an approach that operates within narrative conventions and an approach that is aimed at subverting narrative conventions altogether. Despite the fact that the two approaches are fundamentally incompatible and irreconcilable, there can be perceived some practical complementary relation between the two. Instead of opting for one approach while rejecting the other, it is, in my view, much better to adopt simultaneously what I would like to call "a microstructural" and "a macrodeconstructive" perspective. The former acknowledges textual boundary, but tends to neglect or fail to see the artificiality or arbitrariness of this boundary. The latter encompasses a wider universe as based on theoretical reasoning, intertextual linkage, and mimetic inference. But in stressing that "no narrative can show either its beginning or its ending. It always begins and ends still 'in medias res'" (ibid., 53), the deconstructive position theoretically leaves no room for considering the boundary of single narratives and various relevant distinctions such as that between a closed ending and an open ending. In my view, both perspectives are one-sided, and each needs to be balanced by the other. Or in other words, they are complementary to each other, rather than mutually exclusive.

With the microstructural perspective, it becomes possible to consider the conventional and social forces shaping the beginning and ending of a single narrative. There are various established conventional beginnings, such as "Once upon a time," which function as practical starting points for the narrative. More importantly, the microstructural perspective enables us to perceive the writer's artistry in choosing an appropriate beginning or ending for a story or a narrative text. As we know, a writer's artistry often lies to a great extent in how to begin and end a narrative,[12] in whether / how to start a narrative from the beginning or in medias res, or in whether to give a narrative a closed ending or an open ending. The "closed" ending of a narrative within the boundary of a given text can be described in Miller's words as "the moment of coming full circle in a final revelation at an end point toward which the whole story has been moving."[13] Although the conclusiveness of such an ending is obtainable only within the textual boundary, it should be acknowledged, since such a conclusive ending can, in Miller's words, "fix the characters in a new relation, their final destiny," and cast "retrospective unity over the whole" (ibid., 54), effects that "open" endings would not be able to achieve.

Beginnings and endings are "strategically important points,"[14] and are of vital importance in the reading process. As Marianna Torgovnick puts it, "It is difficult to recall *all* of a work after a completed reading, but climactic moments, dramatic scenes, and beginnings and endings remain in the memory and decisively shape our sense of a novel as a whole."[15] Many narrative theorists have come up with useful classifications of different kinds or aspects of narrative beginnings or endings and have investigated fruitfully their different functions.[16] Only by acknowledging textual boundaries can we proceed to consider the various technical devices involved in beginning and ending a narrative and consider the different degrees of conclusiveness[17] or the difference between narratives that start from the beginning and those that begin in medias res. Indeed, only with textual boundaries can Miller's following observation make sense, "A novel like *Tristram Shandy* breaks the laws of dramatic unity. It lacks the Aristotelian unity of a mimesis copying an action with beginning, middle, and end."[18] If we are to perceive the difference between novels like *Tristram Shandy* and those conforming to traditional patterns of unity, it is surely necessary to preserve the microstructural perspective.

The macrodeconstructive perspective, on the other hand, enables us to break free of textual boundaries, to perceive "the self-serving fictitiousness of most averred originary moments,"[19] and to capture the incessant continuity of fictional events. If we adopt this wider perspective without ignoring the function of textual boundaries, we'll be able to see in a fuller light the writer's artistry, the conventional and social forces involved in shaping narrative beginnings and endings as traditional patterns, and various motivated violations of such patterns. As Miller points out, Western readers' conceptions of narrative and history depend on a shared set of assumptions about causality, unity, origin, and end.[20] Only by going beyond single narratives, can we fully perceive the functioning of the relevant set of shared assumptions.

Narrative inevitably involves an act of selection and so will always point backward and forward from the events it selects. Furthermore, that selection also operates within the space and time of the chosen narrative world—it introduces and complicates some instabilities and tensions rather than others,[21] and of those it generates and complicates, it resolves some, but not all. Miller observes, "Attempts to characterize the fiction of a given period by its commitment to closure or to open-endedness are blocked from the beginning by the impossibility of ever demonstrating for certain whether a given narrative is closed or open. Analysis of endings always leads, if carried far enough, to the paralysis of this inability to be certain whether a story has reached definitive closure."[22] If we adopt the text-oriented microstructural perspective, however, it is possible to tell whether a given narrative is complete in terms of whether the instabilities within the boundary of the text get resolved. If we adopt, instead, the macrodeconstructive perspective and subject narratives to philosophical reasoning, mimetic inference, and intertextual linkage, then no narrative can ever be complete, since it is bound to be a "segment of a larger action" that "always begins and ends still 'in medias res.'"

It is only by adopting both perspectives that one can gain a fuller and more balanced picture of the beginning and ending of the narrative line. While adopting the microstructural perspective, one should not be blind to the artificiality or conventionality of textual boundary as revealed by the macrodeconstructive perspective. Similarly, while adopting the macro-deconstructive perspective, one should not neglect or deny the function of textual boundaries, which is of great importance in literary creation. We can see the joint function of these two perspectives in Miller's words: "The apparently triumphant closure of Elizabeth Gaskell's *Cranford* has its unity quietly broken ten years later by the publication of a continuation story, 'The Cage at Cranford'" (ibid., 53). Only with the microstructural perspective can the "unity" and the "apparently triumphant closure" of *Cranford* come into view, and only by going beyond the single narrative can we perceive the breaking up of that unity.

Free Indirect Discourse and Irony

When it comes to the middle of the narrative line, one common area of interest shared by structuralist narratology and Miller's ananarratology is free indirect discourse. This mode presents a character's speech or thought indirectly (i.e., through the narrator) in the third person and the past tense without a reporting clause (e.g., without "She said that") and often with the character's idiom and subjectivity maintained (e.g., "What a nice gift Mummy had given her!"). To J. Hillis Miller, indirect discourses, especially free indirect discourse,[23] constitute "one of the major resources of story-telling in novels and one of the most important sources of disquieting perturbations in narrative middles."[24]

In Miller's ananarratological book *Reading Narrative*, chapter 13 is entitled "Indirect Discourses and Irony." Miller takes as examples three "innocent-looking passages," one from Anthony Trollope's *The Warden*, one from Elizabeth Gaskell's *Cranford*, one from the opening of Dickens's *Pickwick Papers*. He immediately raises questions after quoting the three passages at length:

> Does not citation perhaps always do violence to what it cites, always quote too little or too much, or too little and too much at once, so that the passage is neither completely free of its paternal or maternal source nor sufficiently provided with it? . . . When I cite these passages here I do something oddly violent to them, or allow them to do something odd and violent to me by citing them. The act of citation changes them radically, if only by putting implicit "scare quotes" around them. They are themselves, however, already, in part at least, citations, already therefore themselves acts of violence. (*Reading Narrative*, 162)

Such questioning and tracing back, which forms a contrast to the sure manner of structuralist narratology, is very characteristic of Miller's investigation, during which he is constantly asking questions, calling into doubt what has been traditionally taken for granted, revealing what has been traditionally hidden.

Focusing on free indirect discourse, Miller asks, "In the passages I have quoted, who is speaking, from what place, and to whom? Whose language or idiom is the reader given, that of the character, that of the narrator, or a mixture of the two? How can one tell, in a given sentence, where the language of the character stops and that of the narrator beings?" (ibid., 164). These questions, however, are also what narratologists usually ask in their analysis of free indirect discourse,[25] a mode that is structurally marked by the combination of the narrator's voice and the character's voice and that is often formally indistinguishable from the narrator's own words (both in the third person, past tense), hence giving rise to ambiguity. While narratologists try their best to answer these questions, Miller's aim is to "try to answer these questions or at least show why they cannot be answered."[26]

Concerning the passage taken from *Cranford*, Miller points out that Mary Smith, the first-person narrator of the novel, speaks at first as a collective "we" for all the Cranford ladies and then uses a comparison that has been made by one of those ladies, Mrs. Forrester: "as if we were living among the Red Indians or the French." This is followed, after a brief introduction to Mrs. Forrester, by a free indirect presentation of this character's "theory," retaining her idiom, her way of speaking. Then there is a shift back to the first person plural, that is, a plunge back into the surrounding collective consciousness of the Cranford ladies as a group: She "being an officer's daughter and widow, we looked up to her opinion, of course." This is followed by the narrator's own thoughts: "Really I do not know how much was true or false in the reports . . . but it seemed to me then. . . ." Finally, this "I" reports, oddly within quotation marks, Miss Matty's words, but transposes them again to the third-person past tense: "Now she did believe that Signor Brunoni was at the bottom of it" (*Reading Narrative*, 165). Miller goes on to comment:

> The passage moves from "we" to "she" to "we" to "I" to another "she," widening and narrowing its focus constantly. The narrative line bends, stretches, vibrates to an invisible blur, divides itself into two, into three, into a multitude that is yet one, comes together again into an unequivocal or univocal one, breaks, begins again, after a brief, almost imperceptible hiatus between paragraphs, and so on throughout the novel.
>
> What is the original line of continuous consciousness (in the sense of the constant presence to itself of a self expressed in a single idiom, an idiolect, a proper language) that is the "source" of all these doublings and redoublings, and to which the line would safely return if its oscillations were allowed to die down or could be damped? The author? The narrator? The author's memory of her younger self and its language? The characters, one by one? The "consciousness of the community," the collective "we"? What attitude does Elizabeth Gaskell have, or does the text have, or are we as readers supposed to have, of judgment, sympathy, understanding, or condescending laughter toward these various imaginary persons? No verifiable answer can be given to these questions. The irony intrinsic to indirect discourse suspends or fragments the narrative line, making it irreducible to any unitary trajectory. (ibid., 165–66)

The two paragraphs seem to be quite different in nature. If the second paragraph is essentially deconstructive, the first is very much structuralist in essence and can be reformulated in structuralist terms:

> The passage moves from "we" to "she" to "we" to "I" to another "she," widening and narrowing its focus constantly. The narrative progresses from the narrator's comment on the community to a comparison given by a character, to a free indirect presentation of that character's words, back to a presentation of the collective consciousness of the Cranford ladies as a

group, then to a presentation of the narrator's present and past thoughts, and finally to a free indirect presentation within quotation marks of another character's words. That is to say, different characters' voices appear in different places of the narration, frequently leading to the copresence of two or more voices or a collective voice. The narrative keeps moving from the narrator's unequivocal or univocal voice to two or more voices or a collective voice, then back to the narrator's single voice, then again to two or more voices, and so on throughout the novel.

This version is essentially similar to Miller's and differs from it only in style or metaphoricalness. As touched on above, in investigating free indirect discourse, structuralist narratologists also pay much attention to the copresence of different voices and to the ambiguity involved. Rimmon-Kenan, for instance, observes: "Even when different segments can ultimately be attributed to identifiable speakers and more so when they cannot, FID [Free Indirect Discourse] enhances the bivocality or polyvocality of the text by bringing into play a plurality of speakers and attitudes (McHale 1978). In cases of an ambiguity concerning the speaker, it also dramatizes the problematic relationship between any utterance and its origin."[27] The "bivocality," "polyvocality," and "ambiguity concerning the speaker" are all structural features of the text. As the first paragraph of Miller's observation indicates, ananarratology and narratology may yield similar results in terms of the description of such textual features. As far as such descriptions are concerned, many narratological distinctions, such as "story and discourse" or "indirect discourse and free indirect discourse," can help enrich the analytical apparatus of ananarratology.

In the second paragraph of Miller's observation, he raises a series of questions, followed by the deconstructive conclusion that "[n]o verifiable answer can be given to these questions." To a narratologist, some questions can be answered: The author is the creator of all the voices in the text, including that of the narrator. But Miller's use of the term "consciousness" may alert us to the fact that the authorial consciousness cannot dominate or control the created consciousnesses, at least in what Mikhail Bakhtin calls dialogic fiction.[28] To a narratologist, the narrator's present voice is what Miller calls the "unequivocal or univocal one." In the passage Miller quotes from *Cranford*, the second paragraph begins with "This last comparison of our nightly state of defence and fortification was made by Mrs. Forrester, whose father had served under General Burgoyne in the American war, and whose husband had fought the French in Spain." In such cases, we only hear the first-person narrator's univocal voice, "to which the line would safely return if its oscillations were allowed to die down." A narratologist would also try his or her best to give an answer to the last question Miller raises, an answer that would be implicitly treated as the most reasonable or feasible interpretation. But to Miller, no answer to this question is verifiable, and any interpretive attempt is bound to fail. As the following section will show, the truth of Miller's opinion may become apparent even to a narratologist when one adopts a macrodeconstructive perspective, going beyond any single interpretive act.

As regards the effect of irony, Miller observes:

> The name for the oscillation of meaning in the passages quoted above is irony. All the passages vibrate with one form or another of radical irony. Since irony is a form of endless looping or feedback, this instability suggests that the interpreter can never go beyond any passage she or he takes as a starting place, if the problem of interpreting it is taken as a serious task. The interpreter remains, rather, suspended interminably in an impossible attempt to still the passage's internal movement so that it can be used as a firm stepping-off place for a more complete journey of interpretation.[29]

To a narratologist, "irony" is just the narrator's (and author's) attitude toward the characters, but to Miller, "irony" is a most important source "of disquieting perturbations" (*Reading Narrative*, 158), subverting the narrative line's stability. In either case, we have at least two divergent voices and consciousnesses (the narrator's and the character's). The final conclusion Miller offers in the above-quoted long comment is that "[t]he irony intrinsic to indirect discourse suspends or fragments the narrative line, making it irreducible to any unitary trajectory." A narratologist, however, will not try to reduce the different voices and consciousnesses to a single one and will not try to "still the passage's internal movement" in the sense of the shift among different voices and different attitudes involved. A narratologist will just take such a movement as an observable textual phenomenon and will proceed from there to interpretation. For Miller, by contrast, "irony" is not chiefly a rhetorical or technical device, but another way of saying that neither individual texts nor indeed the conventions that impart meaning to them have an "origin" or a "foundation." So "the passage's internal movement" is inherently disquieting, making it impossible to have "a firm stepping-off place for a more complete journey of interpretation."

In his specific textual analyses, Miller seems to have taken account of irony both as a rhetorical device and as an inherently subverting force, thus providing a fuller or composite view of the functioning of irony. But of course, Miller's position is still fundamentally deconstructive.

Unreadability/Undecidability versus Ambiguity

To gain a better understanding of the relation between Miller's ananarratology and structuralist narratology, it is worthwhile examining the debate between Miller and Rimmon-Kenan as mentioned at the beginning of this essay. Rimmon-Kenan argues that ambiguity is the coexistence of incompatible, yet equally tenable readings,[30] a phenomenon peculiar to certain literary texts. Such ambiguity "remains a relatively closed phenomenon," "restricting uncertainty to an insoluble oscillation between the opposed members of a logical contradiction ('a' and 'not a')."[31] Miller observes, "Rimmon's definition of ambiguity, however, is too rational, too 'canny,' too much an attempt to reduce the *mise en abyme* of any literary work, for example the novels and stories of James, to a logical scheme. The multiple ambiguous readings of James's fictions are not merely alternative possibilities. They are intertwined with one another in a system of unreadability, each possibility generating the others in unstilled oscillation."[32] To this, Rimmon-Kenan replies: "An analysis of the so-called undecidability of a strictly ambiguous text is bound to yield the exclusive disjuncts from which it hoped to escape. Thus many of Miller's statements about James's story fall into a pattern of mutual exclusives."[33] This point Miller concedes: "No doubt my formulations, like all such formulations, are as Shlomith Rimmon-Kenan says, too decisive, too canny, to avoid being recuperable within such concepts as 'ambiguity' or 'binary opposition.' Precisely. This was the point I was making. My own discourse is necessarily an example of the failure I was trying to identify. Had I succeeded I would have failed."[34]

Although both Rimmon-Kenan and Miller claim that their debate is one between the structuralist approach and the deconstructive approach,[35] it seems to me that they are very much on the same ground concerning the challenge to univocality. In interpreting a literary text, a structuralist critic tends to try to offer what he or she takes to be the most feasible or reasonable interpretation. Seeking for incompatible interpretations is very much a deconstructive practice. More strictly speaking, the aim of deconstruction is to force a text to yield a meaning or conclusion that contradicts what the text ostensibly holds. This textual practice in turn serves to undermine all metaphysical pretensions to origins, foundations, Truth, and so on. This position, of course, is not shared by Rimmon-Kenan, who, however, stresses that "ambiguity renders choice impossible and frustrates the reader's expectations of a univocal, definitive meaning."[36] This is very much in line with Miller's definition of "undecidability," which is:

an effect of the play of figure, concept, and narrative in the work that forbids unification or any making whole. This effect the words of the work
impose on the reader, so that it is not a result of "reader response." Moreover, instead of rich plurisignificance, the notion of undecidability names
the presence in a text of two or more incompatible or contradictory meanings that imply one another or are intertwined with one another, but which
may by no means be felt or named as a unified totality.[37]

The point that Rimmon-Kenan and Miller are of the same stance in
terms of the challenge to univocality may gain confirmation from the following statement by Miller, which appeared about two decades later, in
Reading Narrative:

> As Shlomith Rimmon-Kenan has argued, the meaning of ["The Figure in
> the Carpet"] is fundamentally undecidable. It presents clues or narrative
> details supporting two or more incompatible readings. Therefore all those
> critics who have presented "monological" readings of it have fallen into a
> trap set not only by the story itself, in its presentation of an enigma that
> invites definitive clarification, but also by the critic's false presupposition
> that each good work of literature should have a single, logically unified
> meaning. (*Reading Narrative*, 97)

This concession to Rimmon-Kenan's position here is not surprising, since
her position was half deconstructive, or at least bore a superficial resemblance to deconstruction.

The structuralist nature of Rimmon-Kenan's approach is neatly sum-
marized by Miller.[38] First, the critical discourse of Rimmon-Kenan is
structuralist in "tone" or "style," for it is reasoned, more or less abstract,
given to diagrams and formulations, aiming at mastering texts in a scientific way. The goal of deconstruction is very different from this. As Miller
puts it:

> Deconstruction wants to show the impossibility of mastery, for example
> the impossibility of mastering James's story by means of such an analytical
> tool as Shlomith Rimmon-Kenan's concept of ambiguity. No doubt it fails
> in this. To that moment of failure it has sometimes given the names 'un-
> readability' or 'undecidability,' which, as Shlomith Rimmon-Kenan notes,
> are to be defined as the impossibility of deciding whether or not a given
> text is 'decidable' or 'determinate' in meaning, that is, 'readable' according
> to a common definition of readablility.[39]

To see things in perspective, it seems necessary to adopt again at once
a microstructural and a macrodeconstructive perspective. In terms of one

individual interpretive act of a text in one specific context, deconstructive critics and broad-minded structuralist critics such as Rimmon-Kenan may offer just two or three incompatible readings. A typical case in point is Miller's interpretation of Elizabeth Gaskell's *Cranford*:

> On the one hand, if the reader generalizes from the story of the Reverend Jenkyns and his children, *Cranford* is the story of a failure of masculine authority. . . . On the other hand, the theme of male authority's failure in Cranford gradually turns into its opposite. The narrative solves the problem of how to get the men back into Cranford before it is too late. Seen from this aspect, the theme of *Cranford* is the failure of women to do without men, the failure of feminine authority. . . . Both of these possibilities of reading are supported by the text. What *Cranford* means is not one or the other but their incompatible copresence.[40]

Although Miller's interpretation sounds very much as decisive and canny as that of Rimmon-Kenan, the underlying assumptions are very different. To Rimmon-Kenan, the ambiguity she has found in James's text is the meaning of the text, whereas to Miller, every interpretation is bound to fail to capture the meaning of the undecidable text.

If we adopt a macrodeconstructive perspective, the undecidability or indeterminacy of the meaning of a text may become clearly perceptible: A text means different things in relation to different interpreters in different contexts. Thus, no interpreter can claim that his or her interpretation in one specific context succeeds in capturing the meaning of the text. It is not my intention to equate the undecidability of a text with the difference in readers, however, as is the case with perspectivism. As the above quotation indicates, Miller has clearly distinguished his textual undecidability from perspectivism, which asserts that since each reader brings something different to a text, the text has a different meaning for each reader, and hence that meaning is undecidable. The point I would like to make is that the divergence in readers' interpretations is not only a result of the difference in readers and/or sociohistorical contexts, but also a function of the undecidability or indeterminacy of the meaning of the verbal text itself, a point that can be backed up by the vast literature of deconstructive theory of language.[41] In other words, the divergence in interpretations indicates that the meaning of a text may forever evade mastery and that a critic, however competent, cannot come to *the* correct understanding of a text, not with the help of scientific inquiry or whatever other means.

If we adopt such a macrodeconstructive perspective, the interpretation of a novel by James will not be limited to two or three fixed incompatible readings. Because of the characteristics of human understanding, one critic in one interpretive act will usually come up with no more than two or three incompatible readings, but as time goes on and as interpreters and contexts change, there may emerge numerous different incompatible readings, going beyond the binary opposition "a" and "not a." With this wider perspective, the notion of ambiguity can be replaced by unreadability. When it comes to a specific interpretive act in a specific context, however, Rimmon-Kenan's notion of ambiguity is a workable term in describing the findings of the critic, but it is important to bear in mind that any interpretive act in a specific context is bound to fail to master the meaning of the text, which may remain forever indeterminable, as the continuous debates about the meaning of James's works testify.

The second structuralist feature of Rimmon-Kenan's argument concerns the scope of the texts that are ambiguous or unreadable. To Rimmon-Kenan, "ambiguity" characterizes some, not all, literary texts (e.g., works by James, Gogol, Robbe-Grillet, Sarraute, Pynchon), but Miller, in replacing "ambiguity" with "unreadability," regards "unreadability" as a feature of all texts. Rimmon-Kenan says "one drawback of such a procedure is that it would ultimately do away with the *differentia specifica* of these texts I labelled ambiguous."[42] Miller observes:

> this desire to limit the range of ambiguity and to make it a tool of differentiation is one of the features Shlomith Rimmon-Kenan's procedure shares with that of "science." . . . Shlomith Rimmon-Kenan mentions "James, Gogol, Robbe-Grillet, Sarraute, Pynchon" as writers of ambiguous texts in her sense, i.e., "the 'conjunction' of exclusive disjuncts." It will be noted that all these writers are novelists and that all are "modern." Her study of James is supported by received notions of genre and of literary history which it does not on the whole challenge. This is one of the ways it belongs to that vast collective "scientific" enterprise. The "notion" or "experience" of unreadability, on the other hand, since it is a feature in one way or another of all literary works, tends to break down such generic and historical distinctions.[43]

If we adopt a macrodeconstructive perspective, the meaning of a literary text is indeterminable or unreadable in the sense as discussed above. But if we adopt a microstructural perspective and focus on specific interpretive acts, we may find that some texts tend to yield mutually incompatible readings, while some others may lead to less ambiguous interpretations. But as Miller's admirable interpretation of the ambiguity in *Cranford* shows, ambiguity is not a feature peculiar to modern texts.

That is to say, we should keep our minds open as to the scope of ambiguous texts.

I have been commenting on J. Hillis Miller's ananarratology from the position and perspective of a structuralist narratologist. While I'm fully aware that the basic philosophical grounds of the two approaches are inherently incompatible and irreconcilable, they do seem to a certain extent complementary to each other, especially when we adopt at once a macrodeconstructive and a microstructural perspective. With his characteristic open-mindedness, J. Hillis Miller has perceived the value in narratologists' description of the complexities of narrative structure.[44] On the other hand, if narratologists can keep their own minds open, they are very likely to find reading Miller's works an enriching and perspective-broadening experience. As the present study indicates, Miller's ananarratology functions to broaden the critical and intellectual horizon by questioning what has been conventionally taken for granted, by revealing what has been traditionally hidden, and by deconstructing various conventional or traditional boundaries.

CHAPTER 3

Finding the Zumbah: An Analysis of Infelicity in *Speech Acts in Literature*

Glenn Odom

J. Hillis Miller begins *Speech Acts in Literature* with a promise to show the problematic nature of speech acts in and as literature.[1] Miller's promise has the authorization that comes, as he says "by being 'appointed,' by being given 'tenure,' by having [his] seminar description approved beforehand" (4). My critique of his work carries with it none of Miller's authority. I am perhaps, to cite Miller's citation of J. L. Austin, "Some Low Type" (or perhaps I should say " 'some low type,' " since this is my citation of Miller's citation of Austin, a graduate student attempting to claim authority (ibid.). As such, I will borrow extensively from both the style and words of other theorists in the hopes that some authorization will wear off on me.

This, too, is a promise. It is a promise whose fulfillment begins with the word "Zumbah," but will not end until the Zumbah has been found. My promise, uttered as it is with recognition of my lack of authority, nevertheless creates a responsibility, an obligation to discuss something academically. As Miller points out, the words of others, however polished they may be, cannot bear an individual's responsibility for a discussion: "I am responsible for what I say even if what I say stems from an attempt to say again as exactly as I can just what Derrida says, with abundant citation to prove he said just that" (85). Thus, both Miller and I accept a share of responsibility that stems from the explicit promises we make and the implied promise of an academic text. The significant difference is that, unlike Miller, I keep the promise of my text.

I will use Miller's promises, broken and otherwise, as structural guideposts. This, too, is a promise. Structural guideposts to what? The issue of responsibility and ethics in speech-act theory as manifested in Miller's promised discussion of literature. Miller himself raises the question of ethics repeatedly in his text, but he does not turn this question toward his own writing. If we assume that Miller's book constitutes a form of accurate knowledge on the subject of speech-act theory, then it is paradoxical that Miller's rhetorical structure can produce this knowledge. Of course Miller's misdirections serve to illustrate one of his primary points about the theory he is interrogating: The broken promises, lies, humor, acting, and a whole list of things that, according to Austin, would invalidate the performativity of a certain utterance are illocutionary acts and have a perlocutionary effect of their own.[2] In other words, Miller's speech that acts does so precisely because of the broken promises, not in spite of them. But what actions do his speech make?

Nothing Is Not a Speech Act: The Limits of Austin

In his first chapter, Miller's stated (rhetorically questioned) aim is not to discuss literature, but rather to explicate "how does . . . doubleness or duplicity . . . function in Austin's case?" (*Speech Acts in Literature*, 6). Which doubleness and duplicity? All of it, starting with the title of Austin's text, *How to Do Things with Words*.[3] Miller points out that Austin's text does not meet all of the implied promises in its title: Austin himself makes similar assertions throughout his own lectures. As Miller notes, in Austin's terms, a speech act is "felicitous" if it is not only "efficacious in doing something," but efficacious in "doing what you want it to do, what you intend it to do" (*Speech Acts in Literature*, 18). From the very beginning, however, Austin confesses that while his work is "true," it is only so "at least in parts," and yet this implied infelicity does not stop Austin's text from having an inaugural performative effect.[4] Structurally, Austin's text sets up a series of rules that establish the groundwork of a performative utterance. Austin warns that "If we sin against any one (or more) of these six rules, our performative utterance will be (in one way or another) unhappy" (ibid., 15). For Austin, "unhappy" performatives either are not implemented at all, or are "void or without effect" (ibid., 16). He quickly

points out that "'without effect' does not here mean 'without consequence, results, effects.'" Austin establishes that performative utterances
can fail and still have an effect, "but we shall *not* have done the purported
act" (ibid., 17).

Miller, however, "sins" against several of Austin's rules, but still keeps
his central contract with the reader. Miller's promise of a discussion of
literature is not felicitous in Austin's sense of the term, or not immediately
so, and yet the reader does in fact leave the text with a greater understanding of speech acts in literature. It is as if the groom in one of Austin's
examples has said "I do," but hasn't "done," but then, miraculously, is still
married, carried through by the power of the initial performative act.
Miller keeps the form of his initial promise only by using a series of infelicitous secondary promises. Despite Austin's claim to have catalogued the
intricacies of the performative utterance, Austin is of little help in answering this dilemma, and by the end of his third lecture, Austin is already
reconsidering his initial categories, being "uncertain which is involved in
a particular case" (*How to Do Things with Words*, 38).

Not only does Miller point out the explicit "rueful confession of failure" and infelicitous speech acts in Austin's text (*Speech Acts in Literature*,
13), but he cites other, more subtle inconsistencies, as well. For instance,
in a section on Austin's ideology, Miller points out the "vein of misogyny"
(ibid., 50) that runs through Austin's text. Indeed Austin's examples can
support such a reading because the women in his lecture are constantly
either being wished "to the bottom of the sea" or are making infelicitous
utterances. Miller proceeds to comment that Austin is also culturally and
temporally biased. The character of the author, then, has influenced both
the form and the effect of the text, which, according to Miller is a performative one. Austin, as a white male, has created a text that reinforces the
"vision of history which has the white male English philosopher, not surprisingly, as its evolutionary goal" (ibid., 58).

What, then, should be done with this knowledge? Miller recognizes
that Austin uses this ideology to reinforce a "precious" social structure, to
make possible a judgment of an utterance's ability to keep law and order
(*Speech Acts in Literature*, 55). Miller concludes though, that since such
misogyny and reinforcement of the social order fall outside the definitions
provided by Austin for felicitous speech acts, but nonetheless function as
performatives, Austin "is more subversive of law and order than supportive
of them" due to the internal conflicts of the text (ibid., 59).

What effect, then, does Miller's own subtext have? Miller peppers his
texts with brief biographical details and conjures up a distinctive voice

through his writing. With these tools, Miller begs us to question his own writing in the same way he questioned Austin's. But to what effect? Bias did not stop Austin's text from having an effect, any more than doubts on the part of the groom stop a wedding from being performed, but the perlocutionary effects do not match Austin's intent. It is unclear at that moment in the text whether or not any underlying bias on the part of the author will in fact lead to this subversion of law and order. If such were the case, all writing and all rhetoric, even in pursuit of truth, must be subversive. It follows, then, assuming that all rhetoric is subversive, even as it pursues truth, that the means used, Miller's own lies, do not disrupt a pure system, but rather bring to light the subversion that preexisted. By critiquing Austin's misogyny, Miller has begun to justify his own rhetorical position.

As Miller begins to discuss the disintegration of Austin's logic, he enters into a debate with Austin. I say "debate" because Miller begins "rudely [to] interrupt Austin, even in the middle of a sentence" (*Speech Acts in Literature*, 34). Miller quotes Austin extensively, inserting his own observations in brackets. Specifically, Miller begins to show the way in which literature infects speech-act theory via "learned allusions" (ibid., 34). It is here that Miller begins to tip his hand by remarking that, by alluding to *The Tempest*, Austin is recognizing the power of felicitous lies and illusion and the tension between literary and nonliterary speech.

This literary reference of Austin's shows the presence of literature in speech acts, not speech acts in literature, which was Miller's promised topic. In keeping with my promise to mirror the style of the theorists I am reading, however, I will defer discussion of the importance of this observation and use my promised deferral, instead, to bring out Miller's second point in his interruptions. Austin regularly promises examples and explanations that never come, and frequently these examples are of concepts that Austin has ushered into being by the very promise of these examples. Miller's interruptions of Austin's text then serve to highlight the interruptive moments in Austin's original lectures. When Austin destabilizes the organizational schema of his own text with a deferral, an allusion, or a joke, it is in these moments that Miller makes the structural interruption a literal one.

Eventually it is the interruption of the text that becomes the central focus for both Austin and Miller. Austin excludes humor and duplicity from both his theory and the main format of his lecture, but they are present, nonetheless, in the interjections. The careful reader (as Miller points out) will recognize Austin's attempt at duplicity. Austin wants the reader to be aware of such issues and to see how they serve to draw his theory into question, but by the same token, he recognizes that his specific method of rhetorical analysis cannot directly admit the presence of such difficulties. But in failing to admit the infelicities of structure, Austin's text does not fail in its project of inaugurating a field.

Essentially, then, Miller emphasizes the concept, which runs counter to Austin's claims, that interruptions to logic (humor, irony, literature) can have a performative effect, in this case, an inaugural one. In doing this, Miller allows his own work to be performative, for it is indeed literary and humorous. In his chapter on Austin, Miller demonstrates that the definition of performative is broader than Austin considered, but this changes the grounds for felicity, not ethicality, and thus Miller does not provide full justification for his use of lies to force a "true" content.

Love in a Time of (No) Ethics: Derrida and the Unknowable

The logic from which the above statement on ethics emerges is, itself, called into question by Miller's analysis of the work of Jacques Derrida. Miller ends his chapter on Austin with Derrida's assertion that "[f]elicitous speech acts are parasitic on infelicitous ones, on literature in fact, rather than the other way around" (*Speech Acts in Literature*, 61). Derrida asserts that the meanings of all utterances are fluid, dependent on context, and therefore subject to nearly infinite iterations. Thus, he maintains, neither a humorous nor a literary context can invalidate a performative, although they can alter its effect. This iterability consistently remakes the "self," which Austin cites as the locus for the production of performative utterances, and thus no felicitous performative utterance can exist without the self having first been altered by a series of what Austin considers infelicities. However, in his chapter on Derrida, Miller does not promise that he will explain these concepts of humor and iterability (although he does, in the end, provide an explanation), but rather he promises to explicate the relation of speech-act theory to literature with an "interrogation of literature itself" (ibid., 63).

While Miller mentions literature in the chapter on Derrida, the concept is hardly interrogated there (again, I defer my discussion of this deferral). The opening lines of the chapter also note that for Derrida, speech acts and ethics are "associated with new notions of ethical and political decision, action, and responsibility" (*Speech Acts in Literature*, 62). Miller says: "What Derrida wants to stress is how speech-act theorists tend to leave out or marginalize crucial features of the ethics they espouse" (ibid., 133). Essentially, because Derrida claims that no context can be saturated or completely defined and delimited, no context can completely account for an ethics or an injunction. Injunctions are transcendent, coming from outside of the context, but are at the same time intimately connected to the boundaries of the context. Ethics, in this context, refers to the application of the unconditional demand to a particular set of circumstances, given that Derrida asserts that no such demands can exist wholly outside a context.

Miller's lie at the opening of this chapter on Derrida, the promised discussion of literature, serves to illustrate the new ethics that become the central idea of this chapter via Miller's analysis of Derrida's lectures on the Declaration of Independence and via Derrida's use of the words "Je t'aime." Both these lectures are explicitly involved with the question of ethics, and thus they serve to comment on what Miller himself does with performatives in his text. Derrida's new conceptions of politics and ethics depend on a reversal of speech-act theory whereby the performative utterance "transforms the context it enters rather than presupposing it and being based on it" (*Speech Acts in Literature*, 112). A speech act creates a situation in which it can have an effect. Thus, when Derrida departs from traditional pedagogy in his lecture "Declarations of Independence" and states "I do not teach truth as such," this is not to deny the effect of his lectures or their value.[5] The value lies precisely in the fact that Derrida is reshaping what constituted the truth of the subjects about which he speaks. His speech act has changed the audience, the contractual agreement, and the subject matter. This is what Miller refers to as the "radically inaugural quality of performatives" (ibid., 96). The performative can, in fact, usher into being its necessary preconditions.

This is explicitly not the case in Austin's writing, but the idea of an inaugural speech act is not Derrida's alone. The voice of Ludwig Wittgenstein, whose philosophy becomes the "literature" of Miller's next chapter, can be heard echoing throughout the canon of speech-act theory. In the case of inaugural performatives, Wittgenstein splits the difference between Austin and Derrida: "one forgets that a great deal of stage-setting in the language is presupposed if the mere act of naming is to make sense."[6] In context, naming does not refer to the simple act of labeling someone or something, but rather of ushering into being a system by which ideas can be communicated. These rules, then, make possible the language games that further structure communication. A performative, thus, can usher into being new rules, as Derrida says. Wittgenstein argues, however, that even a performative that creates new rules in fact must follow from something. This "something," the rules that make the rules for a given context, yet do not stem from that context, is, at very least, homologous with Derrida's "unconditional demand."

After discussing Miller, Wittgenstein, and Derrida, who seem willing to allow the rules of performativity to be bent, broken, or recreated, I feel at this point the unconditional demand to allow John Searle to have his say. For Miller, Searle provides the dull foil to Derrida's rapier-sharp wit. Indeed, one has only to page through *Speech Acts* or *Expression and Meaning* to see that they are very different from *Limited Inc*. Searle has filled his work with charts, formulas, equations, and a thorough, if somewhat plodding, progression from term to term. When reading Austin, Miller provides a plethora of quotations, conversations, and analyses. Not so in the case of Searle.

What does Searle himself, rather than Derrida's Sarl, have to say about speech-act theory? Curiously, Searle broadens Austin's concept of performative utterances by claiming, essentially, that all (serious nonliterary) language can be reread as acting (in the speech-*act* sense of the word) and thus is subject to speech-act analysis: "I employ the expression, 'illocutionary act,' with some misgivings, since I do not accept Austin's distinction between *locutionary* and *illocutionary* acts."[7] Searle goes on to create a series of equations to explain the functioning of illocutionary acts (*Speech Acts*, 32–33). These equations utterly remove the idea of context from speech-act theory, and, chapters later, when Searle does get around to discussing context, briefly, he still refrains from talking about a unique speaker. Certainly Searle's text allows space for the existence of context and ego, but, given that Austin makes these concepts primary, it is curious that Searle would leave them out, especially in light of his later critique of Derrida. Even more striking is Searle's own recognition of the potential for inaugural performance. Searle states, clearly, that "the creation of any rule creates the possibility of new forms of behavior" (ibid., 35). He is speaking of constitutive rules, in this case, which are the necessary precondition for a performative. Certainly Searle does not focus on this idea, preferring instead to continue to dissect various rules ad nauseam, but here, at least, his text is not totally incompatible with Derrida's.

Why then the epic battle? Miller asserts that Searle wishes to make a revolution within philosophy, while Derrida wishes to revolutionize the context surrounding philosophy, to call into question the rules of the game. The structures of the texts in question certainly suggest that this is true (*Speech Acts in Literature*, 101–3). If Searle's unconditional demand is a recognition of the rules, and Derrida's demand is a recognition of the limits of the rules, what demand, precisely is governing Miller? If Miller's text is an inaugural performative, what is it inaugurating, and for whom?

The chapter on Derrida closes with the "Je t'aime" example, which pulls together the concepts of unverifiability, iterability, unconditional demand, inaugural performative, and audience reception. When Derrida uses the phrase "Je t'aime," it is already laden with a cultural context to which Derrida adds both a performative and an additional seductive meaning. Miller's mention (or was it "use"—he is intentionally unsure of this) of "Je t'aime" serves to alert the reader to Derrida's expansion of Austin's idea of the performative, but it does so with an example, that, due to its unpublished nature, remains to a certain extent unverifiable. The speech act has created a context in which the audience is led to question even the intent of the speaker. The speech act then requires a response of some sort from the audience, but this response cannot be predicted with perfect accuracy anymore than the speaker's initial intent can be determined. The speech act cannot fail to have an effect, but it could fail to achieve Derrida's desired effect.

The unverifiability of the speech itself (due to its unpublished nature), the unverifiability of the emotions expressed by the phrase "Je t'aime," and the potential for a variety of actions on the part of the audience are, in point of fact, necessary elements of Derrida's revision of speech-act theory. Miller further explains this in terms of Wittgenstein's discussion of private language. In the identification of emotion, a person in fact invents a feeling. Just as Derrida's love-struck subject is not in love until he says, "Je t'aime" (pity those not fluent enough in French to say it), Wittgenstein's analysis proceeds from the idea that a man's emotions are meaningless by themselves and must be put in both internal and external context. Miller goes on to question, "Do these distinctions name different somethings already there or create them by naming them?" (*Speech Acts in Literature*, 167). In fact, Wittgenstein provides a circular answer to this question by recognizing the ability of naming to usher something into being, but simultaneously saying that such an ability relies on context. Via Derrida and Austin, Miller has emphasized the necessity of authority (or the perception of authority), the potential for speech acts to function even in the realm of Austin's exceptions, the ability of speech acts to create their own contexts, and the unverifiability of speech acts. Miller and Derrida both repeat, throughout these chapters, that this fluidity and power of speech acts does not decrease the responsibility of the person speaking, and, in fact, goes hand in hand with ethical demands.

Literature at Long Last:
An Examination of Computers and Wittgenstein

After a brief chapter on Paul de Man's analysis of irony as performative, Miller moves on to the long-awaited "interrogation" of literature, or at least he claims to: "In these final chapters I want to show with one example . . . how a prudent, circumspect, suitably refined awareness of speech-act theories may be helpful or even perhaps indispensable in interpreting literature" (*Speech Acts in Literature*, 155).[8] Before we are actually treated to a direct commentary on speech acts in literature (which is, after all, the title of this volume), we must first develop a "circumspect, suitably re-fined" notion of exactly what the theory is. Apparently Miller does not trust the first 154 pages, or rather does not trust the reader's interpretation (interrogation) of them.

Instead of an analysis of speech acts in literature, Miller treats the reader to an analysis of the end of literature. In order to do this, Miller first reminds the reader about the death of the individual and the undecid-ability of the other, already discussed in his chapter on Derrida. Miller then turns to Ludwig Wittgenstein, the earliest of the major theorists in this text, to provide a summation of the points thus far. As noted twice above, several of the Derridean concepts existed in a slightly altered form in the works of Wittgenstein. Wittgenstein, admittedly, does comment about literature in his books, but the use of a literary theorist is still not the promised discussion of literature.

Of course, Miller has raised the question of the definition of what con-stitutes literature in his section on Austin, so perhaps under his rubric, Derrida and Wittgenstein do indeed qualify. Nonetheless, the chapter deals with electronic communication and passion, and not with direct lit-erary analysis. Miller mentions that Derrida has "contributed to the end of literature" with his commentary on the "new regime of communication" (*Speech Acts in Literature*, 157). Literature can be said to have ended be-cause telecommunication has changed the way the audience receives liter-ature. Notions of self, of distance, of nation, and of the other have changed. These notions form part of the foundation on which literature rests. While Miller discusses this idea more thoroughly in *On Literature*,[9] he does note that "a change in embodiment, such as the one in which we are now participating, will produce corresponding changes in the way words (and, I should add, other sign systems, including graphic ones such as cinema) act on their own to do unforeseen things" (*Speech Acts in Litera-ture*, 157). In other words, our preconditions for naming have changed, thus the name or embodiment of literature has changed. This change now allows a new set of preconditions for some type of spontaneous generation, literature as speech act, ushering in the existence of . . . well, Miller, in a final bit of disingenuousness, calls it "unforeseen things."

Performing a Reading of Proust: A Promise of Things Not to Come?

I no longer must defer my discussion of the ethical effect of Miller's rhetorical strategy, because we now arrive, at long last, at the promised moment with passion fired. As the reader moves into the final chapter of Miller's text, it becomes increasingly obvious that, in fact, Miller has been stage setting, preparing the reader for a radically inaugural performative, which will in turn justify the conditions that Miller has set up through his infelicitous speech acts.

Miller's analysis of speech acts in Marcel Proust's *À la recherche du temps perdu* begins with a two-page rationale for why we should not question him, and then virtually every other page in the chapter contains cautions about accepting things on their face value. Before we are presented with any specific analysis of Proust, Miller warns us not to trust the narrator (*Speech Acts in Literature*, 179). Given the facts that Miller is effectively narrating our way through Proust, that these warnings not to trust are frequent, and that Miller has purposefully misled the reader in prior chapters, the "[m]ore astute critic" (ibid.; as Miller begs us to be) cannot help but question the speech-act felicity of the argument. Miller steps out of Proust's text to remind the reader further that trust in a narrator is "a matter of faith, a performative positing, not verifiable knowledge" (ibid., 183).

Who is this Miller whom we are not to trust, this Miller whose voice is heard so ubiquitously in this text? There is one final task remaining to me, if I am truly to follow the style of those that have gone before. I must return again to the beginning of my paper. "J. Hillis Miller opens. . . . " Who opens? Miller explicitly bases his authority in this book on his context as a teacher at UCI, and this authority does not depend on the material that he chooses to teach or on the manner in which he teaches it. Austin's logic suggests that J. Hillis Miller is an ego, acting, speaking, promising. Derrida suggests the absence of fragmentation of such an ego. Certainly we can see the effects of the action taken by "J. Hillis Miller." These effects, though, are contained within the mark of his name, if one is willing to work some small etymological sleights of hand. "Miller": a person who mills or grinds corn, thus producing a staple of life. Miller, grinder, to mill. "Mill" is related etymologically to "meal," which finally takes us back to the root "mold" and, via the *Oxford English Dictionary*, to "mool," which means friable soil, but also the soil used to fill graves. Certainly Miller has processed the kernels displayed by the dehiscence of these philosophers, but what has he produced? In the end, does the Miller's project leave us with a grave, marked with the phrase "Here Lies Speech-Act Theory?" Here, in *Speech Acts in Literature*, speech-act theory is laid to rest with lies: Here lies Hillis Miller in the laying to rest of speech-act theory. On the other hand, these lies have also milled the grain of Derrida, Austin, de Man, and Miller. Thus, perhaps the lying is not as important as the final product.

Before clarifying the question of the grave site or mysterious final product that results from this book, I must ask another question. Who is being led to this grave? This new notion of ethics must concern itself with audience. Miller tells the reader directly that "if Derrida demands a pardon, you must do something" (*Speech Acts in Literature*, 116). Miller's text is making demands of the reader at all points, both explicitly and implicitly. Given that Miller interprets Derrida as saying that "no unconditional ethical or political demand can exist without a context" (ibid., 130), the question of ethics, within the context of this theory, becomes a question of contexts. The inaugural version of speech acts that Derrida has pointed out or ushered into being himself works to reshape a context via the receiver's perception of the authority of the sender.

What is Miller's text reshaping? What has it buried, or what has it produced? Derrida has already dealt the death blow to speech-act theory and to literature. Miller then raises from this grave a new literature and speech-act theory. He promises a discussion of speech acts in literature, but does not discuss a piece of fictional discourse, a commonplace definition of literature, until the final chapter of his text. Miller allows the readers to assume that he is using a consistent definition of literature, which he indeed describes in his chapter on Austin, but instead allows the definition to shift. Miller does not alert the reader to this shift in definitions until the penultimate chapter of his book, at which point he declares literature to be dead, which should invalidate any attempt to discuss speech acts in literature, unless this speech act is merely a benediction for the theory.

If the reader has been indeed evaluating the illocutionary and perlocutionary effects of Miller's speech acts, this redefinition of literature demands a reevaluation of these effects, but the redefinition of literature is possible only via the broken promises with which Miller began. In the manner in which Wittgenstein claims, Miller provides us with the necessary framework to make an inaugural naming, but, unlike Wittgenstein's process, Miller's naming reshapes the prior rules, creating a new context for further naming. Miller's rhetoric and argument are not shaped by a linear progression or even by an argument where false assumptions are put out in order to argue progressively toward truth. Rather, Miller uses a series of infelicitous speech-act statements to produce a truth that retroactively makes the promises felicitous. If, however, a less astute reader were to stumble across Miller's text, Miller might fail to communicate truth in any form. This, then, puts Miller in the awkward position of being ethical only when surrounded by academics or astute readers.

Throughout my paper thus far, I have self-consciously made excuses and corrections to my own prose. I have emphatically placed my own persona in the writing. Miller, Austin, and Derrida all follow a similar pattern for what I perceive as a similar reason. By constructing a particular self in writing and recognizing that self to be fallible, Miller does not shift responsibility for his words to the "JHM" who speaks within his text. He does, however, forcefully remind the reader of the aforementioned notion of self as a concept created by a series of infelicitous performative utterances. Neither the reader, Miller, nor "JHM" are stable concepts.

The "unconditional" portion of Derrida's ethics may perpetually be lost in the aporia thus created. Are we all a Sarl, bearing equal responsibility as readers and contributors to the text? Where does this leave Miller's writing in terms of our initial ethical question? This question demands a response not only from the writer, but also from the audience, an audience on which Miller can place demands and shape only to a limited extent. It is striking, here, that we arrive back at a question that Austin feels is beyond the ability of philosophy to answer. He states that speech-act theory cannot deal with the perlocutionary effects of speech acts or of speech because the number of variables involved in this are too great. The version of inaugural speech acts presented here, with its fluid context, provides even more ground for variability.

The ethics of Miller's speech act demands, then, as its conditions of being, not felicitous statements and promises kept, but rather a response and an unverifiability. By labeling Derrida's "Declarations of Independence" and Austin's "performative utterances" as speech acts in literature, Miller has performed a naming, an initiatory performative utterance, a calling that demands a degree of response to this text, that mediates our perception of speech-act theory. It is the call that authorizes the response, and it is the potential for infelicity and multiple interpretations that provide the necessary preconditions for a performative utterance to succeed. Of course, my paper, too, has failed in its deferred promise to discuss the specific nature of speech acts in literature, but in doing so, it has created a further call for such a response and attempted to make explicit, as a response, the performative effect on a specific reader of Miller's text.

Since Miller invokes "Zumbah," I also turn to an African concept to elaborate on the ethics Miller displays.[10] In Nigeria *oriki* are "utterances which are believed to capture the essential qualities of their subject, and by being uttered, to evoke them. They establish unique identities and at the same time make relationships between things."[11] These words simultaneously describe something essential and preexisting and shape this existence. The words usher into being new relationships, which provide new ways of understanding old ideas: "*Oriki* opens a channel between speaker and addressee: a channel which is also a bond, both intense and all engrossing. Through it, power flows" (*I Could Speak until Tomorrow*, 248). Perhaps in addressing the issue of infelicities in speech acts, Miller has necessarily bonded himself to this topic, and, in doing so, altered the form of the topic itself. Miller has spoken into being a word where text is literature, literature is speech act, and speech acts are passion. His broken promises, in the end, are not broken, but rather transform their subjects into what was initially promised. Rhetoric such as Miller's cannot be subjected to ethical scrutiny, for the act of examination will change the subject. The lies performed as truth become truth and we all gain a bit of knowledge.

CHAPTER 4

Between "the Cup and the Lip": Retroactive Constructions of Inheritance in *Our Mutual Friend*

Larisa Tokmakoff Castillo

Charles Dickens's *Our Mutual Friend* is a retroactively oriented text, a text that works to undo the events that actuate it. The text begins with an ending, a corpse being drawn from the Thames, and withholds the circumstances surrounding this central event until half of the plot has transpired. While we learn the victim's history much sooner than we do the events leading to his death, his history, nonetheless, is represented inconsecutively—after his demise. We are never to meet the victim himself; we are never to hear his story from his lips; we are never to receive a linear narrative, sequentially organized. Instead, having begun at the end, we must work backward to piece this mystery together. We must depend on the narratives of others to construct the victim's story for us retroactively.

Our experience of reading *Our Mutual Friend*, in which we are forced to reestablish a beginning, corresponds to other sorts of temporal inversions in the text, especially to Dickens's representation of inheritance. Instead of depicting inheritance as a natural point of origin, passed on to succeeding generations, Dickens represents it as something retroactively constructed by an heir. In so doing, Dickens articulates a model of inheritance that corresponds to those of various speech-act theorists, such as J. L. Austin, Jacques Derrida, and J. Hillis Miller, who use the figure of inheritance to disclose their performative theories. For them, as for Dickens, inheritance is not the adoption of a predetermined set of facts that mimic a constative utterance. Instead, inheritance is an act that constructs a seeming set of facts, a seemingly constative utterance. Adopting this position, *Our Mutual Friend* investigates the temporal inversions of inheritance to maintain that performatives contain a force with unknowable consequences outside and unaffected by intention. Moreover, Dickens's text establishes that an attempt to control or mediate intentionality acts as a violence upon others.[1]

The first temporal inversion in Dickens's narrative occurs when Mortimer Lightwood accounts for the mysterious corpse in the opening chapter. When explaining much of the missing context that bewilders the reader, Lightwood additionally introduces the problem of inheritance that structures the text. Thus, at the very outset of the story, the reader understands that the inheritance plot is closely connected to temporal reversal. Addressing the Veneerings and the rest of society, Lightwood reports that the corpse, a "man from Somewhere," was an heir who returned to London after the death of his father, "a tremendous old rascal who made his money by Dust."[2] The father, Old Harmon—whose children long ago renounced him for the tyrannies he once imposed upon them, who was bereft of family, friends, scruples, and kindness, and whose vengeful spirit persists in his written will—leaves his fortune to his estranged son on the condition that the son, John Harmon, marry the mercenary, spoiled, yet beautiful Bella Wilfer. While alive, Old Harmon attempted to control his children's fates by selecting their spouses for them, and after his death, he continues to do the same, imposing on John a wife who is at once completely unknown to him and likely to make him unhappy. In imposing his will upon John in this way, Old Harmon intends to make his son miserable. He becomes the conventional figure of the draconian testator, one whose demands loom over his legatees like a sword suspended by a hair, and his will seems to act as divine law, giving him an absolute authority that demands obedience.

John Harmon initially returns to London with the intention of deferring to the father's command by wedding the woman he has never met, but, on board the returning ship, he reverses his decision and resolves to test Bella's character before marrying her. He hopes that Bella's "enduringly good" nature will supersede her faults, which "have been intensified by her place in [Old Harmon's] will" (366), a circumstance enabling him to marry her for her character as opposed to marrying her for his father's sordid money. He refuses to allow the prospect of a fortune to destroy either his morals or those of another. Armed with such good intentions, however, John's attempt at subversion goes awry when the corpse that surfaces in the opening scene is mistaken for him. Presumed dead by all of London, John must give up his identity as Harmon and must take on the new name and the new identity of John Rokesmith. Thus, we find that in the process of dismantling his father's will, John paradoxically becomes like his father, incapable of completely controlling his intentions. The will itself seems to have triggered a series of events that catapult those affiliated with it into confusion.

The will functions in this way because it is an event that produces a temporal displacement. When enacted, the will does not close itself off, as if it were a circumscribed moment, waiting to be handed to a future generation. It remains open to any number of readings, which all engage, and thus reconstruct, a past. Old Harmon's will sets off the text's principal occurrences: John's supposed drowning, and later, John's attempt to come back to life in order to turn his father's "sordid" money "bright again" (757). In so doing, the will effects actions that function retroactively to erase it, actions that create a different past, and thus, a different will. Not only does John reverse his supposed death, but also, in doing so, he repudiates Old Harmon's testament. Thus, Dickens undermines the linear inheritance plot by depicting the son as the creator of his own destiny. As a critical heir, John defines the document in his own terms, buries the will's authority along with its soon-forgotten author, and thereby disrupts the depiction of the testator as an absolute authority. He reveals that inheritance is no linear narrative, but a retroactive construction of a fictional origin.

Dickens's depiction of the will as a retroactive construction not only reenvisions the linear narrative but also helps articulate a theory of performative speech acts. Intent on demonstrating what happens between the utterance of a speech act and its anticipated completion—in this case, between a testator's enactment of a will and an heir's acceptance (or rejection) thereof—Dickens reveals that many disruptions intervene in the felicity of performatives, or as he so aptly suggests, that "there's many a slip 'twixt cup and lip" (802).[3] By no accident, J. L. Austin, the father of speech-act theory, adopts this very adage in *How to Do Things with Words*, contending that "we distinguish different abstracted 'acts' by means of the possible slips between cup and lip, that is . . . the different types of nonsense which may be engendered on performing them."[4]

This "nonsense" is precisely what *Our Mutual Friend* investigates. While some argue that the text presents the testator as an absolute authority, controlling the prospects of his heirs, and the speech act as a finite, controllable event that comes to a felicitous conclusion,[5] Dickens's text represents the will in various, conflicting ways to reveal that the performative produces consequences exceeding the utterance itself. It characterizes the author's intention as uncertain because the author's speech acts generate effects that no individual can shape. Moreover, by representing inheritance as a speech act constructed by the heir, and not by the testator, *Our Mutual Friend* questions the notion of an a priori, natural origin, demonstrating instead that origins are performatively enacted. Dickens's claims about speech acts, then, initiate a consideration of his role as author—the utterer of a performative act. By undermining intentionality, Dickens reveals that he, like the other authors in the text, never controls the effects of his narrative absolutely. This lack of control, however, is the risk that defines authority. Therefore, his supposed "failures" as author, the inconsistencies that critics disparage,[6] act as moments that work felicitously to articulate what authorship, or performative utterance, means.

Performative theories of inheritance lend strength to Dickens's account of the will as a vehicle articulating the force of performative utterance. Austin, considered by many to be the "patriarch, grandfather, or *capo* of speech-act theory,"[7] discloses the intimate connection between the will and his theory of performatives in *How to Do Things with Words*, a text inundated with the language of wills. Austin calls statements that imply the truth of others "entails,"[8] recognizes that performatives are "heir" to the infelicities that infect all utterances (21), and uses, as one of this most recurring examples of an explicit performative, the bequeathing of a will (5). By using the act of bequeathing as an example to define the performative, Austin links the two so closely as to take the example of the will as synecdochic of performatives generally. Thus, an examination of his use of wills exemplifies the operation of performative utterances.

Austin's use of wills as an example, however, leads him, perhaps unwittingly, to undermine his systematization of a theory of speech acts. In that way, his use of the inheritance trope functions much as it does for Dickens—to undermine authority. As critics of Austin have noted, Austin's attempt to systematize such utterances dooms itself to failure because, as even he notices, the "parasitic," literary forms of language that resist and disrupt such classification and that Austin therefore attempts to exclude from his taxonomy necessarily "infect all utterances" (21–22).[9] Initially, it would seem that the will would conform flawlessly to such systemization because Austin characterizes it as a speech act that seems to elude parasitism. Austin dubs it an "explicit" performative, a "highly significant and unambiguous expression" that comes to a conclusion in its utterance (32), enacting the intention of the speaker completely. Austin's example of the will, however, instead of remaining "unambiguous," puts the explicitness and completeness of speech acts into question. It slips between the distinct temporal moments that constitute the speech act and thereby transforms into another parasitic example, a kind of "nonsense" that infects Austin's delineations with ambiguity.

This shift transpires in Austin's analysis when he disrupts the unity of the explicit performative by splitting speech acts such as wills into at least two moments. While he would very much like to "draw the line between an action we do . . . and its consequences" (111), so as to secure the unity of the action itself, he finds that the "dubiety about what constitutes a subsequent action and what is merely the completion or consummation of the one, single, total, action" is nearly impossible to determine (43). "It is hard," he explains, "to determine the relation between 'I give' and surrendering possession" (43). The problem disrupting the unity of the utterance is the impossibility of pinning intentionality down. It is not enough for one to intend to give a gift if the gift is never handed over. In his consideration of illocutionary utterances, Austin complicates this point further by arguing that:

> Unless a certain effect is achieved, the illocutionary act will not have been happily, successfully performed. This is not to say that the illocutionary act is the achieving of a certain effect. I cannot be said to have warned an audience unless it hears what I say and takes what I say in a certain sense. An effect must be achieved on the audience if the illocutionary act is to be carried out. (117)

Initially, Austin seems to be speaking merely of the felicity of certain performatives. If an effect is not achieved, the utterance is infelicitous. However, when he argues that "I cannot be said to have warned an audience unless it hears what I say," he suggests that the performative is never enacted, either felicitously or not, unless an effect is achieved. If one warns infelicitously, one has never warned to begin with. Here, Austin wants it two ways at once. On the one hand, he insists that the effect of the utterance is not the same as the act itself—that these are distinct. Yet, on the other hand, he suggests that the effect establishes the utterance retroactively. Felicity reconstitutes the initial utterance. If one cannot have performed the act of warning without achieving that effect on one's audience, then the line between act and effect blurs. Thus, Austin's vacillation about what counts as an act's completion eliminates the category of "explicit" performatives, blurs the line between an action and its effects, and opens a gap within the utterance that attracts infelicities and resists completion. He exhibits the slip between the cup and the lip.

Austin's concern about the completion of speech acts becomes important for *Our Mutual Friend* because it puts Old Harmon's enactment of the will into question, thereby undermining his authority. If, as Austin suggests, the performative utterance is not enacted unless an effect is achieved, then the moment of bequeathing is destabilized, if not erased. Austin suggests that when Old Harmon writes a will he does not give his property to another in that act of bequeathing. Only in the moment that John Harmon accepts the terms of the will is the performative act complete. If such is the case, Old Harmon is no longer the agent of his own testament. Instead, his will becomes dependent on the wishes of his son.

According to Austin's reading of speech acts, however, John Harmon has no more control over the speech act than his father because the completion of the speech act is undecidable. When one gives a gift, such as a will, Austin recognizes that "uncertainties about whether anything further is required or not will arise. For example, are you required to accept a gift if I am to give you something? . . . The question here is how far can acts be unilateral? Similarly the question arises as to when the act is at an end, what counts as its completion" (37). While he repeats his previous claim that the performative requires a response to carry it to its end, Austin goes further to suggest that such an end is undecidable.[10] With the future indefinitely postponed, Austin reveals that both an act's completion and an author's intentionality become deferred. Indeed, they must be, for, as Derrida notes, intention "can and should *not* attain the plentitude toward which it nonetheless inevitably tends. . . . Plentitude is the end (the goal), but were it attained, it would be the end (death). This non-end is not an extraneous vestige of the teleological essence of intention, it belongs to it as its most intimate and most irreducible other."[11] Intentionality, essentially bound to a "non-end," cannot be consummated without annihilating itself. It both cannot and should not come to a completion.

In *Our Mutual Friend*, this necessary "non-end" appears in various ways: in Dickens's depiction of Old Harmon's will, which transforms into various, different wills through the course of the narrative; in Dickens's use of analepsis and prolepsis as devices to interrupt a linear narrative; and in Dickens's inclusion of his "Postscript," a continuation of his text indicating his unwillingness to end his narrative—or to see it as complete. Austin, similarly, performs this deferral by leaving his own intention open-ended. Never answering his questions by making explicit, seemingly complete claims, he hands his will to his heirs to consider. His analysis of speech acts is no unilateral act, but works instead to initiate responses from his many readers, who themselves take up the most essential characteristic of speech acts—their "non-end."

Responding to Austin's will, Derrida and Miller have devised their own testaments about the possibility of recuperating an author's intentionality through their invocation of inheritance. By eliminating the possibility of bridging the gap between a speaker's intention and an act's completion, they characterize the will, insofar as the word "will" designates "intention," a misnomer. The term "will" better describes the author's futile insistence on setting parameters by which his text may be read. Both Derrida and Miller critique this tendency in Austin, his compulsion to categorize performatives no matter how impossible the task. His tendency to systematize becomes dangerous because it attempts to marginalize modes of discourse that resist classification and thereby enacts a violence upon those discourses. The violence that Austin imposes, moreover, is compounded when his text is read as a completed document, with him as the originary author whose will must be obeyed. Other "heirs" of Austin adopt just such a reading of his will. These heirs suppose a testator's intention to be both entirely accessible and necessary to retrieve in order to ensure the felicity of his speech act. The heir assumes the capacity to recognize the speaker's intention and imagines that he can fill the gap between the utterance and its completion. He supposes that he can circumvent the problematic fissures that unsettled Austin so as to reinforce Austin's attempted systemization of speech acts. Such an heir conceives of himself as bringing the teleological movement of the performative to an end, his inheritance acting as the completion of the originary act.

Derrida, however, problematizes such an heir's interpretation of inheritance as teleologically oriented by gesturing toward a differing notion of inheritance. "What characterizes a self-proclaimed heir," he explains:

> is the fact that, doubting his own legitimacy, he wishes to be the only one to inherit and even the only one, in a *tête à tête*, to break, now and then, the filial bond of identification, in what is here the height of identification; he alone shall have the right of criticizing or correcting his teacher, defending him before the others at the very moment of murderous identification, of parricide.[12]

In describing the complex, violent relationship between the "father" and the "son," Derrida articulates a model of inheritance that departs from the traditional sense of passing something on to another. The self-proclaimed heir identifies so closely with the father that he feels himself to be almost identical, seeming to know the father's intention better than the father himself. Yet he feels a distinction between himself and his ancestor, a distinction that leads him to doubt his legitimacy. To rid himself of his doubt, he authorizes himself not only as the sole legitimate heir, who protects the aims of the father, but also as the sole critic, who can reinvent the father's objectives as he will. Thus, the heir's self-proclaiming act of inheritance is at once protective and violent—protective insofar as the heir guards the idea of authorial intention (for the sake of his own legitimation) and violent insofar as he undermines the author's intentionality by rearticulating it as his own. He defends the father in the act of parricide.

Miller extends Derrida's consideration of such "self-made, auto-authorized heirs of Austin,"[13] by imagining a scene of deliberation in which such heirs ruminate on their ancestor: "Poor man," they in effect say, "he was a great genius, but he died young, 'at the height of his powers,' leaving us with an incomplete text and a few small problems to solve, a little clearing up to perform. By doing that we can establish a lasting philosophical legacy for him and for ourselves: a clear and unambiguous doctrine of speech acts and a complete repertoire of the different kinds."[14]

In describing such heirs, Miller reveals the retroactive nature of inheritance, the way in which such an inheritance is not something passed on to heirs, like a constative fact, but is a legacy that the heirs themselves must construct, both for the author and for themselves. Their "little bit of clearing up" is an act of interpretation. They constitute the author's text as a legacy, as if it were already complete in itself, and then use the text for self-authorization. These heirs, in other words, attempt to have their inheritance in two contradictory ways. First, by revising the legacy, they undermine the possibility of an absolute will being established, one, that is, that is handed down to them from a self-conscious ego whose intention controls the speech acts he utters. But the heirs also promote the notion of an absolute will by treating their interpretations as a legacy from the past. Such heirs feel compelled to appropriate Austin's text because by authorizing it, they legitimize their own work and status as authors. By producing this legacy of seemingly immutable texts, they devise a body of "truth" to cite from, an "originary" set of rules that work to ground any claims they make.

In these passages, Derrida and Miller put forth a reading of performative utterances by distinguishing two competing conceptions of inheritance: one that sees inheritance as defined, and thus constrained, by the dictates of the father and passed to following generations, what I will call a "narrative of constraint," and one that conceives of inheritance as retroactively constructed, "a narrative of subversion." In the narrative of constraint, the father seems to have absolute authority, his will acting as an implementation of his desire long after he is dead. He seems to reach through time, his hand dictating the actions of his heirs, like a dead man who "sits on all our judgment seats" and whose "icy hand obstructs us."[15] Here, the father's will determines the actions of his heirs absolutely. The will, once enacted, functions constatively, as a fact that cannot be controverted. In the narrative of subversion, the will is performatively constructed after the death of the author, when the heir perverts the testament and transforms it into his own speech act—his own theory of performatives. The first conception posits performatives as felicitous utterances spoken by a unified subject, impervious to the will of others, while the second recognizes that performatives are not felicitously complete, but are self-perpetuating. The heir's act of self-authorization simply produces more speech acts that are marked by undecidability. Thus, the second narrative opens up the possibility of a third, one that conceives of the performative as an act uncontrolled by both testator and heir.

Miller and Derrida reveal that regardless of the narrative one adopts, all heirs are self-authorized, even they themselves. By doing so, they undercut the narrative of constraint and expose the fact that performatives never emerge from a primordial, natural origin. Moreover, by challenging the assumption of such an origin, they force the heir to take responsibility for his own acts instead of treating them as the will of another. The narrative of constraint dangerously operates as a means of avoiding responsibility. It assumes that one's speech acts are not one's own but are acts that belong to an "original" authority to which all responsibility is attributed. In rejecting the narrative of constraint, Derrida and Miller recognize that they must take responsibility for their own responses to the ancestor, regardless of the fact that no individual controls the force of the performative act.[16] Such an assumption of responsibility, such a risk in the face of uncertainty, defines authority.

Dickens presents these two competing narratives of inheritance in *Our Mutual Friend*—the narrative of constraint and the narrative of subversion—to arrive at his position on the force of the performative and the nature of authority. Like Derrida and Miller, he uses this juxtaposition to reveal that the narrative of constraint is merely a fiction. While he initially portrays the narrative of constraint as the story dictating the text, he later undercuts this story of absolute force by introducing a slip between cup and lip—John Harmon's subversion of his father's wishes. Thus, the text as a whole depicts a narrative of subversion, undermining the authority of the father. However, although the narrative of subversion defines the power relations in *Our Mutual Friend,* Dickens often invokes the narrative of constraint to reveal the violences that are imposed upon others when one adopts such a fiction.

Many characters in *Our Mutual Friend* seem confined by such a narrative of constraint. They appear to be without any freedom, powerless under the weight of their fathers' designs. Pleasant Riderhood, Lizzie Hexam, Jenny Wren, Eugene Wrayburn, John Harmon, and even poor Twemlow are bound by their fathers' demands, "aware that they have been thrown willy-nilly into a particular place in the world, and have found themselves already committed rather than able to commit themselves freely."[17] Gaffer Hexam constrains his daughter Lizzie in his life and in his death, making her feel as if she must make a "compensation—restitution" or other amends for her "father's grave";[18] Jenny Wren's father, acting as a helpless child, forces her to "slave, slave, slave, from morning to night" (241); and Lord Snigsworth places his dependent, the terrified Twemlow, "under a kind of martial law" (245). For Pleasant and Eugene, paternal imposition stems from the arbitrariness of their fathers choosing names for them, the child accepting its name, which signifies the father's will, as something indisputable. Pleasant certainly never challenges her condition in the world: "Why christened Pleasant, the late Mrs. Riderhood might possibly have been at some time able to explain, and possibly not. Her daughter had no information on that point. Pleasant she found herself, and she couldn't help it. She had not been consulted on the question, any more than on the question of her coming into these terrestrial parts" (345). "My respected father," as Eugene calls him (shortened to "M.R.F."), names his children as arbitrarily, although with even less personal consideration. Unable to see the purpose of a Christian name, M.R.F. primarily concerns himself with naming their occupation, "prearranging from the hour of the birth of each, and sometimes from an earlier period, what the devoted little victim's calling and course in life should be" (149).

Yet these impositions that constitute one way of reading inheritance are offset by representations of the will as pervertable. Jenny Wren does, after all, refuse the name her father imposes upon her and changes her name to Jenny Wren, thereby solidifying the "dire reversal of the places of parent and child" (241). By reversing the traditional trajectory of inheritance, she is able to tell her father, "I'll circumstance you and control you too" (ibid.). Although Lizzie defers to her father's past and is constantly confined by the stain on his name, she secretively takes on the role of family head by deciding her brother's fate and willfully disobeying her father's first command—of educating both Charley and herself. Eugene refuses to be named by his father and declares to Mortimer that unlike his siblings, and unlike Pleasant, he announced his own birth, only to break with paternal demands more explicitly when he explains to Mortimer that his "intentions are opposed" to those of his father in the matter of marriage (149). Granted, Eugene initially fails to recognize his own intentions in marriage. However, he eventually denies his father's will by marrying Lizzie and rejecting the "Voice of Society."[19] While such behavior on Eugene's part might be expected, even anticipated, Twemlow's rejection of patriarchal authority takes the reader by surprise. Possessing a much more submissive character than Eugene's, Twemlow significantly rebuffs the "father's" command by dismissing Lord Snigsworth's influence. Twemlow's last word, and for that matter the last word of the text, rejects the father's will altogether, for in defending Eugene and Lizzie's marriage, Twemlow asserts that Snigsworth has no claim on him in terms of delicacy: "I could not allow even him to dictate to me on a point of great delicacy, on which I feel very strongly."[20] Through Twemlow, then, Dickens puts the narrative of constraint to rest and reveals that the father's seemingly absolute command is constantly destabilized.

The narrative of subversion, moreover, becomes a necessary component in the process of conversion. Bella and Eugene, the two characters in the text who most notably undergo a moral conversion, realize this transformation only when their fathers' wills are refused.[21] Eugene cannot redeem himself until he marries Lizzie, thereby refusing the wife his father chooses for him. Bella must resist her future father-in-law's will by renouncing the money that is meant to keep her "sordid and vain."[22] Her conversion cannot be accomplished until she rejects the Dustman's money by leaving the Boffins' protection. Mr. Boffin, seemingly ruined by the riches of Old Harmon, transforms into that old "rascal" when he repeats Old Harmon's injustice—of throwing Harmon's son out of the house. With this transformation complete, Boffin becomes the father whose will Bella must refuse. When Bella condemns Boffin's actions and prepares to leave, Boffin, in his best draconian manner, threatens her with disinheritance. This threat, however, becomes the means of her conversion, her way out of the entrapment of the narrative of constraint. Bella's "enduringly good" nature determines that no earthly power could convince her to accept this money, a decision that tests her moral character and that allows her to escape the father's narrative in order that she may create her own.

Narratives of both constraint and subversion enter John Harmon's story, as well, working against one another to facilitate his conversion. While the narrative of constraint is soon undermined, it nevertheless demonstrates the violence of certain performative acts. At the outset, Old Harmon's will seems to be ubiquitous, marking John with a "nameless cloud" that seems to suggest he has undergone a "cruel captivity" (193). John's cruel captivity is the disruption of his ego. Old Harmon's will splits him, setting John's own desires at odds with those of his ancestor. The father's imposition is particularly cruel because it attempts to eliminate John's desire altogether by denying him a name. John functions as a mark on the page of a will, a mere figure of speech with no individuality.[23] He enters the story through the narration of Mortimer Lightwood, who recognizes John only as a testator, as a player in the legality of inheritance. In naming John the "man from Somewhere," Lightwood characterizes him as a kind of cipher with no identity. Only when he describes John's role in the will, his position as inheritor, does Lightwood confer a name upon him, finally addressing him as "Harmon." Only as a beneficiary does the "man from Somewhere" receive an identity.[24] Yet, even as an heir, John has no unified sense of self. The will controls him entirely by splitting his identity, making him "divided in . . . mind," at once "shrinking from" the will and simultaneously claiming that connection.[25] Thus, Dickens initially represents John's self as doubly circumscribed, first defined in terms of the father's will and then dictated by Mortimer's account of him. This narrative of absolute power suggests that the force of the testator's words is all-encompassing, that the testator's speech act, which in this case acts to overpower his son's identity, is a pure performative that magically enacts itself.

In taking the name "Rokesmith," John soon establishes a counternarrative of subversion that puts the father's will and the felicity of the performative into question. However, he soon learns that no narrative—even his own—is within his absolute control. During his soliloquy—in which he reflects on his near drowning, his liminal condition, and on whether or not he should return to life as Harmon—John demonstrates the way in which the imposition of the narrative of constraint persists in keeping him divided.[26] John attempts to undermine the father's control by using his new identity as a means of surveillance to counter the will. However, he has not definitely decided whether or not he will return to life as Harmon. Thus, John remains as divided and bewildered as he felt under his father's influence.

To solidify his identity, John attempts to find a site of origin, the site of his near drowning, which, he hopes, will allow him to redefine himself in his own terms. Yet he finds that origin elusive. At first, he cannot discover it, as he follows a path that "again and again described a circle," which leads him to "the point from which he had begun."[27] Unable to proceed unswervingly, he seems now to be controlled by an outside force, a "secret law" that dictates his chaotic movements (359). Thus disoriented, he finally arrives at the scene of his near drowning, near the Limehouse Church graveyard, not to discover a unified self, but only to wonder at his "fanciful" situation (356), existing as a "living-dead man" (363), knowing, as he says, that "I no more hold a place among the living than these dead do, and . . . that I lie buried somewhere else, as they lie buried here" (356). John perceives his condition as being double—both living and dead, capable of standing and observing the dead while also being "buried somewhere else" (ibid.). By existing as two, he exists in alternate temporalities and in alternate spaces simultaneously—a fanciful condition indeed. He hopes that by returning to the origin of his identity as Rokesmith, he may discover a way to reconcile one self to another, to "pin myself to mine" (ibid.), or to fix his ego to a referent. Yet he cannot control his own story because an unbridgeable gap exists between his experience and his identity. Although he knows himself to be the beneficiary of the will, it is only "Harmon" who can speak as beneficiary. As Rokesmith, he has not the power to manipulate his situation as inheritor. His experiences are always mediated by a figure of speech—an arbitrary name. It is thus that, when John recalls the drowning of John Harmon, he can exclaim, "I cannot possibly express it to myself without using the word I. But it was not I. There was no such thing as I within my knowledge" (366). John cannot speak of himself as "I" because he is no unified subject. He is two, or more than two, and although he might try to "pin myself to mine," he cannot make such a correspondence stick.

Yet while John initially has little control over his narrative, and while there are spaces in his history that he knows "nothing about" (362), he finally asserts his authority to determine his own story when he decides upon a name. He chooses not to come back to life as Harmon, a decision that introduces a slip into the father's intention and transforms the father's seemingly absolute will into John's own. As long as John allows himself to "think it out through the past" (366), rearticulating his inheritance in his own terms, he can choose to leave John Harmon dead and Bella untouched. But in order to construct his own narrative, John must first dictate his own name. John must kill off the "man from Somewhere," the man named by paternal authority, and attempt to articulate an ego that can reformulate the notion of an absolute, chronological inheritance, an ego that can dispense with a search for origins and that can conceive of inheritance as something retroactively constructed.[28] Although Anny Sadrin believes that it is the father who must die for the son to live, we find that the son must "die" as well.[29] Thus, by remaining "dead," John kills off Harmon and takes on the identity of Rokesmith, a bifurcation that enables the narrative of subversion to emerge, the narrative that disrupts the father's intention.[30] John articulates this separation explicitly in recalling Rogue Riderhood's attack:

> I could not have said that my name was John Harmon—I could not have thought it—I didn't know it. . . . It was only after a downward slide through something like a tube . . . that the consciousness came upon me, "This is John Harmon drowning! John Harmon, struggle for your life. John Harmon, call on Heaven and save yourself!" I think I cried it out aloud in a great agony, and then a heavy horrid unintelligible something vanished, and it was I who was struggling there alone in the water.[31]

John recognizes that his ego exists separately from "John Harmon," the "I" acting as a spectator to "Harmon's" drowning. Quite distinct from the "I" who struggles in the water at the end of the scene, "Harmon" never saves himself from the watery depths, but drowns. "Harmon" is the "heavy horrid unintelligible something" that must be cast away so that John's ego can emerge from the water, resurrected as a new person.[32] While John enters the water as a split identity, he seems to emerge as a unified ego—an "I" who can control the narrative. Catherine Gallagher notes that John's suspended animation turns him into either "an omniscient narrator, [who] can see the complete pattern and know its worth" or "an omnipresent narrator, [who] can change the story to create more value."[33] Indeed, John authorizes himself as the author of his own life by choosing death as a means of escaping the narrative of constraint. By thus undermining the father's intentionality that gave force to the absolute will, John demonstrates that the speaker of a performative utterance, in this case the testator, fails to control the utterance's successful completion— that intention carries no absolute force. There will always be a slip between the cup and the lip.

However, although John has subverted the father's intention by discovering an "I" that challenges the father's authority, he does not suddenly adopt a capacity to control the performative. Indeed, he asserts himself for the first time in his drowning scene and thereby rejects the origin of the will, but he does so by rejecting the notion of a priori origins altogether—by performatively constructing an origin for himself and thereby pointing to the arbitrary nature of such construction. His self-actualization has no basis in a greater reality, but reveals that no absolute origin underpins the ego—neither a father nor some other "truth."

Thus, by calling himself an "I," John might momentarily escape the violence that the father imposes, but he does so only to inflict that violence upon himself. In undercutting the assumption that the testator is a unified ego, John also undercuts his own self-authorization. The "I" that emerges in John's drowning scene is no more unified or originary than the father's and can no more clearly shape the direction of the text or bring it to a definitive end than the father can control the will. Instead of one unified narrative emerging after "Harmon's" drowning, two narratives continue to exist side by side—both Harmon's and Rokesmith's. Thus, John remains in his precarious and thoroughly confusing position of being two. By introducing Rokesmith, he attempts to relieve himself of the imposition of a predetermined ego, but by having introduced another "I," Rokesmith, John only widens this gap between experience and identity. He simply adds another rhetorical figure to the mix.[34]

Although killed off by John and "buried . . . many additional fathoms deep,"[35] "Harmon" lingers in the text as a linguistic presence that allows the narrative of constraint to continue as the possibility of what might have occurred had John Rokesmith never been born. When John Rokesmith returns to the Boffins' home after Harmon's "death" in the graveyard, we find that he has not entirely rid himself of his double. Instead, the narrator represents John's experience as two. The narrator tells us that while John Harmon might have intimately approached Bella, "the present John Rokesmith, far removed from the late John Harmon, remained standing at a distance. A little distance in respect of space, but a great distance in respect of separation" (364). In witnessing John's proposal to Bella, the reader cannot observe Rokesmith's actions without simultaneously witnessing those of Harmon. While only Rokesmith speaks directly to Bella, Harmon responds to her behaviors, as well. We are constantly reminded that Bella's mannerisms "would have been very much admired by the late John Harmon" (368); that instead of proposing to Bella, as Rokesmith does, "the late John Harmon . . . would probably have remained silent" (369); or that, in listening to Bella's refusal of him, "the late John Harmon might have thought it rather a contemptuous and lofty word of repudiation" (369). Harmon lingers in the text as an example of the kinds of "nonsense" that infect the completion of the speech act, of the slips between the cup and the lip that undercut the possibility of an absolute will. His presence reminds the reader that no single narrative dictates the text or is capable of entirely marginalizing other narratives.

Rokesmith's narrative of subversion functions as an alternative to the authority of the father, deferring the intention of that author indefinitely. In this story, the son not only undermines the testator's intention by turning the old man's rusty money "bright again" (757), but Bella, resisting Old Harmon's characterization of her as mercenary, develops into someone "loving as well as loveable" (364). By defying Old Harmon's original will, John now has the freedom to choose a wife for himself. He introduces a slip between the cup and the lip by asking Bella to marry him. Because the will makes only Harmon responsible to its dictates, and makes Bella responsible only to Harmon, Rokesmith is at liberty to profess, "I hope, Miss Wilfer, that it is not unpardonable—even in me—to make an honest declaration of an honest devotion to you" (365), and Bella can respond, "I reject it, sir" (366). She has the freedom to say "no" and thus perverts the will herself, just as John undermines it by renouncing his identity as Harmon.

John's perversion of his father's intention and Bella's subsequent rejection of John's reveal the way in which the performative act produces a chain effect, eliciting a response from others that challenges intentionality and that, in turn, instigates additional speech acts. The chain reaction that takes place illustrates that no individual's will, not even one considerably less violent than Old Harmon's, can secure intentionality. John, then, like his father or the author of the text, is powerless to dictate the narrative absolutely. This powerlessness is best demonstrated by the fact that his plot stems from a series of coincidences completely out of his control. He perverts the will through a set of accidents. He cannot know that Radfoot will drown; he cannot know that the Boffins will remain good people; he cannot know that Bella will change. His own attempt at plotting his own story—as well as Bella's—spirals out of his control. Although he thinks out his situation so carefully in his soliloquy, he is unable to account for all the consequences of killing off Harmon, particularly Riderhood's accusation of Gaffer as the murderer of John Harmon. The "consequence he had never foreshadowed, was the implication of an innocent man in his supposed murder" (373). Moreover, the climax of his plot, his final revelation to Bella, stems not from his own action, but from coincidence—from his accidental encounter with Lightwood, the individual, we may remember, who linguistically conveys John into the narrative. Recognizing John as Julius Hanford, the primary suspect in the Harmon Murder, Lightwood obliges John to divulge his identity and thereby transports John into yet another plot not of his own devising. These chance encounters serve as a means of countering a narrative of intentionality. The subversion of control produced by such moments of coincidence illustrates the chasm of possibility situated between an act and its many unknowable effects.

The performative act, in slipping as it does, does not leave only one narrative to emerge, but opens up a space for many unknowable possibilities. No one will is paramount. Instead, the narrative always contains possibilities of perversion that seem to self-generate. Yet, as if intent upon ignoring both the many limitations and infinite possibilities that the performative generates, John writes his own narrative to counter his father's—his own will that imposes on others. "Should John Harmon come to life?" he wonders (362). If the answer is "yes," he will accept his father's contract and thus will accept a fate determined for him. If it is "no," he will determine his own fate, and in the process will shape Bella's fate, as well. By rejecting the will, John hopes that Bella will shed the "faults [that] have been intensified by her place in [his] father's will" (366). He resists coming back to life so that Bella will "develop into something enduringly good under favorable conditions" (ibid.). Thus John, like his father, chooses to dictate the fates of others according to his own moral code, never considering their individual desires. Although in performatively constructing his ego John rejects the "sordid" narrative of constraint that put the old man's money to "its old misuses" of making others miserable (ibid.), his act is no less violent than the strictures of the ancestor. In perverting his father's testament, he merely introduces his own "will" that attempts to control the actions of others. Bella exposes John's violence when she asks him: "Was it not enough that I should have been willed away, like a horse, or a dog, or a bird; but must you too begin to dispose of me in your mind, and speculate in me, as soon as I had ceased to be the talk and laugh of the town? Am I for ever to be made the property of strangers?" (367). Not only is Bella "speculated" upon by Old Harmon, who uses her to plot against his son, but now the son, in turn, acts in precisely the same fashion. Though perhaps with better intentions for Bella's well-being, and perhaps with more personal concern for Bella, John nevertheless imposes his own will upon her when perverting Old Harmon's will.[36] Like the heirs of Austin who consider themselves to be the proper arbiters of the "father's" will, John uses his seemingly benevolent interpretation of his father's will to assert his own authority without taking proper responsibility for his actions. One violent speech act merely begets another.

By representing the many slips between cup and lip that transpire in the reading of Old Harmon's will, Dickens denies the narrative of constraint. Legitimacy, he demonstrates, comes not from deferring to past authors, but is self-instantiated. With this depiction, Dickens suggests that authority has no totalizing force, but always remains contingent upon the wills of others. Authors dictate the contents of their texts but never entirely control the effects of those original performative acts. Dickens exposes the author's limitations in his own text by introducing various beginnings to his text, a subversion of the controlled, linear narrative. He commences his story with the discovery of a corpse, but withholds the events leading up to that discovery until later in the text. In those retrospective moments, Dickens often introduces another narrator, an implementation that puts the originary status of the author into question. Instead of employing one voice to govern the text, one seemingly originary voice that controls every facet of the narrative, Dickens employs many voices, so many, in fact, that "one never knows exactly where the novelist stands because he always stands partly inside his characters."[37] One nameless narrator introduces the text with the account of Gaffer Hexam hauling the corpse from the Thames, after which Mortimer Lightwood undertakes the role of narrator, informing both the reader and the Veneerings of the Harmon history. Even John Harmon becomes the narrator of his own story in the drowning scene and proceeds to account for the sentiments of his split self. But, as Audrey Jaffe notes, the rhetorical device Dickens implements that most undermines absolute authority and the notion of omniscience is the element of surprise.[38] Jaffe compellingly argues that by catching his readers off guard, Dickens demonstrates the author's and the readers' inability to master the text. The flawless narrative is merely a fiction that seduces readers into a mistaken sense of omniscience. Thus seduced, readers are disappointed and disoriented when the narrative takes an unexpected turn. In *Our Mutual Friend*, for example, the "pious fraud"—in which readers learn that Mr. Boffin is, in fact, no villain, but has merely played the part of a miser in order to test Bella's character—seems so contrived as to indicate the text's failure. This letdown is, for many, the greatest frustration of the text. Yet it becomes necessary, in this text that critiques absolute authority, because it startles readers into recognizing their lack of control over the narrative—their lack of omniscience—and by extension, puts the author's power into question.

It might surprise us, then, that Dickens, after constructing a text that consistently undermines the possibility of authorial intention being realized, writes a will for his readers. Or perhaps this ambivalent gesture, of writing a testament in the face of its unattainable fulfillment, is the inevitable ending of Dickens's text. Having insisted on the instability of the performative, Dickens nevertheless feels compelled to write his will, the "Postscript." The "Postscript" takes on a testamentary function because Dickens narrates the story of a train crash he experienced, an accident in which he nearly lost his life as well as his newly completed chapter of *Our Mutual Friend*. "I remember with devout thankfulness," he exclaims, "that I can never be much nearer parting company with my readers for ever, than I was then, until there shall be written against my life, the two words with which I have this day closed this book:—THE END."[39] With these final words, Dickens observes his own literal death and addresses the "death of the author," his incapacity to contain his own text.[40] Dickens represents this lack of control by describing the loss of his text in the crash. Dickens was forced to leave his manuscript in the wrecked car. Only after he made sure he and others were unhurt did he return to extricate his manuscript from the wreckage. The moment of death, either a train crash or a figurative "death of the author," separates an author from his work.[41]

With his death fresh in his mind, Dickens introduces his "Postscript" with a depiction of the relation between author and reader. There, he confesses:

> When I devised this story, I foresaw the likelihood that a class of readers and commentators would suppose that I was at great pains to conceal exactly what I was at great pains to suggest: namely, that Mr. John Harmon was not slain, and that Mr. John Rokesmith was he. Pleasing myself with the idea that the supposition might in part arise out of some ingenuity in the story, and thinking it worth while, in the interests of art, to hint to an audience that an artist (of whatever denomination) may perhaps be trusted to know what he is about in his vocation, if they will concede him a little patience, I was not alarmed by the anticipation.[42]

Dickens indicates that the intentions of the author can never be known, that readers often mistake those objectives as something they are not. Even though the author may have certain designs, Dickens suggests that various "ingenuities" of the story can dictate the course of the narrative in ways that even the author cannot anticipate. Thus, Dickens critiques readers who lose patience with the author for not following his aims exactly— those who refuse to come to terms with being caught off guard. The role of the author is to do the contrary—to disrupt the notion of intention as complete. The infelicities of his text, or the lapses of intention, define authority.

In the same breath, however, Dickens attempts to reestablish his authority when he asserts that the author "must know what he is about in his vocation." Calling upon the convention of authorship, he asks the reader to trust him as an authority, as one who best controls the text. While Dickens momentarily seems to transmute into another Old Harmon, we realize that he, in fact, behaves like John Harmon, performatively establishing his authority in this document by calling on a tradition, an inheritance, that attributes power to him.

Yet in asserting that he may be "trusted" to know his intention, Dickens certainly fantasizes that he omnipotently commands his text. Comparing himself to a "story-weaver at his loom" who can see the "whole pattern" of his text before him (798), Dickens seems to suggest that he can rise above the constraints of the performative. Indeed, Gallagher suggests that the "Postscript" turns Dickens into an "endlessly resilient . . . emphatically male, transcendent subject."[43] As such a subject, Dickens suddenly becomes concerned with clarifying his intentions to his readers so that they might not misinterpret his political beliefs: "That my view of the Poor Law may not be mistaken or represented," he declares, "I will state it" again.[44] While this assertion may suggest Dickens's conception of himself as an absolute author, it equally betrays his recognition that such control is mere fantasy. If the author's intention predominates, and if, indeed, Dickens has such confidence in authorial power, his reaffirmation of his intention in the "Postscript" simply becomes a redundancy that indicates the incompleteness of his novel—his incapacity to control his text. Thus, instead of confirming the writer's authority, this slip on Dickens's part helps us to perceive the contrary.

Dickens's need to confirm his intention might be understood as a symptom of his anxiety about the failure of authorial control, a failure that stems from the possibly "mistaken" interpretations of his readers or, perhaps, from Dickens's confrontation with death in the train crash. Yet while Dickens is suddenly threatened by this loss of authority, he concurrently acknowledges that such authorial power is never contained. Thus, like Austin, who, regardless of his failure in systematizing speech acts, always begins his classification again in order to perform the many slips between cup and lip, Dickens reaffirms his authority over his text to demonstrate the uncontrollable force of performatives. Each attempt to control the text fails, leaving Dickens, like John Harmon, walking in circles in the attempt to find an origin. His attempt to reify his intention corroborates what he suggests throughout *Our Mutual Friend*—that there is always a slip between the cup and the lip. With that, Dickens, like Austin, leaves us his will to execute, no absolute will that dictates our readings, but an open-ended testament that calls upon us for a response.

CHAPTER 5

Hillis's Charity

Jennifer H. Williams

J. Hillis Miller has loved well as a writer, critic, and theorist. For Hillis, one cannot read well without love—reading is a matter of love because one must submit oneself to an uncontrollable performative force that arises when one attends to a radical recognition of difference in the text. Miller's long career teaches us that love is the primary obligation that binds the critic to his or her work because instead of covering over a multitude of sins and acting as a blinding or obfuscating force, love requires the critic to respond to the absolute differences and particularities of each author and work before him or her. Miller formulates love as critical practice in his 1967 essay "Literature and Religion."[1] In that essay, Miller grapples with the very difficult problems of how one ought to read if one is a person of strong religious convictions or if the author of the text has strong religious convictions.

The implications are not inconsequential: At stake is the trivializing of literary study into a diverting pastime and the use of literary criticism to grind one's own ideological axes or to turn religious themes in literature into "something other than themselves" (73). The pursuit of religious questions as they are illuminated by literature is not inconsequential, either. As Miller writes in the preface to the 2000 reissue of *The Disappearance of God*, echoing Paul de Man, "religious questions are the most important."[2] But how, then, to read religion and literature in light of the pitfalls Miller articulates? How do we avoid changing the work into something other than itself? Miller concludes in "Literature and Religion" that "the proper model for the relation of critics to the work they study is not that of scientist to physical objects but that of one person to another in charity" (75). Charity, from the Latin *caritas*, Christian love, is what allows the critic to read with the greatest degree of rigor because it insists on preserving difference, rather than assimilating and classifying. Miller writes, "I may love another person and know him as only love can know without in the least abnegating my own beliefs. Love wants the other person to be as he is, in all his recalcitrant particularity. As St. Augustine puts it, the lover says to the loved one, 'Volo ut sis!'—'I wish you to be'" (75).

St. Augustine is a most fitting source for Miller to turn to for a model of what it means to read with charity, to read with love. Augustine's hermeneutic also rests upon an insistence on caritas.[3] Augustine contends in *On Christian Teaching* that the end of reading is love. Furthermore, we can determine whether or not we have read a text well by measuring the love that our reading produces. Augustine writes: "So anyone who thinks that he has understood the divine scriptures or any part of them, but cannot by his understanding build up this double love of God and neighbour, has not yet succeeded in understanding them."[4] In other words, if our reading does not lead us to love more, then our reading is wrong, and we have not understood the text. To read well is to love well.

But for Augustine, good reading does not just create love. It must be inspired by love. This, however, is where the trouble starts. How do we love something? What does it mean to love? For Augustine, two contrary principles are involved. One must be careful to love rightly, that is, to love something is "to hold fast to it in love for its own sake" (9). Opposed to this is the concept of "use": To use something is "to apply whatever it may be to the purpose of obtaining what you love" (ibid.). When we love something, we "enjoy" it—we take pleasure in it for what it is, in and of itself, in all its particularity. Augustine insists that this is a pleasure that should be specially reserved for only those things that "ought to be loved" (ibid.). The problems start when we love something we ought merely to use and thus take pleasure in a thing that is only supposed to be the vehicle for obtaining what we love. This is loving badly. According to Augustine, "if we choose to enjoy things that are to be used, our advance is impeded and sometimes even diverted, and we are held back, or even put off, from attaining things which are to be enjoyed, because we are hamstrung by our love of lower things" (ibid.).

"Advance," "diverted," "held back," and "put off," "hamstrung," and "attaining" all point to the teleological nature of love in the model of proper love that Augustine proposes because they all figure love as a journey motivated by a particular goal.[5] Furthermore, the problem of use and enjoyment points to the dual nature of love and its tendency to be misapplied by the uncareful reader. This dual nature of love is embodied in many ways by the figures of eros and caritas—love and charity.[6] Eros is dangerous, inappropriate love—it is taking pleasure in something that we ought to use. Caritas, on the other hand, is sacred love—a divine love that is appropriately placed and right for us to enjoy. Caritas is the love that Augustine claims should both inspire and be increased by our reading.

Augustine illustrates these two kinds of love in a parable about travel. Augustine writes:

> Suppose we were travelers who could live happily only in our homeland, and because our absence made us unhappy we wished to put an end to our misery and return there: we would need transport by land or sea which we could use to travel to our homeland, the object of our enjoyment. But if we were fascinated by the delights of the journey and the actual traveling, we would be perversely enjoying things that we should be using; and we would be reluctant to finish our journey quickly, being ensnared in the wrong kind of pleasure and estranged from the homeland whose pleasures could make us happy. So in this mortal life we are like travelers away from our Lord [2 Cor. 5:6]: if we wish to return to the homeland where we can be happy we must use this world [cf. 1 Cor. 7:31], not enjoy it, in order to discern "the invisible attributes of God, which are understood through what has been made" [Rom. 1:20] or, in other words, to derive eternal and spiritual value from corporeal and temporal things. (10)

For Augustine, caritas involves a focus on the end of the journey—on home—while eros involves a "perverse enjoyment" of the rest of the world. To journey properly through the enticements of the world, or to read properly, must involve caritas. Just as the purpose of taking a journey is simply to provide us with a means to get home, our source of true enjoyment and love, so, too, must we use this world, or read it, in order to "discern" the invisible attributes of God. We are to read the world to make the invisible object of our love visible. It is our love of God, then, that inspires our reading, and it is God on which our love and enjoyment are properly fixed. Proper reading, then, is a reading that keeps its goal in sight and attaches its love to that end. That is to say, Augustine would have our eyes and hearts firmly fixed on the destination, whether it be the destination of the journey or of the reading. To love well is to read well. However, Augustine's own claim that our eyes must be fixed on the destination is one that, as I will demonstrate below, is a difficult one to maintain.

Embedded in Augustine's simple story is another danger—that of enjoying reading for its own sake. In the same way, when he warns us that when "we choose to enjoy [or love] things that are to be used, our advance is impeded and sometimes diverted," Augustine employs the figure of travel to depict a misguided love that freezes and leads astray. Just as Augustine cautions against loving the world and thereby not reading within it the invisible attributes of God, becoming enamored of our own hermeneutic practices would be an equally inappropriate slip because to do so would be to enjoy for its own apparent value what should be only a process—a means, not an end. It is to focus on "the delights of the journey and the actual traveling," not the reason for doing so.

At stake for Augustine in both cases is how to extract an eternal value from a worldly thing. Augustine cautions us that "[t]o enlighten us and enable us, the whole temporal dispensation [of the law and scriptures] was set up by divine providence for our salvation. We must make use of this, not with a permanent love and enjoyment of it" (27). The purpose of reading then, and our love, is nothing less than our justification in the theological sense—our salvation. What Augustine proposes is essentially justification by reading. To love the reading, the journey, would be an improper love. Such a love would tempt us to extend our reading and continue it without a thought of bringing it to its proper conclusion. This kind of love is idolatrous. It hamstrings us and impedes us in our search for justification because it seeks to delay the ending of the journey as long as possible. Paradoxically, it also freezes time—it traps the lover in a moment that never progresses. This love wants to go on reading forever. However, is this not, in fact, the kind of love that has tempted Miller to write his many books? By Augustine's standards, Miller is an improper reader by virtue of the fact that he falls into the trap of loving improperly and idolatrously.

To say that Hillis Miller loves literature is no surprise. His students, friends, and colleagues can attest to the fact that Miller's great love for literature is what fuels his prodigious writing, his teaching, his direction of dissertations. The breadth and scope of the authors and works Miller has treated, which at times seems to span *all* of literature, suggests a lover consumed with passion, desperate to know every detail and facet of his beloved and to share that love with the world. Miller has loved particular authors, too. His continued, perhaps even obsessive return to the work of Conrad, Proust, Kafka, Williams, Hardy, and Derrida, to name but a very few, recalls the lover who gazes at the particular features of his beloved again and again without tiring. It also suggests, I blush to point out, that Hillis may be somewhat of a Don Juan—after all, he has loved *so many*. We should leave that question for the time being. Suffice it to say that Hillis has been faithful to all his loves in their turn. To what degree, then, can we say that Miller's work has been one passionate love letter after another?[7] In what ways is literary criticism a declaration of love?

Although Miller cites Augustine's "Volo ut sis," his model of reading differs from Augustine's because he is not concerned with the end, but with the reading—the journey, itself. Miller states that reading well means, in fact, abandoning any expectations or desires for a predetermined end:

> Good reading means noncanonical reading, that is, a willingness to recognize the unexpected, perhaps even the shocking or scandalous, present in canonical works, perhaps especially in canonical works. . . . By noncanonical reading I do not mean a critical relativism or a placing of meaning in the "reader's response," a freedom to make the work mean anything one likes, but just the reverse. I mean a response to the demand made by the words on the page, an ability, unfortunately not all that common, to respond to what the words on the page say rather than to what we wish they said." [8]

Miller shows here that Augustine's second principle of charity undermines the first. What Miller calls the willingness to recognize the unexpected, the ability to respond to the words on the page as they are, as opposed to what we would have them be, can be thought of as Augustinian caritas. Just as Augustine claims in the "Volo ut sis" that to love something is to wish it to be as it is and not as we would wish it to be, Miller claims that the same demand of caritas is always put upon the critic or the reader. Thus, when we read a canonical text and recognize within it something we find scandalous, something we wish were not there, to love the text, in Miller and Augustine's terms, would be not to ignore or efface that scandal.[9]

However, Augustine also insists that proper love should be focused exclusively on the proper goal. Miller's model of love focuses on the individuality of each text—what beckons us and stirs up a desire in us to read. But it is precisely this quality that makes reading for an end impossible. That is, focusing on the goal will always undermine the reader's ability to recognize the unexpected in the text. Augustine's end, after all, is always the same thing—God. For Miller, good reading similarly demands that the reader attempt to make visible what is invisible.

Unlike Augustine, who seemed to know in advance what those invisible elements are, Miller seeks the unknowable "wholly other," something glimpsed in the shocking and scandalous elements in the text that may go unnoticed if the critic wants to control the outcome of his or her reading.[10] Miller continues, "[t]he rare ability to see the object . . . as in itself it really is . . . is the one thing necessary in the good teacher of literature. The strangest and most surprising things are present in those great books if we have the wit to see them."[11] This is a particularly important practice, Miller argues, in texts that are canonical, and thus overdetermined by years of reading, an experience that makes particular books familiar, comforting, and even beloved because of what we come to expect them to say to us. The force of this reading practice is not located within the critic and the critic's desires for the text. Rather, it is the critic's love for the work itself and for reading that causes him or her to put aside his or her expectations and allow the text to be as it is, in all its recalcitrant particularities, whatever they may be.[12] Reading well means, in these cases, resisting the impulse to assimilate and allowing a beloved and intimate book to shock us.

One gets the sense that for Miller, the most terrible fate would be to stop reading, and his delight and joy in reading is writ large across his many books and essays. However, Miller's love of reading is not marked by the volume of work he has produced, but in the method his work tends to follow. We find in many of the prefaces to Miller's books the caution that his selection and grouping of various authors should not be read as an attempt to produce an organic unity,[13] to suggest a historical teleology,[14] or to flatten out the differences between those authors.[15] Miller's criticism is underscored with an attention to difference and the individual characteristics of each work. Indeed, the major similarity among these authors and works is Miller's love of reading them. In what we might take as the emblematic signature of Miller's work, Miller confesses in *Speech Acts in Literature*:

This book began as what I imagined would be a brief introductory chapter to a book I had been writing. . . . As I might have expected, my attempt to read [the work of Austin, Derrida, and de Man] carefully from this perspective and to explain what they say about speech acts to myself and to potential readers of my book . . . got longer and longer and more and more absorbing. Ultimately, that brief introductory chapter became a book on its own. . . . I have taken great pleasure in writing this book. . . . I hope my

readers enjoy my report on these writings as much as I enjoyed my adventures in exploring and explaining them, following a somewhat sinuous track
from page to page.[16]

Miller's confession demonstrates how the focus on individuality necessarily moves away from an end. Miller explains that the 238-page *Speech
Acts in Literature* was meant to be a brief introduction—Miller's intended
goal was to write a book on Henry James. However, his "great pleasure in
writing" the book, along with his great pleasure in reading his authors
("my attempt to read . . . got . . . more and more absorbing"), diverted him
from his goal and instead took him on a sinuous and diverting journey. For
Miller, this is an example of good reading and proper love because it is a
reading that allows itself to be open to the unexpected and the unplanned.
Furthermore, such a love, with its focus on the love of the journey instead
of the goal, is precisely what Augustine warns against when he says that to
love the journey means to never reach the end.[17] But while Augustine
might object, we might celebrate Miller's willingness to be led astray. Had
Miller resisted the pleasures of reading and writing, focusing instead on
the goal of writing a book about James, we would not have *Speech Acts in
Literature*. Miller's critical practice, then, offers a different model of loving
well and reading well—that of loving the journey and thereby loving the
particularities of the individual authors and texts that one reads.

If Miller has succumbed to what Augustine would consider a bad desire,
this improper, idolatrous love, then he is in very good company. In fact,
Augustine himself would seem to be one who loves reading too much. He
too gets caught up in the pleasure of reading when he turns the scriptures,
which ought to be a "homeland" for good Christian readers, into a vehicle
for his larger point that we must read the world to discern the invisible
attributes of God: The scriptures become a metaphor or a vehicle for that
extrabiblical truth, rather than embodying the Truth themselves. In other
words, Augustine does not keep his eyes fixed on the destination. Augustine's other problem is that he chooses to tell a parable to explain the
dangers of improper love.[18] This ensnares Augustine because by using
figurative language he participates in the very thing he warns against—he
delays the communication of his message by conveying it through indirect
means.[19]

This impulse to tell a story is, perhaps, inevitable given the intimate
relationship between love and narrative. Susan Stewart, for example, affirms this relationship when she writes in *On Longing* that "[n]arrative is
. . . a structure of desire, a structure that both invents and distances its

object and thereby inscribes again and again the gap between signifier and signified that is the place of generation of the symbolic."[20] By distancing its object in language, narrative conjures up desire for the object and a longing to close that gap through the telling of its story. Augustine's story about the perils of travel is an apt example of what Stewart means because his story is literally the story of a desire to return home and to collapse distance, but the telling of that story creates the distance that must be crossed to arrive at the longed-for destination.

In the ranks of those who have loved the journey and not the destination, Joseph Conrad is also in that good company of Miller and Augustine. However, Conrad and his characters, for both Augustine and Miller, love improperly. Both he and his characters from *Lord Jim* exhibit different aspects of improper love and thereby exhibit the dangers of not loving as Hillis does. In the author's note to *Lord Jim*, Conrad answers the charge that the novel is too long because he had been "bolted away with" and that the story had "got beyond the writer's control."[21] Although at first denying the story is too long, Conrad confesses that while *Lord Jim* was originally meant to be a short story, it became "a free and wandering tale" because of Jim, the hapless protagonist whose exacting sense of ethics leads him to bear the cross of a mistake made early in his career for the rest of his life, up to a sacrificial death on the remote island of Patusan many years later.

Conrad reveals that his love for Jim causes him to get "bolted away with." He writes:

> I can safely assure my readers that [Jim] is not the product of coldly perverted thinking. . . . One sunny morning, in the commonplace surroundings of an Eastern roadstead, I saw his form pass by—appealing—significant—under a cloud—perfectly silent. Which is as it should be. It was for me, with all the sympathy of which I was capable, to seek fit words for his meaning. He was "one of us." (6)

Jim is a seductive figure—appealing and significant. Conrad's description suggests that Jim's silence is an appeal that elicits interpretation. This call to interpretation requires Conrad to try to read that significance and "seek fit words for his meaning." And he does it with all the sympathy, or charity, of which he is capable. The "one of us" is a gesture of community, neighborly love. But while Conrad may think it is caritas that inspires him to write the free and wandering tale of Jim, Augustine would say that it is eros, the enjoyment of something that ought only to be used, something that causes Conrad to seek to delay the end of the tale. A perverse pleasure in writing and in loving Jim leads Conrad to write his epic *Lord Jim* instead of the short story. For Miller, however, the problem with the love Conrad articulates here is not that Jim's silence creates an irresistible desire in Conrad to seek fit words for his meaning. In fact, Conrad's confession that he had been bolted away with echoes the confession that Miller makes to explain the writing of *Speech Acts in Literature*. Instead, the danger that begins to surface in the text is the danger of classification: Conrad claims that Jim was "one of us." As long as Conrad seeks fit words for Jim, he loves well. But should that seeking become limited or predetermined by what Conrad wants or expects to find, a limit that is suggested by "he was one of us," Conrad fails to love according to the model that Miller advocates.

Lord Jim has much to teach about long journeys and travels, but I will focus here on one lurid scene of butterfly collecting to articulate the failure or perversion of love in the novel from both Augustine's and Miller's perspectives. This scene occurs at the halfway point in the novel. Marlow has followed the misfortunes of Jim for several years now. He has tried to find some job for Jim that would allow him to lead a normal life, but Jim's scandalous past always catches up with him. Stumped when his latest plan fails, Marlow goes to visit his friend Stein, a "wealthy and respected merchant" (122) and an old friend. He is also, we learn, a "naturalist of some distinction," "a learned collector" (122). Marlow tells us:

> Entomology was his special study. His collection of *Buprestidoe* and *longicorns*—beetles all—horrible miniature monsters, looking malevolent in death and immobility, and his cabinet of butterflies, beautiful and hovering under the glass cases on lifeless wings, had spread his fame far over the earth. . . . I . . . considered him an eminently suitable person to receive my confidences about Jim's difficulties as well as my own. (122–23)

The scene of Stein's study is rich with images of heaven and hell, death and life. The beetles are hideous and malevolent little demons; the butterflies are beautiful flying angels, hovering on lifeless wings in a mockery of their former lives. And although both are now dead and pinned to the walls in Stein's study, they have carried Stein's name and reputation far and wide. It seems that Stein is eminently suitable because his study of entomology makes him an expert at finding similarity in the most disparate things—the monstrous beetles and the angelic butterflies are both insects. He is able to share in Marlow's belief that Jim is, at heart, a sailor, a sailor like Marlow himself, "one of us," and thus all they need to do is find the proper conditions under which Jim can succeed. However, this is a project doomed to failure, as the end of the novel attests. In fact, Stein loves badly, and so he cannot counsel Marlow at all. Stein, the obsessed butterfly collector, is a picture of Augustine's love wrongly applied. Stein's love of butterflies is an improper love because he does not allow for individuality and difference, which, as both Miller and Augustine suggest, is the mark of true love.

Susan Stewart's work on souvenirs and collecting again offers a lucid explanation of the forces at work in the singular object that is the collection and its relationship to love and journeying. Stewart argues that the souvenir and the collection are two important devices for the objectification of desire because they are objects that both generate and are generated by narrative. "The souvenir," Stewart explains, "must remain impoverished and partial so that it can be supplemented by a narrative discourse, a narrative discourse which articulates the play of desire."²² These narratives are the stories of the object's acquisition—how the collector came to want and own the object. At the same time, it is the object's ability to generate those stories that condition the relationship between the object and its value as a collected object. That is to say, the object would not have value without the story of the collector's desire behind it, and so the object is transformed into souvenir or specimen by narrative. Finally, Stewart writes, the collection, as a kind of art, is "a form involving the reframing of objects within a world of attention and manipulation of context."²³ The "attention and manipulation of context" that Stewart refers to here is none other than a kind of reading—an interpretation of the object and a refiguring of its context through the production of a story. To collect an object, then, is to read and generate narrative. Stewart's reading of souvenirs and collections shows that Stein's collection of butterflies must have everything to do with the notion of love and readings produced by that love because love and narrative are the two main components that define what the collection is. Stewart adapts Miller's and Augustine's ideas about love to collecting.

The souvenir's relationship to narratives of desire is further determined, according to Stewart, by the fact that the collected object is at once both part of a larger species or genus and at the same time completely unique. That is to say, a collector pursues any object in his or her collection only because he or she is collecting a series of similar things. However, it is the rarity of the object which makes the collector desire the specimen in the first place. Taken as a specimen within a collection, one example among many, that same object gains value as unique, unusual, or rare among the others. In fact, the specimen can be rare and valuable only if it is a part of a larger collection, because it is the context of the collection, as constructed by the collector, that determines its rarity.[24] Ultimately, the end result of the collected object's dual nature, something that is both unique and a mere example, is a kind of temporal and even metaphysical frozenness. For Stewart, the "transformation of labor into abstraction, nature into art, and history into still life . . . eternalize an environment by closing it off from the possibility of lived experience. They deny the moment of death by imposing the stasis of an eternal death."[25]

Collecting, then, is a dangerous form of loving because it emphasizes classification, which overshadows the unique qualities of the object *as object*. That is, the qualities the object had before it was transformed into a specimen in a collection are forgotten in the process of assimilation—the collector must ignore those qualities that do not fit within the context of the collection. Even the so-called qualities that make it rare and unique are specious because they are a fiction generated by the collection and the collector. This process of assimilation and forgetting makes the collection an Augustinian misapplication of love. The collected object is simply one specimen among many, and not a desirable object in and of itself. The collector does not allow the object to be. But at the same time, collections are also perversions of love according to Miller's model because they are governed by a predetermined goal and result in stasis. Taken together, both Augustine's and Miller's approaches reveal that Stein's love is improper because he loves what he ought merely to use and in so doing becomes frozen in time.

Stewart uses the butterfly under glass as an example of eternalized death, which is a most fitting description for Stein and his butterfly collection. When Marlow walks into the study, a study described as a dark "catacomb of beetles" and a graveyard of butterflies (123), he finds Stein in rapt contemplation of a particularly large butterfly:

> His hand hovered over the case where a butterfly in solitary grandeur
> spread out dark bronze wings, seven inches or more across, with exquisite
> white veinings and a gorgeous border of yellow spots. "Only one specimen
> like this they have in *your* London, and then—no more. To my small native
> town this collection I shall bequeath. Something of me. The best."
>
> He bent forward in the chair and gazed intently, his chin over the front
> of the case. I stood at his back. "Marvelous," he whispered, and seemed to
> forget my presence. (123)

The "solitary grandeur" of the bronze butterfly echoes Stewart's argument that the collected object has value insofar as it is rare and unique among other, similar objects—surely Stein would not have been transfixed by a common swallowtail. It is fitting, then, that Stein prizes this butterfly because it is not only a rare specimen in his collection, but also is a rare specimen in the whole world—there is only one other example, in London. At the same time, however, the fact that Stein believes the butterfly is one of only two in the world points to the role his own desire has played in generating the story of the butterfly. He tells Marlow that the butterfly is rare, but his narrative defines the world as the metropolitan world, one made up of London and other cities like it.[26] But Stein cannot possibly hope to account for the existence of every bronze butterfly in the world. His story ignores the possible existence of other collections that are unknown to him, as well as the other bronze butterflies alive and uncollected.

We soon find out the reason for Stein's intense, all-encompassing passion for this particular butterfly, a passion that isolates Stein from Marlow. Marlow continues:

> I was very anxious, but I respected the intense, almost passionate, absorption with which he looked at a butterfly, as though on the bronze sheen of these frail wings, in the white tracings, in the gorgeous markings, he could see other things, an image of something as perishable and defying destruction as these delicate and lifeless tissues displaying a splendour unmarred by death.
>
> "Marvellous!" he repeated, looking up at me. "Look! The beauty—but that is nothing—look at the accuracy, the harmony. And so fragile! And so strong! And so exact! This is Nature—the balance of colossal forces. Every state is so—and every blade of grass stands *so*—and the mighty Kosmos in perfect equilibrium produces—this. This wonder; this masterpiece of Nature—the great artist." (125)

Stein reads with passion, with love, the wings of the butterfly and sees all of Nature writ in its gorgeous markings. Marlow imagines that Stein has literally turned the butterfly into a text as the spots on the butterfly become "tracings" and "markings."[27] Stein seems to see not the butterfly, but the balance of colossal forces—a Kosmos that is justified, "in perfect equilibrium." But this is a reading that seeks similarity and assimilation— Stein can see all of the Kosmos in this single butterfly. Stein has not let the butterfly be as it is—to do so would be to not have caught and killed it in the first place.

Stein reads more than an emblem of Nature in the wings of the bronze butterfly. Stein reads himself into the butterfly and, in holding it, remembers the triumphant moment of its capture. The butterfly becomes both a collected specimen and a souvenir. Stein tells Marlow of the day he caught this butterfly, which turns out indeed to be a particularly rare and perfect specimen. One morning when he was a young merchant living in the Malay Archipelago, Stein kissed his wife and daughter good-bye and left on horseback to meet his best friend. The country where they lived was in the midst of a civil war for the succession of the throne. However, the message from his best friend to come meet him turns out to have been a ruse, and Stein stumbles into an ambush. He feigns death when shots ring out, and eventually seven men emerge from their hiding places in the tall grass. Stein then calmly shoots three men in quick succession. As the other men run off, Stein looks down at the face of one of the dead men and sees a shadow flicker across his face: It is the bronze butterfly.[28] Stein gasps, races after the butterfly and catches it. He says:

> When I got up I shook like a leaf with excitement, and when I opened these beautiful wings and made sure what a rare and so extraordinary perfect specimen I had, my head went round and my legs became so weak with emotion that I had to sit on the ground. I had greatly desired to possess myself of a specimen of that species when collecting for the professor. I took long journeys and underwent great privations; I had dreamed of him in my sleep, and here suddenly I had him in my fingers. . . . On that day I had nothing to desire. (127)

Stein's desire for the butterfly, the perfect specimen that he had previously seen only in books, overwhelms him with emotion. The overpowering emotion he feels at capturing and killing the butterfly is in stark contrast to his matter-of-fact killing of the men—his possession of and relationship with the butterfly comes at the cost of a violent and bloody rift with the community of men. The butterfly comes to symbolize Stein's life made complete—the end of desire, the end of eros. What was once invisible, the stuff of dreams and books, becomes real and tangible in his own hands. In fact, it is also the end of his life as he will shortly lose his wife, child, and best friend and eventually become entombed with his butterflies.

Stein's passion for the butterfly is misdirected. In Augustinian terms, he thinks the butterfly is his homeland and that it is an appropriate object for his love and enjoyment. Instead, according to Augustine, just as the scriptures are a temporal dispensation for us to use for our justification, Stein ought to love the butterfly with a transient love and instead love his wife and child. However, Stein pins the butterfly and turns it into a sacred object—it becomes a goal in itself. Stein becomes pinned just as surely as the butterfly. He continues to read the butterfly over and over again, never progressing, never changing, never finishing his work of writing the catalog for his collection, a project he is immersed in when Marlow finds him. This is a problem which has plagued many a collector. Walter Benjamin wrote of his book collection that the collector has a mysterious "relationship to objects which does not emphasize their functional, utilitarian value—that is, their usefulness—but studies and loves them as the scene, the stage, of their fate."[29] Moreover, Stein does not love the butterfly with the kind of individuality that Miller promotes. Stein has killed the butterfly and values it strictly in accordance with a predetermined set of conditions. While Augustine might object to the infinite generation of text and narrative, for Augustine an instance of loving the journey, Miller would object that Stein's reading of the butterfly is not open to its otherness. Stein is on an infinite journey, but he does not love well in the process.

While Stein fails to read with caritas, Miller's reading of *Lord Jim* demonstrates what this principle of caritas in reading might look like. For Miller, Stein's love of the butterfly can be opposed to Conrad's love for Marlow, a more proper love. Conrad's love for Marlow is one that is governed by a willingness to let Marlow be. Conrad's preface to *Youth* (1917) explains that his relationship with Marlow, with whom he had "grown very intimate in the course of years,"[30] was in part responsible for his continued writing. Conrad writes that Marlow "haunts my hours of solitude, when, in silence, we lay our heads together in great comfort and harmony; but as we part at the end of a tale I am never sure that it may not be for the last time. Yet I don't think that either of us would care much to survive the other."[31]

This picture of intimacy and companionship suggests that Conrad writes stories about Marlow because he enjoys Marlow's company; Conrad's desire and longing for Marlow cause him to continue to generate narratives to bring Marlow back to him. But their relationship is one that Conrad insists is not controlled by him. He writes that "I made no plans" for Marlow's "capture" and that while others think he is the "proper person to throw a light on [Marlow's character] . . . I find that it isn't so easy."[32] By insisting that he has no plans for capturing or pinning Marlow down, Conrad remains open to Marlow's otherness. Moreover, Conrad's love for Marlow does not preclude the possibility for Conrad that he may never write another tale with Marlow in it. Conrad's desire for Marlow does not drive him to predetermine the conditions of Marlow's appearances. For Conrad, there is no end in sight for their relationship and there is no guarantee that it will continue. This indeterminacy preserves Marlow's individuality and thus lets him be.

Miller's love for Conrad and *Lord Jim* matches the love that Conrad has for Marlow. In the novel, Marlow loves Jim as Stein loves his butterflies and beetles. Marlow's insistence that Jim was "one of us," an Englishman and a sailor, means that he cannot accept Jim's failure, abandoning a ship full of passengers on his first job. Marlow ignores those aspects of Jim's character that suggest he was not "one of us," a good sailor, in his constant searching for both a job that Jim can succeed in and an excuse to explain why Jim has done what he has done. While Marlow's love for Jim is improper because it seeks to assimilate him, Miller's reading of *Lord Jim* evidences the kind of love for Jim that is emblematic of what reading well means for Miller. Miller argues in *"Lord Jim*: Repetition as Subversion of Organic Form" that the guiding thread of *Lord Jim* is Marlow's attempt to explain how someone as promising as Jim could fail as magnificently as he does.[33] Such an explanation, Miller writes, "will make it still possible [for Marlow] to believe in the sovereign power" that governs life.[34] Miller's reading of Marlow suggests that Marlow is misguided, although understandably so, in his need to find an assimilating principle—an end, a conclusion of sorts. Marlow goes about trying to construct such an excuse by trying to classify Jim and to determine the kind of person he is, thus treating Jim as an object of collection. Miller writes of Marlow's attempted classification:

> Perhaps Jim is not all bad. Perhaps he can be excused. At other times Marlow suggests that in spite of appearances Jim has a fatal soft spot. He cannot be safely trusted for an instant. . . . At still other times Marlow's language implies that Jim is the victim of dark powers within himself, powers which also secretly govern the universe outside. If there is no benign sovereign power there may be a malign one, a principle not of light but of blackness. . . . To act according to a fixed standard of conduct which is justified by no sovereign power, as perhaps Jim does in his death, is the truest heroism. . . . Perhaps, to pursue this line a little further, the source of all Jim's trouble is his romanticism. . . . The ending is a tissue of unanswered questions in which Marlow affirms once more not that Jim is a hero or that Jim is a coward, but that he remains an indecipherable mystery.[35]

Miller's patience in detailing Marlow's repeated and failed attempts to categorize Jim emphasizes the urgency of Marlow's need to know what or who Jim is. It also ironizes Marlow's position, because in outlining the possibilities, Miller demonstrates a forbearance for Marlow that Marlow does not have for Jim. Despite the long list of possibilities, Miller never offers his own explanation of Jim. Miller allows Jim to remain the indecipherable mystery—as he must in order to be a good critic—to love Jim, or *Lord Jim*, properly.

As opposed to Stein the entomologist, Miller the etymologist seeks neither similarities nor assimilation. Rather, caritas for Miller says to the loved one, "I want you to be in all your recalcitrant particularity." Miller has loved literature by seeking what is different, the absolute alterity of each particular book, its irreducible otherness. That is what it means to love well. Miller's love does not seek to appropriate the other, but to respond to it instead. His work is a kind of justification by reading because it is a reading that tries to respond justly to the call of the other in the text. And Miller loves well because he continues to read and continues to write, never resting in a frozen moment, but always seeking to hear again the call of the other and to respond afresh once more. This is what makes all of Hillis's work a passionate love letter—work inspired by love, loving particularity and seeking difference, allowing the loved one to be. And, in seeking to follow Hillis, my paper, too, has been a declaration of love of its own.

PART TWO

The Politics of Form

CHAPTER 6

"J"; or, Hillis *le mal*

Tom Cohen

> The passage in question in *Cranford* has to do with generation and
> with the passing on of names from generation to generation in family
> crossings. It has to do with the letter f, in fact with a double f. F is
> genealogically derived from G, gamma in Greek, which is another
> kind of crossing, the fork in the road, a truncated X, like Y. The f is a
> doubling of that turn, a *digamma* or "double gamma," as it was called
> in Greek. The cursive or minuscule gamma is y-shaped: g, while the
> capital gamma is like a right-angled turn: G.
>
> —J. HILLIS MILLER, "Line"

No one reads letters anymore. E-mail perhaps, but not letters in the manner of the passage cited above. And one can see why. It is not a matter of
"fashion"—as if close reading, whatever "close" meant, has had its moment. It could simply be that one cannot bear to. One cannot bear to get
near to that space, connected to letteration as sheer form, only not because
of the usual alibi—that it does not provide historical reference and so on.
Au contraire: perhaps it is because of the suspense. It brings us too close to
the virtuality of referents and their catastrophic histories. Perhaps it helps
suspend what seems virtual, what seems there "now," and this itself has
become unbearable to conjure. Maybe the time of the séance is over—and
it is left to deal with how things have fallen out, the distribution of random
pasts, the momentary concretization of intolerably predictable futures.

   At the Irvine conference dedicated to his work and enigmatically titled
"J," Hillis Miller chose to give his keynote address on the "zero" as an
impossible mathematical sign and as a rhetorical figure. Does the "zero"
have something to do with the letter "J" itself that is not apparent—this
other, nonetheless backlooping line and marker? Certainly, the period that
holds the initial "J" in place has been used as a zero (*periodos*, as going
round), much as the "J" has, at different points, represented units, digits.
In Miller's account of the state and status of numeration, which departs

83

from de Man's essay on allegory in Pascal, "zero" appears as a nonentity called forth retroactively by an impasse in numbering. It appears preoriginary to and unlocatable in any genealogy, although it has many: "The origin of the zero seems to fade off into the infinite distance, at some converging point beyond or before Mayans, Arabs, Babylonians, Hindus." And it is not only the zero—a "nothing that is," says Robert Kaplan—that finds itself exposed as placeholder for the absence of number, a "radical heterogeneity" (says de Man) that holds the "double wings" of the two infinities dubiously in place.[1] The "one" does not do too well, either—since it is, in de Man's calculus, a sort of a *Nachkonstruktion* or aftereffect, a "trope of zero." The zero seems to perform as a spectral supplement at the phantom origin of the "n + 1," generating a seriality that then compels spacing or time effects. As a countersignifying backloop, it takes up home almost everywhere—in theology, in capital, in linguistics, in history (innumerable fallacious "ground zeros").

And yet there is something lovable about the zero—utterly ubiquitous and intimate in its nesting into itself: Its sometime rotundity anaesthetizes and is welcome when proliferating at the end of an escalating sum. In its discrete way, the zero, as Miller inspects it, is emblematic for *how* something (or a nothing) inscribes itself into the historical real, like an alien lodger, and where such a program (a way of seeing, of thinking, of using metaphor) *might* be evacuated and reinscribed.[2]

The fact that Miller chose to present an essay on the "zero" for a conference dedicated to his work and entitled simply and enigmatically "J" raises a question. What is the relation between letters and numerical signs, if "J" and "zero" even represent these categories? Miller notes how the zero routinely covers up its own discovery or implantation: its back-looping logic mimes the fact that every time it is discovered, it seems all along to have been there:

The zero seems secretly to have entered into the language needed to talk about it. I mean by this that when the zero enters into equations and equivalences, whether numerical or semantic, it is easily possible to demonstrate that any number is the equal of, homologous to, in some formal semiotic sense the equivalent of, any other number, or that any object is the same as any other object. Seife's example is the proof that Winston Churchill is a carrot. As Seife says, "Used *unwisely*, zero has *the power to destroy logic*."

But if a "zero" or its logics, after all, are subject to use, are essentially to be considered as a sort of *techne*, what would a wise or just use be of what could, in unwise *hands*, simply destroy things? World leaders with advanced nuclear abilities have this same problem. What *uses* does Miller's flâneurlike account of the zero's rhetorical career imply? Is the zero to be considered as a token of what is now called by physicists "dark energy" lodging within number, whose accelerations guarantee, in time, a molecular rip of all constituent bodies and form? Perhaps, if one is looking for the signature of "J," it is in this place or nonplace where "number" seems generated out of its own conflagration.[3]

Whatever it means to title a conference with this letter, "J" is already haunted by a radical technicity. In Hillis Miller's case, the "J" remains a tombstone for a retracted name. Whatever associations this lost name gives rise to, as when Derrida remarks in this volume that it conjures Joseph the Interpreter, even this name is not necessarily accepted as its own by the bottled-up "J." To write "J" is to retract the name, to signal its denial or concealment. It refers to, as if before name *as such*, its refusal of what it nonetheless contains. Without a period stopping it, the "J" might just madly self-replicate—as when a series of cuts or slashes generates a perceptual and spatiotemporal grid. Such a stuttering J J J J might be refined, by the force of repetition, into something like / / / /—all but graphically preceding its Greek or Roman character variations.

Thus in his intricate homage to Hillis, Derrida pauses over the enigma of this abashed initial, and he observes that it looks like the "burial of a bad J"—that it appears, all cut off, in some minor way criminal, an outcast, perhaps to be punished. Yet what is the difference between a good J and a bad J? Is the "J" that conjures rich biblical names and suggests justice and fidelity in fact "good"? Is to be bad, then, to go as if in the other direction (that of a negative infinity perhaps) and retreat to the de-auratic side of the letteral mark, outside any recuperative trope? Or, inversely, might not that refusal of aura be, in a different sense, precisely "good"—that is, insofar as it points as if beyond the spell of names and personification toward a zone in which other teletechnic maps become legible? Why must the "bad J" be buried, so much in the open, as at the crossroads Christians reserved for suicides, those finding no place in the anthropotheological economy in or after death?[4]

* * *

Derrida continued to speculate on what it could be to feel and say, "I, Hillis Miller"—something labyrinthine and phantomatic, no doubt. And he proceeded to honor Hillis with a signal moniker. He conjured an affective being he could, credibly, call "Hillis the Just." One understands, even before Derrida's implosive recasting of *dike* as a performative *à venir* and predicate of "deconstruction": Miller's mercurial migrations between diverse discourses, the tireless networking and undoing in fractal labyrinths, the absence of animus, the generosity, the apparent *fidelity*, if the term is relevant, to whatever had been called deconstruction. Yet the moniker is covertly curselike. Miller is marked. The appellation cannot not recall that of "Aristides the Just" of Athens, a man renowned for being so just that he was ostracized. However pre-Socratic in its inflection and force, in Derrida's rewriting of it, the invocation of the word "just" or "justice" cannot escape soliciting from some quarters prematurely pious or familial associations. And this, just when the extreme opposite, one might deduce at a glance, ought to be mobilized by various deconstructive extensions today, that is, the seeking of discrete points where mnemonic intervention remains possible, less likely to return to familial territory and protection.

Miller signals this resistance in association with the zero, which cannot inhabit anything like justice dependably, given all its inversions and masks. It occurs when he cites de Man in his presentation on "zero" on precisely this: "To the extent that language is always cognitive and tropological as well as performative at the same time, it is a heterogeneous entity incapable of justice as well as of *justesse*." In the name of justice, one renounces the most desirable of its desemanticized projections—a justice so just, so resistant to the calls of affiliation, even, that it is incapable of "justice as well as of *justesse*." It is so just that it acknowledges its injustice or ajustice as constitutive. Whatever language means—this unfortunate prosopopoeia of de Man's, by which teletechnics in all its graphematic extensions is implied—it cannot claim to be "just." Justice cannot *not* wander, perhaps into its opposites, arrest its designees, or compel some rank injustice.

On the same occasion that he received this remarkable honor, which fills out the blocked "J" and gives it again body and goodness, Miller reproduced at the center of his text a counterstrophe by way of de Man's zero that rejects this. The speech act that bestows this moniker (Hillis the Just) is so unique that it cannot but call both the giver and receiver into momentary hiatus. Derrida's name bestowal resists the semimemorializing occasion it arises in response and protest to (symbolic retirement, generational passage)—programming a chain of resistances in advance. There is, however discreetly, a covert tussle of, between, and over (the) "J." At this point, Miller's itinerary assumes a distinct hue.[5]

So I want to address an other Miller or J. Let us call him "Hillis the Bad" or, with a Baudelairean inflection in mind that is directly relevant to his affiliations with de Man and Benjamin: Hillis *le mal*. You think this witty perhaps—but recall Miller's citation of a difference between the wise and unwise uses of zero, the one temperate and curious, the other at risk and destroying. Whatever this bad or evil side is (an appellation redundant if applied to "de Man"), it would appear associated with a certain wound or tear in the fabric of memory, in the familiar, in the house as militarized metaphoric structure, in how the aesthetic and what was once called the political are understood or today programmed.

In speaking of Hillis *le mal*, I am thinking of one who is, in a way, a con.[6] Miller had always been a practitioner of fronts and *proschemata*—able to adopt diverse critical and philosophical histories, roles, and institutional habitats. He has always *passed*. The term *proschema* is one whose use Plato allows his Protagoras, who allegorically explains why a philosopher must adopt roles to disguise and deflect inevitable persecution by the people. Plato had Socrates in mind. Protagoras's technique was to pretend to be teaching old virtues while evacuating and redefining the term *aretē* itself—a prototype of the Platonic *eidos*, another virtual zero term. In his paper on the "zero," Miller wants to give you something for nothing, or a nothing that is something, or some *thing*. He pretends to be the most diplomatic and patient of explicators, as he does here with de Man's remarks on the "zero" as a sort of plug in the universe of numbers and form. Miller comes like your uncle with a suitcase—yet what's in it? It is like the famous contraption that Hitchcock calls a MacGuffin, it covers a black hole of logic, and it is for *you*. Miller tells us of the mathematicians who went mad or committed suicide when trying to think the zero. Yet after examining this very reasonable review of a problem, you get up to go, you want to put it away, but you cannot. You have been pushed into a black hole. Miller thinks it's good for you, even if—per definition—you can't get out (a black hole absorbs constellations, light, space-times).

Now, I am raising this prospect in pop-cultural terms for a reason. There is a problem with the use of the term "ethical" as applied to Hillis Miller (and maybe to what is called "deconstruction"). Let us not understand it too quickly—this ethics of reading. It does not mean that you must be dutiful and rigorous and thorough and respond as a responsible character in tracing the otherness of your readings. That's "Hillis the Just." Maybe. For Hillis *le mal* it means: You have no choice but to go where the tracks and maelstrom *formally* lead, and that is always, always, toward an epistemological black hole buried in the backdrop, like the J.

More: There is indeed an "ethics" to entering this space but it has little to do with will or character—it finds itself at a site whose direction is, de Man might add, irreversible. That's what de Man said of the shift from what he called tropological systems to that "other model" he inadequately called the performative. You can't get back—you must pass through, even if you are unrecognizable after (if there is an after). Some ethics. And yet one can agree with it, almost totally. And the "almost" is, rather, positional, in speculating on what this archival game board seems today, as if irreversibly, being *set* for. All Miller's speculations on reading and critical politics covertly ask not about an exemplary interpretation or a critical concept, which are its pretexts, but—as the metaphorics of the black hole insinuates as it works archival levers—about the ability of a species that has acquired genetic engineering to alter its own preinscriptions. At a time when received epistemopolitical and technoindustrial orders appear to be approaching a certain black hole and impasse as sustainable models, the zeroids on which they are predicated may need to be spectrally dislodged, enphantomed otherwise.

Thus, the "zero," as Miller reads it, is haunting and unbenign. It is not just a "problem" to be considered, since it is constitutive of the logic that would address it. It is not just the plug or bubblegum stuck into aporia that quietly holds numeration or the conceptual order together in forgetfulness. It mimes or gives spellbinding form to—consider it for a moment—the black hole of black holes, a circlet that also marks mnemonic backloops, a wedge against abyssal regress or fracture, a specter become a fact. The ethics of reading does not advise us to return to close readings of literature, such as Miller is mistakenly thought to imply. That is incidental. He delights, it seems to me, in the latter's institutional passing, spurring and fractalizing it en route toward whatever comes next—a mutating archive of which the mnemotechnics of the "book" were but a central dossier. Hillis celebrates literature with a Mafioso's kiss.

This is where Hillis *le mal* returns: Miller knows something other beneath his cover as explicator. It has to do with the structure of hermeneutic programs, mnemonic horizons, how the "senses" are programmed archivally, and how these are controlled, if not self-cancelingly accelerated, through ganglia, nodes, and monads. He wants to contaminate and pass that on—that is, to induce irreversibility. That would be: the instant the tropological dissembles before an event not subject to personification or aura—and just what may occur there. To become irreversible, here, to enter Benjamin's "one-way street," is one means of marking the going under (in Nietzschean parlance) of a mnemonic regime, a template of the senses or archival implant, a way of dissolving an epistemological blind of referential and chronographic maps.

Yet what "is" a black hole—nonsite where a logic folds back to emerge in advance of itself, like the "zero" which, Miller tells us, *was* not, but once in place seems as if it had always been there, fabricating an implanted memory? It is not or not just an "aporia," but an aporia mobilized forward. It opens wormholes in temporal orders, stitching pasts and virtual futures otherwise—and seems very Benjaminian in this: It is proactively oriented toward an intervention in the constructions of experiential time and can suspend—if momentarily—a program one is in the grips of, as if the 3-D before one crackled and dissolved for an instant. I will return to why it should be of interest to a discussion of "aesthetics" what the de Manian moment here may be whereby the aesthetic, so called, is cinematized from a domain of mere play to the phenomenalization of inscriptions, like a film spool from which "experience" or the sensorium is blindly legislated.

To intervene, in this Benjaminian sense, is to intercede performatively in mnemonic systems—in the archive, from which alternative pasts and futures are generated. Miller has given us this exorbitant gift in his suitcase: the black hole. Like the zero, it can be your friend—if you move with it—or it can be your worst enemy. I will suggest why, at the present moment, one may have no option but to enter it aggressively. But by the time you know this, in a sense, Miller has departed. He may even have pushed you in when you went to peek and sat on the lid until the shaking stopped. But now it is irreversible. You will come out otherwise, you may not even recognize or be recognized or be a "you." You will not be rewarded. But there is perhaps an imperative to this, which takes it away from being an ethics of will precisely. I have had the temerity to call Miller a "con," of sorts, like a travel agent whose advertisements mislead. One cannot exactly put up travel brochures for a black hole or its resorts.

Or can you? Have you ever been in a black hole? Have you ever *not*—in a culture or species that fetishizes and occludes, disguises and seeks to repeat, a zeroid figure at the core of its technics? Stop and think: This zero that Miller tells us about, proliferating madly, it is not just for the mathematicians. Look around—it is everywhere on the street: bicycle wheels, phone receivers, spectacles, your raise, your bagel, the moon. It is inescapable, a madness of banalities. Imagine Nietzsche's eternal recurrence, another MacGuffin, as a film set stuccoed with props: That's what you live in.

But it gets worse, these circlets. Hitchcock identified the zero with cinema, the beginning in advance of consciousness of a fully inscribed celluloid strip again and again, inserted before sight, phoenixlike, fired by an artificed light, and has one of his characters refer to a "traveling circus"— that is, a cinematic operation—that had already "folded," that is, collapsed upon itself in advance, imploding representational space. Faulkner, when he wants to insinuate that a titanic black laborer named "Rider" (in which we hear both "writer" and "reader") ruptures temporal structures, writes of a "junctureless backloop of time's trepan"—the surgical intervention at a site in advance of one's own inscriptions, the possibility of altering the archival site from which various presents or futures appear cast. Derrida perhaps calls this nonsite *khōra*.

How does this zero or zeroid figure function? It is, Miller says as much, a kind of *con* too, something one confides in, yet that covers the absence of what it pretends, caught between what de Man calls "the double wings" of the two infinities, positive and negative, large and small, a butterfly at the point of metamorphosis or crossing to another template of memory and morphology. What is a black hole, today, if we are not—and Miller never, strictly, is—talking "literature"? Well, look in the newspapers. The liquidity trap economists predict of deflation (Japan is cited as an incubating model), when the release of capital meant to reverse economic flatlining goes into a black hole of autoconsumption eating up real-estate values: The logic consumes the remedy and accelerates. A black hole. Or again: Imagine a planetary *socius* where the global hyperpower and lead consumer nation—faced with irrevocable data on the evisceration of species and biosystems—instead accelerates the protocols of consumption beyond the point of irreversibility. Then "futures" are consumed, as well, as though (in fact) time were commodified in cooked balance sheets. A black hole. Or again: Imagine an American mediacracy which, in the name of a democracy it has virtually suspended, without any alternative politics or positionality, accelerates the dismantling of any and all oppositional vectors internal or international. A black hole.

The list is just beginning, by the way—it is actually quite extensive today, when all variety of possible futures are being suspended or consumed (the black hole is chronographic as well as, in Miller's term, "topographic"). So you see, Hillis never was telling us about an aporia within mathematics or a nontrope inhabiting literary language. He has just pointed at something, opened the suitcase, and left the room. Miller knows that "we" did not spring from hunter-gatherers to *this*—look around whatever space you are in—in mere thousands of years (that is, circlings by earth of its sun—another zeroid) without the zero from which the "n + 1" takes off or accelerates. Consider what had been called America's "ground zero"—memorialized into a faux trope of one or "n + 1 . . ." on which political schemes and accelerations are grafted in the name of "homeland security," the void specter of interiority.

But this is the familial site of the black hole: You don't know when you are in it, since the program is totalized, and it pulses through every teletechnic device (screens, cell phones, media, memory grids), which it also threatens—on a material level—to redissolve or turn into policial orders. The black hole inhabits the living room or Starbucks, let us say, of the so-called post*global* (another spheroid trope) viewed as a mediatric state. So you might as well go into or through it, irreversibly, implosively, even, if only to arrive as if before the program you ("we") may be inscribed in—in the archival orders that, for Benjamin, would be the only site of intervention. Historicism, which thought itself to accumulate more Enlightenment "facts" that would help (its "n + 1"), for Benjamin just fueled a holocaust that was closing in. Today, perhaps, the totalization of the aesthetic state is more accelerated and replete, more mediatized and void of alternative horizons than that of the fascist encroachment of imperial states—it is not Europe at issue, not even the "global" as trope, but what cannot quite be named the planetary.[7] Any mutation of this anaesthetizing grid might presuppose a retraction of aura, of personification, of anthropomorphism.

* * *

And this is perhaps what de Man meant by the "aesthetic," by *the* aesthetic as a domain in which perception, mnemonics, representation, and the "home" are violently inscribed or maintained. It may name the domain, today, where mediatized perception (heard in the Greek *aisthanumai*) is mnemonically shaped and passively *an*aesthetized.[8] The "aesthetic" converts itself here into the obverse of everything it had, as a general category, been naturalized by when bracketed as "play"—the nonsite from which historical levers and inscriptions appear as if set or hypostatized. The tools and ruptures that Miller harvests while crisscrossing archival legacies anticipate coming wars over such preinscriptions as past models of the "political" deflate before a hyperaesthesia of what may be called today less "empire" (with its retroevangelical tinge) than, perhaps, a totalized (an)aesthetic *state*. Today, this goes for the so-called Right and the Left, philosophy and literature, "man" or "life" and their others—in a mnemotechnic and biomorphic field that, as the "zero" tells us when left flapping, has been more like animation all along.

Hillis the Just? Perhaps. Hillis *le mal*? For sure. They are the same. And nothing is more allied to this evil, in the Baudelairean sense, than the "ethics" Miller pretends to deploy. Even if one is wary today of anything that propels the legatees of Hillis's ticking suitcase to feel memorial or pious, to enter familial zones of academic intrigue and comfort, to *relapse* (this is de Man's word) into illusions of fidelity, just when Hillis, so amiable, so avuncular, all but tells us the opposite with his zero essay. Whatever would seem "irreversible" in de Man's micrological assaults on personification and inscription, prosopopoeia and the aesthetic, perhaps leads here—to a horizon without one, without the "one," without the literalization of "life" as some one biological enclave or homeland.

Now you know why Aristides the Just was cast out of Athens. And why, when an illiterate Athenian stranger, a Snopes-like bumpkin, asked Aristides without recognizing him to scratch the latter's own name on a pottery shard for him (the Athenian could not stand to hear anyone alluded to with that title), Aristides agreed to the request, signing, as with another's hand, what delivered his own exile: "Aristides the Just." But that, then, is the blindness of (a)justice. And that is why entering the black hole (if it is a choice) *seems* ethical. It will not bring you recognition, it will not assure refuge with an academic power at its tediously safe acme. You may not be recognizable when you come out, *if* you come out, and only the event of disinscription, if it occurs, might remain, perhaps without your signature attached. It anticipates a logic beyond mourning, beyond the pretexts of fidelity or its strategic inversions. But it is what remains worthy, I think, for the legatees of this complex, since it is an attempt to keep virtual futures, for the "present," as if in play.

*   *   *

In the remarks cited above by Miller on family crossings and letters, he explains that a passage in *Cranford* "has to do with generation and with the passing on of names from generation to generation in family crossings. It has to do with the letter f, in fact with a double f. F is genealogically derived from G, gamma in Greek, which is another kind of crossing, the fork in the road, a truncated X, like Y." Miller here gives unusual attention to the morphing role of graphic lines and the potential force they retain. One might have difficulty locating the letter J itself on such a map, although it is perhaps closest to what Miller calls, simply, *line*, since it barely disguises its proximity to the most literal and preletteral sort of staff or, if you like, gash. It is one of the unanswered riddles of the "J" conference dedicated to Miller's work: that is, the conference's name.

A more or less vertical bar, the "J" is in the modern era anchored by the spur decorously added by early modern scribes. The letter's genealogy is more dubious—passing back through the relatively unadorned line or digit, derived from a finger, of the Romans or, before them, the Greeks, and spiraling back further to the pictographic hand of the Egyptians, noted as the J's historical source. When a J. is bottled up with a period, or placed alone at the beginning of a signature, it seems heterogeneous. With a little prodding, it can expand into a flagship term like "justice" or a biblical name like "Jesus" or "Jeremiah." Left by itself, it can recede into a preletteral cut or mark, evoke the *hand* as emblem of a *techne* converting the paw into the advent of "man," with its notorious ten digits. Left alone, it cannot be alone or one, but is always lifted from an indefinite series that carves or generates spatiotemporal maps. "J," according to this, passes from the figure of technicity through digitalization, the "one" and the zero—it is, right away, an agency of teletechnic prowess.

Among the contradictions that have shadowed "deconstruction" is how fidelity to a signature or canon, a style or set of moves, a familial enterprise or network, can constitute betrayal of what the term could be taken to mean as a terrestrial and transhistorical project that involves innumerable names and styles. Miller's labors—what he sometimes calls the task of "the critic"—feed horizons of critical combat to come. Fractal reading and the black hole, as critical symptoms, prepare for wars of reinscription over the senses and mnemonics in which the terrestrial would be redecided (or not), its zeros redistributed (or not). And Miller does so by experimenting with the rewriting of archival structures, that is to say, telemnemonics. This task behind Miller's façade eludes various radars. At a certain point, the tropology of family and fidelity—tropology itself—falls away, and there must be a purely infidel moment. Rather than being buried or shy, the grapheme "J" may have all along been ventriloquizing "Hillis Miller" from its anarchival place. Certainly, the digitlike stroke has the power to dissolve the signature's remaining letters into a stuttering row (H-I-l-l-I-S M-I-l-l . . .). It produces a series of fractal cuts, repeating and reassembling "I"s and "l"s. This might gloss the arresting image Derrida conjures in speculating on the affectivity of the one who says "I, Hillis Miller"— and why the "burial of a bad J" may have been a ruse itself. The nearly serial pattern of lines or slashes performs two things: It summons the non-site of inscription in its entirety and, at the same time, suspends or virtually disinscribes that same mnemonic surface.

Miller's incubation of a certain trajectory in late de Man, in his treatment of the zero, raises a question that persists through Miller's essays. It suggests that something may have been obscured by the "de Man affair"— and the "responses" it unleashed. It may or may not be connected with everything that has not happened in critical culture, during a time in which the critical community seemed, for all its sophistications, sleepwalking into a "postglobal" environment it has no distinct strategies to address— dragging the hangover of a glut of historicism and identity politics in its wake. Such an alternative points to something that may have been obscured by de Man's identification with the polemics surrounding "deconstruction" during the 1980s. One could, if one substituted in de Man the vaporous term "language" for something like the media or mnemotechnics, see de Man's trajectory as aimed at intervention in the mnemonic and totalized aesthetico-political orders one encounters today. One has, in any event, the feeling that the critical culture broadly, which seems unprepared for any analysis or response, political or historical, to contemporary transformations, has been sleepwalking. If so, it would be possible to say that the postglobal present persists at a phase during which aesthetic ideology has assumed an increasingly horizonless status, entirely political, a cinematic totalization that brooks fewer and fewer shocks. One might want, in such a reflection on Miller's de Man, to examine various turns not taken: turns that were foreclosed and perhaps did not in all respects quite belong to "American 'deconstruction'" of the '80s. Such a virtual reading of de Man's treatment of inscription might, for instance, supplement something like Benjamin's "materialistic historiography" with micrological engineering to reach into the archival programs themselves, which include *ocularcentrism*, how otherness is configured, the sensorium as a media product, and how the aesthetic is politically registered—or not. Such a trajectory has import in a teletechnic era reflected in the totalized or anaesthetized rhetorical structure, say, of what is called a "'global' war on terror."[9]

CHAPTER 7

The Afterlife of Judaism:
The Zohar, Benjamin, Miller

Henry Sussman

Judaism, so the common myth runs, is the Abrahamic[1] religion devoid of an afterlife. Where first Christianity and then Islam are quite explicit regarding the determination of the life hereafter by the quality of the life lived in this world, picturesque almost to the degree of luridness in representing the conditions, qualities, and experience of Heaven and Hell (and Purgatory, where applicable), Judaism hedges its bets and is far more reticent in the sphere of eschatology.[2] The liturgy of the Days of Awe, the New Year's festivals that stage the collective public acknowledgment of mortal human vices, breeches in morality, and crimes, stresses a judgment before God transpiring from year to year. The afterlife, in the wake of this theology, is the ethical imprint that a person deposits in the memory, communal and individual, of the survivors that she or he leaves behind. If this is the Judaic afterlife, its image is as vague as personal impressions of a fellow human being are idiosyncratic. Even Buddhism, whose theology is far less individual-oriented and rule-driven than Judaism, envisions a much more particular and specific relation between past lives and ones yet to emerge.

This familiar and time-honored cant makes the Christian and Muslim afterworld tantamount to a place or lieu and a time apart. But if we divert our gaze to look past this imagistic literality and allow ourselves to conflate

the afterlife with the spectral, Jewish theology has not been as eschatologi-
cally short-handed as might first appear. It is true that Judaism fully realized its own distinctive version of the afterlife only after Christianity and
Islam established and represented theirs. But once the Jewish afterlife was
inscribed, for all its vagaries and in all the specifics of Christian and Muslim Paradise and Hell that it in many respects evades, it has disseminated
itself to cultural sites far afield and insinuated itself into artifacts and cultural experiments in which its play and connivance have not been divined
even in the present day. I would go even so far as to say that the Judaic
afterlife, inscribed on the eve of European modernity[3] and revising prior
Jewish theology in keeping with the emerging lineaments of epistemic revolution, establishes a spectral setting or lieu unmistakable in its particular
sublimity, poetics, and rhetoric, leaving its imprint on artifacts as diverse
as Kleist's tales, Büchner's prose poems, the Romantic speculations of the
Schlegels and Novalis, Kafka's sublime imagery, obviously, as well as on
Scholem's lifelong project, Benjamin's always-problematical Judaism, and
Celan's poetry.

The specifically Judaic provenance and imaginary surrounding this
spectral scene of writing has been occulted over a significant segment of
its "run." It is incumbent upon us as students of culture to extract and
reconfigure this Jewish revenant or afterlife not in the name of nationalistic celebration or under the imperative of ethnic preservation, but in appreciation of the broad thoroughfare on which the three Abrahamic
religions penetrated and revitalized each other's scripts and scenarios on
the most profound and infrastructural levels. The platform common to
the three major Western monotheistic religions, as well as the spectral
abyss that haunts them,[4] have received an overdue updating and overhaul,
in terms of its conceptual depth and rigor, in Jacques Derrida's religious
explorations of the last three decades. I lean heavily on the conceptual and
architectural support furnished by this work.

The "full-service" Judaic scenario of the afterlife is medieval in its
provenance. The Judaic afterlife achieves its full configuration in the
Zohar, the Book of Splendor, a major element of the mystical movement
and literature in Judaism known as the Kabbalah. Gershom Scholem goes
to some effort to deconflate Kabbalah from the Zohar. The Kabbalah,
for one, is older. In its seminal moment, Jewish mysticism, according to
Scholem,

> did not aspire to an understanding of the true nature of God, but to a
> description of the phenomenon of the Throne on its Chariot as described

in the first chapter of Ezekiel, traditionally entitled *ma'aseh merkabah*. . . . The 14th chapter of the Book of Enoch, which contains the earliest example of this kind of literary description, was the source of a long visionary tradition of describing the world of the Throne and the visionary ascent to it, which we find portrayed in the books of the Merkabah mystics.[5]

Although the Kabbalah claims direct roots in the Book of Ezekiel and the apocryphal book of Enoch and encompasses such works as the eleventh-century Sepher Yezirah, "a compact discourse on cosmology and cosmogany (a kind of *ma'aseh bereshit*, 'act of creation,' in a speculative form), outstanding for its clearly mystical character" (Scholem, *Kabbalah*, 23) and the early twelfth-century Provençal Sefer ha-Bahir, it is in Sefer ha-Zohar, the Book of Splendor, where the Judaic afterlife achieves its full configuration. This multivolume work is a compendium of biblical commentaries or Midrashim, "written mainly between 1280 and 1286 by Moses b. Shem Tov de Leon in Guadalajara, a small town northeast of Madrid" (Scholem, *Kabbalah*, 57).

What the most elemental literary criticism makes obvious, an illumination betokening the compelling need at this juncture for broad-based literary scholars to return, in the sense of a *parcours*, to the canonical texts of a broad range of world religions, is that in the Zohar, the rabbinical contributors to the difficult and technical argumentation of the Talmud, names memorialized in the Mishna, Gemara, and the several registers of commentary around the Talmudic page,[6] have been transformed into literary characters who are seen discoursing with each other (most often in pairs) as they wander through tangible earthly landscapes (sometimes furnished with geographical coordinates). In the Talmud, the rabbis who figure in the Zohar were remote and forbidding surrogates, distant in their conceptual and legal genius. In the Zohar, the myth of their genius is extended in the highly speculative thrust and tone of their comments and in their stunning capability to issue forth in metaphysical, yet precise imagery (we will explore some examples below).

The metamorphosis, in the Zohar, of rabbis into literary characters is a capital development in the cultural history of Judaism. It is an instance in which profound cultural change and interchange are brought about by transformations in narrative. No critic of the past several generations has been more exquisitely attuned to the cultural, metaphysical, and epistemological implications of such a transposition than J. Hillis Miller. We cannot overestimate the sociocultural and tangible historical effects of the subtle, but far-reaching metamorphosis of rabbis who start out as little more than indices or placeholders for the disputations that they propound into full-blooded characters of European provenance and a somewhat modern disposition.

In a Millerian vein, this literary development is tantamount to a mega-speech act, a decisive act of narrative radically reconfiguring certain base positions in Jewish ideology while substantially realigning the Judaic position on the differential platform of the three Abrahamic religions. Miller understands this kind of happening both in terms of the translation between cultural registers and agencies and in terms of the phenomena that arise along the frontiers, no-person's lands, demilitarized zones, and borderlines of textual sites, constructed topographies of reading and thinking. None of these interstitial zones is more treacherous to Miller than the one falling between the particularity of reading and the impulse to theorize.

The experiences of reading and theorizing about the text are so similar, on such intimate terms, that one is tempted to collapse them together. And yet, as Miller specifies:

> A theoretical formulation never quite adequately addresses the insight that comes from reading. That insight is always particular, local, good for this time, place, text, and act of reading only. The theoretical insight is a glimpse out of the corner of the eye of the way language works, a glimpse that is not wholly amenable to conceptualization. Another way to put this is to say that the theoretical formulation in its original language is already a translation or mistranslation of a lost original.[7]

It is more than possible, in the distinctive critical climate configured by Miller, for the segue from the Talmud to the Zohar to perform translation and radical mistranslation.

It is uncanny to what degree Miller's exploration of a biblical text, the Book of Ruth, from which the citation immediately above derives, in terms of the parameters of reading, conversion, repatriation, and translation that it both establishes and violates, could anticipate the transformation of Talmudic figures into Zoharic ones. His reading of the Book of Ruth also accesses the abyssal atmosphere of the landscape through which the rabbis, transformed into characters, stroll together. Miller's reading of the Book of Ruth is itself an extension of a topographical understanding and treatment of the dislocations, distortions, displacements, and interchanges performed in the course of, and by, texts. The integrity of Judaism, or of any cultural community, for that matter, is less a matter of genealogical purity or the systematic exclusion of "external" influences than a strategic rhythm of appropriations and consolidations. This enables the character

Ruth, under Miller's critical gaze, one trained by considerable biblical eru-
dition, to function successfully both as an agent of the ideology of Judaic
commitment, faith, and continuity ("wither thou goest, I will go; and
whither thou lodgest, I will lodge: thy people shall be my people, and thy
God my God" [Ruth 1:16]) and as a talisman for what the story theorizes,
namely, the inevitability and nature of the topographical shifts and intercultural and interlinguistic translations involved in cultural "identity,"
persistence, or perdurance.

For all Miller is taken by Ruth's characterological vividness, strength,
and integrity, the role that he can assign her as an avatar of cultural survival is at most a limited one. This is not by virtue of any flaw or shortcoming in her character or activities, but owing to the limited purview of any
theoretical or quasi-theoretical figure or act. To the degree that Ruth, in
leaving Moab, in assuming refugee status back in Judah, and in marrying
Boaz, functions as a theoretical icon of the topographical and linguistic
transpositions required of cultural persistence, her power and efficacy are
limited, as Miller specifies in the passage cited above, by her definition by
and bracketing within a particular set of conditions, circumstances, and
nuances. This is, in a limited sense of course, the "general" limitation
upon all theoretical acts, themselves blending only too well into the liter-
ary/cultural compositions that prompted them.

Both the figure of Ruth and the Book of Ruth occupy, in Miller's reading, the status of the cultural mainstream or epitome that arises only in a
condition of marginality and displacement and that is irreconcilably alienated from itself.

> Whatever her original language and culture may have been, she can cross
> the border into Israel and be assimilated only by translating herself, so to
> speak, or being translated, into the idiom of a new culture. She becomes a
> proper wife and mother among the Israelites. Nevertheless, she brings
> something of her own, something that resists full translation and assimila-
> tion. The decision to follow Naomi was her own. . . . She is someone very
> much in charge of her own life. Whatever the commentators say, she does
> not seem simply the passive instrument of a historical or divine purpose
> that exceeds her and makes use of her to achieve its own ends. In a similar
> way, literary theory has its own stubborn and recalcitrant particularity. . . .
> It opens itself to assimilation within other cultures and languages. Like
> Ruth, it is prepared to say, "whither thou goest, I will go." (Miller, *Topo-
> graphies*, 330–31)

Miller's reading transpires at the pivot at which Ruth's role as a literary
character and as an ideological paragon fuses with her status as a figure,

both rhetorical and allegorical. It is a seamless suture. Thematically, Ruth may be taken, as Miller demonstrates, both as a figure of fidelity and repatriation and as subject to jarring displacements. Yet this dual loyalty, assimilation, and alienation is built right into her, for she is at the same time the trope of the features of language and culture that she performs. Oddly, it is the invisible seam between her exemplarity and her intransigence as a cipher in language (and specific languages) that mark her with the onus, an extension of Cain's mark, of alienation. Miller is certain not to leave this constitutional marginality and deterritorialization unmarked:

> This book of the Hebrew Bible has been alienated from itself, translated from itself. It has been put to entirely new uses, uses by no means intended by the original authors or scribes. . . . The original writer or writers of Ruth had no intention of using it as a means of legitimating the claim of Jesus to be the Messiah. That, nevertheless, is its "theoretical" function in the Christian Bible. In coming to perform this function Ruth has been alienated from itself. It has been translated in the strong sense of that word. (Miller, *Topographies*, 333)

Alienated from itself on a number of counts, the Book of Ruth may lose control of its initial ideological thrust or semantic meaning, but it joins, at the cost of its appropriation, the only economy of cultural dissemination to which Miller can subscribe: one configured at the linguistic level and operating through events of translation, grafting, and intercultural as intertextual sharing. Indeed, Miller's scenario for the vicissitudes of Ruth is hopelessly tempered by the openness that is the basis of his own exegetical ethics: a susceptibility and openness that is to be maintained at all costs, one including those of clarity, certainty, and political/social/cultural amenity, self-assurance, and self-congratulation.

This open address to what is taken to be the incommensurable and the alien has been as vital an element in Miller's teaching and service as a senior member in the community of critics and intellectuals as it is a persistent feature of his readings and expositions. Miller's gravitation to the permeable frontiers in cultural topography, his insistence on cultural assimilation as opposed to enforced integrity, lends his own writings an unusual openness to adaptation and to the distortions and misprisions that may ensue. They are likely to emerge, for example, even in my own appropriation of his commentary on the Book of Ruth.

Speculating on any enduring lesson to be learned from the displacements and translations embodied by the figure of Ruth, Miller is drawn, again uncannily, in terms of the trajectory pursued by the present essay, to her Romantic emanation as conjured up by Keats in his "Ode to a Nightingale."

> The poem speaks of the nightingale's song as something that has sounded the same in many different places and at many different times over the centuries. The nightingale's song ties Keats's own place and time to innumerable other places, times, and situations in which the nightingale's song has been heard. Thinking of this expands the poet's attention away from his preoccupations with his own suffering, limitation, and mortality to give him a virtual kinship with people in all those places and times who have heard the nightingale. Hearing the nightingale is a momentary escape from the imminence of death, although also a way to experience the desire for death. (Miller, *Topographies*, 334)

One of the emanations of the nightingale's song, which Keats endows with a broad transhistorical and multicultural range, is the one heard by Ruth as she gleans barley in Boaz's fields: "Perhaps the self-same song that found a path / Through the sad heart of Ruth, when, sick for home, / She stood in tears among the alien corn" (ll. 65–67). It is amid the general "limit-experience"[8] performed by Romanticism upon Enlightenment ideology, itself a codification of long-standing and widespread Western aspirations to rationality and utility, that Miller finds a "natural" correlative to the distinctive landscape for displacement and translation that transpires in the Book of Ruth. This is an abyss, a spectral setting of the sort surveyed by Derrida in his engagement with Western theology.

It is not entirely by accident, as we will see in the following tracings of a distinctively Kabbalistic zone of cultural production and imagination from the Zohar into European modernity, that a major Romantic poet and theorist, one who theorized along the lines and within the resources of poetry, chose to deploy the topographical and textual features that Miller unearths in the Book of Ruth. In a parallel fashion, as I hope to demonstrate below, it was a generation of Romantic writers, the likes of Kleist, Büchner, and Hoffmann, that proved most receptive to the place of a Kabbalistic afterlife within the imaginary of German letters.

One way of appreciating Euro-American Romanticism is as a fairly systematic, "retake," recalibration, and reprogramming of all prior Western thought that had currency at the moment. This "reediting" transpired with the declaration and publicity of a trans-European happening or event, and its primary impetus was the accommodation of a broad range of indeterminacies that were infiltrating European ideology on a variety of levels and registers: sociopolitical; epistemological, in the sense of Michel Foucault;⁹ conceptual (there is a reason why sublimity became a big-ticket item at this moment); and rhetorical. Miller's reading of the Book of Ruth demonstrates a subliminal elective affinity between the topography configured by certain works of ancient Hebrew literature, as it among other things theorizes the positionality of its intrinsic ideological and sociopolitical formations, and Romantic literature and theory, which gravitated toward this landscape and its underlying articulations, as they set about, at the infrastructural level, the work of quasi-systematic reprogramming or *tikkun*.¹⁰

The Zohar may itself be read as a limit-experience set to an exegetical procedure and way of thinking, as of living, codified in the Talmud. By the time of its scribing, it inhabited a somewhat different topography from the Book of Ruth, which had been absorbed into a finalized canon and was thereby invested with sacred or transcendental status. Yet its trajectory into modernity follows very much along the lines that Miller has drawn for the values and dislocations of the Book of Ruth. It is indeed against a backdrop of Romantic updatings and appropriations that Gershom Scholem took on, as his life's work, the dissemination, translation, and exhibition of the medieval Jewish mystical literature. It was precisely the Romantic receptivity to a Judaic abyss and afterlife that afforded Scholem some hope for the repatriation of the Kabbalah into the broader sphere of European letters.

Already the Merkabah or Chariot literature of the Rabbinic period, the centuries straddling the birth of Christ, according to Scholem, "refers to historical figures, whose connection with the mysteries of the Chariot is attested by Talmud and Midrash. The ascent of its heroes to the Chariot . . . comes after a number of preparatory exercises of an extremely ascetic nature" (Scholem, *Kabballah*, 15). The Zohar builds upon this tradition of narrativizing the theological paragons of Judaism. The inclusion within the narrative episodes of the Zohar of the Amorim and Tannaim, the Talmudic commentators remembered for the logico-legalistic prose of their discourse, humanizes these rabbis in the sense that Jesus humanizes the principles of Judaism by embodying them, that is, by characterologically condensing them. Ironically, then, the Zohar plays the New Testament to the Talmud's obsessional codification and qualification.

And there is something surely otherworldly, spooky, I would say, but in a distinctly Judaic grain, in the proclivity of the Zohar's rabbis for imagery itself condensing the magical with the metaphysical. In the course of the Zohar's tales, we are made privy to the rabbis' gift for interweaving the logical and conceptually intriguing with imagery "riddled with light," breathtaking in luminosity. Scholem gathered this tendency and poetics of medieval Jewish script under the rubric of "Jewish mysticism." It may well be that the marginal status of Palestine and Israel since the late nineteenth century, combined with Scholem's urgency in establishing the Hebrew University, forced his hand in imputing a revealed foundation to his chosen literature, for his was surely a sophisticated literary and critical mind. Yet what distinguishes "Jewish mysticism" is far more a specific poetics and tonality of imagery that Scholem locates in such works as the Kabbalah, the Sefer Yezira, and the Zohar than it is the claim of direct revelations.

It is in the Zohar that the afterlife of Judaism is first fully revealed. The itinerant rabbis of the Zohar deliver up their images of splendor, which Benjamin would term their dialectical images,[11] in the aftermath of the formal commentaries they have delivered in the various registers of the Talmud. The rabbis of the Zohar expended themselves centuries before in the intricate and obscure discursive involutions of that Talmudic compendium, so vast that it is repeatedly described in oceanic terms.[12]

Their "life" in the Zohar is a revenant, a Second Coming. It is not only the rabbis in the Zohar who are dead. At least figuratively, Judaism is dead, as well. It has died. The idyllic landscape the rabbis traverse as they discourse on a more speculative and poetic level than ever before may not be the Heaven of Jewish faith, but it is an afterlife. In figurative death, that is in exile, and bound up in formalistic legal involution, Judaism is freer and more vibrant than it ever was in life, or as a sovereign nation. Many of the Zohar's folktales take place at night.

* * *

For purposes of the present demonstration, I want to focus on the figure of the stars, above all because their figure resurfaces as a multifaceted motif in Benjamin's criticism. There it ranges in its resonations from an embodiment of metaphysical naiveté that is indispensable to exegesis and inscription at the same time that it cries out for debunking to the constellation of anomalous and dissonant cultural counterforces emerging in the particular archive that every working critic assembles and that becomes indistinguishable from her intellectual imprimatur or signature. But within the framework of the mythopoetic reconfiguration or reformation of biblical and Talmudic sources that is the Zohar, the stars are inscribed within a complex of other figures at once poetically rich and hovering and instrumental to medieval Judaic metaphysics, including nighttime, light, plants, bodies and vessels of water, erotic desire, and clothes. Indeed, the stars form one point in a poetically captivating constellation of images whose interaction lifts the curtain on a modern, literarily full-fledged Judaism, and, as a figure, they become key players in Benjamin's most resilient allegory of criticism.

One could well argue, moreover, that the Zohar's spectral, nocturnal narrative space, in which everything is phantasmatically after the fact, preempts the jarringly concussive space of postmodernity, in which the most disparate and unrelated counterforces, formations, and crystallizations coexist with impunity and in mutual indifference. One of many possible fabulations from twentieth-century literature that could be elicited as an instance of this Kabbalistic space, a phenomenon that could transpire only under the aegis of this specifically Judaic imaginary, is the ironic coda and afterlife at the end of Bruno Schulz's *Sanatorium under the Sign of the Hourglass*. In the sanatorium highlighted by the title, the narrator is afforded one last encounter with his domineering, yet vulnerable father. The father has died, yet is not yet gone. His affective and imaginary power over his son remains in effect. Their last interview transpires in an uncanny time warp that is after life and before annihilation, during a temporal slowdown and deferral, one nonetheless very much in the province and provenance of language. In response to the narrator/son's incredulous question, Dr. Gotard, superintendent of the sanatorium, characterizes the father's status in the following terms: "The whole secret of the operation . . . is that we have put back the clock. Here we are always late by a certain interval of time of which we cannot define the length. The whole thing is a matter of simple relativity. Here your father's death, the death that has already struck him in your country, has not occurred yet."[13] This uncanny legend even goes so far as to suggest that there is something "mystical," in the Zoharic sense, in the temporality of Einsteinian physics, so much at home in the twentieth century. The radical deferral that has settled over the sanatorium, itself a version of the afterlife, corresponds to the temporal setting of the particular folktales that among so many others were capable of riveting Scholem's attention.

The above will I hope serve as a minimal context for a folktale from the commentaries in the Zohar directed at Exodus:

> Once Rabbi Eleazar and Rabbi Abba were sitting together, and then the dusk came, whereupon they got up and started toward a garden by the Lake of Tiberias. Going, they beheld two stars speed toward each other from different points of the sky, meet, and then vanish.
>
> Rabbi Abba observed: in heaven above and on the earth below, how great are the works of the Holy One, be blessed. Who fathoms it, how these stars come from different points, how they meet and disappear?

Rabbi Eleazar answered: Nor did we need to see these two stars to reflect on them, for we have pondered on them, as we have on the multitude
of great works that the Holy One, be blessed, is ever doing.
Then quoting the verse, "Great is the Lord and mighty in power; his
understanding is without number" [Ps. 147:5], he went on to discourse: In
truth, great and mighty and sublime is the Holy One, be blessed.[14]

In a specific setting and location, indeed, in the specific site in the Galilee that was so crucial to the birth of Christianity, two of the seminal
Jewish scholars and litigators of the Talmud meditate, in solidarity and
intimacy, on the sublime phenomenon of the shooting stars that arise,
coincide, and pass each other haphazardly, outside the cadres of meaning
or necessity. Indeed, the discussion is explicitly more about the very condition of such arbitrariness than it is about the most mercurial of the heav-
enly bodies, the shooting stars. The prerogative of thinking people to
meditate on the shooting stars takes precedence over their actuality or
veracity, just as the ontotheological mandate of Abrahamic religion, faith
in a monotheistic divinity, transpires autonomously of the facts and of the
prevailing sociopolitical formation, whose confirmation or approval it does
not require. It is in this sense that the extraordinarily innovative and central Rabbi Eleazar can assure: "Nor did we need to see these two stars to
reflect on them." He agrees with Rabbi Abba that it is ultimately unfathomable "how these stars come from different points, how they meet and
disappear."

The shooting stars' enigmatic trajectory across the sky becomes a legend for a familiar Judaic outcome. The Lord is "Great . . . and mighty in
power. . . . In truth, great and mighty and sublime is the Holy One, be
blessed." The pretext and predetermined outcome of Jewish theology is
faith in God, endlessly reaffirmed faith and commitment, in spite of the
chance, accident, arbitrariness, and sublimity inscribed in the metaphysics
and very image of the stars. This final conclusion known in advance is
only strengthened by these extenuating circumstances. The Kaddish, the
formulaic Judaic response to the unmitigated arbitrariness of death, the
textual talisman, whose repetition, thrice daily for a year after bereavement
and thereafter at specific intervals, is, above all, a responsive series of attributions of omniscience and omnipotence to God.[15] The Judaic gut reaction to death, in other words, consists largely of a subordination of
personal loss, despair, outrage, and related psychological reactions to a
public figuration and affirmation of God's majesty.

But on the way to this fatal, if uplifting outcome, however it might have
been reached in advance, the Zoharic folktale registers a number of key

modifications that have taken place in Judaic parlance. Rabbis Abba and Eleazar are not sages or legal authorities, invested with quasi-divine intelligence and authority. On the Sea of Galilee, one of the primal scenes of Christianity, they have been raptured up from the Talmud and reborn as literary characters, where simply as such they have served as conduits or channels, a key Kabbalistic image, introducing several pivotal traits of modernity into Judaism. Indeed, their rebirth as literary characters, under the enigmatic sign of the shooting stars, coincides with the entry of a Christian and Islamic notion of the afterlife into Judaism. The beloved sages of the Talmud, in other words, as avatars of all Judaism, have to die in order to be reborn, and their rebirth as literary characters coincides with the entrance of figured, depicted, represented death into the sanctuary of Judaism.

But this is not all that is liberated and activated by Judaism's engagement with certain precepts, modalities, and scenes of representation that had been, previously, strictly other. The folktales of the Zohar may coincide with Judaism's acknowledgment of literary characterization and Western eschatology, of Greek as well as Christo-Islamic provenance, but they are also imprinted with a specifically Judaic poetics, one in which the categories of logic and classification are endowed with a vivid sublimity and then literally dance across the stage or abyss of representation, not unlike the track of the shooting stars against the backdrop of heaven. The dance of the divinely inflected creatures or creations of logic across the scene of theological speculation as across the page anticipates by many centuries what Friedrich Schlegel would characterize as *parabasis*.[16] The specifically Judaic afterlife and scene of representation announced in the Zohar was embraced and admitted, if by any mainstream European national culture, into the domain of German letters and into the German literary imaginary, to a far greater degree than into any other. This explains how Walter Benjamin could have credibly set out on his life's work as a herald and scribe of German-Jewish literary relations, however this vocation was ultimately sabotaged by the politico-historical events taking place during his lifetime.

A very fine display of the poetics accompanying the rebirth of the rabbis as literary figures is encompassed by our legend of the shooting stars:

> Acting as guardians over this world are all the stars of the firmaments, with each individual object of the world having a specially designated star to care for it. The herbs and the trees, the grass and the wild plants, to bloom and increase much have the power of the stars that stand over them and look

directly at them, each in its particular mode. The great number of the plants and stars of all kinds emerge at the beginning of the night and shine until three hours minus a quarter after midnight. Thereafter only a small number are out. It is not without purpose that all the stars shine and serve. Some, being at their duty the whole night through, cause the plant which is their special ward to spring up and flourish. Others begin their activities at the advent of night and watch over their own objects until the hour of midnight. . . . So it was with the stars which we saw, which appeared briefly for their set task. When their task is accomplished, such stars vanish from this world. (Scholem, *Zohar: Book of Splendor*, 74–75)

In this vignette, each herb, tree, plant, and variety of grass is the "ward" of a particular star. The sublime multiplication of the stars, and by implication, the vastness of the heavens, is infused into the domestic world of cultivation by means of this dedicated stewardship. In the above passage, for instance, each of the elements in the vegetable kingdom is activated at a different moment in the course of the night. Based on this stately progression of nocturnal vegetable awakening, God has scientifically coordinated a succession of stars the best to oversee the worldly garden.

What is stunning about this image is the juxtaposition between earthy plant life and unreachable stars, impeccable divine planning and spaces and schemes of inconceivable vastness. We are speaking here of "guardian stars," if not guardian angels. The passage builds toward a Foucauldian analogy or similitude between the inconceivable architecture of the heavens and the vegetable biosphere.[17] The poetic effect of this coincidence between two realms, which are, from a human point of view, both inconceivable and uncontrollable, is a specific form of Kabbalistic magic— magical reverie, not magical realism. By means of such a figure as the stars, the Book of Splendor marshals the vastness of the universe in the service and representation of God. The Judaic divinity functions not merely as the transcendental signifier of the work; the *Shekhinah*[18] or divine presence manifests itself in a specific poetics. This poetics choreographs a dance, delirious in its exoneration from the constraints of rationality, but also in its deployment of logic, between the things of our world and the grandeur, multiplication, and endless extension and proliferation characterizing the holy guardians charged with overseeing them, that is, manifesting unwavering attentiveness and intimate, total understanding of them. "The book of the higher wisdom of the East tells us of stars with trailing tails. Comets, which from the skies hold sway and direct the growth of certain herbs on earth, of the sort known as 'elixirs of life,' and influence also the growth of these is brought about by the flash of that luminous tail trailing after these stars across the firmament" (Scholem, *Zohar: Book of Splendor*, 75). Not only is the magnificent, ineffable design of the universe scored into the earth, literally implanted, under the sign of the guardian stars. The heavens, particularly as expressed by the comet's tail, take on a worldly ephemerality within the framework of otherworldly movement and time. Indeed, no figure could intensify fleeting intransience more fully than a comet's instantaneously disappearing traces. The sweep of the comet's tail gives full evidence that the dance that is the exemplary figure for the radiation of divine—that is to say mystical—insight throughout the universe, trips across the heavens, as it does across the earth.

The dance of mystical Judaic poetics, a choreography that is the preeminent poetic trait reaching across a liturgical literature, transpires in a scene or theater that is an afterlife. The dance between the plenitude of this world and the ineffable predestination of the divine plan is rendered all the more vital by the fact that it is staged in a spectral setting in which all telling figures and characters are long dead. This prior death, the transpiration of Jewish mysticism's most striking figures into an afterlife, infuses all Judaic eschatology with an irreducible pretext of irony. This is an irony situated on the very threshold between life and death. Indeed, the contemplation by Judaism of final things becomes a life-and-death matter whose endless potential for humor can be taken in exactly the opposite way. It is one thing for Judaism to suspend certain of its discursive preoccupations and the roles it has assigned to some of its key players in an ironic afterlife, quite another for it to be apprehended as a culture that has prospectively, through some bizarre collective death wish, accommodated its own demise or demission.

Yet if we need any further proof that when Judaism succumbs to the overall Abrahamic tendency toward eschatology it does so with particular vehemence and intensity, we need only examine certain of the folktale commentaries to Genesis in which the afterlife is explicitly invoked. In one of the "basic readings from the Kabbalah" that Scholem translates and assembles in his thin collection of Zoharic folktales, Rabbi Simeon, who appeals directly to God, manages to fend off Rabbi Isaac's impending death, but only for a while. Scholem furnishes this story with the title "The Great Feast," a "parabolic expression of death."

In a dream, Rabbi Isaac's father telegraphs ahead his "portion" in the "world to come." The landscape that Rabbi Isaac is about to inhabit has been fitted out with

seventy crowned places which are his, and each place has doors which open
to seventy worlds, and each world opens to seventy channels and each channel is open to seventy supernal crowns, and thence are ways leading to the
Ancient and Inscrutable One, opening on a view of that celestial delight
which gives bliss and illumination to all, as is stated, "to see the pleasant-
ness of the Lord and to visit His temple" [Ps. 27:4]. (Scholem, *Zohar: Book
of Splendor*, 29)

The kernel of this Zoharic fabulation is once again a biblical verse, a relatively bland celebration of the Lord's temple and of visiting him there.
The extract from the psalm is merely a pretext to a celestial panorama of
immense splendor vastly multiplying upon itself by a constant factor of
seventy. In the approach to the ineffable that Judaic poetics makes through
multiplication and illumination, the latter term embodying Benjamin's
highest hope for commentary, it opens a channel to the iconography of the
Indian religions. The channels of the Zohar, like the *passages* that Kafka
conspicuously installs in the various court settings of *The Trial* and in the
burrow creature's labyrinthine subterranean refuge function both as features in an expansive architecture and as rhizomatic nodes of textual con-
vergence and displacement.[19]

We need to remember that this splendiferous abode, whose channels
and crowns belong to the Sefiroth or formal spheres of Kabbalistic cosmology,[20] belongs to an afterlife, a setting whose being and opening is
conditioned on prior annihilation, the demise not only of particulars, but
of all. The sweep of the comet's tail, the limitless domain of the channels,
and as we will see, the splendiferous garment of the days gain their sense
only in the face of this death, which may be negotiable to a point, but
whose priority and eventuality are final. The only recompense that Judaism offers for the trials and sufferings of this world is a collective splendor,
a state of exegetical as well as cosmological luminosity, and it is conditioned on the undergoing of not a particular, time-specific death, but of
an ongoing death, a death inhabiting an ecology and a condition. The
Zohar figures both our entry to the domain of life and our departure from
it as a display of days, days represented not as invisible units of time, but
as graphic markers, as signs or posters.

Rabbi Judah said: Men's ears are shut to the admonitions of the Torah . . .
in not realizing that in the day on which a human being appears in the
world there appear all the days assigned to him, and these swarm about the
world and then each in turn descends to the man to warn him. And if the
man, being so warned, yet transgresses against his Master, then that day in

which he transgressed ascends in shame and stands isolated outside, bearing
witness, and remains thus until the man repents. (Scholem, *Zohar: Book of
Splendor*, 39)

The days swarm like falling leaves caught in the wind. They are frail and
ephemeral, yet occupy the two-dimensionality of paper and other surfaces
of inscription. At the outset of life, according to Rabbi Judah, they fore-
shadow the successive sequence of life and forewarn of the inscriptive consequences of our deeds. Our actions will be collected in a transcript of
days, and these, in turn, will determine whether we will be inscribed in the
Book of Life or the Book of Death. The swarm of days is thus the pages
of a yet-unbound book, the book of our moral profile. On its basis, we
may be well booked by the highest authorities.

But the Zohar also figures our private book of days as a garment, a
covering, but one with intense symbolic and sociological significance. The
poor quality of an ethical life translates into an inferior mystical garment:

> Woe to the man that has lessened his days before the Almighty, nor left
> himself days wherewith to crown himself in the other world and draw near
> to the holy King. For being worthy, he ascends by virtue of those days, and
> those days in which he did righteously and sinned not become for his soul
> a garment of splendor. Woe unto him that has lessened his days above, for
> the days damaged by his sins are lacking when it comes time to be garbed
> in his days, and his garment is therefore imperfect; worse is it if there are
> many such, and then he has nothing at all for garb in the other world.
> (Scholem, *Zohar: Book of Splendor*, 39–40)

More significant than the moralistic dress code enforced by the seaming
together of the days that unfold in splendor at the beginning and end of
life are the poetic and figurative leaps making the scenario altogether possible. The days first of all coalesce out of an otherwise purely abstract and
nonrepresentational dimensionality of time into markers and signboards
of human life and spirituality. The metaphor of paper or woven days is
then literalized to allow their configuration as clothes or garments, garments with a message far more spiritual than experiential. The textual days
swirl and dance about in the cosmic motion that the Zohar has established
as the very tenor of mystical apprehension and revelation. The swirling of
the days and the radiance of the garments they form join in a *danse maca-
bre*, for the hypervitality of movement and illumination is possible only in
the extended afterlife of Judaism, within the framework of the death that
Judaism has, metaphysically and aesthetically, admitted into itself.

In keeping with its economy of closed allegorical reading, the Zohar puts a moral point on the possible outcomes that the garment of days can signal. "The righteous are the happy ones, for their days are in store with the holy King and make a splendid attire for clothing themselves in, in the other world. This is the secret meaning of the verse, 'and they knew that they were naked' [Gen. 3:17], which is to say, glorious vestments composed of those days had been ruined and no day was left to be clothed in" (Scholem, *Zohar: Book of Splendor*, 40).

But poetically, the Zohar and the Judaism that it would presume to revise have established a figuration and a topography that they cannot contain. Indeed, no specific religious culture could. Set in an afterlife of extended death, the radiance of comets' tails, the palace of proliferating portals and channels, and the garments of days demarcate a distinctive cultural landscape and poetic idiom, but one that was readily transferable to other cultures, theological spheres, and literary and discursive genres. The diaspora of these figures and the imaginary and metaphysical space they inhabit may have illumination to shed on historical outcomes as well as cultural phenomena far afield from Talmudic and Kabbalistic formulation. The figures and their tortuous trajectory are obscured by the general inaccessibility of these sources. But the comets' tails of the Zohar sparkle over a widely diverse, but intrinsically interconnected trail of cultural artifacts.

The afterlife of interpretation, like the abyss of figuration and performance, is rife with irony, a trope and ethos that J. Hillis Miller has studied and on which he has shed light with unusual persistence and radiance.[21] Having entered the terrain of Zoharic interpretation, we now need to broach the possibility, however incredulously, that we are all already dead. All of us, not only our two senior and most eminent rabbis, Rabbi Yose and Rabbi Yaakov, aka Rabbi Eli or Eliyahu,[22] have passed on to that ironically configured domain where, as archivists and protectors of the Law, not the moral law but its script, we synthesize interpretations that are hopelessly after the fact and notoriously beside the point, but that may nonetheless claim a certain effect upon the cultural options of the living, those who continue on a different register, who effectively operate in the domain of action and tangible consequences. All already dead. Rabbi Eliyahu's extrapolation, over the past twenty years, of the spectral dimension pervading and intertwining the Abrahamic religions has been decisive in rendering explicit the distanciation, removal, belatedness, and inchoateness in which our running transcript of cultural commentary, rendered by a rhizomatic community of readers, is sheathed.

The trajectory of the shooting stars in *The Book of Splendor* is the dawn of the flight of the Angel of History,[23] who inscribes his markings on the mystical notepad of the sky. Benjamin's fascination with stars and their aurioles, constellations, and messianic angels, angels whose transformative vision of the world consists in their criticism, is both the endpoint of the modern Judaic reconfiguration of death and redemption in the Zohar and the taking-off point for issues still captivating us today. The comet's tail invoked by Jewish mysticism sweeps over German literature—Goethe's "Egmont" and *Elective Affinities* and Büchner's "Lenz" are only a few of its ports of call—effecting the multifaceted Judeo-German cultural graft noted above and touching down, if only briefly, as a posture of radical exegetical credulity in the work of Benjamin and as a key feature in the abyssal poetic landscape carved out by Paul Celan.[24]

The pivotal irony here is that German Romantic literature could transpire in an abyss ultimately configured by Kabbalistic messianism even where it appeals to the trappings of evangelical theology and, on occasion, anti-Semitic folklore (as abounds, for instance, in Büchner's "Woyzeck"). The "Judaic" feature of this literary space is nothing explicit. It is the irony inhering in the afterlife that persists after the claims of law and sovereignty, and of the actions taken in their name, have been exhausted. It is in this spirit that Jakob Michael Reinhold Lenz, Goethe's "poetic twin,"[25] can go "through the mountains" on January 20, 1778, in search of Johann Friedrich Oberlin (1740–1826), the well-known spiritualist and healer, also the inspiration for Oberlin College in Oberlin, Ohio, where J. Hillis Miller did his undergraduate work.

Büchner, in recounting Lenz's ascent to the highlands where the simplicity of rural life continues unabated, and his quest, amid states of incipient madness, for psychospiritual healing, indeed "fills in" the low road or dark side of mainstream Romanticism, with its polymorphous negotiations of the transcendental so magisterially announced by Goethe. In Lenz's wanderings through the mountains, Frankenstein finally meets his younger brother. The power of Büchner's fragmentary tale (it really is an extended prose poem) derives from many sources, among them its explicit appropriation of the visual effects of the sublime as it irradiates Romantic imagery, particularly in the paintings of Caspar David Friedrich. One could argue, indeed, in parsing the following description, that one of Büchner's primary motives is to furnish Friedrich's landscapes (or Turner's seascapes, or Courbet's caves) with a textual caption in the medium of Romantic prose:

Huge masses of light gushing at times from the valley like a golden river, then clouds again, hanging on the highest peak, then climbing down the forest slowly into the valley or sinking and rising in the sunbeams like a flying silvery web; not a sound, no movement, no birds, nothing but the wailing of the wind, sometimes near, sometimes far. Dots also appeared, skeletons of huts, boards covered in straw, a somber black in color. People, silent and grave, as though not daring to disturb the peace of their valley, greeted them quietly as they rode past. (Büchner, *Complete Works*, 142)

This is a visual landscape configured by the vastness of its zones and the tensions between them. Its sublimity transpires unabated by "human touches" designed to furnish it with scale, the minuscule human figures in Friedrich's *Morning in the Riesengebirge*, or in this verbal canvas, the trail of snowflakes following from a bird, the train or sequence to Kabbalistic comets: "No movement in the air except for a soft breeze, the rustle of a bird lightly dusting snowflakes from its tail" (Büchner, *Complete Works*, 143).

Within this setting, Lenz and Oberlin make an ironic, if not comical pair, both dwarfed by the prospect of reining in Lenz's recurrent madness. I'm arguing here that their partnership, even if its terms are Christological and the redemption it attempts to effect manifestly Christian in its metaphysics, makes sense only in a context of prior ambulatory rabbinic dialogues hopelessly after the fact, the fact of exile, the fact of madness, the fact of endless wandering. This Judeo-German wedding of resources shimmers though the explicitly Christian settings of "Lenz" like the snow crystals illuminating the highland landscape. Oberlin's work is indeed framed by this landscape. The extended description immediately above continues:

The huts were full of life, people crowded around Oberlin, he instructed, gave advice, consoled; everywhere trusting glances, prayer. People told of dreams, premonitions. Then quickly to practical affairs. . . . Oberlin was tireless. Lenz his constant companion, at times conversing, attending to business, absorbed in nature. It all had a beneficial and soothing effect on him, he often had to look in Oberlin's eyes, and the immense peace that comes upon us in nature at rest, in the deep forest, in moonlit, melting summer nights seemed even nearer to him in these calm eyes, this nobler, serious face. He was shy, but he made remarks, he spoke. Oberlin enjoyed his conversation and Lenz's charming child's face delighted him. But he could bear it only as long as the light remained in the valley; toward evening a strange fear came over him, he felt like chasing the sun . . . he

seemed to be going blind; now it grew, the demon of insanity sat at his feet.
(Büchner, *Complete Works*, 143)

In Büchner's cinematography, the engagement between the two men transpires in the flashes of their two countenances, rather than in the exegetical
conundrums they ponder. But an ineffable and fatal intimacy prevails between them. It, too, is grounded in their having, at least for the moment,
entered a mystical engagement with each other, signaled by a loss of
boundaries between them. Enigmatically, the text does not specify who
was "toward evening" overcome by a "strange fear." It is Lenz whose
emotional state is turbulent, but it is Oberlin who may experience limits
in the delight exerted by Lenz's "charming child's face." The highlands
are a place where, very much in a spirit of Christian compassion, Oberlin
assumes the burden of Lenz's madness, yet they are also a Kabbalistic
afterlife in which madness and meticulous human reform or *tikkun* are
one, in which the shimmering dance of nature is also an allegory of understanding and cultural literacy.

The importance of this text as an interface between Jewish and Christian mystical poetics is not lost to Paul Celan. It is precisely as a Lenz

> that the Jew, the Jew and the son of a Jew, and with him went his name, the
> inexpressible, sets out on his wanderings through the mountains. He went
> then, one heard about it, he went one evening, a number had already de-
> scended, he went under cloud cover and shadow that were his own and
> foreign—since the Jew, you know it, whatever he has already, whatever
> belongs to him, that wasn't borrowed, lent out, and never returned—so he
> went out and came there, came to the road, of the beautiful, the incompara-
> ble, like Lenz, through the mountains, who would have been allowed to
> reside below, where he belongs, in the lowlands, he, the Jew, came and
> came.[26]

His name may be this Jew's only possession, everything else having been
"borrowed, lent out, and never returned." Celan alludes to a moment
when the landscape has been largely emptied of Jews. The mountains remain, but not the Jews of the lowlands. This Jew, the Jew of the prose
poem, resides in a spectral afterlife. It is only in this sense that his advent,
his arrival, could be multiple and ongoing. He "came and came." Whether
belatedly and indirectly or not, this Jew comes bearing his only property,
his name, which walks with him and beside him. This figure consists, precisely, in a word, an element of language, the nominative, mystically transformed into a figure, a character, one free to dance and play, like days
woven into garments, to dance within a world suffused with mystical

meaning, a world defined by its role in a consummate exegesis by God. This Jew doesn't encounter many interlocutors. One is the figure of Büchner's Lenz. And of course, the remnants of a family, his cousin and his *Geschwisterkind*: With them he will join a chatter haunting the sublime landscape filled with Jews, as absences and memories as well as voices and figurations.

If Celan was free, in his own postdisaster poetics, to resume both a practice and setting for figuration established in the Zohar, it was Walter Benjamin, who, in his own wanderings on the frontier between Judaic and German letters, elaborated the terms and theory of this grafting, made it historically explicit. Benjamin was long a careful reader of the stars. He had pursued their spectral sway over Paris, in Baudelaire's expletives, in Grandville's cosmic cartoons, since the outset of *The Arcades Project*.[27] He was exquisitely sensitive to the shooting stars' role within the narrative of the Goethean novel in what is arguably his first full-fledged work of literary criticism, his essay on Goethe's *The Elective Affinities*, in which he effects a full crossover between his philosophical readings and his critical ambitions. As late as "On Some Motives in Baudelaire," he still was charting the trajectory as the shooting stars thread the seam between loss and redemption, ritual and industrial time, and poetic inspiration and shock.

Benjamin volunteered himself as the astronomer of the mystical Kabbalistic heavens in the turbulent domain of advanced modernity. He would not allow his readers to overlook Goethe's caption for the last moment in *The Elective Affinities*, when romantic love might win out over social convention, when desire might realize itself instead of capitulating to diversions and dissimulations: "Hope shot across the sky above their heads like a falling star."[28] This burst of hope, set in one of German literature's most resonant and suggestive novels, is all the more poignant for being destined to extinction amid the truisms of *Sittlichkeit* and the economics of bourgeois domesticity. Its short-lived flash reminds us that the broad swath of German letters in Goethe's wake was susceptible to Messianic time. The final one of the two afterthoughts that Benjamin appended to his "On the Concept of History," characterizes this openness: "For every second of time was the straight gate through which the Messiah might enter." Not only does this brief note characterize the hope that briefly flares for the love-crossed modern prisoners of desire in *The Elective Affinities*: It reminds us of Benjamin's explicit desire, one also not realized, to pursue messianic mysticism into the nexus of modern urbanity and shock.

This aspiration, which might seem out of character with his secular sophistication, his commitment, first and foremost, to letters, and his receptivity to social as well as conceptual revolutions of the mind, is spelled out where we are not afraid to read its legend. Given the commitment to fragmentary utterance, to dialectical imagery, and to epigrammatic closure in "On the Concept of History," it is not by chance that in their aftermath, Benjamin should signal his own prior meditations on the afterlife of Judaism: "We know that the Jews were prohibited from investigating the future. The Torah and the prayers instruct them in remembrance, however. This stripped the future of its magic, to which all those succumb who turn to the soothsayers for enlightenment. This does not imply, however, that for the Jews the future turned into homogenous, empty time."[29]

The Jewish future here becomes an afterlife of hope, not of projection. And indeed, Benjamin enlists the words of Joubert to characterize the messianic hope that still suffuses the modern world. "Time is still found in eternity; but it is not earthly, worldly time. . . . That time does not destroy; it merely completes."[30] This time is still accessible in a modernity that has largely degraded the "crowning of experience" consummated by the fulfillment of the wish.[31] This is a modernity in which the folkloric wish embodied by the falling star has been supplanted by "[t]he ivory ball which rolls into the *next* compartment, the *next* card which lies on top," in gambling.[32] In this degraded but captivating time, the wish is served by the one-armed bandit, operated by a spasmodic gesture carried over from the assembly line. "On Some Motifs in Baudelaire" is, after all, a miniature crystallization of the materials gathered in *The Arcades Project* and a roadmap to their many convergences, departures, and collisions. The world configured by both works, the former at an extreme of poetic condensation in critical discourse and the latter at an extreme of archival dispersion, is nothing other than the complex of late-modern commercial, urban, communicative, and technological forces first coinciding in Paris under the Second Empire. Benjamin makes Joubert the mouthpiece for a radical messianic temporality that persists into this configuration. Yet Benjamin is explicitly, ironically, and morbidly aware of its Kabbalistic provenance.

Many were the dreams that failed to be realized in the twentieth century, a period of unprecedented violence, genocide, and the disregard of life. Yet the blueprints for these dreams survive. In the fictive topography configured by a set of obscure medieval rabbis and in certain of the tropes that they tripped into motion, the likes of Benjamin and Scholem accessed a *genizah*, a repository for disrupted dreams, whose parameters mirrored, reenacted, and extended their life.

CHAPTER 8

On the Line

Alexander Gelley

In *Ariadne's Thread: Story Lines*,[1] J. Hillis Miller begins with a fable of reading, a fable in which the reader, although presumably following a (straight) line, is continually sidetracked, led off course, and thus forced into labyrinthine byways. How did the reader get into this trap? He thought he was reading a story, but he finds he *is* that story and can't get out: "These blind alleys in the analysis of narrative may not by any means be avoided. They may only be veiled by some credulity making a standing place where there is an abyss" (23).

What drew me to *Ariadne's Thread* and what keeps me fascinated by that book and its successor volumes is the way that Miller has deployed those twisted bits of string that he took from the narrator of Elizabeth Gaskell's *Cranford*, bits that he used to fashion the nine areas of linear terminology that constitute the frame of his narrative theory. "The model of the line is a powerful part of the traditional metaphysical terminology," Miller writes in *Ariadne's Thread*, and the issue will be how the line is to be taken, whether as "a purely metonymic line . . . [an] organized . . . causal chain," or in the "complex" mode that Miller proposes, as "knotted, repetitive, doubled, broken, phantasmal" (17–18). What follows are nine "topics" which, in effect, constitute the basic categories of his narrative project.

Ariadne's Thread is the first of a series of four books on narrative that Miller published between 1992 and 1998,[2] although, as he explains in the preface to *Ariadne's Thread*, his conception of the project goes back to 1976, when he was completing *Fiction and Repetition*. This series certainly constitutes one of the most far-reaching and provocative studies of narrative that we possess, and it will stand, alongside works by Northrop Frye, Frank Kermode, Paul Ricoeur, Gérard Genette, and Roland Barthes, as a major contribution to the field as it has developed in the last quarter of a century.

The repertory that Miller draws on is immense, but it is selective, and what prompts his choices is worth noting. He does not invoke a criterion of greatness or universality, as Harold Bloom does. Rather, Miller looks for texts that will exemplify, better yet, incite, his theoretical curiosity. His summary of the themes of *Reading Narrative* is revealing:

> The strangeness of Aristotle's *Poetics* and the madness of Sophocles's language in *Oedipus the King*, the Sternean free arabesque that turns into a snake in Balzac, the portmanteau word "Ariachne" in *Troilus and Cressida*, Albertine's lying anacoluthons in Proust's *À la recherche du temps perdu*, sundials facing north in Pater's "Apollo in Picardy," hats on top of hats in Gaskell's *Cranford*—each of these has demanded an attention that exceeds their role as mere examples of some theoretical point. (xvi–xvii)

In *Reading Narrative*, in the course of a brief characterization of Gérard Genette's *Narrative Discourse*,[3] Miller terms his own work one of "ana/narratology," thereby seeking to distance himself from narratology, which he characterizes as "this elaborate act of naming [that] will untangle the complexity of the narrative line and bring all its strands out into the full light of the logical sun" (49). Yet Miller claims that he himself will "try here to untangle the narrative line" by means of deconstructing "all that family of terms by which we habitually coach ourselves or are coached, by novels themselves and by their critics, to spatialize the time of storytelling and to think of it as in one way or another picturable as a graph or plot, a line going from A to B or from A to Z, from womb to tomb, from adolescent awakening to happy tying of the marriage plot, and so on" (49). While Miller's subject matter overlaps with that of critics who are closely identified with narratology or narrative theory—from the Slavic Formalists to Lotman, Bakhtin, Greimas, Barthes, Ricoeur, and Genette—he resists what he sees as their systematizing and ordering tendency.

I am by no means wholly at ease with the label of "narratology." I still feel close enough to the work of Paul de Man to resist Northrop Frye's challenge in his "Polemical Introduction": "Criticism seems to be badly in need of a coordinating principle, a central hypothesis which, like the theory of evolution in biology, will see the phenomena it deals with as parts of a whole. The first postulate of this inductive leap is the same as that of any science: the assumption of total coherence."[4] Nonetheless, as a teacher, I am continually trying to inculcate this "inductive leap" in my students. At the same time, literally in the next breath, I keep testing "the assumption of total coherence" and warning my students that what they think is the law, the rule, the genre is an exceedingly porous container. The "law of genre," this ironic tag of Derrida's essay,[5] is a law of interruption, of transgression, of invagination, a "law" that continually turns the outside in and the inside out.

Nonetheless, Frye's contention that "[i]f criticism is a science, it is clearly a social science" is one that I want to honor in both of its clauses: *if criticism is a science*—the hypothetical, the "inductive leap" that makes it possible to posit concepts, to *think* with conceptual instruments, and then the second tenet, "a *social* science," that is, subject to variable, highly specific constraints, constraints that are disclosed in and through language, certainly, but language that is *situated*, language that is at once expressive and formative with respect to conventions and practices. This I take to be the domain of discourse in the sense of the double genetive of the French title of Genette's *Narrative Discourse*, "Discours du récit."[6]

Ariadne's Thread develops a model of narrative indeterminacy through the story of the labyrinth where Theseus is caught and the thread that Ariadne provides to enable his escape. At the same time, every figure, in the fashion of mythology, becomes subject to overdetermination, so that through a conflation of the word "Arachne," "spider," and the name "Ariadne," there results a combination of savior and prison.[7] The one who is able to negotiate the labyrinth, to lead Theseus out, is by that very capacity the mistress of the web, the agent of entrapment. The story of Ariadne, in fact, is only one layer in a complex palimpsest, and it is this complex that serves as the allegory of narrative for Miller:

> The term *narrative line* . . . is a catachresis. It is the violent, forced, or abusive importation of a term from another realm to name something which has no proper name. The relationships of meaning among all these areas of terminology is not from sign to thing but a displacement from one sign to another sign that in its turn draws its meaning from another figurative sign, in a constant displacement. The name for this displacement is allegory. Storytelling, usually thought of as the putting into language of

someone's experience of life, is in its writing or reading a hiatus in that experience. Narrative is the allegorizing along a temporal line of this perpetual displacement from immediacy. Allegory in this sense, however, expresses the impossibility of expressing unequivocally, and so dominating, what is meant by experience or by writing. My exploration of the labyrinth of narrative terms is in its turn to be defined as a perhaps impossible search for the center of the maze, the Minotaur or spider that has created and so commands it all. (21)

As I understand this, Miller is arguing for a radical discontinuity between "storytelling" and "experience," on the one hand, and "its writing or reading," on the other. This discontinuity ("displacement") is typically labeled "narrative"—in his view a reductive, leveling term—which can never do justice to "experience." So, the argument continues, if understood as "allegory," as the "search for the center of the maze," we can explore its manifold forms, the veritably innumerable paths of the labyrinth.

I find it difficult to account for the sense of "displacement" as used in this passage. In the earlier part, displacement is a continuous relay among signs, as if there were no means of controlling their slippage, of employing signs for determinate ends. But in the middle of the passage, displacement refers to a "hiatus" from "experience," a "perpetual" lapse from "immediacy" to its expression, to what is then denominated as narrative in an allegorical sense. The introduction of personal experience ("someone's experience of life") is itself surprising. Of course, experience can very well serve within a theory of narrative, as in Walter Benjamin's essay "The Storyteller,"[8] where narrative is understood as a repository of cultural experience, and its transmission from generation to generation serves as a gauge of the quality of the life experience of a society. But this is not an issue that Miller pursues in this book. And it is not clear whether "storytelling" is synonymous with narrative or is meant to refer primarily to the *telling*. Not that Miller does not take account of the narrating instance in his interpretations of works, but the issue does not figure significantly in the theoretical framework under discussion.

Miller takes on the founding text of narrative theory, Aristotle's *Poetics*, and argues, taking Aristotle's own model, *Oedipus the King*, as instance, that the primacy that Aristotle gives to plot (*mythos*) in the analysis of narrative should be replaced with, probably, diction (*lexis*), or, better yet, irony, although this last is not included in the *Poetics* as one of the parts of tragedy. In any case, he maintains that the "logocentric" orientation of Aristotle's reading prevents one from recognizing the irrational, aporetic, radically enigmatic elements of the play. So instead of the narrative line as a continuous, unidirectional vector, Miller illustrates his notion of allegory through multiple figures of irregularity or fragmentation—"knotted, repetitive, doubled, broken, phantasmal"—as already cited.

Indeed, the idea that the narrative line is to be conceived as a straight, unidirectional vector may be inferred from Aristotle's definition of plot in terms of beginning, middle, and end, this being, as he argues in *Poetics* 7, the criterion of "an ordered arrangement."[9] But when the elements of a complex plot are introduced, it becomes clear that simple linearity is only a point of departure. Insofar as reversal and recognition are incorporated into the model of plot, either singly or in combination, the "line" takes on more irregular shapes—squiggly, turning backward, and athwart, to account for new details regarding actions that had already been introduced. Thus, insofar as reversal and recognition necessitate a kind of repetition or reenactment at different levels (or from different perspectives) of the premises of the action, the *Poetics* does take account of noncontinuous and irregular forms of linearity.[10] What is addressed in this manner is the tension between the intuitive unity of a given narrative—the nearly simultaneous apprehension of the terminal boundaries, beginning and end— and the discrete chain of transformations that proceed sequentially. This issue is taken up in the Russian Formalists' distinction between *fabula* and *sujet*,[11] where the *fabula* designates the narrative referent or content as conceived in a chronological (although not necessarily causal) order, and the *sujet* designates the process of its articulation, with its multiple forms of displacement, retrospection, and anticipation.

In *Ariadne's Thread*, the aporetic status of narrative analysis is announced in the passage already cited from chapter one, "Line": "The term *narrative line* . . . is a catachresis. It is the violent, forced, or abusive importation of a term from another realm to name something which has no proper name" (21). "Catachresis" is a term with which readers of Miller are familiar. In dictionaries of rhetoric, it is defined as an improper or abnormal tropological denomination, one that cannot be justified on ornamental grounds but is produced to supply some lack in the linguistic repertory. According to Bernard Dupriez, "Catachresis responds to the need to name, with a single word, some new reality or one considered new. Thus to uphold the proposition that if Vietnam went communist, all Asian countries would follow suit one after another, someone created the expression 'the domino theory.' If there is a proper term, the image is not catachretic."[12]

But it is not to manuals of rhetoric, but rather to Jacques Derrida's seminal essay "White Mythology" that Miller appeals, and in that essay, catachresis is part of a larger argument involving the metaphoricity of philosophical concepts: "all the concepts which have operated in the definition of metaphor," Derrida writes, "have an origin and an efficacity that are themselves 'metaphorical.'"[13] Thus there is no nonmetaphorical standpoint from which philosophy could demarcate the field of metaphor. It is not, however, so much for the purpose of disabling the status of metaphor within philosophical discourse that this argument is made as to illustrate the limited duration, the temporal contingency of metaphors, what Derrida designates by the word *usure*, a wearing down and progressive effacement that leads to a ghostly trace of what was once an inscribed sign. That is the sense of the title, faded, blanched mythology: "White mythology [*Mythologie blanche*]—metaphysics has erased within itself the fabulous scene that has produced it, the scene that nevertheless remains active and stirring, inscribed in white ink, an invisible design covered over in the palimpsest" ("White Mythology," 213). In this exposure of the time span of metaphors, Derrida himself draws on Anatole France, on Hegel, and on Nietzsche's 1873 text "On Truth and Lies in a Nonmoral Sense."

I would question whether the temporal inflection of metaphor, of the figurative register more generally, that is found in "White Mythology" supports the kind of radical disablement of metadiscourse that Miller diagnoses. "The impasse of narrative analysis," he writes, "is a genuine double blind alley. It results first from the fact that there is in no region of narrative or of its analysis a literal ground—in history, consciousness, society, the physical world, or whatever—for which the other regions are figures. The terminology of narrative is therefore universally catachresis. Each [element in this terminology] is a trope breaking down the reassuring distinction between figure and ground, base of so much theoretical seeing" (*Ariadne's Thread*, 23–24). Miller rightly argues that the figure/ground distinction is subject to the all too familiar slippage of any metadiscourse, namely, the impossibility of neatly delimiting the "meta," of maintaining a strict segregation between levels of reference. Yet this does not amount to a rationale for abandoning a stratified model, however variable or permeable. It makes a difference whether "line" be taken as vector, boundary, spatiality, sequence, divagation, segmentation, and so on. Each gives rise to distinct forms of separation and continuity, and in fact it is with just such discriminations that narrative theory is concerned. It has never been a question of "history, consciousness, society, the physical world, or whatever" being "a literal ground" for the "region[s] of narrative or of its analysis." The "uses" (Fr. *usage*) of philosophy, understood in "White Mythology" in terms of the temporal economy of *usure*, can never altogether exhaust what is proper to it. There can be no "universal" catachresis that demolishes the system of tropes, since *usure*, the work of depletion, is historically measurable and never altogether reaches its end. There can only be an endless testing of its pretensions. This I take to be the conundrum of "line," the fact that any attempt to restrict it as figure is overcome by unforeseen and uncontrollable mimetic associations.

It is noteworthy that, with the exception of Miller's writings, there has been little work on narrative coming from deconstruction, that is, unless one were to classify certain French thinkers such as Barthes, Tzvetan Todorov, Louis Marin, the early Julia Kristeva, and Genette as deconstructionists, something that, I think, would be resisted on both sides. Paul de Man had very little to say about narrative. There are some tantalizing pages in "The Resistance to Theory" in which de Man contrasts "grammatical codes" with "rhetorical figures," and it is clear that within the former he includes narratology. He writes: "The extension of grammar to include para-figural dimensions is in fact the most remarkable and debatable strategy of contemporary semiology, especially in the study of syntagmatic and narrative structures. The codification of contextual elements well beyond the syntactical limits of the sentence leads to the systematic study of metaphrastic dimensions and has considerably refined and expanded the knowledge of textual codes."[14] Earlier in the essay, de Man had singled out A. J. Greimas as a principal defender of the dignity of "grammar" and had made clear that the assumptions of Greimas and "the entire tradition to which he belongs" commits this tradition to the position that "the grammatical and the logical functions of language are coextensive. Grammar is an isotope of logic." From this it follows "that, as long as it remains grounded in grammar, any theory of language, including a literary one, does not threaten what we hold to be the underlying principle of all cognitive and aesthetic linguistic systems. Grammar stands in the service of logic which, in turn, allows for the passage to the knowledge of the world" (*The Resistance to Theory*, 14). What comes next in de Man's essay is a page about the title of Keats' sequel to his fragment "Hyperion," "The Fall of Hyperion."

One might have wished that, in this fascinating page, de Man would also have considered the kind of narratological issues that Frank Kermode addressed in *The Sense of an Ending*. After all, the word "fall" can be considered not only in the terms of linguistic figuration, but as a species of narrative line, which is exactly what Kermode does (although not with

regard to Keats' poems) in *The Sense of an Ending*. Otherwise, it is in the
essay on Kleist's *Über das Marionettentheater* that de Man deals extensively
with a narrative instance, and here it is the issue of performative dialogicity
that is primarily at stake.[15] I cannot help wondering why de Man, who was
so widely read and so outspoken in his judgments regarding contemporary
theory, never commented in detail about Barthes's *S/Z* (1970),[16] Genette's
"Discours du récit" (1972), or Todorov's *Poétique de la prose* (1970), not
to mention works by Russian formalists like Shklovsky, Tomashevsky, or
Eichenbaum, which were appearing both in French (in an anthology edited by Todorov) and in English in the same period.

Perhaps the outstanding deconstructionist work on narrative, or at least
on the novel, in addition to Miller's books, is Neil Hertz's study of George
Eliot.[17] But I want to turn to another work of Hertz's to pursue some of
the issues at hand. In explicating his title, *The End of the Line*, Hertz refers
to "what Kenneth Burke has named the 'to-the-end-of-the-line mode.'"[18]
For Burke this involved effects of embedding what later, after Burke's
1941 book, came to be termed *mise en abyme*. Hertz, in the afterword to
his book, adopts "the end of the line" to characterize a pattern that had
emerged recurrently in the earlier chapters, namely, a kind of double embedding where the subject of the narrative is first posited as a projection of
the author-artist and then serves as the surrogate viewer of an undecidable
alternative, one that can be, in a sense, named or designated by the medium (whether language or paint), but cannot be represented. The alternative may be—in the instances Hertz discusses—black rock/black water in
versions of Gustav Courbet's painting *La Source de la Loue* or face/label in
Wordsworth's Blind Beggar episode in *The Prelude*, book 7. But in both
cases (and there are others), what Hertz claims is "that the necessity for a
double reading arises not from the presence of a discernible surrogate
within the novel but rather from the requirements of any reading" (220).
What links such instances are "two trademarks of the sublime—
condensed, epistemologically loaded confrontations, and characters designated as surrogates of their authors' activity" (ibid.). For Hertz, the *end* of
the line, the branching that yields an undecidable alternative, serves as
testimony to an epistemological blockage in representation. The line
marks the shift of agency from author-painter to surrogate subject. As a
figure of the double embedding Hertz suggests the diagram of an inverted
T. The stem or horizontal line is cut by a rectangular box to indicate the
shift of agency, and the crossbar of the T (now a horizontal line at the
end) figures the unrepresentable alternative. "Line" here does not chart
narrative segments, but rather relays of viewpoint or perspective.

A very different approach to linearity is developed in Claudia Brodsky Lacour's *Lines of Thought*.[19] While this book does not deal specifically with narrative, it does explore the kind of conceptual formation that underlies terms like "line of thought," "line of argument," and "narrative line." Brodsky Lacour's premise is that the "thinking" that Descartes practices in formulating the autobiographical narrative of *Discours de la méthode* is a kind of architectonic practice, one that represents a decisive moment in the formation of a modern sense of textuality. Her idea of the architectonic, then, is first of all a kind of praxis: "What became apparent to me in the post-Cartesian writings I worked on was that the language of architectonics employed within them was *not* symbolic in the conventional sense. It was pragmatic and functional, even when it took the form of an object; it was active, even when it was explicitly abstract, a means of doing rather than a determined category, schema, or concept" (3).

Lines of Thought treats the figurality of line by way of a concept of architectonic form that brings together Descartes' *Géométrie* and *Discours de la méthode*. "The discursive beginning of modern philosophy," Brodsky Lacour writes, "the founding of the subject of thinking, occurs not as a linguistic picture or image but as line, an iconoclastic line, a 'line of thought'" (8). In probing that famous scene set in a heated room in the *Discours*, she insists on the anomaly of Descartes' thinking: "It takes neither literary nor experiential mimetic form; nor is it method. If it is discourse, it is also the nondiscursive, a discourse of one. What Descartes *thinks* takes the image of what an architect *does*" (32). She focuses on the process that finally yields the unassailable foundation for Descartes' cogito, a process that she terms "manifestation,"[20] rather than "image," "figure," or "drawing"—all these too much allied to a mimetic sense, as if the thinking were in search of a disclosure of a preexistent entity. But the production of the cogito is brought about by a new way of rendering notation, one that has its basis in Descartes' geometry and the new status of the autobiographical subject, the "I" of "Je pense, donc je suis." "Algebraic signs," Brodsky Lacour argues, "are the language of 'intuition,' the discursive means with which 'pure and attentive intelligence' enacts a 'representation'" (72). In the fable of the "I" of the *Discours*, as in the conception of the algebraic equation of the *Géométrie*, Descartes showed the possibility of suspending or bracketing (in the sense of Husserl's *epoché*) content while maintaining the continuity of an enunciation, a "line of thought." "Thinking . . . is the intellectual equivalent of a physical line" (101).

While Brodsky Lacour makes fascinating excursions into the history of philosophy, mathematics, and logic in support of her larger argument regarding the cogito and architectonic form, what is most relevant to the discussion at hand is the way she deals with the temporality of the "I." How is it conceivable, she asks, that the intuition of the cogito, punctual in one sense,[21] can serve as the support of a continuous, unitary subject? "If the act of thinking lasts only as long as itself," she continues, "the *cogito* is the autobiography of thought in which the notation that substitutes for *ce moi*, for all that inheres in being itself . . . denotes its writer and reader while replacing him" (99). Brodsky Lacour grants that "the *cogito* must prove maddening to logical analysis" (102). Her solution is to postulate a linkage to connect the discrete "Is" as the very condition of thinking:

> Just as a line extends from one purely representational point (the coordination of two unknowns) to another (at which the values of those unknowns change), the *cogito* extends from one "je," coordinated verbally with the act of thinking, to another, coordinated verbally with the fact of being that, *in being extended to this second "je,"* the first coordinate entails. Thinking cannot be conducted unless for every point 'during the time' of the act of thinking there is a value, "I." The connection of those points into an intuitional 'whole' . . . is thus less self-reflective than actually productive. (104f)

Just as, in this model, "line of thought" stipulates the continuity of an "I," "narrative line" may be granted a similar function. What Brodsky Lacour's reading of Descartes suggests is that the *middle*, the sequence of incidents that marks the change from beginning to end, is relevant not so much as motivated or causal links, but as a notational line whose content may be bracketed without compromising its function.

I have not, in this paper, attempted to address Miller's narrative project as a whole, but only to take up one strand of its many provocations. Miller himself often betrays a sense of responding to a provocation, although its source is not always discernible. One might say that it is the whole corpus of the Western literary tradition, or at least the way that tradition is normally (routinely) read. His dictum, "close reading is essential to reading narrative,"[22] might be taken as a residue of New Criticism, and this rule is certainly one that will find many interpreters of novels lacking. But Miller takes this tenet in a different sense than the New Critics, in fact in an almost opposite sense. For them, a single local feature—whether of figure, diction, rhythm, and so on—could serve as a key for an interpretation that gathers manifold details in the service of an integral, saturated meaning. Miller, true to another dictum that he proposes—"irony is the basic trope of narrative" (*Reading Narrative*, 157)—is certainly no seeker for closed, saturated units of meaning. For him, irony is Friedrich Schlegel's "permanent parabasis" (156), the "oscillation of meaning" that is "a form of endless looping or feedback" (163), or again, Bakhtin's "radical polylogism" and "microdialogue" (121–22). But while irony is what Miller ceaselessly points to, it is not a primary characteristic of his practice, in spite of his claim to stand alongside a number of master ironists: "I," he writes, "Anthony Trollope, or Elizabeth Gaskell, or Charles Dickens, driven by some sense of lack or deprivation, double myself. I invent another voice, a narrator. . . . I double or split my tongue to give myself, in my muteness, a tongue, but in this act I deprive myself of any tongue, idiom, voice, logos proper to me" (176). What Miller does best is to disclose the kind of double-voicedness that is found in Schlegel, Dickens, Trollope, and Gaskell, and, with something like the zeal of a convert, to awaken readers from their logocentric, monolingual slumbers.

CHAPTER 9

War on Terror

Marc Redfield

Who speaks, and in what mode, when war is declared on terror? What are the conditions of possibility for this speech act; what clumps of historical context cling to it? To what performative felicity could it aspire? Has such a declaration of war indeed occurred? Could it occur or, for that matter, not occur? Both in what the United States government is now calling the "homeland" and in those generally more distant places where the fighting and killing is going on, the world is now enduring the consequences of what the Western media proclaims, over and over, to be a declared war on terror, yet nothing could be stranger—or more strangely familiar—than this declaration. In the pages that follow, I will risk (risk and rhetorical overkill being perhaps inseparable from this topic) the overweening claim that the declaration of war on terror is *the* exemplary speech act of sovereignty in the West, which is also to say that it comes into being as a conflicted, excessive, and, in a sense to be explicated, *literary* performative. Perhaps only an American president, a puissant pseudosovereign in an era of multinational capitalism and technomediation, could have declared this war—if, in fact, it has been declared at all, or even exists at all, except as a symptom, a phantasmatic discharge, cast up in response to the September 11 attacks, but referring back in more diffuse and uncertain fashion to wider, less stable contexts: to the variously military, economic, technical,

semiotic, and ideological forms of domination that we sometimes summa-
rize as Western imperialism and sometimes as globalization; to the career
of modern political and ideological debate since the French Revolution;
even, I will suggest, to modes of ontological and epistemological uncertainty that we sometimes trope as "language," celebrate as "literature," or
(in certain quarters) castigate as "theory."

I

Let me begin again, asking (and to some extent answering) a somewhat
simpler and more specific version of my opening question: Has the United
States declared war on terror? In one sense, no, of course: The United
States has not issued a formal declaration of war since World War II.
Indeed, according to Bob Woodward's account of the Bush administration's response to the September 11 attacks, the president specified, in a
meeting with congressional leaders on September 12, 2001, that "he did
not want a declaration of war from the Congress but would be interested
in a resolution endorsing the use of force."[1] Yet in Woodward's book, as
in the Western media at large, a certain "declaration" nonetheless continues to declare itself. Here is Woodward describing the president hearing
the news of the World Trade Center attacks, a few minutes after the second plane hit: "A photo of that moment is etched for history. The president's hands are folded formally in his lap, his head turned to hear [the
chief of staff's] words. His face has a distant sober look, almost frozen,
edging on bewilderment. Bush remembers exactly what he was thinking:
'They had declared war on us, and I made up my mind at that moment
that we were going to war'" (15).

Michael Moore's mercilessly extended close-up of this distant, "almost
frozen," bewildered sovereign face in *Fahrenheit 911* no doubt offers us a
more satisfying portrait than Woodward's prose does, but the latter's
Gothic figures of etching and freezing suggest nicely, after their fashion,
the ambiguity of sovereign power at the moment of the declaration of war
on terror. It is only here, in Bush's retrospective dramatization of a bit of
his internal life to a journalist, that a declaration of war occurs—or, more
precisely, has *already* occurred: "They had declared war on us." It is the
other, the terrorist, who declares war. The president, in the staged immediacy of his internal consciousness, merely declares war back: "I made up
my mind at that moment that we were going to war." This mingling of
reactive and proactive rhetoric, characteristic of most of the administra-

tion's pronouncements about the war on terror, was to feature largely in Bush's State of the Union Address of January 20, 2004 ("America is on the offensive against the terrorists who started this war. . . . The terrorists and their supporters declared war on the United States, and war is what they got."). War as declaration originates elsewhere: The sovereign, playing, as it were, a *fort-da* game with himself (and if only for this reason I will gender the sovereign male in what follows), relegates sovereignty to the other in order to take it back. The true performativity of war as declaration is thus imagined to take place at a distance, and the sovereign's speech act thereby becomes tinged with constative responsibility. His decisive, but reactive act ("I made up my mind at that moment") subordinates sovereign freedom to factual context: The performative utterance will *also* be a referentially stable description of a preexistent condition. (And in fact, the ambiguously performative and constative utterance "We're at war" seems to have been, if Woodward can be trusted, one of Bush's first articulate recorded sentences in the wake of the attacks.)[2]

The sovereign's double gesture—giving away sovereignty and taking it back—is of course a ruse: one that long antedates the twentieth-century criminalization of aggressive war. If, as Jean-Luc Nancy claims, war is "the *techné*, the *art, execution*, or *operation* [*mise en oeuvre*] of Sovereignty itself," one must add that war, the supreme expression of sovereignty, is also—therefore—the locus of sovereignty's strategic and momentary, but perhaps also symptomatic self-occlusion.[3] The ruse is effective, but its necessity (has any sovereign ever failed to plead necessity, ever simply declared war as a declaration of his own utterly unfettered desire?) suggests that at the heart of sovereignty resides terror: a terror of itself—of the sheer, unrecoverable violence of an absolute performativity. The panic, touched on by Woodward and relished by Moore, that freezes Bush's face as he absorbs the news of the attacks no doubt has something to tell us about Bush himself—about the swagger, hysteria, and incompetence characteristic of this particular man, playing this particular public role—but it also has something to tell us about sovereignty's relation to terror. The absolutely violent act through which war—war and terror, war as terror—enters the world is prior and elsewhere, the fault of the other. The sovereign will no doubt claim the right to "preemptive" violence—but not a whit more. In advance, the "preemptive" strike names itself as secondary, for it is the sovereign's claim that sovereign terror arises in response to the initial, instituting, genuinely *performative* terror of the terrorist. This peculiar wrinkle in sovereignty—this ambivalent abnegation of institutive force, or of what Walter Benjamin would call law-positing violence (*recht-*

setzende Gewalt)—characterizes not just the sovereign's relation to war, but also that of his opponent, the enemy named "terrorist."[4] For, at least according to one dominant narrative, the terrorist has gone to his martyrdom because he believed that, far from declaring a new state of affairs, he was responding to a preexisting situation. "America and its allies" are from this perspective the true "international terrorists."[5] In short: war, as terror, has always already been started by the other, the terrorist. Under such circumstances, sovereign is he who decides on terror—who can call the other a terrorist and make it stick.[6]

The declaration of war on terror respects and exaggerates the complications of conventional declarations of war and gives them an extra twist. If all war requires an enemy, the war on terror declares itself waged against a globalized, absolute, infinite enemy. Practically speaking, this enemy will be Islamic (a fact that deserves patient historical and ideological analysis) and will be given a face and a name (Osama, Saddam), but at least in principle the faces and names are temporary, and the war, having no object except "terror" (we will return to the peculiarities of that object) is limitless and endless, literalizing Kant's claim that, until perpetual peace is successfully declared, war will subtend all human intercourse.[7] Its theater is the earth itself—including the "homeland"—plus any portion of outer space that can be militarized. The war on terror is thus an *absolute* declaration of war: the declaration of an absolute war, an absolutely total war. In the early days after the September 11 attacks, the administration's theological allusions were particularly marked, although usually later provisionally disowned ("this crusade, this war on terror"; "Operation Infinite Justice"; "an axis of evil"). Stress also fell on the war on terror's exceptional character. This war was to be fought "in the shadows" (Dick Cheney). It was to be "a new kind of war . . . political, economic, diplomatic, military. It will be unconventional, what we do" (Donald Rumsfeld). "Americans should not expect one battle but a lengthy campaign, unlike any other we have ever seen. It may include dramatic strikes visible on TV, and covert operations, secret even in success" (George Bush).[8] New, unconventional, even at times—like the futuristic warfare imagined by Walter Benjamin—imperceptible, this war was to surpass all limit, all law, all representational convention or mediation.[9] The declaration of war on terror declares war *as* terror.

Yet this war is undecidably a war and a "war." Its infinite, absolute seriousness and contagiousness (who or what could oppose a war on terror? Who could not say, "I oppose terror; I am fighting that war"?) has about it an unbearable lightness, even, for all the suffering it causes and the damage it does, a kind of silliness, for a war without limits transforms its very prosecution into a sequence of theatrically ineffective gestures. Everything about the war on terror seems perpetually ready to melt into air. It is a war declared—and undeclared and semideclared—by a semisovereign whose words carry enormous force, but whose powers (unlike those of the U.S. Congress) do not (quite) include the legal power to declare war.[10] Its beginning is nearly as uncertain as its end: It scrolls back past the September 11 attacks and the Bush administration's pronouncements to incorporate in its history other attacks, other administrations, other nations.[11] It is uncertainly literal and figurative. It forces ponderous legal documents to pause in midstride to muddle out—I quote here from a brief submitted to the Supreme Court in 2004—whether "the United States is actually 'at war' in the sense of Vietnam, Korea, and the two World Wars rather than in the sense of the 'war on drugs,' which is, and always has been, primarily a law enforcement effort."[12] The war's very existence can seem questionable, as the sovereign himself concedes ("I know that some people question if America is really in a war at all," Bush remarked in his 2004 State of the Union speech). After all, if the war is so absolute as to be at times invisible, how can one tell whether it is going on or not? Where is it to be found, either in the "homeland," where consumers are being exhorted to consume more, or in the areas of the world (or, for that matter, sectors of U.S. society) where direct and semidirect applications of American power have been part of reality for a half-century or more? Do Bush administration policies differ fundamentally from those of the aggressively interventionist (and "terror"-oriented) Clinton administration, or those of previous administrations?[13] That in the wake of the September 11 attacks the U.S. launched visible police, military, and paramilitary actions against certain terrorist groups and attacked Afghanistan and Iraq; that within the United States we are witnessing displays of warlike behavior— the aggressive recruitment of young working-class men to feed the military machine; the programmatic harassment of "Arabs," Muslims, foreigners, and certain sorts of citizens; the semilegalization of torture and of interminable incarceration (this last above all via the abuse of "enemy combatant" and "material witness" provisions); in short, a general and considerable deterioration of human rights and civil liberties—all this does not add up clearly to "war on terror," any more than a terrorist attack, however horrific, comes across without ambiguity as an act of war rather than a monstrous crime. The choreographing of fear and the militarization of public life in the United States will thus at times seem absurd or stagey (as in the case of the much-mocked color-coded terror alerts), while conventional military operations against other sovereign states will always risk being seen, even by gung-ho nationalists, as surrogates for the "real" war on terror. Jean Baudrillard might well tell us, and not entirely without reason, that the war on terror does not exist—or, more precisely, does not *take place*. It goes on, perhaps, but it does not (quite) take place as a determinate event within a determinate space and time.

The declaration of war on terror is undecidably and incalculably performative and constative, real and fictional, literal and rhetorical, consequent and nugatory, radically singular and endlessly iterable and generalizable. It can seem "in a peculiar way hollow or void," as J. L. Austin famously characterized literary utterances.[14] Yet its consequences— legal, political, economic—can seem as traceable as those of any performative. "Declaring" "war," the semisovereign becomes a little more sovereign in and through his own flawed, quasi-fictional exercise of sovereignty.[15] This exceptional declaration of war thus exemplifies the sort of performative that J. Hillis Miller has taught us to understand as "literary"—literary, here, signaling not (as Austin would have it) a performative safely framed and tagged as fictional, but rather a performative that troubles the difference between real and fictional, literal and figurative. Speech-act theory, Miller suggests, is a speech act that exceeds its own theory of itself. It unfolds as a contradiction (relying on a speaker's intention, but subordinating intention to context). It depends on the "parasitic," "nonserious" literary examples it excludes. Like a sovereign declaring war on terror, it downplays its own performativity: Austin's *"How to Do Things with Words* is a truly revolutionary philosophical event attempting to masquerade as a constative statement of fact that does no more than continue a development in thinking long underway."[16]

The analogy between sovereign and text is not as forced as it might seem. Miller's analysis draws attention to the fact that a revolutionary event "definitely does not fit Austin's criteria for a felicitous performative," since it cannot rely upon preexisting laws or conventions: "A revolution is groundless, or rather, by a metaleptic future anterior, it creates the grounds that justify it" (*Speech Acts in Literature*, 26–27). And commenting on the disorder and violence that so often characterize Austin's examples, Miller remarks that, in the Austinian subtext, "we are always skating on thin ice, on the verge of catastrophe" (ibid., 56).[17] In Austin's work, as in Nietzsche's, we hang in dreams from the back of a tiger, for the social order, relying as it does on congenitally unreliable performatives, can at any moment give way (which is why, Miller suggests, "a rhythmic counterpoint of multitudinous references to law, lawyers, judges, and courtroom scenes punctuates *How to Do Things with Words*" [ibid., 56]). In its own way, speech-act theory may be said to wage a little war on terror. And it suggests why the sovereign shies away from himself: The terror at the heart of sovereignty is that of the performative itself, or rather, of the literariness—the radical uncertainty—making the performative possible.

In some ways it has always been clear that a degree of reflection on language becomes inescapable as soon as one has begun to think about sovereignty, war, and terror. For starters, the war on terror is among other things very much a war of words. Sovereign is he, I suggested earlier, who can make the word "terror" stick. It must be added that this Anglo-Latinate word, which has a history we will have to examine, functions as a politically charged site of translation within a globally hegemonic English-language media apparatus. (All political conflicts consequential enough to achieve mass mediatization necessarily involve, as part of their struggle, their translation into the Anglo-Latinate lexicon of "terror": the military, cultural, and economic dominance of the West is thus always also an ongoing act of translation *as* terror-war.) And within that media apparatus a symptomatic slippage occurs, from "terrorist" or "terrorism" to the more general "terror," whereby—we will return to this—the "war" achieves theological stature as a technowar on finitude itself. If we can speak of a terror within sovereignty, a terror that sovereignty exploits and depends on, but with which it is endlessly at war, it is terror in this sense: the rupture of an internal finitude, which is to say a vulnerability to "language" to the extent that we understand language as an uncertain medium, productive of unpredictable effects. Counterintuitive though it may seem, a meditation on the war on terror ultimately entangles us in the seemingly academic and culturally marginal question of "theory" and of a certain war on theory—a war waged in the name of certainty, clarity, referential stability—that forms part of the history and constitution of theory itself. Theory has been blamed for terror at least since the words "terrorism" and "terrorist"—along with, I will suggest, the first drafts of the notion of a "war on terror"—emerged during the early years of the French Revolution. Eventually I will track some of those developments, but first I will invest time exploring the dense, overdetermined notions of war and terror that have become joined at the hip in the Bush administration's signature phrase.

II

To begin with, however, perhaps a few more words about sovereignty, as a way of getting us to war. I have been suggesting that uncertainty and a strategic capitalization on uncertainty haunt sovereignty; arguably this is particularly true in our technomediated era. The major shortcoming of Giorgio Agamben's provocative hypothesis that "the [concentration] camp is the *nomos* of modernity" is its overhasty absolutization of its own terms:

> If . . . the essence of the camp consists in the materialization of the state of exception and in the subsequent creation of a space in which bare life and the juridical rule enter into a threshold of indistinction, then we must admit that we find ourselves virtually in the presence of a camp every time such a structure is created, independent of the kinds of crime that are committed there and whatever its denomination and specific topography. The stadium in Bari into which the Italian police in 1991 provisionally herded all illegal Albanian immigrants before sending them back to their country, the winter cycle-racing track in which the Vichy authorities gathered the Jews before consigning them to the Germans, the *Konzentrationslager für Ausländer* in Cottbus-Sielow in which the Weimar government gathered Jewish refugees from the East, or the *zones d'attentes* in French international airports in which foreigners asking for refugee status are detained will then all equally be camps. In all these cases, an apparently innocuous space (for example, the Hôtel Arcades in Roissy) actually delimits a space in which the normal order is de facto suspended and in which whether or not atrocities are committed depends not on law but on the civility and ethical sense of the police who temporarily act as sovereign (for example in the four days during which foreigners can be held in the *zone d'attente* before the intervention of the judicial authority).[18]

Borrowing heavily (and, it must be said, not always with copious acknowledgment) from Hannah Arendt, Agamben rightly draws attention to the twentieth-century proliferation of "camps" throughout civic space and suggests that the camp, as the space of an "absolute impossibility of deciding between fact and law, rule and application, exception and rule," arguably provides "the hidden matrix of the politics in which we are still living" (*Homo Sacer*, 173, 175).[19] At the same time he fails to note an important double corollary: first, that *there is no such thing as an absolute camp*—even Auschwitz was exposed to systems and pressures larger than itself—and, second, that there is, therefore, no single homogeneous space called "camp" to which the various examples listed in the quotation above can be assimilated without residue. It is simply not the case that "everything is possible" in a *zone d'attente* in the same way that (almost) everything was possible in Sobibor.

The claim that in a late twentieth-century European refugee camp the police "temporarily act as sovereign" is valid, but only and precisely to the extent that one understands sovereign power as fractured, contaminated, and mediated—paradoxically so. "A pure sovereignty is indivisible or it is not at all," Jacques Derrida writes. Yet in order to be indivisible—in order to be the pure instantaneity of the exceptional decision—sovereignty must withdraw from time and language:

> To confer sense or meaning on sovereignty, to justify it, to find a reason for it, is already to compromise its deciding exceptionality, to subject it to rules, to a code of law, to some general law, to concepts. It is thus to divide it, to subject it to partitioning, to participation, to being shared. It is to take into account the part played by sovereignty. And to take that part or share into account is to turn sovereignty against itself, to compromise its immunity. This happens as soon as one speaks of it in order to give it or find in it some sense or meaning. But since this happens all the time, pure sovereignty does not exist; it is always in the process of positing itself by refuting itself, by denying or disavowing itself; it is always in the process of autoimmunizing itself.[20]

This seemingly highly abstract analysis admits of pragmatic illustration. Because it can never be (and yet must be) absolute, sovereignty exploits contingent and unstable zones of ambiguity.[21] The struggle in the U.S. courts over the legal status of the camp at Guantánamo Bay offers a good example of this predicament. Produced as a space of exception—a zone of terror—in the shadow of sovereign ambiguity (Guantánamo, nominally under the sovereignty of Cuba, is "leased" to the United States in perpetuity), this camp proved vulnerable to Supreme Court review to the extent that most of the justices were willing to curtail the sovereign exception precisely by limiting the ambiguity on which it was relying—finding, in the words of the majority opinion authored by Justice Stevens, that writ of habeas corpus applies in "a territory over which the United States exercises plenary and exclusive jurisdiction, but not 'ultimate sovereignty.'"[22] The sovereign claim to exception was absolute, as always—the Bush administration's position was that the court had no business reviewing the case at all—but was checked in this instance by the court's own ("sovereign") decision provisionally to integrate Guantánamo into the polity's rule of law. By simply deciding to hear the case at all, the court, one could say in Benjaminian terms, countered the administration's law-positing power with its own law-positing speech act in order to bring Guantánamo within the fold of law-conserving power. The case could easily have been decided differently or could not have been heard at all: The point is not that the Bush administration was bound to lose, and certainly not that prisoners in this or any other camp have, pragmatically speaking, much hope. (Most of these centers for interrogation and incarceration are in any case better hidden, more mobile, more ambiguously located in the interstices of sovereign power.) The point is rather that the spaces of sovereign exception are always singular, quasi-localized, vulnerable to context, and exposed to contingency.

Agamben is in some respects highly attentive to sovereignty's essential relation to ambiguity. Stressing, like many writers before him, sovereignty's double location "outside and inside the juridical order" (*Homo Sacer*, 15), he emphasizes that the sovereign exception opens the space of law and politics ("the rule, suspending itself, gives rise to the exception and, maintaining itself in relation to the exception, first constitutes itself as a rule") and is therefore "essentially unlocalizable," a "suspension of every actual reference" (ibid., 18, 19, 20). What Agamben seems at times to forget, however, is that this radical state of suspension exceeds its own decisive occasion: Sovereignty draws upon a sheer freedom that it must also evade or suppress.[23] Of the exception as "the structure of sovereignty," he writes, "it is the originary structure in which law refers to life and includes in itself by suspending it"; and, following Jean-Luc Nancy, he gives "the name ban (from the old Germanic term that designates both exclusion from the community and the command and insignia of the sovereign) to this potentiality . . . of the law to maintain itself in its own privation, to apply in no longer applying" (ibid., 28). What he fails to add, however, is that in coming into existence, the sovereign ban splits internally, doubling and resisting itself (as law-positing and law-conserving violence, performative force and constative reference: once again, we recall the sovereign's foot shuffle as he declares war). With this proviso in mind, we may entertain Agamben's imaginative claim that the sovereign ban opens political space by producing *homo sacer*, the man who "can be killed and yet not sacrificed," whose inclusive exclusion founds the city of men.

As the original biopolitical body—the originary inscription of what Agamben calls "bare life" within political life—*homo sacer* is the sovereign's inverted double (as the outlaw who can be killed without consequence by anyone, he is the man over whom all men are sovereign, whereas the sovereign is the man for whom all men are, at least potentially, *homines sacri*). Thus, according to this narrative, "the first foundation of political life is a life that may be killed, which is politicized through its very capacity to be killed" (*Homo Sacer*, 89). Agamben offers these speculations as a meditation on the archaic root of the modern sociopolitical disposition that Michel Foucault calls biopower: modern biopolitics, Agamben suggests, causes "the realm of bare life" to "coincide with the political realm" from which it was originally, if uncertainly, excluded (ibid., 9). As a result, in modernity, the state of exception becomes the rule and the camp becomes the matrix of political space. In other words—it is here, once again, that we have to press Agamben past some of his own formulations—sovereignty suffers and exploits ever more visibly its constitutive uncertainty, even as effects of sovereignty proliferate. It is within this matrix that "the terrorist" becomes the quasi-sovereign's ambivalent *homo sacer*. On the one hand, the terrorist is the sovereign's double as a declarer of war. On the other hand—and for precisely that reason—he is the one who can be "killed but not sacrificed," sometimes immediately (as the object of a newly rehabilitated U.S. policy of targeted assassination), sometimes indirectly (as the illegitimate "enemy combatant" who ought to disappear permanently into a camp where—unless contingencies intervene, as they always can—*anything* can be done to him).

That the modern semisovereign should go to "war" against the terrorist underscores the peculiar ambivalence of their mutual relationship. The last person a properly Agamben-style sovereign would go to war against would be *homo sacer*: As bare life, *homo sacer* is the sovereign's abject double, but he is not an *enemy*. He is an outlaw: He is lower than an enemy, and, being both excluded from and included within the city, he is more ambivalently situated than any enemy could be. The terrorist gives to this structure yet one more twist: He is the enemy outlaw. Capable, like a sovereign power, of declaring war, he nonetheless (as "enemy combatant") falls below the laws of war, and, unprotected by law, becomes bare life to be exterminated. And if "war" has become the name of this thoroughly ambivalent relationship between sovereign and terrorist, this is because, as we must now spend a moment reviewing, in our era, few words have become readier to hand or harder to pin down than "war."

Even if we try to restrict ourselves to the "literal" meaning of the word "war"—"an organized, legitimized, lethal conflict between human communities," to cite one scholar's definitional effort—the notion of war begins to slip through our fingers as we examine the historical record.[24] Restricting our gaze for the moment, and for the sake of convenience, to the last hundred years or so, we see the idea of war balloon and fold into itself, pop and balloon out again: on the one hand, an absolutization of war (the Great War; the World Wars; total mobilization and total war; the unthinkable, unwinnable prospect of nuclear war); on the other hand, an ever-increasing log of undeclared wars, civil wars, "conflicts," acts of pacification and "peacekeeping," local wars of liberation or conquest, "ethnic cleansing." The development of a permanent war economy in the early twentieth century may be said to have begun the process of literalizing Kant's claim about the endless subterranean persistence of war, a literalization that became overt in the era of the "Cold War," when the notion of absolute or total war was married to that of unconventional, undeclared war. Under the shadow of the nuclear umbrella, not just American economic might but "American culture" itself was now to be a weapon of war. All-pervasive though this conflict might be, however, it was also representable as figurative, as falling short of true, literal war, which could now only be nuclear. Contrary, however, to Paul Virilio's assertion that "war today is either nuclear war or nothing," the point is rather that war today is neither quite itself nor anything else.[25] War is always already everywhere, yet defers (as nuclear holocaust) the totality of its arrival. Postmodern theories of war often seek to translate this paradox of war into the idiom of technocratic strategizing: the authors of a recent RAND document *Networks and Netwars* (2001), for instance, define "netwar" as "conflict at the less military, low-intensity, more social end of the spectrum. . . . We had in mind actors as diverse as transnational terrorists, criminals, and even radical activists."[26] Serving multiple ends and devoid of clear points of origin or termination, netwar, in such writings, can at times come across as a militaristic appropriation of the work of Deleuze and Guattari—which should not be surprising: Sovereign power, as we have seen, has no choice but to feed on ambiguity and quite often does so with devastating success.

But it has already become clear that the inflationary spiral of war as a literal notion or condition is inseparable from a rhetorical spiral. The last century witnessed a proliferation of versions of the "war on" formula in Anglo-American culture (a formula that, significantly, seems to have originated in epidemiological contexts, as a "war on typhus," etc.). In recent decades, even literary criticism's small swatch of the discursive universe has known theory wars and culture wars, while the broader public sphere has endured a massively damaging war on drugs and innumerable less consequential "wars" targeting perceived social or moral ills. Although inseparable from the Cold War and related developments as discussed above, these martial tropes (all of which function differently in different contexts and have widely varying institutional motives and resonances) are ultimately assimilable to a hypertrophied, internally dissonant figure of war that seems part of the texture of Western modernity.

Beginning, let us say provisionally, with Hobbes and the grounding of political life itself in an originary *bellum omnium contra omnes*, war has been pressed into service as a trope for—or realization or extension of—consciousness as history (Hegel, Kojève), politics (Clausewitz), class relations (Marx), natural history (Darwin), language and cognition (Nietzsche), the psyche (Freud). More than ever, it seems, *polemos pater panton*: War is the father of all things (Heraclitus). It is at the origin and at the limit, infecting and underwriting the seeming peace of the everyday. If earlier we suggested that the twentieth-century absolutization of war has literalized Kant's admonition that until we successfully perform an oath of perpetual peace we remain either literally at war or suspended within war's potentiality, the abbreviated roll call of famous names given above suggests another way of understanding why it has become harder and harder to tell what war is and whether we would know it if we saw it (a predicament George Orwell allowed his newspeaking totalitarian state to parody with its leadoff epigram "War is peace, peace is war").[27] Might there be a war so cold, a *guerre* so *drôle*, as to be invisible not just to the general public (as Bush suggested portions of the "war on terror" might be), but even to the wagers of war itself? Why not, if "war" has come to name a state constitutive of historical, political, biological, sexual, psychic, or class identity, a condition deeper and older than consciousness? Where would such a war begin or end, and how would one know?

War thus becomes a pressing, yet ambiguous trope: a profligate figure for the human condition that rapidly becomes a figure of its own figurativeness, its own uncertain legibility. Like certain other ideologically and semantically charged tropes, it vacillates between a hyperaffirmation and a deconstruction of its own referential force. On the one hand, war (like "the body") functions rhetorically as the promise of a referential plenitude (or emptiness) beyond representation: It is hell, brute reality, the experience you can't know unless you've been there. In a celebratory register, it becomes sublimity, the generatrix of heroism and matrix of glory.[28] On the other hand (again like "the body"), it crumbles in the grasp and reappears elsewhere.[29] War is what transforms the uncertain into the certain and back again. As Samuel Weber puts it, war's "function is to institutionalize the other as enemy and thus to hold death at bay"; death thereby becomes "a state that can be inflicted upon another, upon the enemy, the result of intentional, strategic planning, a means of establishing control and acquiring power."[30] Yet from antiquity onward, war has been represented as an intensified encounter with the chance (*tuchē*) that weighs on all life.[31] War generates binary oppositions and promises the security and thrill of communal identification and linear narrative, yet in its fog and friction, the best-laid plans go awry. (Appropriately, the English and French words "war" and "guerre" both return etymologically to Old High German "werra," confusion.)[32]

Like sovereignty, war is both inside and outside the law. (If the notion of the "law of war" is in a sense a contradiction, so is that of an utterly lawless war.) In his interesting study *The War Machine*, Daniel Pick provides these paradoxes with a historical nuance, locating the emergence of a "powerful new vision" of war as a "driverless train" in the era of the American Civil War and the Franco-Prussian War: a vision, that is, of war as both a "remorselessly efficient machine" and a "deranged vehicle."[33] As a double figure of technorationalization and irrationalism, he suggests, war becomes a figure for modernity's self-contradictions. Yet that figure always turns out to be a figure of its own potential illegibility, and Pick goes on to suggest that modern writing about war discovers in its object a force that blurs and complicates that object's representation in discourse: "the pen," he summarizes via a reading of Clausewitz, becomes "disturbingly caught up in the 'friction' it describes" (*The War Machine*, 47).[34] Jacqueline Rose, writing in *Why War?—Psychoanalysis, Politics, and the Return to Melanie Klein* mainly about Freud but also about Clausewitz and other writers, makes a similar point: "War . . . operates in Freud's discourse, and not only in that of Freud, as a limit to the possibility of absolute or total knowledge, at the same time as such absolute or total knowledge seems over and again to be offered as one cause—if not *the* cause—of war."[35] The death drive explains war, but the death drive is "the speculative vanishing point of psychoanalytic theory" (*Why War?* 18). Thus, Rose concludes, "The attempt to theorize or master war, to subordinate it to absolute knowledge, becomes a way of perpetuating or repeating war itself" (ibid., 24). The fog of war, at the limit, names a disturbance in the rhetorical status of war itself.[36]

This unruly figurativeness of war—a figurativeness thoroughly implicated in literal violence—generates uncertain crossings between war and "theory." Let me close this brief survey of the career of the figure of war with a glance at Michel Foucault's 1976 seminar at the Collège de France, which was dedicated in part to the question: "Can war really provide a valid analysis of power relations, and can it act as a matrix for techniques of domination?"[37] Foucault unearths a tradition beginning not with Hobbes (whose figure of general warfare Foucault relegates to sheerly "figurative" or "theoretical" status), but with seventeenth-century writers of various political persuasions (from Levellers to aristocratic opponents of royal absolutism) who all understood war as "a permanent social relationship, the ineradicable basis of all relations and institutions of power" (*"Society Must Be Defended,"* 49). Foucault feels a certain sympathy with this tradition, yet remains cautious, unwilling to reduce processes of domination to war: "Is the relation between forces in the order of politics a warlike one? I don't personally feel prepared to answer this with a definite yes or no."[38] "War," here, names a moment where the theorist pauses, uncertain. A hiccup within its own theoretical explication, war is the *technē*, the cunning and the blindness, the divinity and finitude of all sovereignty, including that of theoretical understanding.

III

What, we must now ask, is terror? And what might be made of the glide from "terrorism" to "terror" in Bush administration pronouncements and in the Western media generally? Noting what he claims to be the administration's tendency to favor the former term in 2001–2 and the latter in 2003–4, Geoffrey Nunberg observes that while both words are vague and politically manipulable, "terror is still more amorphous and elastic" than terrorism, evoking "both the actions of terrorists and the fear they are trying to engender."[39] Furthermore, "unlike 'terrorism,' 'terror' can be applied to states as well as insurgent groups"—obviously a fact of some interest to an aggressive sovereign state eager to confront other states. And (particularly as the object of the abstractly oriented phrase "war on," rather than "war against"), terror can be represented as a disease like typhus, an "endemic condition that [can] be mitigated but not eradicated," the object of "a campaign aimed not at human adversaries but at a pervasive social plague." In the idiom of Foucault or Agamben, the war on terror can thus become a dimension of biopolitics: Via terror, the terrorist becomes bare life—a germ or parasite endlessly to be exterminated. Finally, "at its most abstract, terror comes to seem as persistent and inexplicable as evil itself"—or, one could hypothesize, death itself. Death is the sublime "king of terrors," per Edmund Burke's personification, precisely to the extent that it cannot be calculated or known in advance.[40] In this sense, as Burke well understood, "death" is a name for an inadequacy at the heart of representation and knowledge: It is an idea "not presentable but by language," vividly present only when "all is dark, uncertain, confused, terrible, and sublime to the last degree" (*Philosophical Enquiry*, 175,

59). We may expect that, like war, terror will turn out to have a curiously intimate relationship with aesthetics, literature, and theory.

Like so much else in modern American and Western European political and cultural life, our specifically political notions of both "terror" and "terrorism" form part of our romantic inheritance. The capitalized nominative "Terror" has, of course, a historiographical referent: It designates more or less the period between the fall of the Girondins (June 1793) to the fall of Robespierre (July 27, 1794, or 9 Thermidor). Semantically it suggests a collective fear conditioning the social and political order; more specifically, it means a political regime founded on fear and violence and on what in French was (and is) called "mesures d'exception." According to the *Dictionnaire Robert*, the first recorded uses of the French words "terroriste" and "terroriser" date from 1794. One year later, according to the *Oxford English Dictionary*, the word "terrorist" entered the English language in Edmund Burke's fourth "Letter on a Regicide Peace" ("Thousands of those Hell-hounds called Terrorists . . . are let loose on the people") and in the Burkean *Annual Register* ("The terrorists, as they were justly denominated, from the cruel and impolitic maxim of keeping the people in implicit subjection by a merciless severity.").

Although we no longer mean quite the same thing by "terrorist" that Burke did, the word's mutation over two hundred years has been neither clear nor decisive. Burke would have approved its current use in the mainstream media to designate illegitimate organized acts of violence—and whatever he might have thought about the Bush administration's decision to invade Iraq, he would have understood the rhetorical drift from "terrorist" to "terror" that facilitates one sovereign power declaring another illegitimate under the "war on terrror" rubric. Burke's basic claim about the Jacobin government was that it was illegitimate (as he once put it epigrammatically, "the Regicides in France are not France").[41] As we will see in somewhat more detail at the end of this essay, he had himself, to the best of his unsovereign ability, declared war on terror. And in a linguistic sense, he can be said to have won, insofar as throughout most of the world's official channels, the word "terror" now possesses uniformly negative connotations, having lost the suppleness it enjoyed in prerevolutionary aesthetic treatises on the sublime—including, of course, Burke's—and, more pointedly, having lost its affirmative Jacobin meaning.[42] "Terror," Robespierre claimed in his important *Discourse* of February 5, 1794, "is nothing other than prompt, severe, inflexible justice; it is therefore an emanation of virtue; it is less a particular principle than a consequence of the general principle of democracy, applied to the most pressing needs of the nation."[43] After the fall of Robespierre, the word "terror" lost favor as a description of official acts of violence, and in the mid-1790s, "terrorist" became for the first time a category under which people were prosecuted. But the Robespierrist definition of terror did not thereby simply become obsolete.

The association of terror with absolute or divine justice is a Judaeo-Christian topos, and governance through terror is presumably as ancient as human sociopolitical organization itself. What is modern or revolutionary about the Jacobin Terror is its secular appropriation of absolute justice as the prerogative of the state. The Robespierrean naming and claiming of terror offers itself as the performative force of the *patrie*: Terror is the "consequence of the general principle of democracy" because the *patrie* (as democracy's embodied principle) must come into being through an absolute declaration of itself and then must sustain or preserve itself against (as Robespierre says in a previous sentence) "the internal and external enemies of the Republic." Terror (to recall once again Benjamin's useful distinction) is the appropriation of divine violence as law-performing and law-preserving violence. This appropriation—rendered explicit in and as the modern speech act through which the nation or people declares itself—constitutes sovereignty. Sovereignty is terror, a terror that repeats and takes into itself the excess and immediacy of the divine and that, consequently (as we have seen in the context of declarations of war) terrifies itself. Therefore, Robespierre's formulation prudently renders terror virtue's "emanation": terror is to be merely a means, an effectivity subordinate to virtue's stability. Yet like war, terror is both sovereignty's *techné* and the locus of its excess. Sovereignty is thus always waging war on terror, even as it unleashes terror within the space of a state of emergency that defines itself as a war measure (to wit, a National Convention decree of October 10, 1793 that suspended the recently drafted and never to be ratified Jacobin constitution and declared that "the provisional government of France is revolutionary [*révolutionnaire*] for the duration of the war"). Sovereignty occurs as an indistinction between exception and rule that must also be abjured. It is not simply for empirical reasons that the tyrant, in Xenophon's words, has "a soul distracted by fears."[44]

Agamben's intriguing proposition in *Homo Sacer* is that the French Revolution announces the transformation of politics into biopolitics: "declarations of rights represent the originary figure of the inscription of natural life in the juridico-political order of the nation-state." It is thus that "bare life" (the sheer fact, for instance, of being born) becomes the "earthly foundation of the state's legitimacy and sovereignty" (*Homo Sacer*, 127).

This is the matrix of Agamben's broad claim about the camp being the *nomos* of the modern that we examined earlier and thus of his attempt to map, in the wake of Arendt and Foucault, a portion of the ambiguous interface between democratic and totalitarian twentieth-century political formations. Bare life—the moment of the citizen's inscription within the political order, to the purity of which the detainee of the camp is re-duced—is never an extrapolitical fact, but is rather "a threshold in which law constantly passes over into fact and fact into law" such that "the two planes become indistinguishable" (ibid., 171). It is life lived naked under the eye of sovereignty—or, in the idiom we are exploring here, life lived in and as terror. As the linchpin of biopolitics, sovereignty causes us to consider the inscription of terror on the body, or, perhaps better, the po-litical fashioning of a terrified body.

The political nexus terrorist-terrorism-terror thus opens onto the broader historical and phenomenological question: What is terror? Even a cursory review of the historical record soon has us bogging down in complexities and alternatives possibly even more dizzying than those of "war." One would never have done counting the narratives that discover the ground tone of modernity to be terror in the sense of fear: fear pro-voked by the death of God, by the shattering of the Ptolemaic universe and the scientific production of the infinite reaches that filled Pascal with dread, by the socially atomizing and deracinating forces of consumer capi-talism and modern technics, by the nuclear threat, and so on. Like war, fear pops up again and again in the Western tradition as the condition out of which human identity emerges and to which it endlessly returns: Fear generates language (Condillac, and to some extent Rousseau), human self-recognition (Hegel, and especially Kojève), sovereignty and the political order (Hobbes—the Leviathan comes into being in order to protect its subjects from a limitless exposure to terror), ideological interpellation (Al-thusser—what besides sheer terror can one imagine as the affective correl-ative of subjectification at the moment of the policeman's "hey you!"?). Political, social, and psychic life are frequently characterized in critical narratives—the present one, to be sure, included—as sites for the produc-tion, distribution, and overall management of fear. Writing within this tradition, Brian Massumi suggests that "a history of modern nation-states could be written following the regular ebb and flow of fear rippling their surface, punctuated by outbreaks of outright hysteria."[45] Indeed, he asks, "what aspect of life, from the most momentous to the most trivial, has *not* become a workstation in the mass production line of fear?" (*The Politics of Everyday Fear*, viii). That question grows all the more intriguing if one adds to it the question of whether or not we remain capable of identifying fear as such. Massumi seems to take it for granted that we know what terror is, but what happens when, like William James, one wonders whether the most terrifying thing might be the threat of being released from terror?[46] Or when, like Freud, one opens oneself to the possibility that one could be terrified without knowing it, that the unconscious has terrors of which consciousness knows not? How counterintuitive that sounds: Surely it was bad enough to have to entertain the idea that we could be at war without knowing it. Can we not at least be certain of fear—the emotion that wracks the body, freezes it, turns it pale (or, in Homer, yellow-green), invades knees and stomach and sweat glands, opens orifices, turns speech into chatter?[47] What is more real than an emotion that, as a surge of adrenaline, can literally kill us? Yet we have a standard medical term for being terrified without "knowing it": trauma. Fear can, perhaps, be all the more terrible for bypassing consciousness. And even when we "know" fear, what is it that we know? The greater our terror, the greater the shock to identity: The mind goes blank and loses control of the body; the body loses control of itself.

Without pretending here to be able to provide anything akin to a genuine phenomenology of fear, we may pursue a moment longer the peculiar status of "terror" in the modern Anglo-Latinate lexicon of the emotions. Of its near synonyms, "terror" is probably closest to "panic." Both suggest a modality of fear particularly apt to be a group or mass phenomenon. Reflecting on group psychology in the era of mass politics, Freud calls panic (*Panik*) the "collective fear" (*Massenangst*) that accompanies the disintegration of a group when its leader, its common ego ideal, is shattered. Panic not only demonstrates the contagiousness of emotion in a group setting (with no necessary link to an objective cause, "a gigantic and senseless fear is set free"), but also what one might call emotion's impersonality. Since "panic fear presupposes a relaxation in the libidinal structure of the group," it is in essence a communal or structural phenomenon, however sharply felt by individuals.[48] In recent years, good critical work has been done on the irreducibility of affect to individual subjectivity, an idea that, while as old as that of passion itself, may be returned under the terms of a more restricted genealogy to Heidegger's seminal writing on mood.[49] Arguably, no emotion more vividly suggests its own irreducibility to the individual—its more fundamental openness to the political—than panic or terror. And yet the mode of terror's transpersonality resists easy representation. Can terror be a mood in Heidegger's sense—an attunement (*Stim-*

mung), which is to say, "the way of our being there with one another"?[50]
Is it possible to speculate that terror is the attunement proper to what
Agamben calls "bare life"? Perhaps, although whether, in the extreme
spaces of terror, one can still speak of attunement, of being proper to, or
even of being with, in Heidegger's sense, is not to be taken for granted.[51]

We may approach the same point from a slightly different vantage by
noting how differently the notions of "terror" and "anxiety" shoulder
metaphysical baggage. Anxiety, particularly as "the dizziness of freedom"
in the work of Kierkegaard and the early Heidegger, has proved imaginable as intrinsically human, whereas terror, fear, and fright are among
the few emotions—perhaps in the end the only emotions—that, in the
metaphysical tradition, humans and animals are supposed to share.[52] Yet if
"fear" is taken, either in a functionalist or a Heideggerian spirit, as a response to a defined stimulus or object (and thus as the opposite of "anxiety"), then "terror" is arguably not quite that either. When I am terrified,
I freeze in the headlights; my sense of self shatters, and my self-preserva-
tive instincts misfire. What threatens me is neither graspable as an object
per se nor generalizable as the approach of nothingness, death, or freedom. We may risk the following proposal: Terror is the phenomenological
precondition of trauma. Terror names the possibility of *experiencing the
missing of experience*. Terror does not necessarily lead to trauma in the medical sense, but the latter could not exist without the former.[53]

It is possible to understand terror as the experience—or nonexperi-
ence—of what post-Heideggerian thought calls an "event." Jacques Derrida writes of the terror inherent in the idea of the "event in general":
"who has ever been sure that the expectation of the Messiah is not from
the start, by destination and invincibly, a fear, an unbearable terror—
hence the hatred of what is awaited? And whose coming one would wish
both to quicken, and infinitely to retard, as the end of the future?"[54] Fear,
according to Aristotle, "may be defined as a pain or disturbance due to
imagining some destructive or painful evil in the future" (*Rhetoric* 2, 5:
1382a, 21–22). Terror belongs to the event precisely to the extent that the
event per se has never quite arrived and thus can never be mastered or
done away with. The September 11 attacks, Derrida tells us, inspire terror
not because they were horrific in themselves, but because they open the
possibility of another and worse catastrophe: "Traumatism is produced by
the *future*, by the *to come*, by the threat of the worst *to come*, rather than by
an aggression that is 'over and done with.'"[55]

IV

Terror, the ruin of language and consciousness, can nonetheless be thought in relation to linguistic force. Primo Levi, writing of the agony that even sleeping became in Auschwitz, tells us that "one wakes up at every moment, frozen with terror, shaking in every limb, under the impression of an order shouted out by a voice full of anger in a language not understood."[56] Like so many of Levi's generalizations and descriptions, this one powerfully reminds us that the violence suffered by the camp inmate is utterly unnatural. Agamben's trope "bare life" is evocative precisely because it is neither a tautology nor an intensifier plus a noun: Bare life is not *simply* life (whatever that might be). To dehumanize is not to return human beings to a hypothetical state of nature, but rather to reduce them, as Hannah Arendt puts it, to something far worse: "the abstract nakedness of being nothing but human" (*Origins*, 300). The *Häftling*, the prisoner, is interpellated as bare life through a bare speech act, a performative nearly stripped of meaning, understandable only as an order that must but cannot be understood. The attempt to bear witness to such terror is only part of the impossible but necessary task of giving testimony about Auschwitz (only the dead, Levi insists, could give uncompromised testimony), but it is what the survivor must attempt, using infinitely inadequate words.

It is easy enough to accept the idea that literature might have to struggle to remain adequate to catastrophic experience. If "the ideal of truth," as W. G. Sebald asserts, "proves itself the only legitimate reason for continuing to produce literature in the face of total destruction," the path to "unpretentious objectivity" turns out to be excruciatingly difficult.[57] Stories of catastrophic terror exceed "anyone's capacity to grasp them," not just because memory fails ("the accounts of those who escaped with nothing but their lives do generally have something discontinuous about them, a curiously erratic quality so much at variance with authentic recollection that it easily suggests rumor-mongering and invention"), but because the story being remembered resists being put "into any framework of reality, so that one feels some doubt of its authenticity" (*Natural History of Destruction*, 23, 24, 88). Language itself has ghastly powers of normalization that interfere with and threaten to vitiate testimony: "The apparently unimpaired ability—shown in most of the eyewitness reports—of everyday language to go on functioning as usual raises doubt of the authenticity of the experiences they record" (ibid., 25). Language's power to falsify and banalize is one of Sebald's major themes, as is his affirmation of testimony as a *literary* task. To "reveal the truth through literary efforts" is to "quest for a form of language in which experiences paralyzing the power of articulation could be expressed" (ibid., 146, 150). Sebald's unsparing attention to problems of language and form offers us the insight that, pushed to the limit of its possibility, *literature* is perhaps our culture's most rigorous name for the effort to speak truly of terror.

In this context, it is of interest to examine a brace of texts from the mid-1940s that make broad and nonobvious claims about the link between literature and terror and do so from a seemingly quite different vantage. For Jean Paulhan, in his extraordinary and in Anglo-American contexts somewhat forgotten little book *Les fleurs de Tarbes* (1941), literature involves not so much the witnessing as the *imagining* of terror and involves not so much a complicity with terror's victims as with the Robespierrean (or Sadean) sovereign power that seeks to discover in terror the expression of its absolute freedom. "One calls Terrors," Paulhan writes, "those passages in the history of nations . . . where it seems suddenly that what is needed for State governance is not cunning and method, nor even science and technics . . . but rather an extreme purity of soul, and the freshness of a communal innocence."[58] Using the Terror of 1793–94 as the figurative hinge between classicism and romanticism, Paulhan suggests that romantic literature, which is to say modern literature, desires to extirpate conventional linguistic forms—the commonplace, the clichéd, the rule-bound: in short, all the flowers of rhetoric. Modern literature may thus be termed a literature of terror, dreaming of an original, immediate, unmediated expressiveness, a meaning that is being. The key names in Paulhan's account are those of the French romantic and postromantic moment (from Hugo, to Verlaine, to Rimbaud, to the surrealists of Paulhan's own time), and the overarching claim is that modern literature's desire to escape language results in an obsession with language. The more literature tries to reject rhetorical convention, the more its transparency turns refracting and refractory.

Maurice Blanchot, reviewing *Les fleurs de Tarbes* in 1941, radicalized Paulhan's study into a vibrantly paradoxical definition of literature: Terror *is* literature, "or at least its soul," and this soul is condemned endlessly to lose itself in language.[59] This Paulhanian theme returns in Blanchot's great essay of 1949, "La littérature et le droit à la mort" as the needle with which Blanchot lets the air out of Kojèvian Hegelianism.[60] Literature, Blanchot suggests, is the one place where Hegelian negation seems to work perfectly: A writer becomes a writer by writing, acting such that a nothingness becomes something and a possibility becomes presence: "If we see work as the force of history, the force that transforms man while it transforms the world, then a writer's activity must be recognized as the highest form of work."[61] But this perfect model of work crumbles into a haunting sort of unwork or nonwork. The writer's act of negation is global and immediate. He (I will replicate Blanchot's masculine pronoun) is free to imagine anything, no matter how fantastic—like Hegel or Kojève, for instance, he can imagine a world in which slaves become masters—and that is precisely the problem: "Insofar as he immediately gives himself the freedom he does not have, he is neglecting the actual conditions for his emancipation" ("Literature and the Right to Death," 315). Global and immediate, the writer's sovereign negation negates nothing because it offers everything instantly.

We thus begin to enter the uncanny, action-ruining space of what Blanchot calls "the imaginary," and at the same time we begin to register a political desire at literature's heart: a fascination with revolution. Contemplating revolution, the writer, Blanchot writes, "knows he has not stepped out of history, but history is now the void, the void in the process of realization; it is absolute freedom which has become an event. Such periods are given the name Revolution" ("Literature and the Right to Death," 318). At such "fabulous moments," everything seems possible, immediately: "in them, fable speaks; in them, the speech of fable becomes action" (ibid.). And now the title of Blanchot's essay—that intriguing transformation of man and his rights: literature and the *right* to death—begins to explain itself: In its terrible demand for transparency and purity, revolutionary action demands freedom or death, requiring the abolition of the individual's secret particularity:

> This is the meaning of the Reign of Terror. Every citizen has a right to death, so to speak. . . . When the blade falls on Saint-Just and Robespierre, in a sense it executes no one. Robespierre's virtue, Saint-Just's relentlessness, are simply their existences already suppressed, the anticipated presence of their deaths, the decision to allow freedom to assert itself completely in them and through its universality to negate the particular reality of their lives. . . . The Terrorists are those who desire absolute freedom and are fully conscious that this constitutes a desire for their own death. (ibid., 319–20)

To the extent that figures like Robespierre and Saint-Just personify Terror, they are figures of a self-annihilating purity, a death empty of significance and subjective depth.[62] The writer, Blanchot says, sees himself in the Revolution, which "attracts him because it is the time during which literature becomes history." Yet literature also endlessly ruins and renders spectral the transparency and immediacy of terror. A "blind vigilance which in its attempt to escape from itself plunges deeper and deeper into its own obsession," literature "is the only rendering of the obsession of existence." The obsession of existence is, for literature, that of language: "Literature is language turning into ambiguity" (ibid., 321, 322, 341).

If one recognizes in a writer like Sebald a testimonial imperative that is also, in Paulhan or Blanchot's provocative terms, a (modern, postromantic) literary dream of terror as linguistic transparency ("the ideal of truth"), one also recognizes that Sebald's affirmation of literature's ethical task paradoxically translates into endless, scrupulous patience with linguistic deviance and mediation. That double imperative not only rules the literature of testimony, but, as Sebald and Blanchot suggest in their different ways, governs any text we call literary—including, as we saw Miller suggesting earlier, speech acts and speech-act theory, when the act or the theory begins to register within itself the disconcerting uncertainty and singularity of its own performance and terms of expression. The adjective "literary," taken in this sense, is no longer an unambiguous honorific. If I have risked calling the sovereign declaration of war on terror a "literary" speech act, this is not to credit sovereign power with any particular sophistication, though it *is* to suggest both the cunning with which sovereignty exploits its own ambiguity and the finitude conditioning that exploitation. The Paulhan-Blanchot line of speculation has the advantage of compelling us to recognize that sovereignty, with its terror and its war on terror, is not something that literature or critical thought simply oppose from a purely external position. If one accepts the notion that the space of sovereign exception, with all its literally unspeakable horrors, cannot be firmly or absolutely distinguished from the revolutionary moment in which, as Blanchot puts it, "literature becomes history" because everything seems possible, one has affirmed a certain mutual contamination among sovereign, revolutionary, and imaginative force. One has also affirmed, as a literary task, the endless marking of the difference between sovereign power and the revolutionary moment, which is, as Blanchot says, a *fabulous* moment. It is the excess haunting sovereignty, the terror against which it wages war.

The modern literary project as Paulhan describes it—the anguished vacillation between a desire for an unmediated vision and a consciousness of linguistic mediation—is, I have argued elsewhere, a particularly concentrated version of the discourse of modern aesthetics and opens up the kind of reflection on figurative language that, in the last decades of the twentieth century, the Anglo-American academy began to call "theory." And "theory" is in fact another word that, since the era of the French Revolution, has been associated with terror. "Theory" and "theorist" and various cognates ("speculative," "speculation") rank among Burke's favored pejoratives in *Reflections on the Revolution in France* and in his other counterrevolutionary texts. Wordsworth's thirty-line apostrophe to Burke in the 1850 *Prelude* grants appropriately explosive metrical emphasis to Burke's accomplishment as he

> Declares the vital power of social ties
> Endeared by Custom; and with high disdain,
> Exploding upstart Theory, insists
> Upon the allegiance to which men are born.[63]

"Theory," in Wordsworth's or Burke's usage, tends to mean abstractly rational, systematic thought, yet Burke's strictures about theory also tend to grant it an uncanny, spectral, excessive agency. Precisely because the French Revolution "is a Revolution of doctrine and theoretick dogma," it is sublimely uncontainable and threatens to spread across Europe, or indeed around the world, like disease, money, and newsprint.[64]

David Simpson has argued that one can trace late twentieth-century animadversions about theory in Britain and, mutatis mutandis, the United States, back to these eighteenth-century and early nineteenth-century roots, as though denunciations of systematic thinking even today were still haunted by the "ghost of Robespierre, the coldest of the ruthless abstractionists."[65] His remarks help contextualize the frigid inhumanity that antitheoretical writers so frequently ascribe to theory's totemic figure in the American academy, Paul de Man, a critic whose work focuses with exemplary intensity on the ways in which the problematic of reading aligns with that of terror. Reading, for de Man, originates in and returns endlessly to fear—but the whole "theoretical" point is that "fear," at least in this context, is the opacity of a text that must and yet cannot be read with certainty. I cannot do more than gesture here toward a topic that elsewhere I have tried to examine in some detail.[66] Perhaps it will suffice to recall that the allegory of reading that de Man extracts from various texts by Rousseau takes off from a counterintuitive interpretation of Rousseau's parable in the *Essay on the Origin of Language* of the primitive man who, meeting other men for the first time, feels afraid and names them "giants," thereby transforming a hypothesis (the men might be dangerous) into a certainty. "The metaphor is blind, not because it distorts objective data, but because it presents as certain what is, in fact, a mere possibility. . . . By calling [the other man] a "giant," one freezes hypothesis, or fiction, into fact and makes fear, itself a figural state of suspended meaning, into a definite, proper meaning devoid of alternatives."[67] Fear—at least "in theory"—comes into being as the ongoing and always imperfect obliteration of its own constitutive uncertainty.[68]

As the theory of fear (as uncertainty), theory becomes fearful, turning away from and resisting itself and inspiring fear in those who, seeking to put uncertainty (as fear) aside, condemn theory as an excess of enlightened rationality turned obscurantism. The word "obscurantism" is not intended as mine here, but as John Searle's. Here is a quote from Searle's violently negative review of Jonathan Culler's *On Deconstruction* in *The New York Review of Books* in 1983: "Michel Foucault once characterized Derrida's prose style to me as '*obscurantisme terroriste.*' The text is written so obscurely that you can't figure out exactly what the thesis is (hence '*obscurantisme*') and then when one criticizes it, the author says, '*Vous m'avez mal compris; vous êtes idiot* (hence '*terroriste*')."[69] I would suggest that the adjective "terroriste"—we are speaking French here—is organizing this little namedropping anecdote because two centuries' worth of associations, filiations, and figurative transports have woven a context in which obscurity, terror, and reason—here figured as a kind of ruthless ruse, the reader trap of "*Vous m'avez mal compris; vous êtes idiot*"—conjoin to condition the reception of something called "theory." We may seem rather far from romanticism, reading Searle on Derrida, but if one thinks about Burke's early interest in the link between obscurity and terror in the *Enquiry*, about what he says in that treatise about the arbitrariness and power of words, and about the ability of language to achieve sublimity by surpassing its own representational function; if one considers all the ways that "French," as the foreign, but perhaps not quite foreign enough, language of theory, has played a role in the theory wars—Searle expects you to be able to understand these snippets of French, monolingual middlebrow American reader of *The New York Review of Books* though you be; you'd better understand these bits of symbolic obscurity, otherwise *vous êtes idiot*; French, in other words, has always already crossed the Channel and hopped over the Atlantic, even though it needs to be marked off as foreign and expelled—if one keeps all this in mind, the era of Burke and Wordsworth, Rousseau and Robespierre may not seem so very distant after all.

V

That war should be declared (or almost or half or pseudodeclared) on "terror" is, I have been suggesting, perhaps at once the most obvious, overdetermined, and obscure speech act in Western history. It is *the* sovereign speech act, unleashing war as terror and terror as war, yet in doing so, it reiterates and exacerbates the uncertainty of sovereign power, the ambiguity of sovereign enunciation, and the nagging obscurity of the declaration's key words. Having always already been declared, it thus always remains in a sense undeclared and can seem poised uncertainly between a fatality and a choice. As the announcement of a political program or pseudoprogram of absolute (and yet virtual) war, it could, perhaps, be claimed overtly only by a superpower in an era of global mass telecommunication and biopolitical calculation. Thus, the war on terror may be seen not just as one aspect of the ever-tightening regime of modern technics, but rather as the very motto of technometaphysical domination. What other phrase better captures both what Heidegger characterizes as the modern technoproject of regulating and securing (*Steuerung und Sicherung*)—the imperative to objectify and put on order, to stockpile and secure—and that project's dislocation of place, time, and identity?[70]

Yet since we have been provisionally tracing the war on terror back to the French Revolution and the opening of the era of human rights, mass politics, and biopolitical power, it will be appropriate to offer in conclusion a brief study of Burke's counterrevolutionary writing. From the start—from Wollstonecraft and Hazlitt through Arnold and down to our own time—there has been a tradition of reading Burke as both the font or father of modern conservatism and as a self-divided figure, covertly akin to and in sympathy with the revolutionary Jacobin he opposes.[71] Close readings of *Reflections on the Revolution in France* reveal a Burke repeating what he condemns and worrying about the status of borders and distinctions that he not only cannot police, but also cannot help systematically violating. For present purposes, we may restrict attention to the fact that what makes Burke a *modern* conservative is his rejection of divine right in favor of what is in the end, despite numerous rhetorical twists and turns, a social-contract justification of governmental authority ("society is indeed a contract" [*Reflections*, 195]). If Burke rejects the declaration of the rights of men and the declaration of the Republic, he does not reject declaration. A sovereign speech act opens the space of social and political being, although the locus of its power is ambiguous. At times, Burke refers the social contract back to a divine fiat, an "oath," presumably sworn by God to himself, that holds together the universe: "Society is indeed a contract. . . . Each contract of each particular state is but a clause in the great primeval contract of eternal society linking the lower with the higher natures, connecting the visible and the invisible world, according to a fixed compact sanctioned by the inviolable oath which holds all physical and all moral natures, each in their appointed place" (*Reflections*, 195). At other times Burke, whose references to traditional religious faith never come across as very deeply felt, offers a more secular account of society's origins.[72] In both cases, one notes creeping complications.

If the divine "inviolable oath" seems to subordinate the universe and its deity to a strange, superdivine linguistic power, the secular (and equally inviolable) oath emerges out of paradox and fictionality. The fundamental claim of Burkean conservatism is that we never get to the end or the bottom of the contract, which always precedes us. The "People" does not and has never existed in a state of nature: "it is wholly artificial, and made like other legal fictions by common agreement" ("An Appeal from the New to the Old Whigs," 163–64). (Put in more lapidary—even Wildean— fashion: "Art is man's nature" [ibid., 169].)[73] The "legal fiction" of the people has been made by "common agreement"—by a people that is not yet a people, but must be a people in order to decree itself a people. Like the divine oath, the secular one implies an endless sequence of authorities by whom and to whom the oath is sworn. At the origin is a nonorigin, a "fiction"—in the terms we have elaborated, a *literary* speech act.

Fictionality, however, is aestheticized through temporal mediation: man's "art" becomes "nature" by way of a temporality borrowed from the natural order:

> Our political system is placed in a just correspondence and symmetry with the order of the world, and with the mode of existence decreed to a permanent body composed of transitory parts; wherein, by the disposition of a stupendous wisdom, moulding together the great mysterious incorporation of the human race, the whole, at one time, is never old, or middle-aged, or young, but in a condition of unchangeable constancy, moves on through the varied tenor of perpetual decay, fall, renovation, and progression. Thus, by preserving the method of nature in the conduct of the state, in what we improve we are never wholly new; in what we retain we are never wholly obsolete. By adhering in this manner and on these principles to our forefathers, we are guided not by the superstition of antiquarians, but by the spirit of philosophic analogy. In this choice of inheritance we have given to the frame of our polity the image of a relation in blood; binding up the constitution of our country with our dearest domestic ties; adopting our fundamental laws into the bosom of our family affections; keeping inseparable, and cherishing with the warmth of all their combined and mutually reflected charities, our state, our hearths, our sepulchres, and our altars. (*Reflections*, 120)

This famous passage retains traces of the instability of the originary speech act, both in the self-conscious fictionality and literariness of its terms ("philosophic analogy," an "image of a relation in blood") and, perhaps more tellingly, in the strange figure of an impossible, contradictory choice: "In this *choice of inheritance* we have given to the frame of our polity the image of a relation in blood." The oxymoronic figure of choice recurs in Burke's subsequent paragraph, in which "we" are said to choose nature and the breast itself: "All your sophisters cannot produce anything better adapted to preserve a rational and manly freedom than the course that we have pursued, who have *chosen our nature* rather than our speculations, *our breasts* rather than our inventions" (*Reflections*, 121, emphasis added). Inheritance, nature, and the breast are of course three things that one by definition cannot choose. Indeed, the rhetorical function of the figures of inheritance and nature in Burke's polemic is precisely that of marking a fatality and a necessity. It is as an "*entailed* inheritance" that the polity is forbidden to vote itself out of existence and embark on revolution (ibid., 119, Burke's emphasis). Burke's strained, radically fictional figure of choice relays the volatility of the original Austinian speech act upon which modern sovereignty rests.

The haunting trope of the impossible, excessive choice culminates in a passage in which Burke admits into his text, however reluctantly, a revolutionary moment in which a "necessity that is not chosen but chooses" justifies "a resort to anarchy":

> It is the first and supreme necessity only, a necessity that is not chosen but chooses, a necessity paramount to deliberation, that admits no discussion, and demands no evidence, which alone can justify a resort to anarchy. This necessity is no exception to the rule; because this necessity itself is a part too of that moral and physical disposition of things to which man must be obedient by consent or force; but if that which is only submission to necessity should be made the object of choice, the law is broken, nature is disobeyed, and the rebellious are outlawed, cast forth, and exiled, from this world of reason, and order, and peace, and virtue, and fruitful penitence, into the antagonist world of madness, discord, vice, confusion, and unavailing sorrow. (*Reflections*, 195)

Burke's insistence that "this necessity is no exception to the rule" holds only because the rule, as always in the space of sovereign exception, has become indistinguishable from its suspension at the moment of sovereign decision or choice. How can one know whether one is choosing or whether necessity has chosen? Whether one has "submitted to necessity" or whether one has exceeded law, reason, and order in the moment of choice—a choice so excessive as to be that of "inheritance" or "nature" itself? The moment of choice is terrifying, and it is always, in its excess, a choice of war: a war on terror, by way of terror. In Burke's writings after 1790, this theme becomes prominent, above all in the *Letters on a Regicide Peace* of 1795–97, which insist that the war on terror must be a total war, fought without remission or mercy:

> We are at war with a system, which, by its essence, is inimical to all other Governments, and which makes peace or war, as peace and war may best contribute to their subversion. It is with an armed doctrine that we are at war. It has, by its essence, a faction of opinion, and of interest, and of enthusiasm, in every country. To us it is a Colossus which bestrides our channel. It has one foot on a foreign shore, the other upon the British soil. (*Regicide Peace*, 1:19)

The sheer existence of the Jacobins—like the September 11 attacks in Bush administration rhetoric—constitutes an act of war that requires war of us. The war is a civil war, both because Europe is "virtually one great state" such that laws of vicinage or neighborhood apply and because the opponent is everywhere: On the one hand he is the non-European, the cannibal, the Moslem or Jew, yet on the other hand, he is the neighbor next door (ibid., 1:80, 1:82–83, 1:76–77, 2:118). For although the Revolution is always already all too French and foreign, what this really means is that it has no certain origin or end. At one point Burke even suggests that the Jacobin disease originated in England: "I have reason to be persuaded, that it was in this Country, and from English Writers and English Caballers, that France herself was instituted in this revolutionary fury" (ibid., 4:307). More tellingly, in the *Reflections*, Burke savors the image of a double counterfeit and the figure of a line crossed and recrossed as he imagines French revolutionaries being inspired by Britain's own revolution and then themselves inspiring British Jacobins: "We ought not, on either side of the water, to suffer ourselves to be imposed upon by the counterfeit wares which some persons, by a double fraud, export to you in illicit bottoms, as raw commodities of British growth though wholly alien to our soil, in order afterwards to smuggle them back again into this country, manufactured after the newest Paris fashion of an improved liberty" (*Reflections*, 110–11).

The figure of the line is Burke's master trope, on which all law and prophecy hang: "The speculative line of demarcation, where obedience ought to end, and resistance must begin, is faint, obscure, and not easily definable. It is not a single act, or a single event, which determines it." (*Reflections*, 116).[74] And it is the inevitable blurring of the line even as it is drawn that generates terror and counterterror. Burke and Robespierre, skewed doubles, root out conspiracies that proliferate infinitely, prosecuting a war in which sovereignty and terror define each other in and through their mutual uncertainty. Giving us literature, theory, human rights, and biopolitics, romanticism declared a war on terror that continues to shape our lives. We will never be certain of that declaration's locutionary shape, illocutionary status, or perlocutionary reach. Thus, sovereign power will always exert itself where and as it can, calculating and capitalizing on a situation that resists calculation. But let us give the last word to Kant, whose essay on perpetual peace summons us to another (if never completely other) war on terror: a war on war on terror that imagines as its fabulous possibility and goal a perfect speech act—a declaration of peace. To be a true declaration of peace, the peace declared would have to be perpetual and the declaration would have to be absolute: absolutely transparent to itself and its medium, made without reservation, without the reserve of secrecy, without limit. It would be an utterly felicitous and sovereign speech act, as unmediated and instantaneous as Robespierrean justice; only such a terrible and sovereign speech act could pronounce the end of war. It is also, to be sure, an utterly fabulous, literary speech act, as Kant slyly reminds us as he opens his treatise under the sign of a fictional, uncertain, impossible imperative:

Toward Perpetual Peace

Whether this satirical inscription on a Dutch innkeeper's sign upon which a burial ground was painted had for its object mankind in general, or more particularly the rulers of states who can never get enough of war, or merely the philosophers who dream this sweet dream, is something that need not be gone into [*mag dahin gestellt sein*]. (*Werkausgabe*, 11:195)

American Literary Studies and American Cultural Studies in the Times of the National Emergency: J's Paradoxes

Donald Pease

Unlike many of the other contributors to this volume, I regret to say that I never had the occasion to study under Hillis Miller in graduate school. And until October of 2002, I had never enjoyed the benefits of J. Hillis Miller's prodigious gift for collegiality.[1] When I undertook a course of graduate study in the field of American literature nearly three decades ago at the University of Chicago, I did so under the tutelage of James Edwin Miller, Jr., in the methodology of the myth-symbol school of literary interpretation whose dominance of the field of American literary studies was undermined in part by the practices of deconstructive reading that J. Hillis Miller fostered. J. Hillis Miller's work has nevertheless played a significant role in shaping my understanding of the reconfigurations of the field of American Studies and in clarifying the complicities between discourses produced within the field of American Studies and United States governmental policies.

In an effort to explain the part that Miller's work has played in my understanding of both of these developments, I intend to follow the itinerary of Miller's project along two different tracks. In the first two parts of this essay, I intend to correlate an account of the part that poststructuralist theory played in transforming the orientation of the field of American Studies—from the aesthetic ideology of J. Edwin Miller's myth-symbol school to the multicultural initiatives of American cultural studies—with a discussion of an essay in which J. Hillis Miller productively interrupted the transition from American literary studies to American cultural studies.

But in addition to analyzing the significance of Miller's work for the field of American Studies, I will use what Miller calls "inaugural performatives" to scrutinize the complicities between the literary and cultural practices produced within the field of American Studies and the state's rationales for war. At the conclusion of this itinerary, I hope to demonstrate how these tracks are intertwined dimensions of J. Hillis Miller's paradoxical praxis by showing how the inaugural performative Miller produced to disrupt the transition to cultural studies might be mobilized to unsettle the state of emergency that President George W. Bush inaugurated when he declared the war on terrorism.

From the Myth-Symbol School of American Literary Studies to American Cultural Studies

With the exception of Henry Nash Smith, the founders of the myth-symbol school of American literary studies—R. W. B. Lewis, Leslie Fiedler, and Leo Marx—were, like James Edwin Miller, Jr., veterans of the Second World War. After the war's conclusion, these soldier-critics produced a patriotic fiction in whose name they could retroactively claim to have fought the war. The national myth they created linked their need for an idealized national heritage with the epic narrative through which that idealization was imagined, symbolized, and supplied with characters and events.

Myths are machines responsible for the construction, representation, and regulation of a people. The myth about the nation that the founders of the myth-symbol school invented was at once a narrative about the national heritage and a metanarrative in which these soldier-critics installed the idealized representations of the nation to which they desired to return. Because metanarrative involves a universal subject in a transhistorical action, Kenneth Burke has characterized it as the "justifying myth" for materially specific national events.[2] The myths and symbols that the founders selected would supply the members of disparate interpretive communities with the paradigmatic narrative through which they went about representing, codifying, explaining, and thereby resolving their own conflicts.

The idealized representations invented by the founders of the myth-symbol school of interpretation came to name, that is, to entitle, the master texts of the field of American literary studies. These masterworks engaged a prototypical American self (*The American Adam*), in an epic quest (*Errand into the Wilderness*) to liberate our native land (*Virgin Land*) from foreign encroachments (*The Machine in the Garden*). While each of these foundational texts provided a slightly different account of the metanarrative that defined the practices of Americanists, all of them presupposed a utopian space of pure possibility where a whole self internalized this epic myth in a language and a series of actions that corroborated American exceptionalism.[3]

Each of the foundational signifiers sedimented within the national metanarrative possessed a performative dimension that would bring about belief in the conditions that they represented. In their original usages, collective representations like the "American Adam," "virgin land," the "American frontier," and the "errand into the wilderness" had reference to historically specific cultural agents, objects, and events. The national metanarrative converted such raw sociopolitical data into collective representations through which it made sense of things, retroactively transforming them into the foundational origin of the national order for which it also supplied the rationale, transhistorical concepts and descriptive taxonomies foundational to the national community's acts of interpretation. This circular logic peculiar to the myth-symbol school then facilitated acts of reading that transformed the hermeneutic register on which these collective representations operated. The themes anchored within the national metanarrative thus supplied the transformational grammar through which the state shaped the people's understanding of contemporary political and historical events.

The fact that Americanists could agree upon an encompassing vocabulary and consensus over their methodology and objects of analysis (myth and symbols) as well as the conventions for interpreting them formed the bases for the autonomy and coherence of their field. At once a mode of inquiry, an object of knowledge, and an ideological rationale, the discourse produced within the myth-symbol school of American literary studies facilitated an interdisciplinary formation that enabled Americanist scholars within the disciplines of literature, history, politics, sociology, and government to undertake cooperative projects. This interdisciplinary formation was constructed in reaction against what its practitioners described as the fragmentation of knowledge accompanying specialized academic disciplines. Through this interdisciplinary approach, the field of American Studies collaborated with the press, university system, publishing industry, and other aspects of the cultural apparatus that managed the semantic field and policed the significance of such value-laden terms as "the nation" and "the people." By this means, the logic of the nation as a knowable "whole" was grafted onto the concept of interdisciplinarity that was made to serve the state with the ideological function of making one out of many.[4]

As a model of the civic behavior that it would also bring about, the national mythology thus was part of the aesthetic ideology of the nation-state. U.S. citizens educated in the myth-symbol school used its technology to rework daily life into images that authorized belief in the isomorphism of the U.S. people, territory, and national culture. Following its deployment as the grounding mythos for the national pedagogy, the U.S. metanarrative that the myth-symbol critics invented thereafter solidified into a relatively autonomous system for the production of meaning that resulted in a semantic field by which individuals were persuaded to live demonstrably imaginary relations to their real conditions of existence.

In its relationship with the collective representations embedded within the national metanarrative, the myth-symbol school performed a quasi-regulatory function. The mode of reasoning developed within the myth-symbol school circumscribed the questions Americanists might ask and established the criteria and rules of validity for their responses. Its foundational concepts framed the questions determining the production of knowledge and exerted control over their interpretation. Indeed the state's powers of governance depended in part upon its recourse to the national metanarrative as a regulatory intertext that transmitted a normative system of values and beliefs from generation to generation.[5] When they subordinated actual historical events to these mythological themes, government's policymakers constructed imaginary resolutions of actual historical dilemmas. After the U.S. metanarrative was instrumentalized to justify the state's imperative to rebuild and develop nations worldwide, scholars in American Studies crossed international as well as disciplinary boundaries. By pitting their artistic and scholarly freedoms against the repressive cultures of the Soviet bloc, Americanist scholars enshrined U.S. liberal democracy as the subject and telos of universal history.

Upon being harnessed to the reason of state, the U.S. metanarrative supplied the metarules and the grounding assumptions underwriting the narrative grammar through which to determine what would and what would not count as an Americanist perspective. When it extended the logic of the reason of state into the everyday lives of the citizenry, the national metanarrative supplied the people with the fantasy that their everyday activities contributed to the United States' mission to restore the rule of law internationally. Rather than restricting its governance to the civic sphere, this U.S. metanarrative produced an imaginary space wherein citizens were encouraged to believe that their daily exercise of rights and freedoms participated in the efforts through which the United States conducted a global war against the Soviet empire.

The national mythology did not merely facilitate the aestheticization of the political, it was a fusion of politics and art that resulted in the production of foreign policy as a work of art. U.S. foreign policy was grounded in the credo of American exceptionalism, which required the belief in the United States as a unique political formation. The national metanarrative invented a tradition corroborative of this belief.

However, in the 1970s, the growing opposition to the Vietnam War undermined the state's use of the national metanarrative to justify state policy. The war effected what John Hellmann has described as a radical disruption in the nation's self-representations: "When the story of America in Vietnam turned into something unexpected, the nature of the larger story of America itself became the subject of intense cultural dispute. On the deepest level, the legacy of Vietnam is the disruption of our story of our explanation of the past and vision of the future."[6]

Shared opposition to the Vietnam War resulted in a counterculture composed of social-activist, feminist, civil rights, and gay and lesbian scholars. The aspiration for radical social transformation within the new social movements led to the repudiation of the national metanarrative propagated within the myth-symbol school for its complicit identification with the "exceptionalist" state apparatus.

When the founders of the myth-symbol school described the national metanarrative as expressive of the national will, they endowed it with what might be called a monopoly of symbolic (as opposed to actual) violence. As the instrument of the people's will that state officials invoked when they spoke as representatives of the sovereign people, the national metanarrative supplemented the state's monopoly over the right to exercise actual violence. During the Cold War, the national metanarrative produced what might be called a structural repression of the people's right to question the Cold War's rationale. As the harbinger of the patriotic values in whose name the Cold War was fought, the national metanarrative supplemented the authority of the state upon whose sovereign powers it depended for the efficacy of its governing representations.

In ascribing the source of the state's power to declare war against North Vietnam to the sovereign will of the people, President Johnson performed the bait and switch maneuver constitutive of the state's sovereignty. If sovereignty pertains to the agent who monopolizes the power to exercise legitimate violence, it was the state's restriction of the people's power to exercise legitimate opposition to the state's acts of violence that constituted the precondition for the state's sovereignty. But when the opponents of the Vietnam War disclosed the groups—African Americans, Latin Americans, women, Native Americans, gays and lesbians—who lacked representation within the national metanarrative, they explained that the sovereign will of the U.S. people was an invention that the state had fashioned at the nation's border, where it decided who was assimilable to the national identity and who was not.

Their demystifications of the national mythology permitted a dramatic reshaping of the nation's social and political landscape. Arguing that their task was to break the constraints of an enveloping imperial culture, architects of the new social movements repudiated myth-symbol pedagogy as a specific form of the construction of citizenship and citizens and of normative cultural reproduction. Whereas the myth-symbol school presupposed the narrative of the birth of a nation made sacred by the nation's exceptional mission, opponents of the war agitated on behalf of countercultural attitudes that moved away from the privileged standpoints provided by myths, symbols, and other unifying paradigms to reveal the field's internal critical limits. Challenging the hegemonic understanding of objects of study, identities, and scholarship that had predominated, the proponents of the countercultural movement formed academic programs in African American Studies, Latino/a studies, Asian American Studies, Native American Studies, Gay and Lesbian Studies, and Women's Studies.

Throughout the late 1970s and 1980s, activist scholars who received their academic training under J. Hillis Miller and other members of what was then called the Yale School (Paul de Man, Geoffrey Hartman, Harold Bloom, Jacques Derrida) employed deconstructive tactics and poststructuralist stratagems to clear the ground for the emergence of disciplinary sites for feminists, critical race theorists, and members of the newly acknowledged ethnicities. Henry Louis Gates on behalf of African Americans, Barbara Johnson in support of feminists, Ramon Saldivar in the promotion of Chicano/as, and Lee Edeleman and Judith Butler in the advancement of gay and lesbian causes had all put poststructuralist theory in service to their radical transformation of the academy.[7]

In "authorizing" these new fields of knowledge, poststructuralist theory altered the conditions for the production of academic knowledge by dismantling the metanarrative that had formerly regulated the field. The national metanarrative promoted belief in a national identity that was seen as noncontingent and in its essence grounded in an absolutely prior, utterly unique, inside core wholly identifiable with the sovereign will of the U.S.

people. But poststructuralists argued that the coherence of this narrative was possible only to the extent that an inside was supplemented by the alternative narratives it excluded. Since the counternarratives that it excluded were crucial to the self-enclosure of the inside of the national meta-narrative, the sovereign national will that it was said to represent required the supplemental act of the exclusion of such alternatives.

The identitarian social movements required theorization as a precondition for their academic placement, yet these theoretical practices also required social practices for their implementation, their elaboration, and in some instances, their correction. The negotiations that poststructuralist theory effected between academic and social realities led to the reconceptualization of the cultural phenomena of patriarchy and heterosexuality as structures of oppression that foster sexism, racism, homophobia, and cultural imperialism.

In adding the knowledge that the constituent disciplines of American Studies had traditionally excluded, the concepts of racism and sexism revealed a fundamental insufficiency in the way these disciplines were normally organized. Racism and sexism were structural realities that were at once insistently present to traditional disciplinary perspectives yet persistently absent from their terms of analysis. Reconceptualizations of race and gender undertaken during this period inspired the formation of disciplinary subfields and academic programs that refused either to accede to the dominant assumptions of American Studies or to be reduced to its categories.

Poststructuralist theory brought into crisis the myth-symbol school's canonical objects of analysis, protocols of reading them, and the interpretive narratives that had secured this field identity. Advocates of the myth-symbol school attempted to repair the conceptual ground of a field whose fissuring into multiple programs and subfields had exceeded their epistemological grasp. In the face of the opposition mounted against them, members of the myth-symbol school attempted to accomplish a dramatic resolution to the protracted epistemological crisis by undertaking a meta-theoretical exercise in boundary management. They represented this crisis as the effect of the conflict between the field's consensus paradigm and the imperatives for change that had been forged within the social movements.

J. Hillis Miller's colleague in the Yale School, Harold Bloom, entertained such an aversion to the unregulatability of what he called the emergent "School of Resentment" that he invented a mythopoetic apparatus that was designed to control the dynamics of both social and disciplinary change. As a critic raised on the belief that literary studies depends upon

British Romanticism's version of the myth-symbol school for its positive valuation, Bloom assessed the significance of emergent literary formations in terms of the loss or preservation of mythological themes. In a series of books—*The Anxiety of Influence, A Map of Misreading, Agon*—that he published through the '70s and '80s Bloom attempted to transform the myth-symbol paradigm into a psychopoetic tropology designed to synchronize the field's entire history within an encompassing psychodrama. But Bloom's efforts to reintegrate the terminology, practices, and tactics of poststructuralist theory within his revisionary mythos did not persuade the members of the emergent "subdisciplinary" and interdisciplinary formations to reorganize themselves in their projects in terms of Bloom's paradigm.

But after these new social movements were institutionalized, tensions developed between activist projects and the theoretical formations through which they were reconstituted as academic programs. The radicality of poststructuralist theory might have gone to the roots of Americanists' relationships to disciplinary processes and conventions, but it took grassroots activism, as theory's opponents now declared, to change the conditions of history. By the 1990s, scholarship in the field of American literary studies was eclipsed by research in a new interdisciplinary formation called American cultural studies.

But upon acquiring institutional power, the practitioners of American cultural studies routinely represented what was explicitly political about their enterprise as involving their ability to stress the performative over the "merely" theoretical aspects of their practice. The Americanist critics who had obtained institutional legitimacy by supplanting the myth-symbol school as the organizing matrix for Americanists' scholarship now invoked the social logic of multiculturalism to regulate the relations between these newly formed academic programs and the heterogeneous social movements out of which they had emerged. In transforming the U.S. multiculture into a more or less coherent image of American cultural studies, these new Americanists had in effect erected a justifying myth for their projects that they did not want deconstructed. Rather than recalling the key role that poststructuralist theory had played in the emergence of the new field, Americanist cultural critics characterized poststructuralists as engaged in an effort to replace political activism with a theoretical culture all its own.[8]

From Literary Studies to Cultural Studies: The J-Turn

By the time I was promoted to the rank of associate professor in American literature at Dartmouth in 1981, American cultural studies had become an interdisciplinary formation that supplanted the myth-symbol approach as the organizing matrix for scholars in American Studies. As a mode of explanation, an object of study, and an agent of change, multiculturalism supplied the new field with an encompassing imaginary out of which Americanist critics produced a legitimating rationale for their disciplinary praxis. I then subscribed to the sentiment that Eric Cheyfitz has recently elevated into a credo: that American literary studies must be supplanted by American cultural studies or risk losing its relevance altogether.[9]

In the initial symbolic act that I performed upon receiving tenure in 1981, I pledged my allegiance to the prerogatives of American cultural studies by writing a critique of what I characterized as the conservative effects of J. Hillis Miller's deconstructive readings on the emergent field. In the essay, I condemned Miller for deploying deconstruction as a cover for the incompleteness of his commitments to the disparate theoretical formations—the dramatism of Kenneth Burke, the phenomenology of Georges Poulet, and the poststructuralism of Jacques Derrida—with which he had identified in the course of his academic career:

> Miller, then, in his serial adaptation of significantly different critical positions, never completely coincided with any one critical position. Thus in place of a coherent development of a critical project, we find in his career a curious symmetry, discernible mostly in the disjunction between the critical position he claims to represent and the language he uses to describe that project. Throughout Miller's "later" criticism we find traces and remnants of his earlier positions. Unlike those dangerous supplements Jacques Derrida is fond of locating in traditional texts to unsettle their apparent coherence, remnants of Miller's earlier positions, functioning as if they were the return of repressed elements from what we might call the critical unconscious, confer a sense of coherence and integrity upon Miller's later criticism. Indeed, these remnants allow Miller to ensure the claims of the newer criticisms by drawing on the "principles" of outmoded critical positions.[10]

In rereading the essay, I now realize that it had less to do with J. Hillis Miller's commitments than with my own desire to mark a decisive turning point. The criticism of Miller for his "incomplete conversion" to poststructuralist theory was expressive of my continuing attachments to the myth-symbol school. My condemnation of J. Hillis Miller for his putative failure to complete the transition from one field identity to another displaced the desire to repudiate my own former identifications with the myth-symbol school in which J. Edwin Miller had educated me.

The object of my desire was a mythological event—the complete and irreversible transition from American literary studies to American cultural studies. But this desire was itself underwritten by the belief in American cultural studies as a totalized academic field. In criticizing Miller for his failure to annul his previous affiliations, I had tacitly ascribed to his project a grounding assumption that was as totalizing and ideological as that of the myth-symbol school, namely, that his poststructuralist theory had supplied the metaphysical grounding for an entirely different field of academic inquiry. But J. Hillis Miller's commitments to what he has described as the "ethics of reading" required that he refuse either a coherent field identity or a metaphysical ground for his reading practices.

Rather than aligning his critical project with this transformation of the organizing matrix of the field of literary studies, J. Hillis Miller addressed the relationship between literary studies and cultural studies in two essays that reflected slightly different orientations in Miller's relationship to the two academic formations.[11] In the essay that he published in 1992, "The Work of Cultural Criticism in the Age of Digital Reproduction," Miller questioned the legitimating narrative through which cultural critics justified the transition from literary studies to cultural studies. In the essay that he published in 1998, which appears in extended form as "Literary Study in the Transnational University" in *Black Holes* (1999), Miller redescribed cultural studies as an aspect of the study of literature that promoted the "ethos of dissensus" he believed necessary to resist the incursion of globalization on the transnational university.

In "The Work of Cultural Criticism in the Age of Digital Reproduction," Miller questioned the teleology that represented cultural studies as an epistemological advance over literary studies. Miller posed this question by juxtaposing a close reading of Walter Benjamin's "The Work of Art in the Age of Mechanical Reproduction," a text that had been elevated into one of the foundational texts of the field of cultural studies, with a critique of the progressivist claims expressed by the advocates of the computer databases undergirding the Thoreau project. Miller did so in an effort to dismantle the assumption that underpinned both of these cultural practices, namely, that new technologies necessarily mark an advance in the production of knowledge.

Miller's refusal of these assumptions required that he demonstrate how the computer databases in the era of digital reproduction are comparable to the technology that mass-produced artworks in the era of mechanical reproduction. Both of these information-storage systems, he showed, were underwritten by genetic narratives that presupposed the self-evident explanatory force of context. The genetic narratives linking these technologies to literary works simply revalorized the assumptions of historical scholarship that represented the relationship between text and context in terms of the relationship between an effect and its cause. "To say that a cultural artifact is rooted in the culture from which it arises and can only be understood within that context, or to say that big computer bases will allow an understanding of the genesis of a work like Thoreau's *Walden*, is to yield to one form or another of the genetic thinking that remains an almost irresistible trap for thought" ("The Work of Cultural Criticism," 28).[12]

Benjamin's essay on the effect of mechanical reproduction on the work of art and the Thoreau database project were especially suited to Miller's purposes in that each of these exercises in cultural studies appeared to ratify what Miller designated as the eight invariant presuppositions upon which the field of cultural studies was founded:

1. Cultural studies tends to assume that a cultural artifact "can best be understood if accompanied by an attempt to understand the work's historical context."

2. Cultural studies presupposes "a crossing or breaking down of traditional disciplinary separations."

3. Practitioners of cultural studies "deliberately attempt to break down the assumption that there is an agreed upon canon of works that ought to be the center of humanistic works."

4. Cultural studies tends to assume that a cultural artifact has its best "purchase on the world if it remains understood in relation to some specific and local people, a people defined by language, place, history, and tradition."

5. Practitioners of cultural studies tend to define themselves through a series of binary oppositions: "elite versus popular, hegemonic as against marginal, theory as against praxis, cultural artifact as reflection of culture as against art as maker of culture, and so on."

6. Cultural studies has "an uneasy relation to theory."

7. Cultural studies' "uneasy relation to theory goes with an attitude toward reading that is somewhat different from either that of the New Criticism or of so called Deconstruction."

8. Cultural studies is "explicitly political." ("The Work of Cultural Criticism," 13–18)

According to Miller, these presuppositions of cultural studies necessarily involve its practitioners in one or another combination of three unavoidable aporias. Each aporia discloses the structural interference between an already constituted cultural discourse and a knowledge production structured in the displacement of that discourse.

The first aporia refers to cultural critics' presupposition of the linguistic and ethnic specificity of any "authentic" culture. But as soon as a cultural critic transforms an artifact from an "authentic" ethnic culture into an object of disciplinary knowledge, that knowledge inevitably effects the artifact's forcible doubling—into itself and the representations of it archived within the field of cultural studies. And since the cognitive aspect of the knowledge production necessarily undermines the "authentic" dimension of the artifact's cultural context, the coherence of the knowledge produced about the artifact depends upon the foreclosure from the field of cognition of the violence effected by the cultural critic's knowledge production.

The second aporia has reference to cultural studies' double and contradictory orientation. Cultural critics have been simultaneously involved in a celebratory and preservative relationship with the cultures they would empower and in a concerted effort to disempower the dominant culture. As soon as a cultural critic transfers a cultural artifact produced within an "authentic" minority culture onto an alternative context that they hope will empower new forms of group solidarity, however, that artifact's cultural context also undergoes a displacement from itself. Following this transference, the cultural context becomes at once different from and irreducible to the cultural knowledge through which cultural critics aspire to preserve that context within the field of cultural studies.

Each of these first two aporias allude to cultural studies' contradictory representation of the sociohistorical context of the cultural artifact. Cultural critics' representations of these contexts are at once epistemological, when the context operates as an explanatory framework of the culture's activities, and preservative, when the context locates the sedimentation of the culture's invariant particularities. Insofar as the explanatory aspect of the context produces knowledge about the culture, it inevitably brings about the alteration, rather than the preservation of the sociohistorical dimension of the context. But insofar as the resistance that cultural critics have mounted against such alterations requires them to describe the culture as fully enclosed and self-determining, such efforts at cultural preservation risk replicating totalizing models of cultural nationalism.

Both of the first two aporias are in fact versions of the third aporia, which reveals the contradictory assumptions inherent to the performative praxis underpinning the field of cultural studies. Cultural studies scholars have presumed that their cognitive intentions will govern the performative aspects of their projects. Since there is no cognition that can guarantee the outcome of the performative use of language, however, the performative and constative dimensions of linguistic acts cannot be construed as either structurally homologous or symmetrical. Moreover, although cultural critics always have worked from within preexisting subject positions, the effect of the performative dimension of their speech acts has been irreducible to the deliberative act of conscious, willing subjects.

As we have seen, advocates of the new field had elevated multiculturalism into the legitimating metadiscourse of the field of cultural studies. But J. Hillis Miller dismantled this justifying myth by exposing the contradictions between the political aspirations of cultural studies and its practical effects within the academy. Rather than subverting existing structures, Miller observed, the knowledge that cultural critics hailed as culturally empowering instead made it easier for university administrators to assimilate the marginalized groups into academic rationalities corroborative of dominant power structures. University administrators routinely overcoded the terrain of cultural studies with normative presuppositions about identity, ethnicity, gender, sexuality, and race, categorizations that contributed to their management of the university multiculture.

Insofar as they are organized out of the imperatives of Enlightenment rationality, university archives constitute the most powerful mechanism for the incorporation of cultural differences. The knowledge about marginal cultures and subcultures produced within the field of cultural studies inevitably supplied university administrators with added instruments of regulation. Administrators in colleges and universities across the United States now routinely deploy the discourses produced within the field of cultural studies as templates through which they reorganize heterogeneous communities into the manageable spatial grids that serve the interests of governance. "Since the university is at present one of the most powerful institutional mechanisms of assimilation," Miller cautioned in the wake of this reflection, "how can cultural studies avoid participating in the work of assimilation they would resist?" ("The Work of Cultural Criticism," 46–47).

When programs in ethnic studies have been constructed on the model of area studies, to name but one example of such cooptation, they have served the university administration in the manner in which area studies once served the foreign-policy interest of the state. A cultural critic who intended to produce new knowledge about Korean American literature might believe that he or she has thereby transformed this ethnic tradition into an oppositional site from which to contest the educational apparatus of the state. But insofar as the knowledge produced about its traditions adds Korean American culture to an archive that constitutes the basic instrument of Western Eurocentric hegemony, this knowledge instead simply legitimates the university's traditional function of socializing subjects into the state.[13]

But after he revealed the double binds and culs-de-sac into which these aporias inevitably lead, Miller did not negate cultural critics' aspirations for social change. Miller instead concluded the essay by declaring that their goal of "working for a more just social order everywhere" has "my wholehearted allegiance" ("The Work of Cultural Criticism," 54). Upon announcing his solidarity, however, Miller then added the following conditional phrase, which shifted the aim of his allegiance away from the conditions of social justice that cultural studies had presupposed (conditions that simply had reaffirmed the regnant standards of the "unjust" hegemonic culture) and onto a condition of justice that had not yet materialized: "The work of the cultural critic, like the cultural product she or he studies, can and should be performed in the name of a justice and democratic equity that has not yet come into the world and that can now only be indistinctly imagined" (ibid., 57). This added conditional phrase did not merely shift the objective to which Miller pledged his allegiance, it also realigned the field in the direction of an aporetic project that, in lacking a place in the field of cultural studies as it was then configured, might also transform the field.

In this addendum, Miller restricted the ambit of his solidarity to "cultural critics who realize that these goals cannot be obtained by adopting the presuppositions about history, culture, and the relations between culture and history of the hegemony that is being contested" ("The Work of Cultural Criticism," 57). In adding this factor of critical vigilance, Miller dedicated his work to the achievement of just social arrangements that not only have not yet been imagined, but that would be impossible to realize out of the presuppositions organizing the field of cultural studies. Rather than identifying with any of the preconstituted field identities, Miller has added to them the different identity that emerged with his pledge of allegiance to the aporias out of whose exclusion the field of cultural studies had been constituted. Miller's revision of the constitutive aims of cultural studies underscored the engagement with these aporias as crucial to the accomplishment of his new aims: "Such appeals (to the democracy to come) cannot escape the impasse of seeming to depend on standards or concepts that pre-exist the appeal, here justice and democratic equity, standards that are parts of the contested hegemonic culture" (ibid.).

But how can a cultural critic go about embracing the goals of cultural studies without internalizing the field's presuppositions as the means of attaining them? And how can Miller make critical vigilance about the three aporias he has spelled out the point of departure for a just "democracy to come"? How can we differentiate cultural groups without falling back into one nationalism or another? How can we imagine self-determination without reinstating liberal ideas of individualism and subjectivity, and how can we exercise power without effecting injustice?

In answering these questions, Miller instructs cultural critics in how cultural studies might act within these aporias in a way "that would preserve and productively transform cultural difference in the new technological condition, while at the same time working for a more just social order everywhere" ("The Work of Cultural Criticism," 54). Miller's instruction conveys the following dual responsibility: "The work of artist or of cultural critic is a response to an infinite demand not only from the heritage to which the artist or critic must be faithful, but from the 'other' of that heritage" (ibid., 57).

The elements of the critic's dual responsibility are most clearly in evidence at the site of the second of the aporias constitutive of cultural studies: the double and contradictory orientation that requires cultural critics to empower and preserve oppressed minority cultures and to disempower the dominant culture. Cultural studies instructed its practitioners in how to ignore the contradictoriness of these dual injunctions. But as long as the cultural critic who attempted to empower minority cultures did not conceptualize the new cultural formation he or she effected as utterly incommensurate with the social logic through which the dominant culture distributed and regulated social empowerment, the newly empowered minority cultures simply reproduced the dominant culture's social logics. Miller was unlike the cultural critics who ignored this aporia in that he installed what he called the critic's "inaugurative responsibility" in an engagement with the ineluctable differences between these cultural formations.

What interests Miller in this inaugural scene is the critic's reception of dual responsibility as an infinite demand. If what is infinite in the demand of a putatively democratic culture refers to what is missing from its condition of democratic inclusiveness, the addition of what the existing structure of the heritage is presently lacking also constitutes a response to that infinite demand. But if the "other" of the heritage names the part of the heritage that must be excluded in order for the heritage to appear self-contained, the critic's response to the "other" also reveals what brings those powers of exclusion to their limits. In producing a response to the demand for democratic inclusion of what the heritage has excluded, the critic is taking up a position that is lacking in the existing heritage culture and that would perforce add what is lacking to that heritage. But as the part of the heritage that has no part in the present order, this nonparticipating part will have posed the infinite demand to the cultural critic to inaugurate an alternative to the existing heritage.

Rather than sharing a common ground, each of these venues—the heritage, the "other" of the heritage—is articulated on the basis of its difference from the other. The demand placed upon the critic to respond to these noncomparable injunctions should be construed as infinite because it is not informed by or motivated by any knowledge concerning the form the coming democracy should take. This doubly binding obligation does not involve the critic in the continuation of the heritage, but in the production of an alternative in the name of the "democracy to come." The contestation over the form of the future democracy is the sign of what is infinite in the demand. Receptivity and openness to the other are demanded, rather than knowledge. The cultural critic's aporetic praxis had been understood to be underpinned by the cognitive presuppositions of a repeatable methodology. The dual responsibilities to which the critic now would be obligated are betrayed by the very knowledge in which the method requires them to be formulated. The infinite demand of the "other" of the critic's heritage could not derive from that heritage. And the critic's heritage could not supply the ground for the "other" of that heritage. Each of these demands undoes the other. The critic must support this intolerable and insupportable difference without reducing these asymmetrical demands into either an opposition or a resolution. Without the cultural critic's ongoing negotiation, each venue would threaten either to detach itself from or collapse into the other.[14]

It is the cultural critic's dual obligation—to the already universalized heritage as well as to its "other"—that discloses the impossibility of a democratic culture's ever achieving universalization. As a part of cultural studies that had no existing place in the normative order, Miller's aporetic praxis supplements the field with the demand from a future that is unassimilable to the contemporary organization of the field. A democracy to come cannot extend present social arrangements into the future because its status as unassimilable to existing modes of categorization describes the conditions of its futurity. Any effort to subsume the democracy to come into preexisting categories renders what is to come merely a latent possibility of the present organization of things. The tempo of Miller's aporetic praxis supplants the present with a futurity that can never become present and that is not the future of the present order.

While the performative praxis that Miller has added to the practice of cultural studies can never be assimilated to the field's normative disposition, this nonassimilable part can be excluded from cultural studies only through the erasure of the dual obligation that refounds the vocation of cultural studies—to achieve the democracy to come—as an infinite task. The demand to achieve the democracy to come remains ever-present, but without any rules that would predetermine or constrain the decisions through which it might be accomplished. Moreover, since the responsibility to a democracy to come exposes the finitude of all existing constraints and rules as the precondition for the demand to move beyond them, the condition of judgment informing the critic's decision at the site of this dual responsibility turns doing justice into an infinite task, as well.

In light of these observations, "The Work of Cultural Criticism in the Age of Digital Reproduction" might be described as having illustrated what Miller meant by the critic's inaugurative responsibility to these aporias by producing an instance of it. Miller's aporetic praxis hollowed out a site within the field of cultural studies wherein Miller could reflect critically upon the disparity between the field's presuppositions and the aporias they occluded. That reflection took place at the site between the already articulated field and the other of the field inaugurated with Miller's aporetic praxis.

The essay bore the burden of the paradoxes Miller's praxis conveyed. The aporias upon which Miller reflected exposed an alterity within the field's normative presuppositions, yet it was the cultural critic's foreclosure of these aporias that had empowered these norms to regulate the field. In writing in the name of his allegiance to the aporias that brought those norms to the limits of their regulative powers, Miller was at once authorized, yet deauthorized by the existing normative understanding of the field. Because these aporias were granted no part in the field of cultural studies, Miller's essay described how the field was in part constructed out of the exclusion of his aporetic praxis.

But after Miller added this deconstructive reading of presuppositions that the field of cultural studies had stabilized itself by excluding, he neither founded a new field nor recommended the restoration of literary studies. Whereas his colleague in the Yale School, Harold Bloom, had agitated on behalf of a complete reversal of the trajectory from literary studies to cultural studies, Miller's aporetic praxis jammed the machinery of Bloom's mythopoetic technology at the site at which Bloom otherwise would have executed this U-turn in the academic itinerary of cultural studies. The impasse that Miller installed at the site at which Bloom would complete this reversal inscribed what might be described as a "J-turn" in the spatial relationship that literary studies enjoyed with cultural studies. Miller's aporetic praxis does not pass from American literary studies to American cultural studies. It almost returns to literary studies, but without the rule of its metanarrative.

Overall, "The Work of Cultural Criticism in the Age of Digital Reproduction" performed an exercise that, in exposing the field's presuppositions to the aporias they had occluded, took the field to the limits of its provenance. But this deconstructive reading of the presuppositions underpinning the discourse of cultural studies could not be unproblematically classified under the sign of either literary studies or cultural studies. The demand for a complete transition from the one area of inquiry to another was grounded in the assumption that literary studies and cultural studies constituted organized totalities. In replacing the transition with this ineluctably paradoxical site, Miller's essay might be described as an enactment of the claim that cultural critics could not abandon the deconstructive readings of literary studies for the political interventions of cultural studies because these two projects are inextricably intertwined.

From Inaugurative Responsibility to Sovereign Performatives

When Miller discussed the challenges that confronted the cultural critics who aspired to realize the "democracy to come," he drew parallels to comparable challenges within the realm of Realpolitik. The real threat to democracy arises, Miller explained, when a sovereign state pretends to know what a true democracy should be and thereafter tries to impose that ideal globally. The language that Miller invoked to describe the work conducted within the field of cultural studies also revealed potential complicities between the discourse cultural critics invoked to justify their practice—the preservation, rescue, and empowerment of oppressed cultures in the name of social justice—and the nation-making and nation-preserving acts undertaken by the representatives of sovereign states. By way of such homologies, Miller correlated the projects taken up by cultural critics with the then-contemporaneous political concerns about the nature of the democracy that would be adopted by the emergent nation-states in Central and Eastern Europe, the occupation of Kuwait, the ethnonationalist wars in the Balkans, and the Gulf War.[15]

At the time that he wrote the essay, President George Bush had actualized this threat when he undertook the first Gulf War to inaugurate what he called the "New World Order": In the following passage, Miller discusses the "inaugural" performative within the context of such "inaugural" acts of a sovereign state power:

> On the one hand, performative praxis can be thought of as working on the ground of whatever is—the pre-existing disadvantaged culture that is to be rescued and empowered. If it has such a ground, it is in danger of perpetuating the injustice of the past, even if only in the form of a symmetrical reversal. On the other hand, performative praxis can be thought of as inaugural, as bringing something hitherto unheard of into the world. For this, the bringer must assume responsibility. ("The Work of Cultural Criticism," 55)

The adjective "inaugural" that Miller associates with his aporetic praxis was itself a term commonly reserved to describe a range of activities associated with the sovereign exercise of state power. An "inaugural" event might refer to the founding of a state, or to the official state ceremonies responsible for the initiation of a president into a term of office, or to the enactments through which a president announces an official agenda.

Every inaugural activity of a sovereign state includes an inaugural performative. And the inaugural dimension of a state's actions might seem to have taken place as a consequence of the state's having responded to the dual injunctions underpinning its enactments—the infinite demands of the national heritage and its "other": Insofar as what the inaugural performative adds also exposes the limits of an already constituted national heritage, the inaugural acts of state might also be described as having taken place as a response to the infinite demand of that heritage. Moreover, insofar as such acts are the result of the state's sovereign power, the state's inaugural praxis brings into existence what is "other" than the national heritage.

But while a state's inaugural acts may appear to have taken place at the site of these dual injunctions, the state has in fact rendered the "other" of the national heritage that its acts have instantiated virtually the same as the already existing heritage. The state has effected this equivalence by retroactively assigning the sovereign people joint responsibility for the action that the state has inaugurated. In doing so, the state has eradicated the possibility of responding to the demand of what is "other" to the national heritage.

The state's inaugural performatives thus supplant the contradictory subject of dual responsibility with the political fiction of dual sovereignty.

Whenever the state inaugurates an action, it characterizes the figure responsible for the action as a double agent. This double agent is constructed out of the superimposition of the sovereign will of the people upon the sovereign will of the state. As a consequence of this doubling, the state eliminates the possibility of dual injunctions.

The connotative reach of the "inaugural" quality of this performative praxis has thus placed its operations in a differential relationship with the state agencies responsible for the rescuing and empowering of cultures, the perpetuation of social injustice, and the inauguration of a national people. At certain moments in the essay, Miller alludes to these connotations in order to propose that the projects undertaken by the advocates of cultural studies have verged on replicating the sovereign state's presumption that it grounds a unitary and coherent "multiculture": "Insofar as the project of cultural studies is expressed in terms of hierarchies of power—hegemonic, white, Eurocentric power as against the powerlessness of women, minorities, and Third World cultures—how can they avoid merely reversing the hierarchy, the putting out of power of those in power and the empowering of those now without power? Might this not replace one tyranny with another symmetrical one?" ("The Work of Cultural Criticism," 52–53).[16]

Were it not for the role that American literary studies manifestly played in legitimating the state's rationale for the Cold War, Miller's suggestion that cultural critics and sovereign states were involved in analogous practices might seem historically counterfactual. The idiom that cultural critics have deployed to articulate their demand—"that social and intellectual justice be rendered to those who have been oppressed by society generally and by the university" ("The Work of Cultural Criticism," 48)—also supplied evidence corroborative of Miller's claim. The cultural critics who have invoked the discourse of social justice forged within the political domain to legitimate their work within the field of cultural studies have associated their disciplinary practices with the discourse of rights that regulate the relationship between a sovereign people and a sovereign state.

But after they are thus explicitly linked with the discourse of rights, the aporias of cultural studies must be redescribed in terms of the unavoidable contradiction between a disempowered group's desire to break free from the state's essentializing categorizations and the group's need to accept the state's categorizations as the precondition for representing within a court and under the state's jurisdiction the wrong performed against the group. Rights presuppose the regulated relationship between the state and the categorizations that the state has imposed on individuals and groups to distinguish between legitimate and illegitimate bearers of rights. Before the United States government will recognize a cultural group's demands for social justice, the members of that group must agree to express their demands within the state's official terms and categorizations. But since those official taxonomies have implemented the social logic that has enabled the state to achieve the group's oppressive marginalization, the very terms through which the group's members would give expression to the injustices they suffer might simply add another instance of injustice.

After thus remarking his anxieties over the potential complicities between cultural critics and the state powers to which they have been ostensibly opposed, Miller gave expression to the infinitely more ominous fear that the means whereby cultural critics have gone about achieving this reversal "might be some kind of war. I mean a shooting war in which people are killed. Cultural studies must find some way to work for the self-determination for all groups while not falling into the trap of this kind of nationalism" ("The Work of Cultural Criticism," 53). Miller credits Walter Benjamin as the first cultural critic to have recognized that all "efforts to render politics aesthetic culminates in one thing—War and war only can set a goal for mass movements on the largest scale while respecting the traditional property system" (ibid., 52). But Miller believes that the efforts by cultural critics to fashion aesthetic remedies for political dilemmas pose a corresponding danger.

Walter Benjamin arrived at his insights at the time that German National Socialism entered into collaboration with German aesthetic ideology to promote the illusion that the political state is a work of art. And J. Hillis Miller is scrupulous in expatiating upon the significant differences between cultural critics' desire to empower culturally oppressed minorities and German National Socialism's efforts to propagate a single, racial, and national culture across the globe. But Miller nevertheless characterizes cultural critics' aspiration to aestheticize politics as contributing to a corresponding danger:

> As soon as you think of yourself as defined in important ways by your membership in some group, for example, some disempowered minority, it is extremely difficult to avoid thinking of that group as having an essential rather than merely historical and contingent existence. And it is all too easy, even if you know nationalisms are contingent constructions, to justify some return to essentialist thinking on the grounds that political expediency justifies it. ("The Work of Cultural Criticism," 49)

His reflections on the Nazi war machine supplied the context for Benjamin's composition of "The Work of Art in the Age of Mechanical Reproduction." But the first Gulf War was the milieu in which Miller composed "The Work of Cultural Criticism in the Age of Digital Reproduction." Miller occasionally made explicit the connection between the images Benjamin invoked to illustrate the dangers attending the centralized state's aestheticization of politics and the media technologies responsible for transmitting images of the first Gulf War: "Benjamin's example is Marinetti's celebration of the Ethiopian colonial war, but World War II was a spectacular confirmation of Benjamin's insight, as has been the television treatment of the Gulf War" ("The Work of Cultural Criticism," 35).

After offering a video still of the 1991 bombing of Baghdad entitled "Desert Storm: The War Begins" as a spectacular illustration of Benjamin's insight, Miller introduces the following example as more probative of the truth of this claim:

> An example from our own day, though not one from which human figures are lacking, is the recent presentation on American Public Television of a series called "Making Sense of the Sixties." This was being shown at the very moment that the United States plunged itself into a war in the Middle East not entirely unlike the Vietnam War, though there are of course differences in the character of the enemy as well as in the rapidity of the allies' disengagement from the Gulf War. ("The Work of Cultural Criticism," 26)

Because spectral images of war haunt Miller's essay as well as Benjamin's, it is impossible to read Miller's observation that "photographs become standard evidence for historical occurrences . . . they are also invested with a hidden political significance" without interpreting it within the context of the efforts by the United States to conceal the signs of its devastating violence in the images it transmitted of the Gulf War ("The Work of Cultural Criticism," 26). When Miller introduces his commentary on Benjamin's assertion that "Atget photographed empty Paris streets . . . as if they were scenes of a crime" with the query "What crime is that?" the images of the civilian populations eradicated by the smart bombs' devastation force their way into the reader's visual field (ibid.).

It was the state's decision to occlude actual scenes of human carnage during the Gulf War that constituted its chief difference from the war in Vietnam. After they were harnessed to the war machine, the new computer technologies' contribution to the war effort was aesthetic in that it regulated the representations of the enemy's obliteration within the scenes through which the media transmitted the war. These state-of-the-art technologies facilitated an official state spectacle that at once celebrated the state's awesome powers of annihilation and yet regulated the representations of their horrific effects.

As the media eliminated the distance separating the viewer's perspective from the military action, their aestheticization of state violence enabled the sovereign people to participate in the war as an extension of the technology through which it was visualized. The televisual record of the war did not represent the action. It produced a fantasmatic structure that embedded U.S. citizens in the project of war. As the television screen replicated the incoming missile's aerial view, the conflation of the television screen and the smart bomb's lens secured the fantasy that this was not a representation, but an enactment of the sovereign power to remake the world in the image of U.S. democracy. And once the war's enactments were articulated to the nation's patriotic fiction, that fiction represented the state's show of force as an expression of the sovereign will of the U.S. people to propagate the U.S. model of democracy worldwide.

Miller's effort to undermine such collaborations between the technologies of cultural studies and states at war led to his instruction in aporetic praxis at a site between a national heritage and the "other" of that heritage that states must perforce exclude as the precondition for the production of "sovereignty." Miller articulated the relationship between the sovereign actions of the state and inaugural performatives in terms of the logic of mutual exclusion. An inaugural performative is unlike the declaration of a sovereign state in that it exceeds the context in which it takes place and is not reducible to the act of a conscious, willing subject.

The referents of sovereign performatives are fixed, immobilized, and regulated in positions of subordination, but inaugural performatives place entire political ontologies between quotation marks. The effect of these quotation marks is to denaturalize existing social arrangements and to designate them as occasions for political debate and alternative constructions. Whereas the sovereign subject is regulated on the basis of the presuppositions that the excluded have no entitlement to occupy the position of the normative agent, the inaugural performative emancipates the subject from the ontologies to which it was restricted and releases the subject into a future of multiple significations.[17]

Whereas the contradictory subject of an inaugural performative is exceeded by the performative that he or she practices, the sovereign subject believes that he or she is the agent of the will governing a performative's stated intention. The sovereign subject that is retroactively assigned responsibility for the performatives through which he or she is effected is modeled after the example of the sovereign power of a head of state. The sovereign dimension of a declaration of state is evident in the attributes of unilateral, nonreciprocable efficacy that authorizes its power to bring into existence and enforce the state of affairs that it declares.[18]

When he represents the sovereign, autonomous subject as constituted out of the foreclosure of the aporias inherent to performative praxis, Miller's point is not that you cannot exclude these aporias, but that their forcible exclusion produces the illusion of sovereignty at the expense of inaugurative responsibility. If the political question of the democracy to come involves deciding at the site of these aporias, the sovereign, autonomous subject might be described as constituted out of the foreclosure of politics.

Miller cites war as the limit case for cultural studies because it supplies an enveloping context though which to illustrate the consequences of cultural critics' foreclosure of the aporias informing their practice. Miller's performative praxis has involved his restoration of the aporias that the war apparatus has obliterated. Insofar as the Persian Gulf War could not preserve Kuwaiti culture without representing its conflicts into terms corroborative of the U.S. rationale for war, the media transmission of the war spectacularized the aporias that cultural critics foreclosed. Miller restored these aporias in the similarities he adduced between the actual violence exercised by the state in its "liberation" of Kuwaitis from Iraqi occupation and the symbolic violence exercised by cultural critics in their empowerment of local cultures' self-determining transformations. The homologies Miller adduced between the state's actual and the cultural critics' symbolic violence reside in their shared desire to impose preexisting models of self-determination on the culturally oppressed. In restoring these aporias, Miller took the ground out from under the state's rationale.

As we have noted, at the time J. Hillis Miller was composing "The Work of Cultural Criticism in the Age of Digital Reproduction," the Bush administration was declaring the Gulf War to be the inaugural moment of a "New World Order." The Bush administration invoked the multiplicity of cultures as an apt representation of that new order. But Miller dismantled this justifying metanarrative when he disclosed the aporias upon which that rationale foundered. The academic multiculture and the Gulf War displaced what Miller meant by the "democracy to come" with the fantasy that the U.S. (multi)culture was as at once the origin and the goal of democracy worldwide. Miller's interruption disclosed the wrong that Bush committed in the name of the New World Order against the possibility of a democracy to come.

The democracy that emerges from Miller's aporetic praxis differs from both of these models in that it would instigate an openness to what could not be assimilated to any familiar concept of culture. Miller's aporetic praxis avoids articulating cultural practice to a social order's preexisting categorizations. "We" who name the collective subject of its inaugurative responsibility emerge out of nonassimilative encounters with other cultures and with something that is other than culture. "We" are constantly reconstituted by acts of self-constitution born out of an infinite, impossible responsibility to forms of justice and democratic equality that are not yet part of the political order and that can emerge only within the democracy to come.

By contrast, the state's inaugural performatives differ from the performative praxis of "we" who name the collective subject of its inaugurative responsibility in that the state's actions supplant the contradictory subject of dual responsibility with the political fiction of dual sovereignty. The state's erasure of this site of dual responsibility becomes clearest when a state declares war.

When a state inaugurates war, it monopolizes both positions of sovereign agency—the people's and the state's. When at war, a state declares itself at once the sovereign will of the people and the power to which the people must appeal for the protection and defense of their sovereign will. In wartime, the people become the hostages of the sovereign powers of the state. But if the state is at once the representative of the people's will and the monopoly of legitimate power that endows the people's will with the quality of sovereignty, the state forecloses the possibility of the emergence of an "other" of that heritage.

The state of war attenuates the reach of the subject's responsibility to loyalty to the state, and it demands that "others" be construed as either friends or enemies of the state. When the state declares war, "we the people" speak only of and from the patriotic metanarrative founding the people. A people at war demands to know in advance that "we" are intact, self-contained, and utterly defended. Rather than being construed as an infinite demand for responsibility, during wartime, alterity is represented as a potential threat to the state's survival. And the state's heritage is reduced in scale from an infinite demand upon the responsibility of the subject to the dimensions of the already constituted order that the state must defend in the name of survival.

After the state declares a war, the "other" of that heritage is doubled, as well—into the enemy of state and the emergency powers that the state must exercise to defend the people against the threat. Described as a threat to a nation's way of life, the "other" of the national heritage is transformed from a figure that is different from the heritage, hence capable of producing a different heritage, into the threatening enemy whose opposition must be wholly overcome.

The declaration through which a state inaugurates a war materializes a site whose surplus violence renders it unassimilable to the terms of the national heritage. In undertaking the war, the state is neither within nor outside the order that it protects. The state situates itself within that order, but it occupies the position of the exception to it. To defend the order it also represents, the state must declare itself an exception to the order it regulates. In taking up the site of the exception, the state institutes an alternative to the normative order, an alternative called the state of emergency.

The emergency state is marked by absolute independence from any juridical control and any reference to the normal political order. It is empowered to suspend the articles of the constitution protective of personal liberty, freedom of speech and assembly, and the inviolability of the home and of postal, telephone, and Internet privacy. While the state of emergency supplies the occasion for the state to enact its monopoly over the legitimate use of violence, it also renders the site of the exception at which the state exercises this violence vulnerable to being declared an illegal usurpation of the people's sovereignty. During a state of emergency, the state produces its monopoly by placing limitations on the people's rights. And at the site of these limitations, the people can inaugurate a praxis that divides the people into those who consent to the state's restriction on their rights and those who declare the right to question the state's right to inaugurate the war in their name. Claude Lefort has described the paradoxical status of the people's declaration of rights as follows:

> By referring the source of right to the human utterance of right [the French and American declarations of human rights] made an enigma of both humanity and right. . . . [It was] an extraordinary event, a declaration that was an auto-declaration, that is a declaration by which human beings, speaking through their representatives, revealed themselves to be both the subjects and objects of the utterance in which, all at once, they named the human in one another, "spoke" to one another, appeared before one another, and in so doing, erected themselves into their own witnesses, their own judges.[19]

But the people who declare the right to question the state's arrogation of the power to speak and to act in their name can no longer be described as the sovereign people. As we have seen, the state attributed the sovereign power through which it regulated them to the people themselves, so that the people would depend upon the state's authorization as the precondition for the enactments of their rights. In questioning the state's right to act in the name of the sovereign people, the people inaugurate a right at the site in which the state's sovereign performative reaches the limits of its power. Their inaugural praxis demarcates the distinction between the people whose sovereign rights describe the individuality through which the state regulates them and the people whose right to question the state does not derive from the state. Unprotected by the mantle of sovereignty, the right to have this right produces a people who can emerge only with the dismantling of the emergency state. By claiming the right to say and do what the state will not, this people questions the legitimacy of the state's monopoly over the exercise of violence. Whereas the state installed the sovereign subject as the sine qua non for the bearer of rights, their inaugurative practice effects a people who, in lacking any part in the order over which the emergency state rules, do not demand the state's sovereign power as the guarantor of their right to question the state's rights. And insofar as they have questioned the state's sovereign powers, neither can they represent their demands within the context of the sovereign rights authorized by the state. As a people who have added a right that the national people are lacking, this singular people's infinite demand for rights cannot be met within a nationalist provenance.

J-J: Critical Witness to an Inaugural Event

Having differentiated the inaugural performative that Miller produced during the First Gulf War from the declaration through which the state initiated that war, I want to explore, by way of a conclusion, the ways in which Miller's aporetic praxis might be deployed to disrupt the emergency state that Bush inaugurated when he declared the "war on terrorism." That exploration will turn on an account of the difference between the "community of dissensus" that emerged from the inagurative praxes Miller found at work in the field of American literary studies and the Homeland Security state that George W. Bush inaugurated with the declaration of a war on terrorism.

At the outset of these remarks, I described Hillis Miller's influence on the field of American Studies as confined to the role that the poststructuralist critics trained by him and by other members of the Yale School had played in opening up the field of American literary studies. The concerted initiatives of those critics constituted the precondition for the emergence of American cultural studies. But I have now arrived at a moment in which I must account for the role that Hillis Miller himself played in the field's transformation.

In order to explain that role, I need to turn to the one essay in which Miller, upon encountering the core texts produced within the field of American literary studies, afforded them the following description:

> The important books on United States literature, from those by F. O. Matthiessen, Charles Feidelson, Jr., R. W. B. Lewis, and Perry Miller down to more recent work by Roy Harvey Pearce, Sacvan Bercovitch, and Harold Bloom, have been devoted not so much to describing as to attempting to create the unified national culture we do not in fact have. They characteristically do this as a complex, performative scholarly ritual that masquerades as objective scholarship. They appeal to such general concepts as the frontier ("Go west, young man"), the American Renaissance, the American Adam, a certain use of symbolism, the Puritan ideal, the unity of a canonical poetic tradition from Emerson, Dickinson, and Whitman through Crane and Stevens to Ammons and Ashberry, and so on, in incoherent multiplicity. . . . Each scholar makes up his or her idea about the unity of American literature, and each idea is incompatible with the others.[20]

Unlike J. Edwin Miller and other critics trained within the myth-symbol school, J. Hillis Miller does not restrict his description of the master texts within the field to a horizon of expectations circumscribed by the national metanarrative. In taking the ground out from under the metanarrative through which they had formerly been organized and transmitted, Miller dismantles the frame narrative governing the relationships between these texts. The national metanarrative had formerly laid down the law for determining what would and what would not count as an example of Americanist literary scholarship. Miller's withdrawal of the frame narrative that had previously governed the production of Americanist literary scholarship also dissevers scholars in the field from the grounding assumptions about United States culture that had been sedimented within that narrative. In the absence of a grand Americanist narrative that would assimilate their works to its categories, the Americanist scholars under Miller's description were now required to invent criteria that would create a unified culture that the United States does "not in fact have."

After he describes these works as the result of their groundless founding acts, Miller renders each of these master texts contingent, rather than foundational. It was the national metanarrative that supplied regulatory intertext responsible for the linkages interconnecting each of these master texts to the field. In Miller's conceptualization of them, what these works share are the negative traits of their differences from one another and the ungroundedness of the condition of their emergence. These negative traits cannot not be subsumed under the mythological themes and collective representations of a synthesizing metanarrative.

These texts are inaugural in the sense that they do not result in a cumulative body of knowledge. Their incompatibility propagates an incoherent multiplicity of conflicting accounts of the national culture. In lacking the metanarrative that had formerly integrated the field, each added a part that became the occasion for the particularization of an alternative universalization of American literary studies. Rather than recapitulating the assumptions of the justifying myth, each new work in the field made up an entirely different America. Each work thus differs from itself or within itself by the presence of its own other. Whereas critics trained in the myth-symbol school interpreted American literature as the revelation of the national identity, what the agents of these inaugural performatives reveal cannot be accounted for by intention or by the antecedents in the tradition to which their works belong. Each inaugural performative pushes the parameters of the field to its limits. Here the conceptual structures give way to other configurations.

Insofar as the account that J. Hillis Miller has added to the field of American literature has dislodged the metanarrative through which the field of American literary studies had formerly been regulated, Miller's intervention might be described as having reenacted in the late 1990s the deconstruction accomplished by the Yale School poststructuralists in the 1970s. But instead of transforming American literary studies into American cultural studies, as had his predecessors, Miller's dislodgement was instead inaugurative of a community of scholars organized around what Miller has called an "ethos of dissensus." The members of the dissensus community that Miller has envisioned have been unlike the cultural critics who populated the field of American cultural studies in that they do not embrace the global logic of liberal multiculturalism. The relations between the members of the community are not regulated by equivalences and are not reducible to a coherent identity. The community's openness cannot not be assimilated to any familiar concept of culture and cannot not be reduced to an acculturative association with another culture.

Miller at first selected the term "dissensus" to describe the property of reciprocal incompatibility shared by the core texts within the field of American literary studies. But when he then transferred the term to describe the relationships that pertained between the members of the field of American literary studies, he treated dissensus as their common trait. Their dissensus community has been organized out of decentered and nonhierarchical groups, each of which is already differentiated from within and open to radical reconceptualization from without. The continuous rifting between Americanist scholars over the significance of what they have done thereafter has become the groundless ground of their community.

If Miller's dissensus community sounds counterfactual and difficult to imagine, it actually constitutes the only community to which cultural critics who have situated their practice at the site of dual responsibility could possibly inhabit. When Miller describes these works as the outcome of each critic's desire to create a unified culture that the United States is in fact lacking, he indicates that each work has been the outcome of the critic's response to the infinite demand from the heritage—the ungratifiable desire for a unified culture—as well as from the "other" of that heritage—in this case, the critic's act of responding to that demand. In adding the act of creating the unified culture that "we do not in fact have," the critic particularizes an alternative universalization of U.S. culture. In adding what is lacking, these inaugural performatives produce a futurity for the United States that cannot become present within any of its existing conceptualizations.

Miller initially published this account of American literary studies as a community of dissensus within the context of Bill Readings's claim that the transnational university of the twenty-first century no longer needs a national ideology. According to Readings, the transnational university is a function of the processes of globalization that no longer require citizen-subjects because it serves the economic interests of transnational corporations, rather than of nation-states.[21] But as we have already considered, the stratagems of the myth-symbol school transmuted American literary nationalism into a transnational enterprise that served the global ambitions of the Cold War state. After Miller demonstrated how American literary scholarship effected an ethos of dissensus, he rendered the field unassimilable to the structures of governance of the transnational university, as well as of the global state.

In the late 1990s, J. Hillis Miller placed the inaugural performatives he added to American literature into the service of undermining the transnational university's powers of co-optation. But in his September 20, 2001 address to the nation, George W. Bush invoked the metanarrative upon which these texts had formerly been grounded to effect a shift in the nation's governing self-representation—from a secure, innocent nation to a wounded, insecure emergency state. Given the renewed use to which President Bush placed the national metanarrative, I find it especially important, at this juncture of the discussion, to recall J. Edwin Miller's instruction on the demands that the nation's mythological heritage placed on those trained within the myth-symbol school of American literature. That is because if I take up an analysis of Bush's address by way of the instruction in only one of these practices to the exclusion of the other, I sacrifice what J. Hillis Miller has described as my dual responsibility.

The figure that I encountered when, in reflecting on my account of their histories, I reach the threshold separating American literary studies from American cultural studies, is Janus-faced, composed of both Millers. What J. Edwin Miller celebrated as a fully enclosed field, J. Hillis Miller describes as inherently incomplete and subject to change. This Janus-faced figure enunciates dual contradictory injunctions—to the heritage out of which I have emerged, but also to those formations out of whose exclusions that heritage has constituted itself, that is, to the site of a performative praxis that is structured in an interference between the knowledge produced and the performative forces productive of the knowledge. The newly constituted knowledge cannot appear within the already constituted field without doing violence to the constituting power that is inhabited by what the previously constituted knowledge has excluded. But when the contradictory instructions of these two J. Millers are intertwined, the resultant figure repeats contradictory injunctions—to respond to Bush's address in terms of the infinite demand of the myth-symbol school in which I was trained and to the "other" of the tradition out of whose exclusions that heritage has reconstituted itself and in which an inaugural performative takes place.

I have already discussed how the grand mythological themes—"virgin land," "redeemer nation," "the American Adam," "an errand into the wilderness"—supplied the transformational grammar through which the state shaped the people's understanding of contemporary political and historical events. After they subordinated historical events to these mythological themes, government's policymakers felt empowered to fashion imaginary resolutions of actual historical dilemmas. But the catastrophic events that took place at the World Trade Center and the Pentagon on September 11, 2001 precipitated a "reality" that the national metanarrative could neither comprehend nor master. In his September 20, 2001 address to the nation, President George W. Bush represented 9/11 as an act of war in the sense that it brought about the destruction of a core tenet of the national people's patriotic fiction concerning their relation to the land.²² Bush's address provided a symbolic reply that inaugurated a symbolic drama that was partly autonomous of the events that called it forth. The address to the nation was designed to lessen the events' traumatizing power through the provision of an imaginary response to a disaster that could not otherwise be assimilated to the preexisting order of things:

> On September 11, enemies of freedom committed an act of war against our country. Americans have known wars, but for the past 136 years they have been wars on foreign soil, except for one Sunday in 1941. Americans have known the casualties of war, but not at the center of a great city on a peaceful morning. . . . Americans have known surprise attacks, but never before on thousands of civilians. . . . All of this was brought upon us in a single day, and night fell on a different world. . . . I will not forget the wound to our country and those who inflicted it. . . . Our grief has turned to anger and anger to resolution. Whether we bring our enemies to justice or bring justice to our enemies, justice will be done.

The executive phrases in Bush's address allude to and replace mythological themes embedded within the national narrative. Specifically, the state's symbolic response to 9/11 replaced "virgin land" ("Americans have known wars, but for the past 136 years they have been wars on foreign soil") with "Ground Zero" ("Americans have known the casualties of war, but not at the center of a great city on a peaceful morning") and the "Homeland" ("Americans have known surprise attacks, but never before on thousands of civilians") as the governing metaphors through which to come to terms with the attack. The spectacular military campaigns in Afghanistan and Iraq that followed Bush's September 20 address accomplished the conversion of these metaphors into historical facts.²⁴

When George Bush cited the historically accurate fact that "with the exception of a Sunday in 1941" (and of 1812, which he didn't mention), the United States had not been subject to foreign invasion, he linked the public's belief in the myth of a virgin land with the historical record. But when he did so, Bush did not supply the U.S. public with historical grounds for the collective belief in a virgin land. The myth that America was a virgin land endowed the historical fact that U.S. soil had rarely before been subjected to foreign violation with a moral rationale: This virgin land was inviolate because the American people were innocent. In describing the surprise attack as a "wound to our country," Bush interpreted this violation on mythological as well as historical registers.

The state of emergency Bush erected at "Ground Zero" was thereafter endowed with the responsibility to defend the "Homeland" because the terrorists' violation of virgin land had alienated the national people from their imaginary way of inhabiting the nation. This substitution anchored the people to a very different state formation. It also drastically altered the national people's foundational fantasy about their relationship to the national territory, redefining it in terms of the longing of a dislocated population for their lost homeland.

The events of 9/11 enacted a violence against a foundational myth that led to a situation in which the need for a myth and the recognition of the impossibility of the myth coincided. But in his September 20 address to the nation, President Bush turned this foundational violence into a justification for a change in the myth that the nation tells itself. On September 20, Bush superimposed the foundational myth of a virgin land over the act of violence directed against the myth. Bush's declaration did not describe a state of affairs; it invoked this traumatized myth so as to bring a state of affairs about. Bush's deployment of this foundational trauma to implement a change in foreign policy changed 9/11 into a decisive turning point in U.S. relations with the rest of the world. But Bush installed this change in policy through the abrogation and repudiation of the very universal principles—national sovereignty, democratic freedoms—to which he appealed.

The state's symbolic response to 9/11 effected a major reorganization of the regulatory fictions through which the state exercises governmental rule. The narrative organized around the virgin land metaphor entailed the collective wish to disavow the historical fact of the forcible evacuation of indigenous peoples from their homelands. But the narrative accompanying Ground Zero has linked the people traumatized by the events that took place on 9/11 with the Homeland Security state that as emerged with the loss of belief in the inviolability of the native land.

The shift in dominant narratives from a secured, virgin nation to a violent, insecure state of emergency justified the state's inherent transgression of the nation's foundational fantasy as the basis for the monopoly over the exception. In establishing the prerogatives of the emergency state at Ground Zero, George Bush conscripted the traumatic power of the events that took place on September 11, 2001 as the preconditions for the preemptive strikes through which the state would compensate for them. The Bush administration thereby supplanted the loss of the mythological credo that underwrote U.S. exceptionalism with the arrogation of the power to occupy the position of the exception to the laws of the world of nations.

With the enemy's violation of the rules of war as rationale, the state suspended the rules to which it was otherwise subject and violated its own rules in the name of protecting the people against a force that operated according to different rules. The Congress's passage of the USA Patriot Act (Proved Appropriate Tools to Intercept and Obstruct Terrorism) into law effected the most dramatic abridgment of civil liberties in the nation's history. This emergency legislation subordinated all concerns of ethics, of human rights, of due process, of constitutional hierarchies, and of the division of power to the state's monopoly over the exception.

As 9/11 dislocated the national people from the mythology productive of their imaginary relation to the state, Bush linked their generalized dislocation with the vulnerability of the "Homeland," which thereafter became the target of the security apparatus. But the Homeland that emerged as the justification for the state's exercise of excessive violence was not identical with the land mass of the continental United States. The Homeland Bush invoked to "authorize" these emergency actions did not designate either an enclosed territory or an imaginable home. The Homeland secured by the emergency state instead referred to the unlocatable order that emerged *through and by way of the people's generalized dislocation from the nation as a shared form of life*.[24]

The state refashioned the Homeland Security state out of the image of Ground Zero. The Homeland demarcated a rent in the social order where sovereignty is utterly dissevered from the will of the people upon whom the state had putatively depended for the legitimation of its monopoly over the use of force. But the Homeland Security Act did not even pretend to derive its legitimation from the sovereign will of the people. It forcibly dispossessed the U.S. peoples of their way of life in the name of protecting that way of life. As the unlocalizable space the population was ordered to occupy when the state entered the site of the exception to the normative order, "the Homeland" named the structure through which the state of emergency was realized normally. Insofar as "the Homeland" named what emerged when the population became dislocated from the conditions of belonging to a territorialized nation, its security required the domestic emergency state to extend its policing authority to the dimension of the globe.[25]

The state's symbolic response to 9/11 did not simply violate the normative order, it redefined what counts as a legal norm. These redefinitions disrupt the entire social edifice by undermining the mores that have regulated the intersubjective collective of the polity. The point of the state's redefinitions was not that the state's actions could not be judged according to already existing criteria—the point was that it changed the criteria by which it should be judged. With the Homeland Security Act, the state separated the people from the rights that the state secures. Then the USA Patriot Act declared the people lacking in the power to question whether or not the state possesses the right to dissever the people from their rights.

If the emergency state names the exception to the rule of law, the Homeland gives substance to the state's power to enact the exception, in the sense that it supplies the state's exception with a material space and tangible bodies. The entirety of the people has been taken outside the polis and moved into the space of the Homeland, where the people are asked to construe their rights of freedom and equality as secure only insofar as they do not act upon them. But after the entirety of the national people were relocated within the Homeland state, all of the people became the part of the whole that the emergency state was required to exclude in order to constitute the state's monopoly over the limitless use of power. But if all of the people designate that segment of the people that the state must exclude in order to declare its sovereignty over the limitless exercise of power, then the state must be described as lacking a national people to govern.[26]

The constitutive duplicity of the people's "sovereignty" is rendered visible in the following paradoxes: The emergency state has deprived the Homeland people of their right to exercise their rights in the name of protecting them from an alien way of life, but the emergency state can promise the people the future restoration of their rights only by supplanting the way of life in which those rights can be recognized as the national people's. As hostages of the state, the inhabitants of the Homeland state are no longer the national people endowed with sovereign rights, and the people who are to be restored those rights in the future are lacking a national form in which those rights can be exercised. The infinite demand from the other to "we the people" and the infinite demand from "we the people" who have become other than ourselves converge at the point at which these aporias become visible.

Lacking a national heritage and lacking the sovereignty through which to give expression to a national alternative to the heritage, the people who emerge at the site of these redoubled losses must inaugurate what Miller has called the "democracy to come." This singular people will have come into existence as and through the truly inaugural performative through which "we" declare our right to have rights. In responding to what has replaced the sovereign national people in the wake of 9/11, "we" cannot reinstate another metanarrative through which the emergency state will authorize its monopoly over sovereignty. We can inaugurate a people with the right to have rights only when our claim to rights takes place without grounds, when our declaration of the right to have rights takes the ground out from under the sovereign state's foundational acts of violence.

Insofar as the emergency state's exceptions to the rules of law and war are themselves instantiations of the traumatizing violence that lacks the grounding of norms or rules, they resemble the traumatic events upon which they depend for their authority. As such, these sovereign performatives will maintain their power to rule only as long as "we the people" remain captivated by the spectacles of violence the state has staged at the site of Ground Zero. Should the people of the "democracy to come" inaugurate a performative praxis that exposes the emergency state as itself the cause of the traumas it purports to oppose, its exceptions will be exposed as the criminal violations of a terrorizing state. And at that moment, the Homeland state may disappear into the pomatum within which it was inaugurated.

PART THREE

Justices

CHAPTER 11

"J" Is for Just a Minute:
It's Miller Time When It Shimmers

Peggy Kamuf

When I heard the beginning of a phrase repeated a propos of this gathering, "J is for . . . ," it was inevitable, even fatal that I would complete it first in a certain way: "J is for just a minute." In the idiom of my family, that is something one said—above all my father used to say it—to force a pause, a little more patience when he was being pressed for answers or decisions. By itself, it's a bit of nonsense, a kind of useless mnemonic device, which is why it could usually effect the pause it asked for. Maybe it was also something said in cops and robbers films of the '30s, I don't know. But the line almost always got a laugh from us because Jay is also the nickname of one of my brothers, short for James, and as a child he was anything but patient. So the phrase was an insider joke about misnomers or something like that.

None of this is the least bit pertinent, of course, for the purpose here. I've begun with such nonsense only because it is what I have to set aside so that the phrase can return to the general language, or at least to our general convention around the initial "J" in the name J. Hillis Miller. Before dropping the phrase, however, I'll just remark that although "just a minute" names an increment of time, the temporal reference can be merely incidental to pragmatic uses of the expression. If I say "I'll be just a minute," then I've more or less promised to keep track of the clock, whereas an indignant "Now, just a minute, sir!" probably has little to do with the minute hand on a watch. Still, the saying always explicitly or literally invokes a very conventional figure of time, its pure logical, mathematical figure. ("Minute" comes from the name of a mathematical fraction in medieval Latin.) This is my pretext (or excuse) for trying to say something—but necessarily not nearly enough and therefore finally very little—about the immense subject of time for J. Hillis Miller. Miller time: that is my inevitable theme. "J" is for J. Hillis Miller on the subject of time.

It goes without saying that, as a theorist of narrative fiction, Hillis Miller has made temporality, temporal form, or temporal relations a focus in many of his readings. If temporality is, as he insists, "a determining principle of theme and technique" in the novel,[1] it is narrative form that also determines a predominant idea of temporality, or perhaps one should say its dominant ideology. This is an insight Hillis Miller shares with Paul de Man, who once remarked that "it is very difficult not to conceive the pattern of one's past and future existence as in accordance with temporal and spatial schemes that belong to fictional narratives and not to the world."[2] Like de Man, Miller is always working to draw this difficulty into the open, which he does by replacing already narrativized temporal schemes with linguistic ones. One of the narrative sites to which both Miller and de Man return repeatedly is Proust's grand novel. I'll try to say something more about the magnificent essay Miller titled "Fractal Proust." But first, I want to put in place a few elements from two earlier essays in which Miller approaches texts that, as far as I know, de Man left alone.

The essay on *Mrs. Dalloway* in *Fiction and Repetition* (1982) carves a reading of that novel's temporal schemes out of sustained, scrupulous attention to the floating past tense of a narration that, as Miller puts it at one point, "shimmers momentarily between the narrator's past and Clarissa's past."[3] What "shimmers" in Miller's syntax is more precisely the verb "was" as lifted from a sentence at the beginning of the novel. This shimmering briefly occludes or fogs the condition of indirect discourse, whereby the sentence would supposedly record the narrator's recollection of Clarissa's recollection of a repeated scene from the latter's own youth. In that scene, the one from Clarissa's past, the air *was* fresh and calm "in the early morning." ("How fresh, how calm, stiller than this of course, the air was in the early morning.")[4] Because it is also early morning when this recollection resurfaces, Miller remarks that the reader is "left with no linguistic clue . . . permitting him to tell whether the 'was' refers to the present of the narration or to its past."[5] Hence the shimmering, as he calls it, which is said to be "momentary," that is, it lasts for just a moment before the two moments are separated out again and the briefly dazzled reader can once again determine distinctly different times, past and present, but also this one's time from that one's. What shimmers for a moment is something like time arrested between all the linguistic tenses and thus beyond them, but not strictly speaking beyond language. There is, Miller writes, "no linguistic clue," but this absence of a mark or this unmarking is also a marking to the extent it can be read. That is what Miller is doing, as one for whom, in Blanchot's terms, reading has become a serious task.[6] He is remarking that it shimmers when one approaches the edge of language, in an arrested time without time, or at least without narration. Miller dazzles us with his readings because he is always getting us to look into the places where language gleams at the edge of an immensity of darkness.

This chapter on *Mrs. Dalloway* moves from one shimmering surface of Woolf's text to another. Because, like Melville's *Confidence-Man*, Joyce's *Ulysses*, or again, like classical tragedy, this novel sets its narration to the measure of one solar day and night, it is always the sun, in one way or another, that is glowing above or at the horizon. Surely Miller is right to insist that nothing could be less like Proust's depiction of memory's difficult retrieval than "the spontaneity and ease of memory in *Mrs. Dalloway*" (184). Still, as his own "Fractal Proust" would later make apparent, Proust's novel is ruled or overruled by a "solar myth" that, as we'll see, Miller reads through to the place of its and the sun's arrest. But *Mrs. Dalloway* is likewise being read here as solar myth from the moment Miller remarks its repetition of "the temporal form of many novels" in "an incomplete circle, time moving toward a closure which will bring together past, present, and future as a perfected whole" (177). Thus, what Miller calls the "solar myth," taking the phrase over from de Man, has a natural affinity, so to speak, with a common temporal form of narrative. Woolf adopts this form, but also investigates its implications. "Implications" is Miller's word, and it can be taken to name precisely a certain folding in of the myth of solar form whereby each of the novel's principal characters situates a desire that he characterizes at one point as the universal desire to "take possession" of the continuities between present and past, and between one mind and another, "to actualize them in the present" (192). In another formulation, he writes of "the universal desire to bring into the open the usually hidden continuities of present with past, of person with person, of person with the depths of himself" (194).

Miller hesitates to declare that the novel depicts a general failure of this universal desire to actualize temporal continuities, that is, to make them present in the present. He writes that the desire, "the general urge toward lifting up and bringing together" moving each of the characters, including Septimus when he plunges onto the railing, "fails in all of its examples," but then he quickly adds "or seems in part to have failed" (194). However, as regards narrative temporal form, Miller can be more or less categorical: "everything in a conventional novel is labeled 'past.' . . . If there is no past in the cinema, there is no present in a novel" (188). A conventional novel would thus always necessarily fail to actualize, make present, temporal continuities. As for Woolf's quasi-conventional novel, this necessity or impossibility gets remarked in the double temporal form that Miller analyzes. The shimmering effect we earlier saw him point to arises from this doubling repetition of a temporal difference whose linguistic mark can also be suspended, momentarily, like a light blinking off and on.

When, however, he comes to read the famous last two sentences of the novel, it is not a shimmering he remarks within the repetition, but rather the gap holding open any temporal closure. Here is how Miller's analysis of these lines begins:

> I have said that *Mrs. Dalloway* has a double temporal form. During the day of the action the chief characters resurrect in memory by bits and pieces the central episode of their common past. All these characters then come together again at Clarissa's party. The narrator in her turn embraces both these times in the perspective of a single distance. She moves forward through her own time of narration toward the point when the two times of the characters come together in the completion of the final sentences of the novel, when Peter sees Clarissa returning to her party. Or should one say "almost come together," since the temporal gap still exists in the separation between "is" and "was"? "It is Clarissa, he said. For there she was." (199)

Miller's incomparable reading of these last two sentences stretches over the final three pages of the essay. Countless and far-reaching implications of this linguistic, literary marking of temporal division are unfolded there, for example: "Literature for Woolf is repetition as preservation, but preservation of things and persons in their antithetical poise. Time is rescued by this repetition. It is rescued in its perpetually reversing divisions" (199). The temporal shift between the last two lines, "is" to "was," follows a shift in the narration. If time is being rescued here by the gap spacing out a repetition, then its rescue is effected by the fiction of narration or of a narrator. What is rescued, that is, is not the time of some mortal or other, not mortal time, but the time of a nonpresence in language, which speaks here as well in Clarissa's sudden disappearance from the realm of the living present. Clarissa is, and then in the next sentence, she was no more. Miller repeats this last sentence again before remarking more of its implications:

> "For there she was." With this sentence, "is" becomes "was" in the indirect discourse of the narrator. In that mode of language Clarissa along with all the other characters recedes into an indefinitely distant past. Life becomes death within the impersonal mind of the narrator and within her language, which is the place of communion in death. *There* the fragmentary is made whole. *There* all is assembled into one unit. All the connections between one part of the novel and another are known only to the agile and ubiquitous mind of the narrator. They exist only within the embrace of that reconciling spirit and through the power of her words. (200; emphases added)

The repetition by Miller of "There," "There" poses or performs the ground on which fiction rescues time. It is ground as the absence of ground, as absence, as language. "There she was" is spoken by no one, by the speech in absentia that is writing, figured here as the fiction of a narrating voice belonging to the only one for whom the fragmentary can become whole and all be assembled in one unit: it belongs to the narrator, that is, to no one.[7] The whole and the unit take form solely by virtue of what Miller calls the "circle of narration," which, when it is complete and the narrator's last words recorded, "past joining present, the apparently living characters reveal themselves to be already dwellers among the dead" (199). There she was, and there she "is" still, *Mrs. Dalloway*, but undeniably in the mode of not being there, without presence, although not without the life that language confers through its capacity endlessly to summon the dead, to be as Miller puts it, "the place of communion in death."

Notice that Miller writes "communion"—not "communication," or "community," or "commonality," but "communion." Other shards of Christian vocabulary are scattered through this essay, which speaks, for example, not just of the rescue of time, but of its resurrection ("The novel is a double resurrection" [ibid.]). Such echoes of Christian or biblical time, of time's eternity, are never entirely missing from Miller's discourse, it seems to me, but they also return there like so many ghosts, so many "dwellers among the dead," unresurrected as elements of a whole faith in the body's resurrection. The rescue he discerns rescues nothing from death. On the contrary, it is death, the realm of language, that rescues time from the mortal ties that otherwise bind every appearance to a disappearance without trace.[8]

To rescue time, for Miller, as he reads and writes it, would be to rescue, retrieve, refind, if not resurrect or resuscitate, the shimmering, blinking effect of "*perpetually* reversing divisions." Of language, in other words. What we call "time," as Paul de Man insisted, is a linguistic predicament. In his great essay on Proust, Hillis Miller cites one of the places where de Man says something like that, in his own essay on Proust in *Allegories of Reading*, the essay famously titled "Reading (Proust)." Here is de Man as cited by Miller:

> the unbridgeable distance between the narrator, allegorical and therefore obliterating figure for the author, and Proust is that the former can believe that this "later on" could ever be located in his own past. Marcel is never as far away from Proust as when the latter has him say: "Happy are those who have encountered truth before death and for whom, however close it may be, the hour of truth has rung before the hour of death." As a writer, Proust is the one who knows that the hour of truth, like the hour of death, never arrives on time, since what we call time is precisely truth's inability to coincide with itself.[9]

Miller's readings of Proust, especially those gathered under the fractal analogy, are so luminous, with the light they shed into every corner of Proust's work, that it's difficult to approach them with anything other than gratitude for his lucidity as a reader, for the unoccluded view he offers of the word landscapes uncovered by his work and practice of reading. Of course, no less can be said and no less gratitude is owed for all he has written, according to that conjunction of self-similarity and self-dissimilarity that creates a fractal pattern and that he traces out in the example of Proust. "Fractal Proust" thus comes to take up its place in a pattern of fractal Miller. Whatever description one might attempt of the latter, it would have to take account of a fractality that each time, with each repetition and change of scale, is patterned on the fractal iterations of each of its examples[10]—something therefore like a fractality squared, fractality to the next power, a proliferating series of fractal iterations that trace the fractal iterations in the idiom of the other's text.

One of the great achievements of "Fractal Proust" is to have formalized a general principle of reading out of the necessity of reading Proust's unfinished and unfinishable work as a fractal, that is, according to the synecdochic or metonymic principle of part for whole. But as a general principle of reading, fractality immediately breaks up any principle of generality and disseminates the fractions in infinite examples, each of which is an example tending to infinity, to infinitely different infinities. There is perhaps no better modeling of what we call reading than Miller's description, through Proust's example, of fractal iteration. But to think fractally with Miller is to think precisely beyond the model, beyond the model of the model, the generality of model, and toward the analogy, which poses the similarity no less than the dissimilarity of the terms held in relation, as if in "their antithetical poise," to recall Miller's phrase for Woolf's narrative technique.

Reading is a fractal, which means that, as de Man asserted, it is impossible to read reading, and thus, as Miller insists and demonstrates, it is impossible to limit the pertinence of the analysis of "reading." When I say he demonstrates this, I have in mind Miller's constant and consistent "analogizing" between reading and literature, on the one hand, and everything that, beyond the language of literature, demands to be thought and responded to: new communications technologies, the institution of the university, and within it, the ideas of literary studies and of cultural studies, politics in both the broadest and narrowest senses, and ethics. The ethics of reading are fractal, which is why their responsibilities are infinite.

It is thus less to detour from than to broaden this pattern if, before returning finally to "Fractal Proust," we consider first Miller's reading of another narrative text, "Bartleby, the Scrivener." The extraordinary essay on Melville's tale in *Versions of Pygmalion* bears Miller's fractal signature as just sketched: the unoccluded embrace of another's language, a reading that each time is molded to its fractal object, to the self-dissimilar pattern that "extends in principle down to infinity."[11] For although "Bartleby" may be about a thousand times briefer than Proust's *Recherche*, it is no less inexhaustibly infinite, no less finally unreadable, unreadable to the end.

Miller ends this essay by remarking on the tale's "inexhaustible power to generate commentary,"[12] but it is commentary from readers turned to stone by the petrifying action of the text's essential and irreducible silence about its eponym, Bartleby. "Who is he?" is the ontological question the narrator, and therefore also the reader, can never answer in the present. Bartleby *is* not present with a full ontological presence for, as Miller writes, he "is not so much mortal, like the rest of us, as already dead. He is a ghost come back from some realm beyond the grave to haunt the living and to interrupt all those everyday activities of our common humanity" (*Versions of Pygmalion*, 163). For the reader, it is the experience of an impossible narration that, like a ghost, interrupts everydayness with the imperative demand to be read. On the one hand, Miller writes, "the story demands to be read, with an authority like that of Bartleby himself over the narrator. Imperiously, imperatively, it says, 'Read me!' On the other hand, it cannot be read. It demands an impossible task, and the reader remains paralyzed by the text, called upon to act but unable to act" (ibid., 175).

Just as the narrator's paralysis manifests itself in "wandering vagrancy" (*Versions of Pygmalion*, 177) as the tale progresses, the readers of the story are as if compelled to generate commentary that, as Miller puts it, never "seems to get quite to the point, as if it too were fugitive and vagrant" (ibid.).[13] In other words, to avoid paralysis, one flees the point, the pointedness, and the evidence of a Bartleby who *is* already dead, if one can say that.

And, of course, that is precisely what the narrative does say for having been written after the death of Bartleby. From the first mention in the lawyer's narration, Bartleby *is* not, he *was*: "Bartleby, who was a scrivener the strangest I ever saw or heard of. . . . Bartleby was one of those beings of whom nothing is ascertainable."[14] There is nothing at all remarkable about this past tense, to be sure, nothing that even begins to resemble the elastic temporality of Woolf's past narration. On the contrary, Melville's narrative technique seems thoroughly conventional in this regard and its temporal frame never in doubt. Miller, for example, need not take it much into account for his hauntological analysis, but that is not to say he could not find there as well points of support for that analysis. To demonstrate this and by way of a small tribute to this great essay, I offer a brief reading of two specific moments from Melville's text that Miller does not mention, but that his analysis strongly illuminates all the same.

Because, as Miller emphasizes, all the narrator's strategies are suspended from the other's passive immobilism, his being already dead, one could say that the lawyer-narrator undergoes the ordeal or has the experience of impossible decision. In this regard, Melville's tale, as Miller reads it, would configure a deconstruction of decision's classical concept. This concept, which seems indispensable for both an ethics and a politics, has to be deconstructed wherever it presupposes the identity and self-presence of a metaphysical subject. In numerous recent texts, most published since Miller's 1990 essay on "Bartleby," Jacques Derrida has brought to the fore such a rethinking of decision, for example, in a 1998 essay collected in *Papier machine* in French and in *Negotiations* in English:

> a decision that I *am able* to make, the decision that is *in my power* and that indicates the passage to the act or the deployment of what is *already possible* for me, the actualization of my possible, a decision that only depends on me: would this still be a decision? Whence the paradox without paradox

that I am trying to accept: the responsible decision must be this impossible possibility of a "passive" decision, a decision of the other-in-me who [or that] will not acquit me of any freedom or any responsibility.[15]

Miller shows us how to read "Bartleby" as a displacement of this impossible passive decision. The narrative, that is, displaces itself, and the narrator flees along the axis of the necessity that it be the other-in-me who decides. But before the flight begins, the impossible will have already happened. How does the text show this to be the case?

Whereas Melville's temporal frame is that of a largely conventional and stable retrospective first-person narration, it is, as so often in Melville, the spatial relation that calls attention to itself and that seems to bear an extra charge of meaning. Indeed, the question of Bartleby's occupation, or non-occupation, becomes indiscernible from his occupancy of a corner in the lawyer's office. The text bears down from the outset on the configuration of the space into which Bartleby is introduced, or rather, into which he is enfolded: behind the "glass folding-doors" that divide the office, and then again behind an "old green folding screen" that the lawyer sets up to keep his new scrivener out of sight, but within earshot ("Bartleby," 19). All of these details and many more fill out the narrator's description of this curious arrangement that enfolds Bartleby into the space of the office and the narrative. It is a complex topology that both holds an outside apart from an inside and brings an inside within an outside according to a structure that folds in or invaginates the limit between the external and the internal. Invisible, in his corner, Bartleby thus figures as an outside-inside, interiorized but held apart, along the invaginated border of the relation to the other.

However curious it may be (and Melville's inexhaustible commentators have rarely failed to remark this curiosity),[16] the movement of folding Bartleby into the economy of the narrator's affairs, which both incorporates him into and separates him from the corps of copyists, is recounted as a deliberate, decisive, and resolute set of actions on the part of the lawyer. "I resolved," he writes, "to assign Bartleby a corner by the folding-doors, but on my side of them. . . . I procured a high green folding screen, which might entirely isolate Bartleby from my sight" ("Bartleby," 19). However, in the order of the narration, this resolution or decision to redivide interiority occurs only *après coup*, after the *coup* that is Bartleby's sudden appearance, one morning, at the office's outer threshold. And although one would not call it a shimmering moment, nevertheless, the *coup* leaves its mark in a temporal vacillation that, as Miller says in general of this text (or of any literary text), demands to be read. Here is the moment that does not so much shimmer as shiver, that is, send a shiver, a trembling, across the threshold dividing the narrator's time from the time of the other: "In answer to my advertisement, a motionless young man one morning, stood upon my office threshold, the door being open, for it was summer. *I can see that figure now*—pallidly neat, pitiably respectable, incurably forlorn! *It was* Bartleby" (ibid.).

Standing outside the door, before he crosses any threshold, Bartleby would have presented himself as *already* within. Is that possible, or is it not precisely the im-possible arrival of the other that happens? There, on the threshold, an event of decision takes place that the narrator must allow to take place *already within him*, even before the other passes through the door. Everything that is impossible about this *already* can be read when the narrative executes a jump within its temporal frame in order to present Bartleby as he appeared "one morning" on the threshold. "I can see that figure now. . . . It was Bartleby." The figure he says he can see now *was* Bartleby, already. Already in the past this figure presented itself as in the past, and thus as its own specter. It is *as if* he said that Bartleby stood there dead, already dead in the past present, figuring his future death as already happened. It is *as if* the narrator could say that is who or what he saw arrive at his door one morning. It is also by means of the figure of an impossible or rather ghostly present tense that the hallucinating narrator says: "I can see that figure now." The figure allows him to say the impossible decision that takes the other into the "self," the other who must already be there in order to make the decision to come within.

The narrator gives us this impossible figure, so to speak, above and beyond what belongs to his own account as a possible subject. In other words, by figuring the act of no possible subject, the *récit* differentiates itself from the narrator's own discourse. It is in this placeless place of the *récit*, of the *récit* without subject, that the impossible comes to be traced and inscribed. The instant of impossible decision makes a hole in the narrator's discourse, and the *récit* lets one read this hole as what the other does, by arriving, to time, to the instant, the mad instant of decision. With the arrival of the other, the impossible happens: The instant divides, and a decision will have been made in that place that belongs properly to no one subject and that is present to no one, that is no one's present. The subject of decision has already absented itself in the other. This is what happens. And this is what the discourse of the narrator can say only backward, after the death of the other who was *as if* already dead when he took the first step onto the threshold.

These threshold lines describe or inscribe something like the im-possible task that Miller's essay on "Bartleby" traces so finely through to a certain paralysis. Here, in place of paralysis, there is a leap over the threshold of decision, an event that the narrative economy can never account for within the retrospective temporality of a subject. As the threshold of temporal/spatial difference with every other, as, in other words, the condition of (im)possibility of an ethics, this shivering, liminal event is presupposed by Miller's reading at every step. The same may be said for the second passage to which I'll now turn and which traces the contrary movement of Bartleby's expulsion across the same threshold.

Here is how the narrator recounts the decision that eventually expels Bartleby in the direction of the Tombs:

> When again I entered my office, lo, a note from the landlord lay upon the desk. I opened it with trembling hands. It informed me that the writer had sent to the police, and had Bartleby removed to the Tombs as a vagrant. . . . These tidings had a conflicting effect upon me. At first I was indignant; but at last almost approved. The landlord's energetic, summary disposition, had led him to adopt a procedure which I do not think I would have decided upon myself; and yet as a last resort, under such peculiar circumstances, it seemed the only plan. ("Bartleby," 42)

Once again, the narrator lets another decide, but this time it is another who seems to stand clearly outside the one recounting this act and its effects. This other is anonymous, unknown, named only by his legal title: Here, he is "the landlord," elsewhere simply "the lawyer." It is thus this anonymous other who has decided the thing from somewhere well outside the narrator. The anonymity of the decision is further stressed by the matter being turned over to the police, so that it is finally the law, that is, no one, who or that decides. Combined with the remark about the landlord's "energetic disposition," all these features of the act underscore the narrator's own passivity.

But what about this passivity? Through what does it pass? Through whom? Who lets whom decide what? The decision to transfer Bartleby to the Tombs seems clearly to oppose, at least on the level of the narrated story, the original decision made to hire Bartleby. And yet, it is not at all clear that these acts can be opposed in their shared structure of passive decision. Instead, the relation between them would be a relation within the im-possible time of decision, the time of the other in me who divides the time of the instant and of the present.

To see this relation more sharply defined, one may once again look closely at the language of the passage. If upon Bartleby's initial arrival, the mark of the impossible time or tense was a "now" implying a certain "already" ("I can see that figure now"), his departure will have been no less marked by a time or tense without possible present: "The landlord's energetic, summary disposition, had led him to adopt a procedure which I do not think I would have decided upon myself; and yet, under such peculiar circumstances, it seemed the only plan." Note first the play among verbal tenses here: pluperfect, past conditional, present, imperfect. This play brings out the remaining irresolution of the decision that would probably not have been made by the one speaking. But what is thereby so tenuously affirmed ("I do not think . . .") if not once again the narrator's experience of im-possible decision because it belongs to the other already and always enfolded *in* him? This is the condition of decision's im-possibility, that of deciding "upon myself," as he says in a syntax that can be understood in multiple ways. It can be read first as a simple emphasis on the subject: "myself, as for me, unlike the energetic landlord, I would not have decided upon such a procedure." One may hear also an echo of the expression "to take something upon oneself," that is, to take responsibility for it. The narrator's phrasing could thus be heard advancing a rather unconvincing denial of his responsibility for Bartleby's arrest. But there is still another, less idiomatic possibility held in reserve by this syntax, according to which the narrator would seem to be saying: "I would not have decided this by myself, me alone and on my own." That is what would have been impossible for him and in him. Him, that is to say, already the other, another, him acting and from the outset, on the threshold, *like* the totally passive Bartleby, *as* Bartleby. No, he says as the other and speaking already, always from the place of the other, "I do not think I would have decided upon myself."

If indeed, as I've already indicated, Miller's reading presupposes and illuminates all these liminal events in Melville's tale, then I cannot have offered him anything here that is not already encompassed by his reading. So, predictably, I will have failed to bring Hillis something he does not already possess. And if ever I thought to say more than my bedazzled admiration, then I should right away abandon the promise to return to "Fractal Proust."

But "J is for just a minute." And just a minute will be all it takes to point, just to point to the shimmering final pages of that text, which Miller brings to a close around what he calls "the nadir in all Proust's work, the low point beneath which it is impossible to sink."[17] What cannot sink any further is nothing less than the sun, stopped, arrested in Marcel's narrative by the shattering effect of "O sole mio" artlessly bellowed from a Venetian gondola as the hero stands paralyzed in his will to integrate the fabled city into the designs of his self. Miller writes: "The self, deprived of all the usual fictions that have constituted it, is without will to impose its ordering power on the external world, on other people, and on itself. Time stops" (*Black Holes*, 479). This is the culmination of Miller's reconstitution of Proust's "solar myth," a culmination that can only ironically be called a nadir inasmuch as the arrested, paralyzed sun remains high in the sky instead of sinking as it should into the depths of darkness and what Miller calls "the hidden homeland of otherness" (ibid.).

Perhaps it is in order to underscore this irony that, in the midst of his reading of this nadir moment of the will, Miller poses the following comparison or analogy: "The defiance of the sun causes it to stand still in the sky, as the sun stood still when Joshua commanded it to do so, against all naturalistic possibility (Josh. 10:12–13)" (477). This analogy is slyly inappropriate, hence the irony: Whereas Joshua's command is a supreme expression of will, the will of a man through whom speaks God's will that victory be assured to Israel over its enemies, Proust's novel records a nadir moment of the will's disintegration, a crushing defeat for the hero, who recovers only once habit kicks in and the sun also sets again. Perhaps however, rather than irony, Hillis was pointing to the inexhaustible reversibility of the Occident's solar myth, the immense fractal pattern of which this novel would finally be just one infinitesimal part. Or perhaps, and this will be my last guess, he was just having fun with the biblical allusion, teasing his reader into going to look for herself. He cites chapter and verse, so he has made it easy. The book of Joshua 10:12–13:

> Then spake Joshua to the Lord in the day when the Lord delivered up the Amorites before the children of Israel, and he said in the sight of Israel, Sun, stand thou still upon Gibeon; and thou, Moon, in the valley of Ajalon.
> And the sun stood still, and the moon stayed, until the people had avenged themselves upon their enemies.

And then the scribe, the scrivener, or the scripturalist of the book of Joshua points to the provenance of this incredible story in another scripture, another text, another book. "Is not this written," he asks, "in the book of Jasher?"

Yes, to be sure, it is there, the time of a shimmering, arrested sun. It is there in the book of J . . .

CHAPTER 12

Three Literary Theorists in Search of o

J. Hillis Miller

Nothing that is not there and the nothing that is.

—WALLACE STEVENS, "The Snow Man"

In a quite remarkable recent essay, "Auktorialität: Die Nullstelle des Diskurses" (Authoritality: The zero point of discourse), Wolfgang Iser uses the mathematical zero as a figure for what he calls "the authorial instance [*der auktorialen Instanz*]."[1] The authorial instance is the generative source of a literary or philosophical text. I want first to juxtapose Iser's essay to two brief essays by Maurice Blanchot that also explicitly use "zero" as a figure for a starting point or origin. I will then turn to Paul de Man's Pascal essay.[2] The juxtaposition of Iser and Blanchot brings to the fore what is seemingly arbitrary, but by no means insignificant, in the direction one goes in thinking about the relation of zero to one. Iser takes the zero, the authorial instance, more or less for granted as his starting point. The problem, for him, is how to get from zero to one and how to see one as a representation of zero or as authorized by the zero. Blanchot, on the contrary, takes the one as his starting point. The problem, for him, is how to get back to zero. Whether either of these theorists makes a truly rhetorical, as opposed to grammatical or logical, use of zero is not all that easy to decide, as I will show, but I would like to give them the benefit of the doubt.

Iser

Iser's essay is characteristically rigorous, circumspect, learned, and original. He begins by observing that authorial authorship or authority lies
outside the text's discourse, while making it possible, just as zero lies outside the number system, but makes it possible. Iser depends, as I have, on
Brian Rotman and Robert Kaplan for his understanding of zero, for example its relation to the vanishing point in Renaissance perspective painting.[3]
"There is nothing prior to zero," says Iser: "as a number, it signifies the
absence of all numbers, which makes it the initial condition of counting.
[Der o ist nichts vorgegeben, und als Zahl bezeichnet sie die Abwesenheit
aller Zahlen, was sie zur Ausgangsbedingung des *Zählens macht*]" (E, 1; G,
219). This is not quite what the authorities say. They say that zero is a
number and not a number, both inside and outside the number system.
Of course, moreover, what is prior to zero are the negative numbers. Zero
is halfway between minus one and one. This may be important, since the
fact that there is nothing prior to zero ("Der o ist nichts vorgegeben") is
crucial for Iser. This is an equivocal phrase, at least in English, since it can
be read to mean that the nothing that is comes prior to zero, as well as
that nothing comes before zero, according to an ambiguity that always
seems to appear when anyone, including me, starts talking about zero.
Zero both is and is not. It does not exist and yet is one something. Iser
wants to use the assumption that nothing is prior to zero as an analogy for
the authorial instance: "As that which makes discourse possible authorial
authorship [*auktoriale Urheberschaft*] resides outside of discourse, and it becomes the zero point [*Nullstelle*] because it relates to nothing prior to itself
[*sie auf nichts ihr Vorausliegendes bezieht*]" (E, 1; G, 219).
    Iser is clear later on in the essay in ruling out any appeal from the
authorial instance to the psychological makeup of the author or to his
social, historical, or ideological placement. The translation that Ingo Berensmeyer uses for the fundamental phrase that echoes through Iser's
essay, "der auktorialen Instanz," is "the authorial instance." This is ac-
ceptable, since it carries the odd-sounding German word over into an English cognate. The semantic range of the two words, however, is somewhat
different, even though they have the same Latin root. "Instance" in English means "a case or example, a legal proceeding or process, a suit"
(though I never heard the word used to name a legal proceeding); a step
in a proceeding, and a prompting or request, as in "He called at the instance of his wife." The word is derived from the Latin "instantia," meaning presence, perseverance, urgency (*American Heritage Dictionary*). Surely

the most common English meaning is "example," as in "for instance." Most people, I, for instance, before I looked the word up, do not even know that "instance" means a legal proceeding. In German "Instanz" means only "authority, court (of justice); stage (of proceedings)," not ever, apparently, "example" (*Cassell's German Dictionary*). "Der auktorialen Instanz" therefore means authorial authority, but with overtones of a court of justice's sovereign power, beyond which there is perhaps no appeal. The etymological root of "Instanz," as of "instance," suggests something that "stands in," in the sense of being firmly planted, posited, laid down as a self-sustaining foundation on which a solid edifice may be built.

The problem that concerns Iser throughout his essay is how one can imagine the transition from the authorial instance to the actual text of a philosophical or literary work. More precisely, he attempts to find what traces there are in the work itself of the "Instanz" that authorizes it. How does one get from zero to one? What evidence does the one give of the authorizing authority of its source in zero? In brilliantly succinct and concentrated readings of a series of works, Montaigne's *Essais*, *Robinson Crusoe*, *Gulliver's Travels*, *Oliver Twist*, *Vanity Fair*, Kierkegaard's *On the Point of View for My Work as an Author*, Nietzsche's *Ecce Homo*, and Beckett's *Ping*, Iser searches for signs of the authorial instance in these works. In *Robinson Crusoe*, the authorizing source is present figuratively in the fictive editor's fictive attestation, outside the work itself, to the literal truth of Crusoe's fictive story. In *Gulliver's Travels*, the text itself contains a somewhat similar self-authorization in the fictive Gulliver's preface containing a certification by his fictive Cousin Sympson that "the Author was . . . distinguished for his Veracity." This eighteenth-century procedure is a circling from fiction to fiction or a lifting oneself by one's own bootstraps. It indicates an anxiety to make a (fictive) claim for the referential truth-value of a fiction. "This demonstrates," says Iser, "that generation possesses neither validity nor authority [*weder Geltung noch Autorität besitzt*], which is why the postulation of a truth claim remains a predominant characteristic of the representation of authorial zero points [*der Verbildlichung auktorialer Nullstellen*]" (E, 6; G, 223).

In Kierkegaard or Nietzsche, the affirmation of authority is achieved through a doubling or masking. Kierkegaard, notoriously, adopts various personas and pseudonyms. Nietzsche expresses himself by speaking through Wagner, Schopenhauer, or Zarathustra. In Beckett's *Ping*, the authorizing zero has wandered into the text, as opposed to being indirectly represented. Beckett's zero point of discourse appears, Iser asserts, in the repeated semantically empty word "ping" that disables even further an already fractured syntax. If the zero of authorial authority is ever going to appear in person, or as such, it must appear as a nonsense word, a mere sound. One might call this the zero degree of articulate speech: "Ping!"

Iser's argumentation is logically rigorous. It depends on a series of assumptions or steps that are repeated in different ways for each example. One assumption is the impossibility of facing directly or of expressing directly the zero point of the authorial *Instanz*. If it appears, it must appear indirectly, or as "mirrored," or "veiled," to use two of Iser's recurrent metaphors. Even more important for Iser, however, is the motif of doubling. Doubling is fundamental to his theoretical model and to his reading of the various works. The absent or effaced authorial *Instanz* is mirrored in the doubling of personages or perspectives or voices within the texts. Iser calls this "binarity." Instances are the doubling of Montaigne into a *moi* that he is and a *moi* that is the spectator and recorder in words of that *moi*; the doubling of Crusoe by the editor of what he has written; or the doubling of Gulliver by his cousin; or the masking of Nietzsche as Wagner, Schopenhauer, or Zarathustra; or the doubling of author by narrator in Victorian novels; or Kierkegaard's pseudonymous writings; or even the dissolution of any imaginable enunciator of *Ping* into innumerable conflicting and contradictory possible points of view. "Ping" itself, the sound of the word, is "a duplicate of the authorial zero point [*Duplikat der auktorialen Nullstelle*]" (E, 18; G, 237).

Doubling as a universal component of Iser's general model is expressed apodictically in the last paragraph of his essay, apropos of carefully reserved comments he has made about Foucault's discussion of the famous "death of the author." "[T]he authorial zero point," says Iser, "becomes operational through its doubling in discourse [*Die auktoriale Nullstelle durch ihre Verdoppelung im Diskurs operativ wird*]. Moreover, the authorial zero point neither says something about the empirical individuality of the author nor about certain author functions. As zero point, it does not signify anything [*bezeichnet sie nichts*], which is why nothing needs to be imported into this absence. The zero eludes taxonomic attributions, but it is, as in counting, the condition of generativity [*die Bedingung des Hervorbringens*]" (E, 21; G, 240). Doubling occurs in two ways in Iser's model, in the doubling or mirroring of the zero in the author's discourse, as when Iser says "'ping' is the duplicate of the zero" (E, 17; G, 236), and in doublings within the text in which each speaker makes the other its authorizing authority, in the circular lifting by one's own bootstraps I have identified.

The difficulty with Iser's model is easy to see. He still has not, and in fact cannot, explain in his own logical or rational terms how you get from zero to one. The doubling and redoubling of zero is still zero, not ever one: $2 \times 0 = 0$. You cannot get from zero to one except by an unauthorized leap that says the zero is a one, one number in the number series. One or two or ten million times zero is still zero. Iser has missed an opportunity to describe the process of generativity he sees in these texts in truly rhetorical terms, that is, to see these "doublings" or "mirrorings" as performative catachreses posited or imposed on what remains unknowable, the zero, even though it is instantiated as the generative source of the catachreses that veil and unveil it at the same time. These catachreses are "performative" because they are freely posited in a speech act (any mirroring or doubling is as good as another, because none is a mirroring in the sense of "mirror image") and because they are not and cannot be validated by cognition. The zero does not "generate" the one. The one, however, any one, "generates" a glimpse of the zero that is at the same time its hiding or covering over by a false or fictional name.

Iser, who is nothing if not immensely intelligent and perceptive, approaches an understanding of this at two points in his essay. One place is in his comments on what Montaigne means when he says his intrinsic *moi*, the me that he really is, is not prior to his writing, but is generated by it: "Je n'ay pas plus faict mon livre que mon livre m'a faict, livre consubstantial à son autheur" (cited E, 3; G, 221). The other place is in Iser's brilliant analysis of the emptiness of Nietzsche's proleptic anticipation of just what the transvaluation of all values will be like when all the false ideals or ideological idols have been destroyed. Only then can Nietzsche's sovereign authorial authority express itself directly into the vacuum left after the universal ruin of humanity's ideals. Nothing comes of nothing. Nietzsche's authorial *Instanz*, like all authorial instances, is a zero. This means that Nietzsche can say nothing whatsoever except empty promises about what will come to fill the gap when his work of destruction is accomplished.

Nothing comes of nothing, and yet something obviously does. The whole of modern mathematics emerges from zero. In the most concrete and material way possible, Defoe invents Robinson Crusoe and then sits down with pen, ink, and paper to write down Crusoe's fictive adventures. Those of us who can read can then relive those adventures whenever we pick up the book and begin to read the first words. No language about doubling or about generativity (a covert personification) will fill the gap between zero and one. Nevertheless, it is crossed every time a new work of literature or philosophy is invented, as indeed it was crossed when zero was invented, out of nothing.

Blanchot

The mental space we enter when we read Blanchot rather than Iser is quite different. Even so, the texts both writers generate are, in places, concerned, in strikingly diverse ways, with zero. In two essays, in two different books, out of the immense number of essays Blanchot wrote over the years, inventing them who knows how, zero is the explicit focus of attention. One is a review essay in *L'amitié* (Friendship) of Claude Lévi-Strauss's *Tristes Tropiques*, entitled "Man at Point Zero." The second essay I will discuss, although it was published first, is called "The Search for Point Zero." That essay mentions Mallarmé, Proust, and Barthes. It is part of a prolonged meditation, in a series of essays in a section at the end of *Le livre à venir* (The book to come), on the question "Où va la littérature? [Where is literature going?]." It seems to be going straight into the abyss. Blanchot's concern is with the disappearance of literature, or with literature as disappearance. Literature disappears into that silence Blanchot names, in "The Song of the Sirens," as the silence of the Sirens when they will have sunk into the sea.[4]

In their relation to zero, the direction of the two Blanchot essays I will discuss is, as I have said, just the reverse of the movement for which Iser's essay attempts to account. Rather than taking the zero point of the authorial *Instanz* as a starting place and trying to show how to get from there to one, the work, Blanchot takes for granted the author's ability to write endlessly, as, for example Proust did, but he defines that writing as a "recherche" for point zero. Zero for Blanchot is not a unique generative source within each author. It is an impersonal zero point on the horizon, or in the depths, or somewhere out of this world. The literary effort is oriented toward this point. Literature attempts to reach and speak for that point, as well as to speak in response to it, responsibly. Blanchot's essays are extremely subtle. Each makes many different moves, impossible to recapitulate without a lengthy analysis. The upshot of all of them, however, including the two I will discuss, is an affirmation of the failure to reach the goal of the zero point. If Iser shows, perhaps inadvertently, that it is impossible to get from zero to one, Blanchot shows, deliberately and patiently and carefully, over and over, that it is impossible to get from one back (or forward) to zero.

"Man at Point Zero" begins with a reflection on the awe nonscientists feel for the work of scientists, or for those who claim scientific status, such as Lévi-Strauss. Blanchot, correctly, acknowledges our disappointment when a great scientist, such as Einstein or Oppenheimer, tries to draw moral or political conclusions from his scientific discoveries: "when Oppenheimer tries to improve [*enricher*] our 'common sense,' he only makes us think by way of the contradiction between the force, the seriousness, and the authenticity of his science and the insignificant conclusions he elicits from it for the benefit of popular thought."[5] On the basis of this sad fact, Blanchot asks, in effect, what good Lévi-Strauss might be for those who are not ethnographers.

Far from arguing, as many did at that time, that the methodology of structural anthropology could be appropriated for the humanities, Blanchot derives a quite different lesson from *Tristes Tropiques*. He begins by acknowledging, as Lévi-Strauss does too, that "[t]he ethnographer is the uneasy companion of imperialism" (E, 75; F, 89). The ethnographer destroys what he or she studies, by an irresistible and infinitely sad "power of volatilization" (E, 76; F, 90). Once Lévi-Strauss has been among the Nambikwara, they will never be the same again. Nevertheless, Blanchot defines Lévi-Strauss's quest, and that of ethnography in general, as a search for "man at point zero." Ethnography is an attempt to reach back to "originary possibilities of which human societies are the constant implementation [*mise en oeuvre*]" (F, 78; F, 92). Of course, as Rousseau, Lévi-Strauss's hero, already knew, and as Lévi-Strauss's work discovers again, this search is always a failure. You cannot get from one back to zero. Why not? Because "it is true that in one sense there never was a beginning, not for anything nor at any moment [*il est vrai qu'en un sens il n'y ait, pour rien et à aucun moment, de commencement*]" (E, 79; F, 93). The Derridean rejection of identifiable or attainable origin, by any remounting the stream of time, so to speak, is already rigorously present in Blanchot. On this point, Blanchot is no doubt one of Derrida's "sources," or, it might be better to say, they worked simultaneously at similar demystifications of the myth of origin.

Why then this "attraction of beginnings," this fascinated "interest in what is first" (E, 78; F, 92)? Blanchot's answer takes him some distance from Lévi-Strauss, but by way of Lévi-Strauss's Marxism. What Blanchot says is a good example of the political orientation of his thinking. This orientation is sometimes forgotten or ignored in discussions of Blanchot's work. Making use of a figure drawn from the way travelers by sea hypothesized a zero meridian, by crossing which they would be transformed and able to begin their lives anew, Blanchot affirms that the fascination with man's zero point is oriented, in the end, not so much toward the past as toward the future. It is focused on the impossible dream of a destruction of false ideologies and of the dehumanizing effects of modern technologies so man (*sic*) could begin again: "one must either perish or begin again; perish in order to begin again [*il faut périr ou commencer; périr afin de commencer*]. This, then, would be the meaning of the task represented by the myth of the man without myth: the hope, the anguish, and the illusion of man at point zero" (E, 82; F, 97).

The operative words here are "myth" and "illusion." Our political and personal dreams may be driven, motivated, by this illusory myth, but it is an illusion nevertheless. At one point in his essay, Blanchot makes a provocative comparison between the myth of man at point zero and imaginary numbers in mathematics, most notably the square root of minus one, or "i." This does not exist, but nevertheless it is generated as a heuristic necessity in computation. Point zero may be illusory, but the search for it is imaginary, like "i": "It is also easy," says Blanchot, "—and perhaps useful—to denounce the illusory character of this search for point zero."

> Not illusory, however, but imaginary [*Non pas illusoire pourtant, mais imaginaire*], almost according to the meaning given this word by mathematics: *imaginary* is the reference to a man without myth, as is *imaginary* the reference to the man dispossessed of himself, free of all determination, deprived of all "value," and alienated to the point where he is nothing but the acting consciousness of this nothing [*la conscience agissante de ce rien*], the essential man of point zero, whose theoretical model certain analyses of Marx have proposed and in relation to whom the modern proletariat discovers itself, defines itself and affirms itself, even if it does not truly satisfy such a schema. (E, 79–80; F, 94)

Blanchot's reference here is to Marx, but he might just as well have referred to Nietzsche's dream of emptying humankind of all prejudices and idols, leaving an *Übermensch* at point zero ready to begin again.

What Blanchot says recalls Wallace Stevens's endless and endlessly failed attempt through the written meditations of his poems to "get it right" at last and capture in words the "primitive like an orb," "the giant of nothingness," "the idea of man," "major man."[6] Stevens's search is for what, in "A Primitive Like an Orb," he calls "sleep realized," "the whiteness that is the ultimate intellect / A diamond jubilance beyond the fire" (Stevens, 433). Stevens's search, too, was for man at point zero. His search, too, never reached its goal. The word "zero" is not a big word in Stevens's poetic vocabulary, insurance executive though he was, no doubt using zero all the time in his office. I do not remember that Stevens ever uses "zero" in his poetry, although I may have forgotten. I had thought of calling this present essay, "The Comedian as the Letter Z," but that would not work for Stevens himself. "Nothing," however, is a key word for Stevens. Stevens's name for "man at point zero" is, in one early poem's title, "The Snow Man." The snow man is the man who has been cold long enough, who has lived close enough to the zero degree, to behold, as my epigraph says, "Nothing that is not there and the nothing that is" (Stevens, 10).

Blanchot's "Man at Point Zero" does not seem to have much, except indirectly, to do with literature or with its rhetorical analysis. The second Blanchot essay I shall discuss, however, "The Search for Point Zero," from *The Book to Come* (*Le livre à venir*), exemplifies what is said in the unsigned and anonymous note at the beginning of the English translation of *The Book to Come*. That note is given a whole, mostly blank, page to itself, as if it had fallen from the sky onto the page: "Maurice Blanchot, novelist and critic, was born in 1907. His life is wholly devoted to literature and to the silence unique to it."[7] Just what is this "silence" that is unique to "literature," whatever *that* is? Blanchot devoted his life to trying to figure out just what literature is. "The Search for Point Zero" is, like "Man at Point Zero," an essay in the guise of a review. In this case, it looks like a laudatory review of Roland Barthes's *Le degré zéro de l'écriture*.[8] It deflects Barthes, however, in the direction of Blanchot's own concern for the neutral, "le neutre," as one name for the murmuring silence of the imaginary or for the space of literature where everything is turned into image. Blanchot's essay is not very Barthesian. Its endpoint is explicitly un-Barthesian.

The essay begins with an intransigent recognition that the rise of new media (radio, television) is transforming literature. Literature, however, has already in the past two centuries been transforming itself from an agreed-upon social institution to a tormented search for the essence of literature. "Literature" as such begins to exist only when it is no longer protected by social assumptions, for example by the conventions of the novel, the dominant nineteenth- and twentieth-century form of so-called literature, with its use (in French) of the *passé simple* and of indirect discourse in the third person. Literature begins to approach itself only when it begins to shatter and disperse, when it enters "the tension of a search that calls everything in question [*la tension d'une recherché qui remet tout en question*]," when it poses or receives "the demand that rejects the very horizon of a world [*l'exigence qui rejette l'horizon même d'un monde*]" (E, 204; F, 249).

This new literature about the question of literature, which Blanchot especially associates, not unexpectedly, with Mallarmé, Kafka, and Beckett, begins with a sense of heady liberation. The writer feels that he or she can now at last say anything and everything. The writer no longer has to obey conventions and proprieties. What freedom! The writer ends, however, by perceiving "that he has at best devoted all his strength to searching for only one single point [*à ne rechercher qu'un seul point*]" (E, 205; F, 249). This is that zero point the essay's title names.

What happens to abort that search is defined by way of distinctions Blanchot borrows from Barthes between language, style, and writing: the common language everyone speaks in a certain place and time; the style that is the unique result of a given writer's temperament; "writing [*écriture*]." The first two are relatively superficial or contingent, but "literature begins with writing [*La littérature commence avec l'écriture*]" (E, 205; F, 250). That seems clear enough, but the rest of the essay shows that the search for the zero point of literature must, in the end, dispense even with writing, especially when the latter has erected a temple consecrating as sacred certain procedures and modes of writing as ritual necessities. (The reference once more is implicitly to Mallarmé, in this case to his appropriation of religious terms to describe the act of literature.) The true writer in search of literature's zero point must refuse to enter that temple or must deliberately destroy it. True writing ends by destroying itself and lapsing into silence. "[T]o write," writes Blanchot,

> is first of all to want to destroy the temple before building it; it is at least, before passing over its threshold, to question the constraints of such a place, the original sin that formed the decision to enclose ourselves in it. To write is finally to refuse to pass over the threshold, to refuse to "write." [*Écrire, c'est finalement se refuser à passer le seuil, se refuser à écrire.*] . . . To write without "writing," to bring literature to that point of absence where it disappears [*Écrire sans "écriture," amener la littérature à ce point d'absence où elle disparaît*], where we no longer have to dread its secrets, which are lies, that is "the degree zero of writing," the neutrality that every writer seeks, deliberately or without realizing it, and which leads some of them to silence. (E, 206, 207; F, 251, 252)

The remainder of the essay sketches the consequences of passing into the realm of fiction or the imaginary, where everything is turned into image. Things become infinitely distant, and the self is dissolved. The conditions on which we enter the true realm of literature are "that the world, where we have only things to use, first of all collapsed, that things have become infinitely distanced from themselves, have recovered the inalienable distance of the image [*le lointain indisponible de l'image*]—that is why I am no longer myself and can no longer say 'I.' A formidable transformation" (E, 207; F, 253). The example of this Blanchot provides is Proust, who, by dint of perpetual writing, dispossessed himself of himself until it is not "Proust the man" who writes, but writing itself, literature itself: "We say Proust, but we sense that it is the entirely other who writes, not only someone else but the very demand of writing, a demand that uses the name Proust but does not express Proust, that expresses him only by disappropriating him, by making him Other [*en le désappropriant, en le rendant Autre*]" (E, 208–9; F, 254). It is perhaps not necessary to observe at this point that if Blanchot is right about literature, and he is, then much academic study of literature is beside the point, irrelevant, however valuable may be the information it gives as a support of semantic, thematic, biographical, or referential readings. Such information, however, does not help identify what is literary about literature. It displaces attention to literature's thematic "contents" or to its contexts in biography or social conditions, falsely assumed to be able to account for it.

Blanchot's "The Search for Point Zero" ends, after a passing swipe at the legion of novels that are not literature at all, however carefully or carelessly written, to a radical revision of Barthes' degree zero of writing. That zero degree, says Blanchot, is not just the neutral, featureless style that Barthes finds exemplified in Camus. It is a more dangerous, more destructive, more lethal neutrality. In that neutrality, everything, including literature itself, disappears into the zero point of silence, the silence of the drowned sirens, or into that interminable and dead/deathless murmur that comes not from me, but from infinitely outside me and that so fascinates Blanchot in all his "writing." The orientation reverses once more. Now it is not the writer speaking as he or she moves forward in the search for the zero point, but the zero itself, in a stuttering speech that is the equivalent of a terrifying silence. "By directing us, through serious thought," says Blanchot, with only a hint of irony, "toward what he called the zero degree of writing,"

> Roland Barthes perhaps also designated the moment when literature might be grasped. But the fact is that at that point it would be not only a bland, absent, and neutral writing [*une écriture blanche, absente et neutre*], it would be the very experience of "neutrality," which one never hears, for when

neutrality speaks, only one who imposes silence on it prepares the conditions for its hearing, and yet what there is to hear is this neutral speech; what has always been said cannot stop being said and cannot be heard [*cette parole neutre, ce qui a toujours été dit, ne peut cesser de se dire et ne peut être entendu*]. (E, 209; F, 253)

To express this in terms of my figure of the relation of zero to one: The only way the writer can make the zero speak is by falsifying it, by imposing silence on it, so the writer's speech, which is not yet at the zero point, can be heard in its place. The speech of the zero point itself, although the search for it motivates all real literature, is a neutral speech, a murmuring of the always already said that cannot be heard and so cannot be distinguished from silence, the true song of the Sirens. The more faithful to his or her vocation or calling the writer is, the more certain he or she is to end in silence, as for example Arthur Rimbaud did. If any writer ever gets to the zero point and disappears into that black hole, we will never hear of it, not, at least, in anything he or she writes.

de Man

To the most rigorous example I know of a truly rhetorical exploitation of zero's propertyless properties I now turn.

Paul de Man's "Pascal's Allegory of Persuasion" is one of its author's most brilliant and important essays. Andrzej Warminski makes it the focus of his introductory essay for *Aesthetic Ideology*, the volume in which the essay is collected. The endpoint of the essay is a recognition that the disjunction between justice and power, in Pascal's *Pensées*, arises from a general disjunction between cognition and performance as functions of language: "To the extent that language is always cognitive and tropological as well as performative at the same time, it is a heterogeneous entity incapable of justice as well as of *justesse*."[9] This concluding insight is reached by way of an intricate argumentation that begins with a discussion of Pascal's distinction between nominal and real definitions, followed by an analysis of Pascal's mathematics, including the zero in Pascal's thought. De Man then proceeds through by reading several of Pascal's *pensées*. He shows that they remain within cognition and take the crisscross form of a chiasmus, a version both of proportionality (A is to B as C is to D) and of tropological exchanges. Finally, the *pensées* dealing with the relation between justice and power are shown to be different. They introduce something like the zero and are therefore inassimilable to the chiasmus structure: "the tropological field of cognition is revealed to be dependent on an entity, might, that is heterogeneous with regard to this field, just as the zero was heterogeneous with regard to number" (69). The narrative of this heterogeneity, the accounting for it in language, for example the discovery that it is impossible to inscribe the pairs *présence/absence* and *plaisir/déplaisir* into a neat chiasmus structure, is said to be "what we call allegory": "The (ironic) pseudoknowledge of this impossibility, which pretends to order sequentially, in a narrative, what is actually the destruction of all sequence, is what we call allegory" (69). De Man calls this knowledge "pseudo" because the impossibility in question cannot be known, only gestured toward. It is ironic because, as de Man demonstrates in "The Concept of Irony," another essay in *Aesthetic Ideology*, irony is disruptive of all narrative or dialectical sequence. It suspends or pulverizes any sequential story or argument. He says "what we call allegory," rather than just "allegory," to call attention to the way the constantly interrupted or broken narrative in question here is outside the order of cognition. You can call it anything you like, but all the names would be catachreses, performatively imposed names for what has no literal name, either nominal or real. "We [whoever that "we" may be. De Man himself? Some collective entity, including me, the reader?] call it allegory" by a performative fiat, a speech act, like naming a baby.

What is the role of Pascal's zero in this argumentation? The central statement, the culmination of de Man's discussion of Pascal's logic and mathematics, is the following characteristically cheeky assertion: "To say then, as we are actually saying, that allegory (as sequential narration) is the trope of irony (as one is the trope of zero) is to say something that is true enough but not intelligible, which also implies that it cannot be put to work as a device of textual analysis" (61). What in the world does this mean? De Man tells us we are not going to find it intelligible, so why say it unless as a kind of challenge: "Understand it if you can! I challenge you to do so, but don't blame me if you fail. I will have told you so." How can something be true, able to be formulated in a neat proportional aphorism (allegory is to irony as one is to zero), and yet be unintelligible? Does not de Man, in spite of what he says, put his insight to work "as a device of textual analysis" in the discussion of the disjunction between justice and power in the *pensées* read at the end of the essay? The odd formulation, "to say then, as we are actually saying," mixes, no doubt deliberately, "mention" and "use," the cognitive and the performative, in the distinction between "someone might say" and "I declare that I (disguised as we) am now actually saying." This anticipates the cognitive/performative disjunction with which the essay ends. What de Man is saying is unintelligible insofar as it is a speech act, not a constative statement, since, in de Man's speech-act theory, performative speech acts are radically foreign to the order of cognition.

The context of this "not intelligible" formulation does not help much toward making it intelligible. De Man has been concluding what he has to say about the way "the numerical series are interrupted by zero" and is now moving on to ask whether anything like that happens in the dialectical theological and epistemological formulations of the *Pensées*. "It is possible," says de Man, "to find, in the terminology of rhetoric, terms that come close to designating such disruptions (e.g., *parabasis* or *anacoluthon*), which designate the interruption of a semantic continuum in a manner that lies beyond the power of reintegration."

> One must realize at once, however, that this disruption is not topical, that it cannot be located in a single point—since it is indeed the very notion of point, the geometrical zero, that is being dislodged—but that it is all-pervading. The anacoluthon is omnipresent, or, in temporal terms and in Friedrich Schlegel's deliberately unintelligible formulation, the parabasis is permanent. Calling this structure ironic can be more misleading than helpful, since . . . (61)

Then follows the formulation I cite above about the (tropological) relation of zero and one being proportional to the (tropological) relation between irony and allegory.

The context tells us at least that de Man is shifting from mathematical terminology to rhetorical terminology, but to odd rhetorical terms or odd uses of them that are beyond easy intelligibility. "Anacoluthon" names a failure in following, such as a sentence that begins in the first person and shifts in midsentence to the third person. De Man, however, is talking about a pervasive anacoluthon, a failure in following all along the line. He proposes, that is, a form of anacoluthon that does not really make sense. A "parabasis" is interruption or suspension of a dramatic illusion, as when a character or the dramatist steps forward on the proscenium and speaks in his or her own voice about the drama as a fictive illusion. "Permanent parabasis" is Friedrich Schlegel's definition of irony. It is "deliberately unintelligible" because a permanent parabasis would be a suspension without anything other than itself to suspend or without anything that had not been already suspended at every point throughout the dramatic action, as if by a perpetual disillusioning commentary addressed to the audience. Calling the structure de Man is trying to describe "ironic" may be more misleading than helpful, since irony, like zero, cannot be defined in either of Pascal's senses of definition, nominal or real.

Trying to understand the Pascalian zero may allow me to defy de Man's prohibition and at least get an "(ironic) pseudoknowledge" of the relations between irony, allegory, zero, and one. That would permit a truly rhetorical (as opposed to semantic, thematic, or semiological) application of zero, if not necessarily an intelligible one.

However it is approached, even with the most powerful tools of rhetoric, zero seems to remain mind-boggling. In the discussion of Pascal's *Réflexions sur la géométrie en général: De l'esprit géométrique et de l'art de persuader* that opens de Man's essay, he begins with a description of the way geometry succeeds because it uses only nominal definitions that do not depend on anything outside the closed code for their intelligibility. Geometry uses only *"definitions of name [définitions de nom]*, that is to say, [gives] a name only to those things which have been clearly designated in perfectly known terms" (Pascal cited by de Man), whereas real definitions bring in the question of correspondence to something external to the code, that is, they are "axioms" or "propositions that need to be proven" (55).

De Man's unraveling of Pascal's system, or demonstration that it unravels itself, proceeds through a recognition that one is both a number and not a number to the more disruptive recognition that the zero is radically not a number, both necessary to the establishment of the system and wholly outside it, heterogeneous to it: "There exists, in the order of number, an entity that is, unlike the *one*, heterogeneous with regard to number: this entity, which is the *zero*, is radically distinct from one. Whereas one is and is not a number at the same time, zero is radically not a number, absolutely heterogeneous to the order of number" (59). The introduction of the zero allows for a reconciliation of number and space, but this happens at a price: "the coherence of the system is now seen to be entirely dependent on the introduction of an element—the zero and its equivalences in time and motion—that is itself entirely heterogeneous with regard to the system and nowhere a part of it. The continuous universe held together by the double wings of the two infinites [the infinitely small and the infinitely large] is interrupted, disrupted *at all points* by a principle of radical heterogeneity without which it cannot come into being" (59). De Man's account of zero, the reader will note, differs from that of the authorities I refer to in footnote three. They say "zero" is both a number and not a number. De Man says "one" is both a number and not a number, whereas zero is radically not a number. This displacement from zero to one of the formula "both a number and not a number" and the relegating of zero to "radical heterogeneity" is essential to de Man's use of zero as parallel to irony, that is, to his use of zero as a figure for a linguistic problem.

At this point, de Man shifts to another register and argues just that, namely that the aporia here is not a mathematical but a linguistic dead end. "The notion of language as sign is dependent on, and derived from, a different notion in which language functions as rudderless signification and transforms what it denominates into the linguistic equivalent of the arithmetical zero" (59). "Rudderless signification" is a wonderful phrase. It figures signification as like a boat drifting without a rudder, hither and thither as the wind and waves take it, although most likely ultimately on the rocks. Although de Man does not say so here, in so many words, what he is actually saying is that the name "zero" differs from all the other names for mathematical entities by being a catachresis, that is, a transferred name for what has no name and is unknowable.

> It is as sign that language is capable of engendering the principles of infinity, of genus, species, and homogeneity, which allow for synecdochal totalizations, but none of these tropes could come about without the systematic effacement of the zero and its reconversion into a name. There can be no *one* without zero, but the zero always appears in the guise of a *one*, of a (some)thing. The name is the trope of the zero. The zero is always *called* a one, when the zero is actually nameless, "innommable." (59)

"One" is straightforwardly and intelligibly both a number and not a number. Zero, however, is unnameable. It can only by an abusive transfer be called a one, one something. The trope in question here is catachresis, which means just that: "abusive transfer." To say the zero is always *called* a one is to call attention to the way the trope called catachresis is always a speech act, a groundless performative. "I call this zero a something, a one." This equivocation about the zero is present in different forms in set theory and in the ambiguity in mathematics between saying zero is a number, the first number in the series of numbers, and saying zero is a meta-number, a number about the absence of any numbers, therefore outside the system of numbers. De Man accepts the second definition of zero, but refuses the first. For him, zero is not the first number in a series of numbers, but something altogether outside the system of numbers, heterogeneous to it, although inside it, too, as its ungrounding ground. As the condition of the system, zero cannot be thought within the system of numbers or signs, although it does not exist somewhere outside the system, either.

What does de Man mean when he says "allegory (as sequential narrative) is the trope of irony (as the one is the trope of zero)"? Can this
gnomic aphorism actually be put to work as a device of textual analysis,
whatever de Man says to the contrary? Since neither irony nor the zero is
knowable, able to be confronted phenomenally, any trope for them will be
a catachresis. De Man's sentence might be rephrased by saying allegory is
the catachresis of irony, just as one is the catachresis of zero. The word
"zero" is already itself a catachresis, an abusive name for something unknown, unknowable, and unnameable, "innommable." This is so because
the word "zero" implies that what it names is something, some thing, a
one. To call it zero or to call it one comes to the same thing, since it has
no proper name. It is not an etymological accident, without significance,
that the word "zero" and the word "cipher" have the same root, Arabic
"sifr." The double meaning of "cipher," as zero and as a name for any
number, is hidden also in the double meaning of "zero," as one something,
and as an abyssal nothing at all. De Man finds this duplicity present in
Pascal's somewhat inconsistent distinction between "néant," which is the
zero as something, as a number, and "zéro," as Pascal's name for the unknowable that makes infinitesimal calculus possible, as well as being what
allegories are about.

In a throwaway line at the end of the first paragraph of "Pascal's Allegory of Persuasion," de Man says, "The difficulty of allegory is rather that
this emphasis on clarity of representation does not stand in the service of
something that can be represented" (51). Clarity of representation, he has
just been saying, is necessary in allegory not as "an appeal to the pagan
pleasure of imitation" (51), but so the objects that are the vehicle of the
allegory can be clearly recognized. The tenor of the allegory, however,
what the allegory is an allegory of, is one version or another of the unknowable: zero, irony, death, or what Friedrich Schlegel called "chaos,"
or the performative dimension of language, language's "power," as opposed to its "justice." These names are all posited pseudonames for that
unrepresentable blankness or radical otherness that allegories allegorize.
Irony, as a pervasive disruption of intelligibility in an entire discourse, is
like performative speech acts in being alien to cognition. This explains
why de Man, rather surprisingly, puts irony on the side of performative
language in "The Concept of Irony": "Irony also very clearly has a performative function. Irony consoles and it promises and it excuses" (de
Man, *Aesthetic Ideology*, 165).

The impossibility of representing what allegory represents also explains
why the Pascal essay is called "Pascal's Allegory of Persuasion." This title

no doubt plays on the "of" as both subjective and objective genitive. It is an allegory about persuasion and an allegory belonging to persuasion. All allegories are allegories of persuasion. This is true not only in the sense that they persuade, but also in the sense that what they allegorize is the unknowable speech act we call persuasion. Persuasion is the dimension of rhetoric that uses language as a power to bring people to act and believe in a certain way, unjustly or justly, you cannot be sure which. It is in this sense, moreover, that all allegories are allegories of allegory, that is, emblematic expressions of their own mode of working, which is to be persuasive. Or, to put this another way, all allegories are allegories of reading, since what they "stand for," or "stand in for," as placeholders, is their own unpredictable performative effects on readers, readers good and bad. If one is to zero as allegory is to irony, then it can be said that de Man's originality, not entirely authorized by Pascal, is to take Pascalian mathematics, with perhaps an admixture of modern set theory (de Man, after all, was an engineering student at the University of Brussels), as an allegory of the working of allegory. This, I claim, is a truly rhetorical use in literary theory of zero's strange properties.

CHAPTER 13

Justices

Jacques Derrida

I

J'aurais dû commencer, I should have begun, even before an exergue, by wishing my translator, Peggy Kamuf, "good luck," while thanking her from the bottom of my heart.

Je me dis d'abord, I say to myself first, that my French *J* will have been lost from the first letter of the first word. I'm not talking here about my first name, but about my *je*, my I and my *jeu* with *je*, my play with I. *Je* (I) will have withdrawn, effaced itself from the first letter of the first word. *Je est un autre*. I is another one.

Nevertheless, I and I alone should answer for such an effacement.

J'en suis responsable. I am responsible for it.

The one who says "je," "I" is responsible for it here, as always. Moreover, responsibility always seems to return to someone who says "je," "I." This is how what is called law and perhaps justice work. This is how one understands the words of law, right, and *justice* in the culture where our tradition and language draw their breath. Everything in this culture that acts, thinks, and speaks intentionally, everything that does something, and especially with words, in the perfomative mode, must be signed, implicitly or explicitly, by a responsible *je*, I. Austin stresses the point: The condition

of the pure performative, the temporal modality of the felicitous and serious performative, is the *present*. At least implicitly. But it is also the full
presence to itself of a first person, thus of what is called in French a *je*. In
other words, of what you call an I, thereby making the *j* of the *je* disappear.
So many untranslatable Js, already!

Je me suis si souvent demandé, I have so often asked myself, perhaps for
more than thirty-five years, from the depths of my friendship and admiration for him, how one could be J. Hillis Miller. *Quel est son "je" à lui?*
What is his own *je*, his I?

And what taste could this *je*, this I have?

The taste I have for him or the taste he has for others and for me, is it
the same? Is it the same as the one he has for himself? One may very well
doubt that it is. This doubt likewise takes on a very perceptible flavor in
me, an obscurely immediate sense. We are moving here in that strange
geometry where the nearest and the most distant are but one and the same.
The most similar and the infinitely other return in a circle to each other.
How does J. Hillis Miller *himself* feel when he says "je," "I," or when he
has the feeling of "himself"? These borders of the I are vertiginous, but
inevitable. We all rub up against them, make contact without contact, in
particular as concerns our dearest friends. This is even what is astonishing
about friendship, when it is somewhat alert. It is also vigilant friendship
that startles us awake to this strange question: What does it mean for an I
to feel itself? "How does he *himself* feel, J. Hillis Miller? J. Hillis Miller
himself, the other, the wholly other that he remains for me?"

This question is not necessarily a worried or painful one. At bottom, it
is rather confident. It even lets itself be taken over by the contagion of
that incomparable serenity that, rightly or wrongly, I tend to attribute to
J. Hillis Miller. But it is revived and renewed constantly through all that I
have shared with him for so many decades.

"How does J. Hillis Miller *himself* feel *himself*?": This is a reverie that
I would like to share with you today. What is it to *feel oneself* [se sentir]?
To *feel* oneself, to sense oneself in the sense in which one lets oneself be
affected also by a feeling or a sensation? One cannot imagine this affect
without the figure of some *contact* with oneself, without an autoaffection
of touching and, more precisely, without that kind of intimate tactile sensi-
tivity that is enigmatically called *taste*.

Perhaps it is a matter here of what Gerard Manley Hopkins, in the
great texts that J. Hillis Miller has taught me to read, called "selftaste."
Selftaste constitutes all "selfbeing," all "selving," Hopkins tells us, "my

selfbeing, my consciousness, and feeling of myself, that taste of myself, of *I* and *me* above and in all things."[1]

How to accede to the "taste of myself" of another? How to feel or get a sense of the "taste of myself" of a very close friend, when proximity does not prevent the altogether close from remaining also an unknown? This is the question that has constantly plagued me during this long life of friendship I have had the unique chance to share with J. Hillis Miller.

For the exergues—they will be long and there will be two of them—I am going to turn things over, *justement*, to the specter of Gerard Manley Hopkins.

On two occasions, Hopkins appeals to the *just*. On two occasions at least, he names *the just*.

The Just: This is the nickname I am giving today to J. Hillis Miller, from where I think I feel, where I get the sense that he senses himself and has the taste of himself. This taste, his taste, would also have the taste of justice and rightness. "The Just": This is the name I think I have always set aside for him, in secret. It is the name of a virtue, to be sure, and an exemplary sense of responsibilities before others and before works, texts, the signatures of others. But it is also a gift that cannot be acquired, a simple way of being that one does not choose, a cheerful and natural "that's the way it is."

Hopkins does not name only the just; he also uses the word *justice*, but otherwise than as a noun. He has the magnificent audacity of an unusual verbal form: to *justice*, *justicing*, the act of doing justice, of justi*fying* justice, of *putting* justice *to work*, operating a justice that, by rendering justice outside, in the world and for others, remains itself, remains the justice it is, carrying itself out in the world without going out of itself. *To justice* is intransitive even if justice, *by justicing*, does something, although it does nothing that is an object. Justice shines forth, it radiates, and so does the just. That is what I wanted to say about Hillis. The just one has a gift. For Hopkins, it can only be a gift from God, who nevertheless leaves us free to be just in our own names and to say "je," "I" at the moment of being just. The just has the gift, he has the grace and the power to see to it that justice comes about outside itself in itself. He succeeds in making it happen that justice be justice, that justice *justices* without this being a simple tautology. It is given to the just, and the just gives himself the power to see to it that justice be produced justly, precisely, *by justicing*, as the justice it is, that it must be, and that it will have been. In the beginning will have been the verb: *to justice*.

With extraordinarily complex Latin roots, overloaded with Greek memory, the word "justice," as we know, can become a common abstract noun. The substantive *justice* names a concept. It says an idea, a value, a quality, a manner of judging, a judicial apparatus, always a juridical figure of right and of law. In its nominal form, justice can also designate in English the title or status of a person. Justice is the first person of a judge who can thus say "I," which the thing, the concept, or even the allegory that bear the name "justice" cannot do. I learned this use of the word "justice" the day I was married, in Boston in 1957, by a justice of the peace.

But there is a more important event for me, today, when I want to pay homage to the justice of the just that J. Hillis Miller has always been for me.

Which event? In a very rare case and by grace of a poet justly cited by J. Hillis Miller, *justice* can become a verb. It then designates a way of being, of shining forth, of radiating, and of acting, a way of doing things, most often with words, with the performative force of a speech act: *to justice*. To justice would be to produce justice, cause it to prevail, make it come about, as an event, but without instrumentalizing it in a transitive fashion, without objectifying it, but rather making it proceed from itself even as one keeps it close itself, to what one is, namely *just*, closest to what one thinks, says, does, shows, and manifests. The one who thus justices does not refer in the first or the last place to the calculable rules and norms of law. He is just by essence, just as he breathes. He does what is just, he accomplishes the just in a spontaneous manner. A spontaneous manner means freely, but especially as something that flows from the source, that emanates from its own source, *sponta sua*. Justice proceeds and *emanates* (it is thus *emanent*) from the one who justices, but this way of being and of doing, this manner of emanating remains also *immanent*, interior, in any case inseparable from the just himself, from the source of justice insofar as it justices. I will thus speak to you of a "just" that is just with a justice at once *immanent* and *emanent*.

That is why one must go back—this is decisive and will be my point of departure—to the apparently inventive performativity of a poetic event that, in order to say this, enriches the English language with an unheard-of usage. But through the poet, through his genius and ingenious performance, language itself affects us with this event. Language here is speaking an English that is heavily laden with an obscure Latin memory: *jus, jus jurare*, to swear an oath, an expression that must be understood, Benveniste tells us, as a verbal and ritualized formulation, as a speech act, if you will, rather than as the content of the oath (*sacramentum*).

My quotations of Hopkins will have a point in common. They are both expressions of praise. Praise of God, praise of man. God and man, both are the just, both are just ones. One of these expressions of praise resembles a performative, the other a constative. I say "resembles" because the frontier—and Miller is very aware of this risk—is not very certain between performative and constative, as is so often the case, and especially when one speaks *to* God *about* God.

What seems unique, when these two quotations are juxtaposed, is a certain chiasmus. In one case ("Thou art indeed just, Lord"), one seems to be dealing with the performative writing of an apostrophe or a prayer. But the performative of adoration includes a constative description ("Thou *art* indeed just, Lord"). In the other case ("the just man justices"), a statement of the constative type describes a way of being, let's say an ethics, and above all a way of doing that is essentially performative (to justice).

How is that? How does this chiasmus work? In its grammar and its logic, the poetic phrase resembles a constative. It describes the just man, namely, that just man who is today my subject. It also praises this just man. This just man is a man who "justices." But because he is just, inasmuch as he is just, in an immanent way and through emanation, he does or renders justice in a performative fashion. As for the other statement, which is just as poetic, it resembles a performative, an address, an apostrophe. The poet is now speaking *to* God; he raises up toward him his praise, that is to say, strictly speaking, a hymn. A hymn is always performative; it is an act of faith, an orison, a prayer. Devotion is engaged there as a promise of faithfulness. But the same statement also claims to *describe*, in a constative manner; here it describes justice as an attribute or predicate of God. It does everything to be just, in a performative manner, with the essence of God thus defined, but in order to adjust the rightness of its statement.

As far as I know, of these two writings of Hopkins, J. Hillis Miller cites only one, precisely the one that uses in a constative manner the word "justice" as a verb that nevertheless implies an action of a performative type. It is naturally thanks to Miller's book *The Disappearance of God* that I discovered this poem. I repeat that the verb describes a performative, but is not itself, in its structure, a performative. It says (and I will come back to this again) "the just man justices. . . ."

The contrary is true about the other poem that, in the performative mode of the hymn and of praise, claims to state what is the case. I will first read the several lines that J. Hillis Miller does not quote. I find them in a poem from 1889. It itself carries an exergue of a Latin quotation that will be like the *incipit* of the poem: "*Justus quidem tu es, Domine, si disputem tecum; verumtamen justa loquar,*" which becomes in Hopkins's language and beginning with the poem's first lines:

Thou art indeed just, Lord, if I contend
With thee; but, sir, so what I plead is just.

Since John the Evangelist, it is classic to address God, in the performative form of prayer, praise, and hymn, by calling him "the just," *justus* ("Justus quidem tu es, Domine," "Thou art indeed just, Lord"). Since at least the Gospel of John, to be just is one of the essential attributes, one of the proper names of God to which the prayer is addressed. In his famous *Mémorial*, the little paper found after his death that had been sewn into his garment eight years earlier, Pascal quotes from John's Gospel, when the latter cites the words and prayers of Jesus (we thus have the chain of transmitted words in "J": Just (God), Jesus (his son), John (the evangelizing disciple): *Pater juste, παπηρ δικαιε "Père juste, le monde ne t'a point connu, mais je t'ai connu.*" The King James Version translates this prayer by replacing *justus* or δικαιε with "righteous": "O righteous Father, the world hath not known thee: but I have known thee, and these have known that thou hast sent me."[2]

I insist again that the grammatical and logical form of the statement "Thou art indeed just" is constative. It is a question of describing the essence of God. God, you are always just. Always just, God is always right, *you* are always right, even when I contend with you so as to ask you, in a manner no less just, why sinners prosper. But we easily see that this descriptive and definitional, predicative, constative form is carried away and contained by a performative address, by an apostrophe close to praise and to the hymn. "Praise him," in the words of Hopkins that Miller often cites. It is an act of faith in God whose designs and whose justice surpass understanding. God is love, he is a friend. He is called with the vocative "my friend." This so very powerful friend could do me more harm than an enemy, but he does not. Here's the continuation of what I just quoted:

Wert thou my enemy, O thou my friend,
How wouldst thou worse, I wonder, than thou dost
Defeat, thwart me?[3]

As for the other lines that I will take as an exergue, J. Hillis Miller cited them and interpreted them in his magnificent reading of Hopkins, at the

end of *The Disappearance of God* (*DG*, 316), forty years ago. Many of you
were not born then, others were still young students. As for me, I had not
yet met a person or read anything of a work that will have mattered so
much for me throughout the rest of my life.

> . . . the just man justices;
> Keeps grace: that keeps all his goings graces;
> Acts in God's eye what in God's eye he is—
> Christ—

These are poems. J. Hillis Miller specifies the abbreviated reference,
P., for the edition of the *Poems* he is using. As for all the other citations,
by far the most numerous, they are signaled in the body of the text itself
by the letter *J* (an abbreviation chosen, as if by chance of course, for *The
Journals and Papers of Gerard Manley Hopkins*).

In the luminous and new interpretation that J. Hillis Miller proposes of
Hopkins and of these lines in particular, one might see at work, already,
forty years ago (but I will not overuse this retrospective teleology) everything that we are now almost accustomed to admire in the most recent
books: the inventive rigor of analysis, to be sure, but also the double concern with correctness and justice, the properly ethical care to articulate,
out of responsible fidelity to the other's text, theological, ontological, epistemological, literary questions; and to do it, preferably, while privileging
performativity or rather the question of the performative. There is here a
typically Millerian gesture, even if, in 1963, one did not yet have recourse
to the lexicon of Austinian speech-act theory, and above all to the prob-
lematization of the categories of performative and constative. This is one
of the strengths that always impresses me the most and that one must
salute as the courage of justice itself, but also (and I'll come back to this)
as his ethics of reading, which is also an ethics of writing and of teaching.
The Millerian gesture consists of always taking account, in order to render
an account, in order to do it justice, of what is most idiomatic in the opus,
in the operation itself, in the inimitable signature of the text studied, in
what *The Ethics of Reading*, precisely, will call the *example*, the ethical necessity of the singular example. As we read in the first pages of the latter
book, "There is no doing, in this region of the conduct of life, without
examples."[4] Miller's exemplary justice consists of paying essential attention to the irreplaceability of the example.

In the case of this line of verse, the idiom is not only the unique example, the odd use of the verb *to justice, justicing*. The interpretive approach
to this line mobilizes, precisely like its signature, like one of his signatures,

another of Hopkins's idiomatic inventions, namely, the strange and uncanny word "scape."

In the passage I'm preparing to read, the density of a word becomes unforgettable through Miller's grace and work. It is a question of the irreplaceable singularity of the word "scape." This word carries an enormous charge. It condenses and concentrates everything at stake in the Millerian interpretation. To put it quickly and abstractly, it is a matter of demonstrating that all the performativity put to work by Hopkins presupposes an ontology, a theology, and more precisely an epistemology, thus a knowledge of the constative type. This then is a presupposition. It is the postulated condition for the event, or even for the "felicity" of these performatives. There must first be a convention, itself performative, that stabilizes the consensus on the subject of this presupposed, so that poetic performativity takes on meaning and value. Or perhaps the poem itself is the production of this prior consensus in the very experience of writing-reading. At this point, reading and writing are indissociable. Hopkins's poetic invention, his very *oeuvre*, gives itself as the reading of the work, *l'oeuvre*, of God. The experience of Hopkins's reader is also called on to become writing in the same sense. The poetic act, the experience of the language, would thus be inseparable from these acts of Christian faith, in truth, from Christ himself. What is remarkable in the Millerian deciphering is the analysis of a *double performative*: After having elucidated the doctrine, that is, the constative knowledge, the ontotheology, the theology, or the epistemology that serves as presupposition or foundation of the performative stratum of the poetic act, one must bring to light a still more profound foundation. The stratum of the foundation has a constative appearance, to be sure. But it becomes a credible consensus only through a more originary engagement and thus through an initial performative, through the preperformative of a pre-event that precedes and prepares everything.

All of this comes to be itself signed, in some way, by the word "scape." This passage turns around the question of the poetic rhyme. It is above all a question of what, for Hopkins, makes of all men the rhymes of Christ. "All things rhyme in Christ," Miller recalls (*DG*, 313). To demonstrate this practically, poetically, to write it in a language that is at once faithful and new, Hopkins must take a step beyond cognition and recognition, beyond the "recognition that all things rhyme" (ibid., 316). But if I have read Miller correctly, this step beyond "recognition" finds itself guaranteed, assured, founded by a "doctrine," thus by a teachable theory, an ontotheology. This is what Miller then calls Hopkins's "epistemology." I am going to read this passage while interrupting the quotation several times:

"The doctrine of the common nature takes Hopkins one all-important step beyond the recognition that all things rhyme. The latter led to a sense that all nature is integrated, but is foreign to man. Hopkins's doctrine of Christ allows him to integrate man in the great chorus of created things. Man too is a scape of Christ" (*DG*, 316).

I interrupt my quotation for the first time.

"Man too is a scape of Christ." What does "scape" mean here? It's a word of Hopkins's that we will elucidate in a moment. We will follow Miller when he analyzes its history and what one could call its reinscription in Hopkinsian poetics. This will be worth a detour. I continue the quotation:

"Man too is a scape of Christ, and reflects Christ's image back to Christ at the same time as he affirms his own selfhood."

Before I pursue the analysis of this sentence ("Man too is a scape of Christ, and reflects Christ's image back to Christ at the same time as he affirms his own selfhood"), allow me to evoke a memory and to cite a fragment from a long letter Hillis sent me from Yale on June 25, 1977. Just a fragment because I must resist the temptation of anamnesis prompting me to reread the whole letter that recalls for me so many happy memories, between Yale, Paris, Geneva, and Zurich. Hillis says to me, toward the end of his letter:

I am in the middle of my NEH seminar for college teachers (on narrative theory), am trying (with some difficulty) to write my paper on Béguin [the accent on the é is added by hand because the letter is typewritten and there are no accents on the American keyboard], Balzac and Trollope for the Geneva colloquium. I shall argue that the model for literary creation and for moral action for Balzac, and for Béguin the critic, is God the Father, whereas the model for Trollope and his characters (as well for a different kind of criticism) is God the Son, but that the imitatio dei and the imitatio christi come in the end strangely to the same, since, as you say, all analogy is of the word, and to imitate God is of course to imitate Christ, that is to be Christlike, what G. M. Hopkins calls an "afterChrist." It will be hard to say all this and still keep on the right side of my old friend Georges Poulet, who is supposed to translate my essay into French, because in the end the imitator of Christ is the one who uses language performatively, that is, to bring something absolutely new, without measure, into the world, and at that point the imitatio Christi and the imitatio diaboli come to be the same thing, as Hopkins, Trollope and Balzac partly knew, though perhaps Béguin didn't.

Well . . .

After that, Hillis talks to me about all the work he has underway, including "a long essay on Shelley's 'The Triumph of Life,' which will go in *The Linguistic Moment*." He ends like this: "It is a way of demonstrating that *I must* [underlined] get out of the chairmanship when my term is up."

"Man too is a scape of Christ, and reflects Christ's image back to Christ at the same time as he affirms his own selfhood."

"His own selfhood": the "selfhood" of man. How is the "selfhood" constituted of a man who is but a "scape of Christ" and a reflecting image of the son of God? The first thing at stake in this great text by Miller is thus the question of the "self," or, as I would say, of ipseity. In Hopkins's extraordinary lexicon, what comes to effect, identify, think, prove this selfhood, in truth that by which selfhood affirms and produces itself, affects itself, "selves" itself, operates its own "selving," as Hopkins will say, is not thought, consciousness, or reflection but *taste*.

What is taste?

The great question of taste thus precedes here, and by a long way, all its consequences in the literal or metaphoric experiences of the *langue* (tongue or language), from gastronomy to the aesthetics of the fine arts, to literature, plastic arts, and poetry. I regret not having reread this text of Hillis's when I was writing *Touching, Jean-Luc Nancy*, for I would have learned a lot about the mysterious relations among taste, taste of self; the autoaffection that constitutes selfhood through the sensed experience of self, this autoaffection consists of touching oneself in taste, of tasting oneself in that "selftaste" that Miller tells us is "inimitable" and, quoting now Hopkins, "unspeakable" (*DG*, 272). "When I turn within I find only my own inimitable taste of self," Miller notes. Or yet again, to explicate Hopkins's word "unspeakable," to speak in turn of the "unspeakable," Miller takes himself as example when he says "I" in what is at once a pedagogical and rhetorical manner, but also in order to signal that, ontologically, grammatically, I am the only one, *un je*, an I is the only one able to say of himself, autoreferentially, autodeictally, that he is himself, in his selftaste, ineffable, that I alone can say and only say what exceeds language in the experience of my selftaste: "If it would be impossible to explain, to someone who had never tasted them, the taste of alum or clove, so it is even more impossible to explain to another man how I taste to myself. My selftaste is, literally, 'unspeakable.'" (*DG*, 271).

The isolation, the insularity of whoever is "selved"—and one should say "severed," "separated," "cut off," "removed"—is the experience of a "selfbeing," a "selfhood," a "self-awareness" that, long before *thinking itself*, long before the cogito, senses the taste of self. Miller gives the best formulation of the Hopkinsian version of the cogito: "I taste myself, therefore I am, and when I taste myself I find myself utterly different from everything else whatsoever" (*DG*, 271). To be sure, Descartes also defines the cogito by a certain "feeling," *sentir* ("But what then am I? A thing that thinks. What is that? A thing that doubts, understands, affirms, denies, is willing, is unwilling, and also imagines *and has sensory perceptions* [*et qui sent*]").[5] But to feel or to feel oneself, *sentir* or *se sentir*, is not specified by Descartes as taste. Either literally or figuratively.

Speaking dogmatically or elliptically, one could assert in two words that love and friendship are born in the experience of this unspeakable selftaste: an unshareable experience and nevertheless shared, the agreement of two renunciations to say the impossible. As for hatred, jealousy, envy, cruelty, they do not renounce. That is perhaps why they go together more often with knowledge, inquisitorial curiosity, the scopic drive, and epistemophilia.

As concerns selving, the privilege of taste, among the five senses, deserves a minute and patient analysis. Limiting myself to the least one can say, I will underscore that taste is the only tactile sense to share, with the sense of touch in general, the privilege of autoaffection, of the touching-touched for which the most frequently given example is the touching-touched of the fingers. But unlike all the other surfaces of the skin, taste is at once contact with the outside and contact with self inside the *mouth*, *lips, and tongue*. And the mouth, lips, and tongue are places of passage for speech, voice, and ingested food, thus for interiorization in general—along with autoaffection, idealization, mourning work, introjection, or incorporation, and so forth.

As I already suggested a moment ago, I am haunted by the question that a friend always asks about a friend, at once closer than another and infinitely other: What is J. Hillis Miller's "selftaste"? This question is perhaps more attentive, more surprised, more *interdite* as one says in French about what takes away your breath or speech; thus it is more questioning, more faithful than the question that amounts merely to wondering: "*What is J. Hillis Miller*" or "*Who* is J. Hillis Miller? What does he think of this or that? What does he do?" All these latter questions suppose that of self-taste. They all come down to asking oneself first of all: How does one feel within oneself? What is the singular and solitary taste that one feels in contact with oneself, at every moment, when one is oneself J. Hillis Miller? It is as if the question of selftaste went looking *behind* the name of someone to gain access, in secret, to the secret of his forename, his before-the-first first name. Why has the same J. Hillis Miller himself paid such sharp and lucid attention to this question of selftaste? For example and in a privileged way, to selftaste in Hopkins, in a singular context where the signature of a great poet remains indissociable from the experience of a thinker, linguist, philological etymologist with a keen passion for Greek and Latin, but above all of a highly cultured Christian theologian, and moreover so very Catholic, which ought to have distanced him from Hillis—not to mention from me.

Since the selftaste of selfhood, in its selving, remains indissociable from the scape, how is one to understand this latter word? One would have to follow closely here (but I will not be able to do so) all the stages and meanderings of the Millerian demonstration. As one knows, Hopkins, from a very young age, already as an undergraduate and in his first diaries, loved to indulge in etymological speculations. For example, he discovered with glee, in a dictionary by a certain Jamieson, the existence of the word "scape." It is another form of "skep" or "skip," meaning "basket" or "cage." Well, Hopkins forges the word "inscape," the use of which seems to be absolutely determining for his whole discourse, where poetics, the view of the world, and theology are mutually conditioning. They condition each other in truth in the signature of a Hopkinsian invention that came to countersign a possibility of the English language and its whole filiation. Miller goes straight toward this inscape. "Inscape" looks like an inimitable seal; it seals and signs Hopkins's work. The author of *The Disappearance of God* writes for example (but it's just one example among many others):

> His own word inscape always implies the sense of a skeletonlike structure which captures and encloses an inner principle of life, as a basket or a cage may imprison a wild bird of the air. The inner pressure of instress, permeating nature, is the true source of inscape, and brought into the open by it. This word is *in*-scape, the outer manifestation or "scape" of an inner energy or activity—not external pattern which is pleasing to the eye as design: "All the world is full of inscape and chance left free to act falls into an order as well as purpose: looking out of my window I caught it in the random clods and broken heaps of snow made by the cast of a broom." (*DG*, 289)

What is it I want to suggest with this reference, in the spirit and the opening of my question "who is J. Hillis Miller the Just?" What is the

selfhood of his selftaste, of that autoaffection that itself is implicated, precisely, in the performative force of the neologizing and idiomatic statement "The just man justices"? These idiomatic neologisms ("scape,"
"inscape") belong to the same series as "selftaste" and "justicing." Each
unique and irreplaceable time, a singularity exceeds the generality of the
language. It thus overflows the language itself. The singular says itself, but
it says itself as "unspeakable." What is strange and "queer" here is that all
this comes down to an experience and, in Hopkins's own words, to a sort
of theory of the queer, if not to the impossible uncanniness of a "queer
theory." And without hesitating to define the taste for the "queer" as a
"vice," or rather the becoming-vice of a virtue, the great Catholic poet
himself elaborates, theorizes, and formalizes his invention, at once his creation and his discovery, the truth of this "pattern" that he calls the inscape.

How does the word "queer" impose itself on Hopkins? How does it
come to qualify a kind of compulsion to vice? A famous letter to Robert
Bridges analyzes the common and analogous "pattern" that is found to be
at work in painting and in music as well as in poetry: "As air, melody, is
what strikes me most of all in music and design in painting, so design,
pattern or what I am in the habit of calling 'inscape' is what I above all
aim at in poetry" (*DG*, 281).

This inscape can in no way be reduced to the meaning or the thought-
out content of poetry, even if it requires them. Whence its untranslatabil-
ity, which is very near to its unspeakableness. The inscape exceeds the
meaning and is its own end, "inscape for the inscape's sake": "Poetry is
speech framed for contemplation of the mind by the way of hearing or
speech to be heard for its own sake. . . . Poetry is in fact speech only
employed to carry the inscape of speech for the inscape's sake—and therefore the inscape must be dwelt on" (*DG*, 282).

Miller insists that this motif, this end in itself of the inscape as "uniqueness of pattern," owes a lot to what Duns Scotus calls *haecceitas*, the ultimate principle of individuality. And he cites Hopkins again, just at the
point where the latter has recourse to the word "queer": "Now, it is the
virtue of design, pattern, or inscape to be distinctive and it is the vice of
distinctiveness to become queer. This vice I cannot have escaped" (*DG*,
281).

It is his destiny, his virtue, but also his vice, not to have managed to
escape the inscape. He was not able to escape the becoming-vice, the be-
coming-queer, of this virtue. Well, at the precise moment at which the
poem puts to verbal work such an inimitable pattern, it begins to resemble
what remains unspeakable in the selftaste of a man. When Miller notes

this by saying "A poem should have the same unspeakable stress of pitch that a man's selftaste has" (*DG*, 281), he remobilizes Hopkins's words in a passage where the latter is questioning himself, as I was doing a moment ago by wondering, in a childlike fashion, "*comment, justement, comment au juste*": "How precisely can one be J. Hillis Miller the Just?" "How can one be someone other than oneself while one is oneself?" "How can one be someone other than one's friend?" This is also to say: "How can one not or must one not, necessarily, be like him, oneself as himself?" It is thus that Hopkins describes at the same time his solitude and the unspeakable singularity of this selftaste, on the basis of which all the same he speaks, addresses himself to another, and gives to be shared just that, the unshareable of his own taste. This radical solitude, the isolation, or the insularity he analyzes belongs to the tradition of the *ultima solitudo* of Duns Scotus. I cite here again J. Hillis Miller so as to honor the key that was generously confided to me for my keynote address. Here is a key to Miller by Miller:

> The selftaste of Hopkins is what Scotus calls the *ultima solitudo* of man. At the deepest center of selfhood a man is alone. Each member of a group of such selves will be completely isolated from all the others. God must now be defined as the most individualized and unique person. As the most exquisitely tuned of all, God is the most isolated of all. God is the key which fits no finite lock. (*DG*, 330)

What is thus given to us to think, to the point of vertigo, is perhaps the divine character of solitude. But it is above all this, which we are not always ready to think: the terrible and uncanny solitude of God. God is alone. Of course, the solitude of human singularity is in the image of that of God. But God is the most solitary of all his creatures. As he is unique, exceptional, as he is alone in being God, by essence, by definition, par excellence, as he is all alone, as he is alone in being so alone, he is more alone than anyone, and he feels alone, so alone. His selftaste must have the terrifying flavor of solitude. But each time that we ourselves are alone, we begin to resemble him a little, he who is, himself, absolutely alone, isolated, insulated, or even abandoned in his absolute uniqueness, and in the hyperbole of his very ipseity. And if he is the just, he is that insofar as he is alone and exceptionally alone. A just one is always more alone than any other. Whence arises in us, by virtue of this analogy, a kind of pity, compassion, and thus love for what must be the suffering of such an implacable solitude as that of God. We are tempted to pity God, who is infinitely alone, still more alone, infinitely more alone than each of us. The movement of praise, prayer, hymn, address to God the Just thus proceeds also from this compassion that is born in us from the very solitude of our own selfhood, our own selftaste. If we are alone in our ipseity, and in our selftaste, how still more alone God must be, but also how well we understand him, how consenting and compassionate we are!

But this very compassion cannot cross the abyss of solitudes. On the contrary, it only makes the abyss deeper. It is a little as if we were asking ourselves: How can one be as alone as God? How to endure this uniqueness? And what can be the selftaste of God the Just?

It is still the same question. If it is the same, that is because it is borne by this doctrine of the univocity of being according to which the word "being" has the same sense for God and for his creatures. God *is* God, therefore God *is* alone, alone in *being* God, and he *is* alone *as* we *are* alone, and each time, the word "being," the copula "to be" in "he is alone" and "we are alone," has the same sense. Being is there *univocal*, and that is why, by analogy, we understand the solitude of God: He is alone like us, which pains us very much, and that is why we love him. We do not love him (this is at least the hypothesis I am risking for the fun of it) because he is a sovereign and all-powerful father, generous and formidable, giving and forgiving. We love him because he is alone, the poor fellow, the loneliest of all beings, and thus as vulnerable, in his divinity, as an abandoned child. This is not necessarily Christian thinking, as you might well suspect, even if it could become so, for example, for a Catholic like Hopkins, although it is not exactly his argument or his language here. This solitude of the unique, at once ineffable, abandoned, and vulnerable, mute as a child, is also what we imagine with regard to all those we love, friends and lovers. It is here that arises the "queer," the properly ontotheological dimension of which I will specify in a moment, but also perhaps its excess, in prayer, over ontotheology. And because it's a matter of representing to oneself God, this other, as an abandoned child, infinitely unique and vulnerable, thus mortal to the point of an immortality that can also look like hell, the thinking that I am describing in this way resembles the thinking of an old man. At whatever age it comes to us, it is the thinking of the greatest old age. Is it not the thinking of someone who is already, since forever, older than what he or she loves or pities in this manner?

Still, according to the powerful gesture that consists of exhuming a constative or preperformative stratum of presupposed knowledge beneath the layer of poetic performativity, Miller is right to insist, here again, on the Scotist ontotheology that subtends this whole poetics of the inscape. As we know, Scotus, the thinker of the univocity of being, the thinker for whom the word "being" has the same meaning for God and for creatures, was Hopkins's indisputable master. Hopkins misses no opportunity to recall this. And precisely on the subject of the inscape. He writes for example: "just when I took in any inscape of the sky or sea I thought of Scotus" (*DG*, 314).

One could demonstrate, although I won't have the time to do so here, that this doctrine of the univocity of being is the ultimate origin and the very experience of absolute solitude that we were speaking of a moment ago. It is the origin of what is queer in the inscape, but also in *being*. To be is to be queer. Is it the equivalent of "uncanny" or *unheimlich* according to the use Freud and Heidegger make of these words? The question is unlimited. If it's a question of translation, it will remain open, beyond the multiplicity of languages, where the analogic transfer involves also the equivocity or univocity of being, where selftaste exceeds both the analogy and language:

And this [my isolation] is much more true when we consider the mind; when I consider my selfbeing, my consciousness and feeling of myself, that taste of myself, of *I* and *me* above and in all things, which is more distinctive than the taste of ale or alum, more distinctive than the smell of walnutleaf or camphor, and is incommunicable by any means to another man (as when I was a child I used to ask myself: what must it be to be someone else?). Nothing else in nature comes near to this unspeakable stress of pitch, distinctiveness, and selving, this selfbeing of my own. Nothing explains it or resembles it . . . searching nature I taste *self* but at one tankard, that of my own being. The development, refinement, condensation of nothing shews any sign of being able to match this to me or give me another taste of it, a taste even resembling it. (*DG*, 271)

What is the paradox of these statements? To be sure, they depend, as Miller has clearly shown, on Hopkins's whole poetics, which itself implies an ontology, the one that poses the univocity of being. And yet they constitute an exception to that ontology, as soon as no taste of self resembles any other, not from one man to another, or from one living being to another, or from a finite living being to God. There is only the unique. The law is always a law of exception.

One of Miller's daring moves that most seduced, convinced, and impressed me, and not only in the reading of Hopkins, is the articulation of this poetics of selftaste and inscape with the *thought* of the hidden God. I say "thought" of the hidden God because it is perhaps more and something other than a knowledge, a philosophy, or even a theology, including a negative theology. It is a question of thought, experience, the experience of thought and literary writing, of the very literary experience that, throughout *The Disappearance of God,* Miller interprets so lucid and faithfully, so justly, with *justice et justesse,* justice and correctness, in the works of five English-language writers, so as to uncover there an inflexible necessity.

God is hidden not only because one never sees him himself, but because he never *responds* to anyone in person. This is what we are taught by the thinking of literature, by literary responsibility, on the side of the writer and of the reader. Just before citing Hopkins once again ("God, though to Thee our psalm we raise / No answering voice comes from the skies"), Miller had described in a striking fashion this situation of modern literature, beginning in the nineteenth century. He calls it a "religious situation," but it is a religious site whose place is, by essence, deserted. It is a nonplace deserted by God, who has withdrawn from it or separated himself from it. Like the most solitary anchorite in the world. And like a writer. What Miller then says about presence, and above all about impossible presence, involves his discourse, quite evidently, already in 1963, in a deconstruction *avant la lettre*: deconstruction, therefore, as justice. I no longer remember who it was who dared to say that deconstruction is justice. Contrary to the persistent rumor, Miller did not convert, one fine day, to deconstruction. The latter is already at work beginning with his first book. One has just to read. One recognizes the taste of it in what he says about the singularity of taste, the limits of language, *logos,* thus logocentrism, and especially about what exceeds and divides presence:

> God does not exist as a manifest being, immanent in the works of the creation. When I ask where my throng and stack of being comes from, nothing I see can *answer* me. When I turn within, I find only my own inimitable taste of self. Neither within nor without is God anywhere *directly present to me*. He exists only as a necessary deduction from my discovery of myself as the most highly pitched entity in the creation. Having created me and the rest of the world, he has apparently withdrawn from his handiwork, and lives somewhere above or beyond or outside, occupied with his own inscrutable activities. He is a God that hides himself. This is the religious situation in which many men of the nineteenth century find themselves, and it is the situation which is described in Hopkins's early poems. (*DG,* 272–73, emphases added)

And after the blank between two sections of his essay, Miller quotes Hopkins. The latter is speaking *to* God who does not answer; he addresses the other *performatively,* in order to point out *constatively* that the other never answers (as many, indeed almost all philosophers, say about the animal, in sum—the animal can make signs but never knows how to answer—and as Lévinas says of the dead, who are not annihilated, but simply no longer answer; I believe there is much that can come from following the path that leads us to this historical observation: the so very heedless attribution of nonresponse to the animal, to God, and to the dead). Hopkins speaks *to* God and of God; he invokes and states:

> God, though to Thee our psalm we raise
> No answering voice comes from the skies (*DG*, 273)

2

Have I reached the end of my exergues, and thus of my hors d'oeuvres? Is there room, in a poetics of the "queer," like that of Hopkins's, for some hors d'oeuvre (*ex ergon*)? In truth, there is nothing but hors d'oeuvre and nothing is hors d'oeuvre, nothing is outside the work. My epigraphs, in sum, were but a preliminary reflection on this at once interminable and impossible thing that is called the exergue. Every hors d'oeuvre (*ex ergon*) resembles first of all the reflecting part of that about which or the one about whom he is speaking or to whom he addresses himself, namely, par excellence, the work of the other that is hidden and does not answer, even if I cannot dispense with answering to it and for it. To abandon or pursue an exergue is finally the same renunciation and the same insistence.

Let us insist. For someone who, like me, writes only in French; for someone who, like me, was raised in the cult of the idiom and in the culture of French letters; for someone who, like me, has been confused for almost his whole life by the immemorial and uncanny *règle du jeu*, the rule of the game between the French *G*, which is pronounced like the English *J*, or the English *G*, which is pronounced *J* in French; for someone like me, whose selftaste has always distilled its nectar from a certain taste of the French language; for someone like me, who, for better or worse, mixes the taste of the French language with everything, it is difficult, without first having strayed in the labyrinth between the two languages, between the two ways of speaking, to accept to pronounce the same letter from one language to the other. It is difficult, I say to myself, to begin imprudently to say "je," as I did by saying:

J'aurais dû commencer, I should have begun. . . . *Je me dis d'abord*, I say to myself first that my French *J* will have been lost from the first letter of the first word. I'm not talking here about my first name, but about my *je*, my I and my *jeu* with *je*, my play with I. *Je* (I) will have withdrawn, effaced itself from the first letter of the first word. *Je est un autre*. I is another one. Nevertheless, I and I alone should answer for such an effacement. *J'en suis responsable*. I am responsible for it.

So many untranslatable Js, already!

So many letters involved, already, *dans le jeu*, in the game we are asked to play and in the rules of the game, *les règles du jeu* that are imposed on us here, today.

Among so many letters, and among those that I have received, for thirty-five years, from Hillis and that are all very dear to me, there is one that seemed to forecast today's lecture and keynote, from more than thirty years' distance. It dates from 1969. In a moment I will read its postscript. This postscript came down like a verdict on my original sin, on the first wrong against friendship I committed against Hillis, against his name, his hidden first name, precisely, *justement*, as to his letter *J*. I still blush when I think of it.

When they impose the use of certain letters of the alphabet on a Frenchman or a nonnative speaker, allowing, for example, "J" to make the law, the *règles du jeu*, these rules of the game are perverse. They invite us to cheat; they provoke us to break the law by speaking a language other than the language of the law. That all laws are perverse is no doubt something that will have always kept J. Hillis Miller going. Among all the originalities that are increasingly recognized in his immense *oeuvre*, Miller is well known for having constantly exposed his work as theoretician of language and of literature, within and beyond the Anglo-American and Victorian fields, to the question and the demands of the law (and not merely the ethical law, but also the juridical and political law). None is presumed to be ignorant of the law, as we say. The terrible paradox of the law, what destines it to terror and terrorism, is that, despite its universal structure, it is formulated always in the performative of an event in a national language or in a singular idiom that none is presumed to ignore. That is to say, in the literality of a letter. Is the literarity of literature simply foreign to the literality of this letter? This is another question that, in so many diverse forms, will have traversed, crisscrossed, tormented Miller's very singular work.

This paradox is further sharpened when the content of the literal prescription is the privileged use, in the title and in the name of a text, and thus in its dominant theme, of a single letter: *J*. And not merely of a letter that is not pronounced the same from one language to the other, but that twice comes at the head: at the head at the head, *en arkhē*. At the beginning of the beginning, at the beginning as title and at the beginning of the word must be, not the *logos*, but the letter *J*. For example, "Justices."

For two reasons. First of all, because the title is the heading on the letterhead, *l'entête*, of the text. (*Entête* is moreover a possible French translation, literal and published by A. Chouraqui, of *Genesis*, at the beginning of the Bible.) But also because this letter must figure the initial of a common noun or a name, even of a proper first name. And when it is the initial of a proper first name, it lets itself be heard as what I will call an absolute, sovereign letter. The use of this singular initial, especially in the Anglo-Saxon world, has always seemed to me obscurely related to the subtle rites that oversee, in certain Hebrew traditions, for certain mystics or apophatic theologians, the approach to or avoidance of the name of God, of the God hidden, precisely, between living speech, appellation, and writing. In the name *J*. Hillis Miller, the *J*. is never completed; it interrupts its own movement, remains alone, followed by a kind of final period or expectant point. In French, one might call it a *point de suspension*, but a single suspension point that therefore resembles a full stop. Closure, absolute interruption, separation, secret. This is indeed what happens with the *J*. of J. Hillis Miller, at least in ordinary situations, whether one writes it, sees it, or hears it mentioned. In all these cases, in all these uses, which are uses of mention (that's right, I said *mentioning* uses), and, I suppose, except for official documents like a passport, the *J*. remains alone and stands like the absolute initial the rest of which one does not have to know. The *J*. remains without the rest. But this situation is restricted, I repeat, to uses that consist of *mentioning* the name, whether on the cover of a book, some document or other, or as an address on an envelope, or else orally, when one mentions it to designate J. Hillis Miller as a third person: for example, if one says or writes "He, J. Hillis Miller, is the great professor and the famous great theoretician of literature and of so many other things, who, and so forth. . . . " On the other hand, the *J*., as initial of a first name, is never *used*; one never makes *use* of it; it is always silenced. It is always passed over in silence when, performatively, one *calls* the bearer of this name, J. Hillis Miller. When one calls him, one calls him Hillis, or Mr. Miller, or Professor Miller, but never J. Hillis or J. Hillis Miller. Here is someone, close to us, a great friend, an eminent colleague, a respectable professor, whose work we are going to celebrate under the sign of his *J*., the ineffaceable initial and the absolute incipit of all his names. Well, throughout his whole life, this man, J. Hillis Miller, will never have been *called J.* or *J. Hillis*. No one, I assume, will ever have addressed him by saying, "Hi, J.!" or "Hi, J. Hillis!" *J.* is like someone to whom one will never be able to speak. *J.* is a phantom whom no one will ever have dared to address in a vocative fashion, in the space and time of a performative apostrophe. It is like a hidden God in his name, a God to whom one would not even be allowed to destine a prayer, a hymn, a praise. This is to say that today, since I intend to praise him, I will perhaps speak *of J.* and *of J.* Hillis Miller, but I will never address him, I will in no case speak *to* J., only *to* Hillis. I will speak *of* J. Hillis Miller but I will speak only *to* Hillis.

Now, with your permission, I confess and make public my original sin, namely, the first wrong I committed against *J.* as against the hidden God of this first name. In 1969, I had known Hillis for a year; we were already linked by friendship, thanks to another Hopkins, this time Johns Hopkins. We were then teaching together, and we already had our Tuesday lunches, a tradition that continued from Hopkins to Yale and still continues at Irvine thirty years later. Well, I was at the time foolish enough and thought myself clever enough to believe I was capable of deciphering on my own the hidden first name behind the *J.* I was also ignorant enough of American customs to exhibit presumptuously the result of my supposed discovery. I thus wrote to Hillis, no doubt more than once (I have no archive of this), letters whose envelopes bore the address: John Hillis Miller. I probably committed this wrong very many times, to Hillis's amusement or irritation, when I received from him, on June 2, 1969, a long, beautiful, and richly detailed letter (where it was a question of Nietzsche, *Beyond Good and Evil*, of différance, of the cogito, of Poulet once again, of time and space, of an article soon to appear by de Man on Poulet in *Critique*, etc.). Then, in two lines, came a postscript. Here it is: "By the way, my first name is 'Joseph,' not 'John,' not that it matters in the least, since I've never used that name in any case!"

Exclamation point. By saying that he had "never used" it, he meant that no one, no one in the world (except me, in sum, and then wrongly!) had ever used it to call him, in the performative, vocative, and apostrophizing mode of address. No one had ever addressed him by calling him "Hi, J. Hillis!" or "Hi, Joseph Hillis!"

Here then is the initial of a name before the name, here is the initial of a hidden first name that, by a sort of sacred prescription, it is forbidden to approach or pronounce in ordinary life and every day. Something like a divine first name hidden in the name. Is it forcing things to sense here an analogy with everything Hillis has taught us to think, from the beginning, under the title of *The Disappearance of God*? For a long time, I have wondered, in general and not just on the subject of the strange phenomenon of his *J.*, how Hillis felt, how he lived, within himself, between him and himself, this singularity of the relation to the singularity of his name. And I still wonder if, and how, across the incredible richness, impressive diversity, and secret continuity of all his works, one can identify, as one might identify a key, the law of this relation to self, this taste of self that must link him to something that, before the name, would resemble a hidden first name. The theme of what he calls, in 1963, the "gradual withdrawal of God from the world" (*DG*, 1) is recalled once again, beginning with the exurge of the final chapter, the one Hillis devotes to Hopkins. It is a quotation from Isaiah (45:15): "Verily, Thou art a God that hidest thyself." Address to God: The hidden God is apostrophized, he is called by his name, but called at the very moment when this performative appeal describes, states, defines the absence, withdrawal, separation, the inaccessible secret that forbids us the very essence of God, thus the form of his substantial presence. The essence always says a presence. Here, the essence is called absence, *in absentia*. To say to God, "You are hiding" is another way of saying, at least in the language of ontotheology: As for you, you are not, you do not even exist. A performative contradiction, *n'est-ce pas*. How can one say to someone "you do not exist"? Unless behind the aspect of a peaceful constative, this declaration were a declaration of war, a threatening or murderous performative. This is the whole history of relations between faith and prayer, on the one hand, and ontotheology on the other. I think it was, from the beginning, a focal point of the Millerian meditation. As Heidegger notes in *Identität und Differenz*, to the God of the philosophers, to the God of ontotheology, to the *Causa Sui*, to the Ground of what is, one can address neither prayers, nor sacrifices, music, nor dance. I would add: neither a poem nor literature in general.

What then is one doing when one makes a mistake with the hidden name of God? I don't know if Hillis kept my letters and my envelopes. I hope he has not preserved the archive of the offenses I committed against his hidden first name. The wrong of which I repent did not consist merely in having claimed to reveal publicly and display a hidden first name on an envelope readable in the world and by everyone. But also to have done so, in the very act, doubly wrongly: by exhibiting the presumed body of his first name and by substituting for it another. According to a Jewish tradition that Lévinas discusses, when a mistake in spelling or transcription of the name of God comes to alter a manuscript, this manuscript must be neither destroyed nor burned (for one does not annihilate the name of God) nor preserved (for one does not keep the trace of such a blasphemy).

The parchment must in that case be buried. One must hide it and put it in a safe place, but keep it at the same time invisible and illegible. Moreover, a mistake with the name of God can be destined only to illegibility; it is illegibility itself. But there are veritable cemeteries of faulty manuscripts, underground libraries, special collections, and they are earthquake-safe. What is more, are not all our libraries made up of, even full of such buried blasphemies? What I have just done by confessing is a little like the burial of a bad *J*, an intruder, John having come to usurp the legitimate place of Joseph.

This is a violence that befell so many Josephs in the Bible. Concerning Joseph the fiancé or the husband of Mary (not to be confused with Joseph of Arimathea, the one who asked Pilate for Christ's corpse), the New Testament, as has often been remarked, has finally too little to say. That constitutes a first injustice. But it is true that Matthew describes him, *justement*, as a "just" man. When Mary discovers she is with child by the Holy Spirit, "Joseph her husband, being a *just* man (Matthew underscores δικαιοσ, *justus*), and not willing to make her a publick example, was minded to put her away privily" (Matt. 1:19). As for the other Joseph, the first one, the one from the Old Testament and Genesis, the favorite son of Jacob, the one who was called "master of dreams," Freud's ancestor, you recall that his brothers threw him into a pit and sold him for twenty pieces of silver to a caravan of Ishmaelites that took him to Egypt (Gen. 37:23–28).

It is thus under the sign of these two testaments and these two Josephs that I wanted to inscribe this admiring and grateful homage to my friend Joseph Hillis Miller: Joseph the carpenter, Joseph the Just, on the one hand, and Joseph the reader, the master in deciphering, on the other, the one who, like Hillis, knew how to recognize the stakes and the political future of his decipherings, how to take into account the evolution of sciences and techniques, of modes of production and archiving of knowledge, and who in Egypt was also, as is well known, that incomparable man of the institution who, in the words of a pharaoh vis-à-vis whom he jealously kept his independence up until the end, passed for "a man discreet and wise."

To these two Josephs from the Old and the New Testaments, I could have added, or even preferred other Josephs. These other Josephs are the inhabitants of a literature with which Hillis is familiar, authors or heroes of fiction who, each one in his irreplaceable singularity, all had the privilege of being recognized and seeing a place set aside for them in the Millerian architectonics. I am not suggesting that the first name Joseph is the

key here of a crypt (for if I had to bury my fault, namely, the guilty substitution of the name John for Joseph, one can also say that Joseph had already been encrypted and reduced to silence in the initial *J.*, since Hillis
tells me he "never used that name"; well, I say to myself in order to lessen
my guilt somewhat, without this strange crypt, I would never have made
the fatal mistake). Although I have resisted it, the temptation would have
been great to bring back under the first name Joseph, as with the key of a
crypt, all the voices that are crossing in Hillis's work. For despite the immensity of the trajectory and the impressive diversity of so many works
devoted to Victorian literature, more generally to English, American,
German, and French literatures, to literary theory, to rhetoric, to linguistics, but also to teaching, to the university institution, to the history and
the problems of canons in mutation, to so-called cultural studies, to new
technologies, to ethics, politics, painting, all of these new advances putting
to work theology, philosophy, linguistics, the pragmatics of speech acts,
and so forth, one may wonder if, across the incredible multiplicity of these
voices, some invariable signature, for which one would search out precisely
the key, the musical key, does not come to seal and dissimulate the unity
of a selfhood, of a selftaste, but also and by the same token, of a single
vocal timbre, of a single character, in the sense at once of personality, soul,
psyche, or psychology—and of the literal graphism. Is there, in this sense
of the word "character," a characteristic seal of Joseph Hillis Miller? By
convoking here so many witnesses named Joseph, haven't I, by means of
successive approaches and variations, been conducting a sort of experimentation that attempts to identify such a "character"? When I formulate
such a question in this way, I am referring once again to something Proust
said and that already in 1963, more than thirty years before his wonderful
studies of Proust (among the most remarkable I have read, even in my
language, and I am thinking in particular of "Fractal Proust" in *Black
Holes*), Hillis placed in exergue to the very opening of *The Disappearance of
God*. As translated by Miller, Proust said in his *Pastiches et mélanges*: "For
a writer, as for a musician or a painter, the multiplicity of works provides
that variation of circumstances which makes it possible to discern, by a
sort of experimentation, the permanent traits of character."

Before I greet in passing the other Josephs that I thought I should invite
by confiding to them the key to this celebration, allow me to confide in
you what I have the effrontery to believe, despite or because of my original
sin. This: It would be just to grant me here, besides the privilege of senior-
ity, a few other privileges. My right to the key, to the keys, would be first
of all the right of my discourse to link indissociably emotion to reflection,

the personal inflection of admiration and affection with the more neutral tonalities of theoretical, philosophical, even institutional analysis. For nothing in the world would I have passed up the chance to recall publicly that it has been given to me, like a benediction, to know Joseph Hillis Miller for more than thirty-five years, to have had the honor of teaching at his side and most often thanks to him in all the American universities that have welcomed me, from Johns Hopkins, between 1968 and 1974, to Yale, from 1975 to 1986, to Irvine, since 1987; the honor also of having shared with him more than with any other, through I don't know how many countries, colloquia, meetings of all sorts, the intellectual adventure that signs and seals our lives—and this always while breathing with him the air of serene friendship and unfailing loyalty. Those who know the world a little, and within it the academic world, will agree with me: The thing is more than rare, no doubt it is unique, exceptionally exceptional. Whether it is language, history, style, gesture, character, all kinds of idio-syncrasies, selfhood and selftaste, so many differences separate us, Hillis and me, which is all too obvious and everyone here knows this, in the first place both of us know it. Well, never has the shadow of a dispute, never has the least cloud transformed these singularities into discord. The credit for this goes to what I call Hillis's justice and, what is not to be distin-guished from it, his ethics of friendship. Hillis is just in friendship, and first of all in his work of reading and writing. I dare to think that it is the same thing, the same spirit and the same law. The same relation to the law.

I want to speak now of this probity by evoking, besides the two epony-mous Josephs of the two Testaments, a few Josephs who are more literary, who were no doubt, in one regard or another, their descendants. As I tried to show elsewhere, in *The Gift of Death*, literary writing, in the strict and modern sense of the word, remains, whether it knows it or not, the child of the Bible, an at once faithful, sacred, attested, and unforgivably unfaith-ful heir of the holy scriptures from which it constantly, without confessing it, asks forgiveness for a perjury while repenting before them.

I could have looked for these heirs of the Old and New Testament Josephs, and I would have found them, in the person of Joseph Conrad, for example, the author of *Lord Jim* (here we have already two Js, one of which, Jim, forenames all the Jameses that haunt Miller's work, starting with a certain Henry, not to mention a certain Joyce). As regards Joseph Conrad, Joseph Hillis Miller has luminously reinterpreted what is called his "nihilism," but especially what *Victorian Subjects* mentions in passing, namely, "the complex use of multiple narrators."[6] This allusion is meant to draw our attention again to the braiding and bunching of the multiple narrative voices to which Miller, in every reading, is intent on doing justice, and to all the keys that might have set the musical key, today, for my modest lecture.

I could have looked for other heirs, and once again I would have found them, in the direction this time not of authors, like Joseph Conrad, but of characters. Think, for example, of the Joseph in *Wuthering Heights*. In *Fiction and Repetition*, this Joseph rejoins a theory of phantoms, precisely, but also a theory of literary and novelistic spectrality. One sees there a cohort of egos pressing together, a lively crowd of singular *je* or I's; one witnesses their *unheimlich* return in the figure of the living dead come out of their crypt: "With that 'I' the reader brings back also the moment in the fall of 1801 when his 'I have just returned' is supposed to have been written or spoken. By way of that first 'I' and first present moment the reader then resurrects from the dead, with Lockwood's help, in one direction Hindley, Nelly, Joseph, etc."[7]

Or, again, the conclusion of the chapter, that moment where the dispersion of the Josephs, the infinite solitude of the homonymous Josephs engages the play, *le jeu* of the multiplicity of *je*, of I's, of the words (*je*, "I"), where the anguish of justice, of the universality of the law kept at bay by dissociated singularities, tightens in our throat and cuts off our breath. We have difficulty speaking and breathing each time a *je entre en jeu*, each time an I enters the game, that is, when what is most universal, the most commonly shared thing in the world, namely, the possibility and the right to say "I," the very condition of the homonymy of all the *Je* and Josephs, is also reduced to the most singular, the most solitary, the most untranslatable, the most unshareable, the most "unspeakable," like selftaste itself. This nameless taste, this incommunicable taste will always prevent homonyms or homophones from becoming synonyms.

Joseph is anyone whatsoever. A pseudonym for anyone whatsoever. Me or the wholly other. But Joseph is all the same irreplaceable. *Comme tout autre*: like every other as being wholly other. And every other is anyone whatsoever. There are only exceptional *examples* that at the same time found and defy the universal law. One day it will be necessary to study the untiring work on the question of *exemplarity* from one end to the other of Miller's work. To read a text, to respond to the injunction of its singularity, is always to bind and bend oneself to an example. In a very fine essay destined first of all for the University of California Humanities Research Institute on the theory of translation, on the translation of theory and the "travel of theory," an essay that is itself the unprecedented study of an example, the biblical Ruth, where "the story of Ruth can be taken as a parable of the translation theory," Hillis writes: "There is no work of theory without examples. The examples are essential to theory."⁸ But at the same time, *The Ethics of Reading* reminds us that

> no choice of examples is innocent. It is a somewhat arbitrary selection for which the chooser must take responsibility. On the other hand, there is no doing, in this region of the conduct of life, without examples. This is as true of philosophical treatises on ethics as it is of literary study, as I shall demonstrate by means of an example from Kant. . . . Without storytelling there is no theory of ethics.⁹

Isn't this the best way of saying at the same time the origin and the end of ethics? Its end as eschatology and its end as limit, its term and its death? The limit itself? Isn't this the condition of any ethical injunction? Of any metaethical question about ethics? But also the inevitability of a failure, of an intrinsic betrayal and perjury, which are imminent to fidelity itself? Isn't it above all what gives us to think justice in its essential link to law, as well as its irreducibility to law, its resistance, its heterogeneity to law? Which would amount to seeing a suddenly looming justice break the surface, a justice that will always exceed law, but without which law itself, *by justicing*, would never begin to exhaust itself going after justice.

That, it seems to me, is the endless path Miller is pursuing. After having named Joseph in this discourse on the spectral resurrection of the dead (I cite again: "By way of that first 'I' and first present moment the reader then resurrects from the dead, with Lockwood's help, in one direction Hindley, Nelly, Joseph . . ."), Miller concludes, and it is as if the word "I" were inaugurating, in the first person, the very grammar of all spectrality, as if the "I" still wore, like a mask, the "I" of a revenant:

> Words no different from those we use in everyday life, "I have just returned," may detach themselves or be detached from any present moment, any living "I," any immediate perception of reality, and go on functioning as the creators of the fictive world repeated into existence, to use the verb transitively, whenever the act of reading those words is performed. The words themselves, there on the page, both presuppose the deaths of that long line of personages and at the same time keep them from dying wholly, as long as a single copy of *Wuthering Heights* survives to be reread.¹⁰

Among so many other originalities, I would like to insist on what is most singular in Miller's work, on what detaches itself remarkably, as inimitably Millerian, within the landscape of the most notorious affinities, proximities, resemblances of the last two or three decades. What calls and is called, under the name and the signature of J. Hillis Miller, would be an untiring and permanent urge to *answer*. To answer responsibly in his name, for his name, to be sure, but while answering for responsibility itself. To answer for responsibility, and for what ties and obligates it to justice, is to think responsibility by formulating and formalizing its possibility, as well as its aporia. Ethical responsibility (which is also to say juridical and political responsibility) that is exposed not only in what is called life or existence, but in the task of deciphering, reading, and writing. This is a task to which, as we know, Miller has devoted, that is, given, all his gifts: as teacher and writer, but also as citizen, and citizen of the world, and even beyond all citizenship, without any other title. No one says better than he this *necessity*, if not this *truth* of response. The distinction of necessity from truth appears in the very epigraph of the Wellek Lectures, delivered right here in 1985, under the title *The Ethics of Reading*. A quotation from *The Trial* by Kafka says something about this tension between *truth* and *necessity*. What the priest confides to Joseph K. remains in a certain way without any response other than a melancholy sigh: " 'No,' said the priest, 'it is not necessary to accept everything as true, one must only accept it as necessary.' 'A melancholy principle,' said K. 'It turns lying into a universal principle' " (" 'Trübselige Meinung,' sagte K. 'Die Lüge wird zur Weltordnung gemacht' "). In the last chapter of the book, "Re-vision: James and Benjamin," Miller, like the man and like Joseph K. before the law, explains to us why he must answer before the law that is the other's text, but also how, having to respond by adding something of his own, by countersigning, he risks, he *even must* risk, with the performativity of his response, doing more or less than answering faithfully to the text's demand; he must risk lying, then, by not responding loyally even while responding in the most upright manner possible—that is, also while reading himself, while analyzing vigilantly his *selftaste*, while also analyzing, through examples, writers who likewise, already, read and analyze themselves:

> My question throughout this book has been whether reading can also be an ethical act, a performance, part of the conduct of life, with its own measurable effects and consequent responsibilities. My focus throughout has been on only one corner of this field, those places where we can see an author reading himself or herself. . . . Such passages, I have implicitly claimed, are therefore exemplary for interrogation of the question of the ethics of reading. In following through one small arc of the trajectory of that prodigious act of re-reading as re-vision which is recorded in James'

"Prefaces," I want to make James' text my law. I want to follow what he says with entire fidelity and obedience, to see whether what he says about the ethics of reading may be made the basis of a universal legislation. This book has explored various acts of self-reading in Kant, de Man, Eliot, Trollope, and now James. It has also been itself all along an example of what it is about. I have performed acts of reading of my own which are both responses to an ethical demand made by the texts I have read and at the same time ethical acts themselves which may have performative force in their turn on my readers. This power of acts of writing and then of reading to engender a limitless chain of *further* [my emphasis] such acts is in fact one theme of that last paragraph of all in the last preface, the preface to *The Golden Bowl.*[11]

It would be interesting to reread, in the same spirit, Miller's own re-reading of himself, here as well in a preface: the 1975 preface, written at Yale, to the second edition of *The Disappearance of God.* Among so many other things, one is convinced of the necessity of conceiving literary criticism as an "international enterprise," of the necessity of "generosity" in reading, "a willingness to accept what one finds in an author and to go all the way with him"; and finally the necessity of "self-subverting insights," "the analogue in literature and in criticism for Gödel's incompleteness theorem," according to which "any formal system will lead ultimately to conclusions which cannot be encompassed within its original assumptions."

The risk and the aporia will always have to disturb this responsibility. It will always be deprived of certitude, knowledge, and assurance. To be sure, it must surround itself with science and vigilance, it belongs to the *Aufklärung* of modern times and times to come, but nothing ought to dissipate every shred of darkness in it. To respond faithfully, to obey loyally the text's demand, as with any injunction whatsoever, I must not only listen and read, I must write in order to put to work and to the test the maxim of a universal legislation. I must sign a new text, issue another pledge that, however faithful it may be, will still signify something else as well and thus will risk betraying the demand, betraying it out of fidelity, in order to exert an unforeseeable and, by definition, improvident "performative force" on readers, to convince them of what I write and give myself to be interpreted, for example as reader and decipherer of James, and so forth. And when I speak here of writer and reader, I could just as well speak of professor and student, lecturer and listener. On the next page, analyzing the necessarily religious character of this "vocation," "of this "response to a demand or a call," Miller declares that the "I must," in the case of James or Kant, is "free and bound at the same time." How can one be free and bound at the same time? How can one not be?

That is why I wanted to associate here the two figures of Joseph: that of Joseph the Just from the New Testament (*dikaios, justus*, says Matthew) and the other, older figure of Joseph the decipherer from the Old Testament, this favorite son of Jacob, the reader and incomparable interpreter of oneiric or fantastic texts that were also laden with ethico-political significance, as close as possible to what orders the decision of the state and the sovereign, namely, the pharaohs of every age.

Well, one would be wrong to see in Joseph Hillis Miller, the author of *The Ethics of Reading* (the book that could have given its metonymic subtitle to all other books by the same author), a pacified, serene, confident, even moralizing or right-thinking thinker, a thinker who would have sought to moralize a deconstruction so often and so stupidly accused of being perverse or amoral, cynical, skeptical, nihilist, or relativist. The interminable debate with ethics remains for Miller, it seems to me, a fight that is tormented, risky, bold, aporetic, constantly obliged to reinvent probity and loyalty with every "example," with every "I," with every "text," with every singularity, with every "other"—and this does not enclose him either in the library, in bibles, in what is called books, in the books of literature, or especially in the university.

I will not be able to give here the long demonstration that would be required—and that I believe possible, of course. I must be satisfied in conclusion with evoking its spectral and metonymic silhouette by recalling for you the passage of Kafka's Joseph K. in the Millerian corpus. To simplify things, I could have followed the continuous thread that, over thirty years, goes from the *Deus absconditus* of Hopkins to the *Deus absconditus* of Kafka and Joseph K. as these are read in *Tropes, Parables, Performatives* (1991). This book, coming almost thirty years later, is the faithful heir of *The Disappearance of God* (1963). For this time again, whether it is poetic or narrative, the literary experience is given to be deciphered as the undecipherable justice of a being *before the law* of someone (Joseph, in other words, anyone) for whom the law never presents itself in person and withdraws while deferring itself forever. What counts here above all, in this wandering that we are familiar with today, is that the name of Joseph K. becomes in Miller's view the pseudonym or the metonymy, the other name or even the nickname, of *all* Kafka's characters. Without exception, even though each one of them is exceptional. For they are all, like all *je* and all I's, without exception, exceptional. All are Josephs, and we are all

the Josephs of this allegorical metonymy. To the point that the superpower
of the name Joseph is right away lost in anonymity. And, I would say in
French, "c'est justice." Justice is thereby rendered. The becoming anonymous of these pseudonyms, of these homonyms, of these eponymous me-
tonymies, makes me think of that cryptic operation in which the forename
Joseph came thus to hide itself, *Josephus absconditus*, behind its initial, in
the full name of J. Hillis Miller. And one of the sins that I must have
committed at the origin, by substituting John for Joseph, will have been to
risk evangelizing and Christianizing a name that hovered at the frontier
between the Old and New Testaments. Like Kafka and like the Joseph K.
deciphered by Joseph Hillis Miller. Kafka would never have been able to
"make the leap from the tragic vision to Christian faith, or even to the
point at which the possibility of Christian faith might be entertained. His
closest approach to Christianity is probably to be found in an important
chapter of *The Trial*, 'In the Cathedral.'" This is the moment when Joseph
K. sees on the wall of the cathedral "a picture of Christ being lowered into
the tomb." Miller deciphers there the most "dreadful" moment in the
history of Christianity. It is the unique moment when the intercessor dies,
the disappearance of the man-God. The unique instant when the translation between human and divine speech gets interrupted. Like this analogic
translation or transfer, the deciphering then risks becoming impossible.
Returning to the Scotist doctrine of Hopkins, one could say that along
this seismic fault the very univocity of being, and thus the inscape, is no
longer reliable. Is this not the origin of modern literature? It is the time,
says Miller, "which Hölderlin's poems describe, the hard time, when the
gods are no longer present and are not yet again present to man. And this
is Kafka's time too. For it is as though not only Joseph K. *but all his characters* [my emphasis] had been condemned to endure permanently the terrible time between the death of Christ and his resurrection."[12]

This time opens and sketches out, for the being "before the law," a
space, a placeless place, an endless spacing. Miller continues: "This is the
time when, as in the priest's parable to Joseph K., one stands forever at
the door which is the beginning of the way to the Law, the promised land,
and yet forever put off by the statement that this is indeed one's very own
door, but that one may not yet enter it" (*Trope, Parables, Performatives*,
29–30).

You recall that the guardian in fact says to the man from the country,
"No one else could ever be admitted here, since this gate was made only
for you [*nur für dich bestimmt*]. I am now going to shut it." The prison
chaplain also says to Joseph K.: "I belong to the Law. So why should I

want anything from you? The Law wants nothing from you [*Das Gericht will nichts von dir. Es nimmt dich auf, wenn du kommst, und es entlässt dich, wenn du gehst*]. It receives you when you come and dismisses you when you go."

And here is the return of the *Deus absconditus*: "One may compare Kafka, then, with Pascal, for whom the mystery of Incarnation, the joining of the two worlds through the God-Man, alone could provide an escape from the contradiction of the two. Only Christ, the *deus absconditus* made present and manifest, could, for Pascal, provide an avenue from the world of *divertissement* and ambiguity to the higher realm which is the simultaneous affirmation of the yes and the no. . . . For Kafka God remained 'absconditus,' yet, in making this testimony, he did, in a way, testify to God's presence."[13] Hopkins, Kafka, Kafka's Joseph K.

In the filiation of Joseph the ancient, the Egyptian Jew, the political sage, the interpreter of the dreams and phantasms of sovereigns, I would be tempted to inscribe, so as to pay him the most admiring tribute, all the political, politico-institutional, geopolitical, technopolitical vigilance of Joseph Hillis Miller. This is not talked about enough as I see it. I hope that people will soon reread and take away the lessons from all Miller's texts on the ongoing transformation of geopolitical life, on the effects of new technologies in the university institution and in democracy, on the political stakes and implications of "cultural studies" in the university, and on so many other burning questions. As a very rich bibliography and dozens of titles could attest, these political questions, in both the wide and the narrow senses, have never been dissociated, in his work, from so many readings that will have opened the most necessary paths within literary fields (and not just Anglo-American or Victorian), in the fields of philosophy, psychoanalysis, painting, architecture, and so forth. One of the latest proofs is to be found in *Black Holes*, in particular in the chapter titled "The Transnational University," with its subchapters on "Cultural Studies and the Ontopolitological," "The Other Other," and "The University of Dissensus."[14]

I do not have the time to enter the rich territory of so many texts like this. Permit me, in conclusion, to leave the last word to Hillis. He recalls, better than anyone else, the sociopolitical and historical stakes, the extra-linguistic, extrarhetorical, and especially extra-academic stakes that one must learn once again how to analyze rigorously *within* what is thus being exceeded. I purposely cite two relatively old texts (1987–88) so as to underscore that it is not a matter of some recent evolution. And the second of my quotations will make apparent a continuity that goes back to *The Disappearance of God* from forty years ago.

In *The Ethics of Reading*, Miller explains how the responsibility of the response exceeds *on the one hand* the presumed interior of a purely internal reading, such as the interior of a text or of an academic institution. *On the other hand*, it exceeds the limits of an ethics in the direction of politics, the social, or the juridical. I say it without intending any ironic provocation: *The Ethics of Reading* exceeds the ethics of reading; it overflows both mere reading and morality in a narrowly conventional sense. It goes "further" than a mere ethics of reading, and in the following passage, I will underscore the word "further." Miller writes:

> By "ethics of reading," the reader will remember, I mean that aspect of the act of reading in which there is a response to the text that is both necessitated, in the sense that it is a response to an irresistible demand, and free, in the sense that I must take responsibility for my response and for the *further* effects, "interpersonal," institutional, political, historical, of my act of reading, for example as that act takes the form of teaching or of published commentary on a given text.[15]

The other quotation would no doubt go in the same direction. But, *on the one hand*, over and above a second essay on Hopkins, in *Victorian Subjects*, it links up again with *The Disappearance of God* (especially as regards the interpretation of an epistemology and an ontotheology subtending the poetic performative, which Miller unmasked beneath Hopkins's poetics, a layer that he here calls, in the text I am going to cite, "ideology"); and *on the other hand*, it suffices to dissuade us from thinking that, beneath the more or less clandestine name of Joseph, which has been our guide throughout, hides "some identifiable secret behind any veil," or even, on my side, a secret original sin that it would be a matter of bringing to light or, still less, of psychoanalyzing. I cite in conclusion a few lines from "Literature and History: The Example of Hawthorne's 'The Minister's Black Veil.'" This was a lecture given in 1987 to the American Academy of Arts and Sciences, but I refer, of course, to the later book, published in 1991, *Hawthorne and History*, and especially to the chapter "De-facing it: Hawthorne," which considerably enriches and systematizes this question. I remember having heard, at the University of California, Irvine, one of Hillis's most stunning lectures, "The Minister's Black Veil." Here finally is this excerpt. Hillis is in the process of rereading himself and, as he so often does, he takes the measure of the responsibilities of his reading:

> Certainly my reading of "The Minister's Black Veil" would exemplify this claim for an indispensable social function of "rhetorical reading." I have

shown that Hawthorne's story does not merely reaffirm the Puritan version of the traditional language of parable and apocalypse, the notion that here below, in this mortal life, each of us veils a secret sin that will be unveiled at the general resurrection. At the same time, such a reading shows, the story puts that ideology in question. In doing that, the story functions as a powerful uprooting of the ideology of an opposition between realism and allegory on which Hawthorne's own self-analysis and deliberate procedures as a writer depend.[16]

NOTES

INTRODUCTION
Dragan Kujundžić

1. For a comprehensive overview of J. Hillis Miller's work, including an exhaustive bibliography, see the *J. Hillis Miller Reader*, ed. Julian Wolfreys (Stanford, Calif.: Stanford University Press, 2005). For another "offshoot" of the conference dedicated to J. Hillis Miller, particularly in relation to "J," I take the liberty of drawing attention to "J," a special issue of *Critical Inquiry*, Spring 2005, edited with an introduction, "Journey With J on the Jour J," by Dragan Kujundžić, devoted to the texts by J. Hillis Miller and Jacques Derrida.

2. J. Hillis Miller, *Charles Dickens: The World of His Novels* (Cambridge, Mass.: Harvard University Press, 1958; Bloomington: Indiana University Press, 1969); J. Hillis Miller with George Ford, Edgar Johnson, Sylvere Monod, and Noel Peyrouton, *Dickens Criticism: Past, Present, and Future Directions* (Cambridge, Mass.: Charles Dickens Reference Center, 1962). Larisa Tokmakoff Castillo analyzes the vitality of these "early" works on Dickens by J. Hillis Miller in "Between 'the Cup and the Lip': Retroactive Constructions of Inheritance in *Our Mutual Friend*," included in this volume.

3. J. Hillis Miller, *The Form of Victorian Fiction* (University of Notre Dame Press, 1968; 2d ed., Cleveland: Arete Press of Case Western Reserve University, 1979); J. Hillis Miller, *Victorian Subjects* (Hertfordshire, UK: Harvester Wheatsheaf, 1990).

4. J. Hillis Miller, *The Disappearance of God: Five Nineteenth-Century Writers* (Cambridge, Mass.: The Belknap Press of Harvard University Press, 1963; New York: Schocken, 1965; Urbana: University of Illinois Press, 2000). The essay on Gerard Manley Hopkins from the *Disappearance of God* is analyzed extensively in Jacques Derrida's "Justices."

5. J. Hillis Miller, *The Ethics of Reading* (New York: Columbia University Press, 1986).

6. J. Hillis Miller, *Others* (Princeton, N.J.: Princeton University Press, 2001).

7. J. Hillis Miller, "The Critic as Host," first published in *Critical Inquiry* 3 (Spring 1977) and reprinted, with Jacques Derrida's "Living On/Border

Lines" and essays by Harold Bloom, Geoffrey Hartman, and Paul de Man, in *Deconstruction and Criticism* (New York: Seabury Press, 1979). Also reprinted in *Theory Now and Then* (Hertfordshire, UK: Harvester Wheatsheaf, 1990) and quoted here from the most recent reprint (Durham: Duke University Press, 1991), 170.

8. Ibid.

9. J. Hillis Miller, *Speech Acts In Literature* (Stanford, Calif.: Stanford University Press, 2001), includes essays on J. L. Austin, Jacques Derrida, Paul de Man, Ludwig Wittgenstein, and Marcel Proust. In the present volume, *Speech Acts in Literature* is given an attentive assessment in Glenn Odom's essay "Finding the Zumbah: An Analysis of Infelicity in *Speech Acts in Literature*."

10. J. Hillis Miller, "Border Crossings, Translating Theory: Ruth," in *Topographies* (Stanford, Calif.: Stanford University Press, 1995), 336–37.

11. J. Hillis Miller, *On Literature* (New York: Routledge, 2002).

12. Jacques Derrida, "'Le Parjure,' *Perhaps*: Storytelling and Lying"" in Jacques Derrida, *Without Alibi*, ed. and trans. Peggy Kamuf (Stanford, Calif.: Stanford University Press, 2002), 165.

"J" IS FOR *JOUISSANCE*
Juliet Flower MacCannell

1. J. Hillis Miller, *The Disappearance of God* (Cambridge, Mass.: The Belknap Press of Harvard University Press, 1963).

2. J. Hillis Miller, *Others* (Princeton, N.J.: Princeton University Press, 2001), 253, n. 3.

3. J. Hillis Miller, *Speech Acts in Literature* (Stanford, Calif.: Stanford University Press, 2001), 147.

4. Paul de Man, *The Rhetoric of Romanticism* (New York: Columbia University Press, 2000), 118–19. De Man's thesis on language might be compared with Lacan's. Lacan speaks of the unary trait as the first "violence" that language—or really, the signifier—does to the subject. But in Lacan, the senseless (if pseudo) violence of installing language is followed by the protectiveness built in to a symbolic order. This second part of Lacan's theory is what de Man would reject in favor of what Lacan also recognizes as the equally violent *excess* that language inadvertently institutes. For the psychoanalyst, the subject must learn to "deal with" the excess, the repetitive violence generated by language. De Man's concerns, by contrast, are purely formal and unconnected to the subject of the unconscious, while Lacan's are.

5. "J. L. Austin," in Miller, *Speech Acts in Literature*, 6–62.

6. The reader is referred to my recent essay, "More Thoughts on War and Death: A Reading of Jacques Lacan's *Seminar XVII*," translated into Slovenian by Alenka Zupanãiã, *Razpol* 13 (2003), ed. Mladen Dolar: 157–91. This can

now be read in English in *Reading Seminar XVII*, ed. Russell Grigg and Justin Clemens (Durham: Duke University Press, forthcoming). In this essay, I explicate in detail the changing fate of *jouissance* in his four discourses as Lacan's strong meditation on capitalism and its version of excess.

7. Fredric Jameson. *The Political Unconscious: Narrative as a Socially Symbolic Act* (Ithaca, N.Y.: Cornell University Press, 1981).

8. Jacques Lacan says that *jouissance* is the only real substance in psychoanalysis.

9. *A Thousand Plateaus* speaks of a courtly poetry that becomes a "permanent plane of consistency of desire," a consistency that looks like *jouissance*—indivisible, refractory to linguistic distinctions and logical partitionings: "There is, in fact, a joy that is immanent to desire, as though desire were filled by itself and its contemplations, a joy that implies no lack or impossibility and is not measured by pleasure since it is what distributes intensities of pleasure and prevents them from being suffused by anxiety, shame and guilt," Gilles Deleuze and Félix Guattari, *A Thousand Plateaus: Capitalism and Schizophrenia*, trans. Brian Massumi (1980; Minneapolis: University of Minnesota Press, 1987), 155–56.

10. This is Rousseau's turn of phrase in his autobiographical letter to the censor, M. de Malesherbes. He writes: "Had all my dreams become realities, they would not have been enough for me; I would have imagined, dreamed, desired still [*encore*]. I found in myself an inexplicable void that nothing could have filled; a certain launching of the heart toward another sort of enjoyment [*une autre sorte de jouissance*] of which I had no idea and of which I nonetheless felt the need. . . . This in itself was enjoyment [*jouissance*] because I was transpierced by it with a very vivid feeling and an attractive sadness that I would not have wanted not to have." Jean-Jacques Rousseau, *Quatre lettres à M. de Malesherbes*, ed. B. Gagnebin and M. Raymond, in *Oeuvres complètes*, vol. 1 (Paris: Bibliothéque de la Pléïade, 1960), 1140–41 (my translation).

11. *Jouissance* has now gained a name for itself as a tool of cultural critique (Slavoj Žižek, Mladen Dolar, Alenka Zupanäiä), of political and economic analysis (Juliet Flower MacCannell, Joan Copjec), and of the clinic of psychopathology (Nestor Braunstein, Willy Apollon, Jacques-Alain Miller).

12. Sigmund Freud, "Civilized Sexual Morality and Modern Nervousness," in *The Standard Edition of the Complete Psychological Works of Sigmund Freud*, vol. 9, trans. James Strachey (1908; London: The Hogarth Press and the Institute of Psycho-analysis, 1959), 181–204. See also his "Instincts and Their Vicissitudes," *Standard Edition*, 14:117–40, and his "Civilization and its Discontents," *Standard Edition* 21:64–145.

13. Lacan, in his late work, rediscovered the "enjoyment" of letters in a different way than he had earlier. He began to spell it *"jouis-sens"* or "enjoy-

meant"—a supplemental *jouissance*, an enjoyment taken from and in the very free play of differential language as such. This late Lacan extended Freud's initial insight that art is a special way of satisfying drive. Two Lacan pieces, one on James Joyce ("Le sinthome") and the other on "Lituraterre" (both delivered in his Seminar XXIII, 1975–76) treat art a bit differently from the purloined and insistent letters of his earlier seminars. In the Joyce seminar, Lacan devised the term *sinthome* to designate a signifier that is a primary agent for both the expunging of *jouissance* (metaphorically) and for its (metonymic) reconveyance.

14. Paul de Man, "Kant and Schiller," in *Aesthetic Ideology*, ed. Andrzej Warminski (Minneapolis: University of Minnesota Press, 1996), 134.

BROADENING THE HORIZON: ON J. HILLIS MILLER'S ANANARRATOLOGY
Dan Shen

The author would like to thank Jiwei Ci, James Phelan, Barbara Cohen, Emma Kafalenos, Shlomith Rimmon-Kenan, and J. Hillis Miller for their helpful and generous comments on an earlier version of this essay. The author would also like to thank Brian Richardson for sending a helpful reference book from the United States.

1. J. Hillis Miller, "The Figure in the Carpet," *Poetics Toady* 1 (1980): 107–18; Shlomith Rimmon-Kenan, "Deconstructive Reflections on Deconstruction: In "Reply to Hillis Miller," *Poetics Today* 2 (1980–81): 185–88; J. Hillis Miller, "A Guest in the House: Reply to Shlomith Rimmon-Kenan's Reply," *Poetics Today* 2 (1980–81): 189–91.

2. J. Hillis Miller, *Reading Narrative* (Norman: University of Oklahoma Press, 1998), 49.

3. S. H. Butcher, *Aristotle's Theory of Poetry and Fine Art, with a Critical Text and Translation of The Poetics* (New York: Dover, reprint, 1951), 31, quoted in Miller, *Reading Narrative*, 8–9.

4. Wallace Martin, *Recent Theories of Narrative* (Ithaca, N.Y.: Cornell University Press, 1986), 81.

5. Vladimir Propp, *Morphology of the Folktale* (Austin: University of Texas Press, 1968), 26–63.

6. Gérard Genette, *Narrative Discourse*, trans. Jane E. Lewin (Ithaca, N.Y.: Cornell University Press, 1980), 33–85.

7. Ibid., 36.

8. Ibid., 39.

9. Miller, *Reading Narrative*, 57–59. See also Edward W. Said, *Beginnings* (New York: Basic Books, 1975); Jacques Derrida, "Outwork: Prefacing," in *Dissemination*, trans. Barbara Johnson (Chicago: University of Chicago Press, 1981), 1–59.

10. Sophocles, *Oedipus the King*, trans. Thomas Gould (Englewood Cliffs, N.J.: Prentice-Hall, 1970), 1, quoted in Miller, *Reading Narrative*, 10.

11. Miller, *Reading Narrative*, 10.

12. See Brian Richardson, introduction to *Narrative Dynamics*, ed. Brian Richardson (Columbus: Ohio State University Press, 2002), 251–52. Richardson's introduction (249–55) also offers an overview of prominent issues in the theoretical work on beginnings and endings of narrative.

13. Miller, *Reading Narrative*, 54.

14. Gerald Prince, *Narratology* (Berlin: Mouton, 1982), 72.

15. Marianna Torgovnick, *Closure in the Novel* (Princeton, N.J.: Princeton University Press), 3–4, quoted in Peter Rabinowitz, "Reading Beginnings and Endings," *Narrative Dynamics*, 312, n. 2.

16. See, for instance, James Phelan, "Beginnings and Endings: Theories and Typologies of How Novels Open and Close," in *Encyclopedia of the Novel*, ed. Paul Schellinger, 2 vols. (Chicago: Fitzroy Dearborn, 1998), 1:96–99; Peter Rabinowitz, "Reading Beginnings and Endings," in *Narrative Dynamics*, 300–313; Meir Steinberg, *Expositional Modes and Temporal Ordering in Fiction* (Baltimore: Johns Hopkins University Press, 1978); Steven G. Kellman, "Grand Openings and Plain: On the Poetics of Opening Lines," *Substance* 17 (1977): 139–47; and David H. Richter, *Fable's End: Completeness and Closure in Rhetorical of Fiction* (Chicago: University of Chicago Press, 1974).

17. See Richter, *Fable's End.*

18. Miller, *Reading Narrative*, 74.

19. Richardson, *Narrative Dynamics*, 249.

20. J. Hillis Miller, "Narrative and History," *ELH* 41 (1974): 455–73.

21. For "instability" and "tension," see James Phelan, *Narrative as Rhetoric* (Columbus: Ohio State University Press, 1996).

22. Miller, *Reading Narrative*, 55–56.

23. Stylisticians, linguists, and narratologists draw a distinction between indirect discourse (e.g. "She said that her mother had given her a nice gift") and free indirect discourse ("What a nice gift her Mummy had given her!"). The former displays greater narratorial control, presenting character's speech in the subordinate clause (subordinated to the narrator's reporting clause), editing character's words in a neutral reporting style, while the latter "frees" characters' words from heavy narratorial control—from subordination by omitting the reporting clause, characteristically retaining characters' idiom and subjectivity. J. Hillis Miller has not made the distinction, but he uses the plural term "indirect discourses" to indicate that there is more than one form of indirect discourse. The phenomenon he focuses on is "free indirect discourse" as such. It should be noted that one difference between J. Hillis Miller and structuralist narratologists is that Miller is less interested in developing a

terminology and a method of analysis than in finding ways to interpret in depth individual works of literature.

24. Miller, *Reading Narrative*, 158.

25. See, for instance, Brian McHale, "Free Indirect Discourse: A Survey of Recent Accounts," *Poetics and Theory of Literature* 3 (1978): 249–87; Genette, *Narrative Discourse*, 172–76; Shlomith Rimmon-Kenan, *Narrative Fiction: Contemporary Poetics* (London: Methuen, 1983), 110–16.

26. Miller, *Reading Narrative*, 165.

27. Rimmon-Kenan, *Narrative Fiction*, 113.

28. See Mikhail Bakhtin, *The Dialogic Imagination*, trans. Caryl Emerson and Michael Holquist (Austin: University of Texas Press, 1981), and Mikhail Bakhtin, *Problems of Dostoevsky's Poetics*, trans. Caryl Emerson (Minneapolis: University of Minnesota Press, 1984).

29. Miller, *Reading Narrative*, 163.

30. See Shlomith Rimmon-Kenan, *The Concept of Ambiguity: the Example of James* (Chicago: University of Chicago Press, 1977).

31. Rimmon-Kenan, "Reply to J. Hillis Miller," 186.

32. Miller, "The Figure in the Carpet," 112.

33. Rimmon-Kenan, "Reply to J. Hillis Miller," 186.

34. Miller, "Reply to Shlomith Rimmon-Kenan's Reply," 189.

35. Rimmon-Kenan, "Reply to J. Hillis Miller," 186; Miller, "Reply to Shlomith Rimmon-Kenan's Reply," 189.

36. Rimmon-Kenan, ibid., 186.

37. Miller, *Reading Narrative*, 97.

38. Miller, "Reply to Shlomith Rimmon-Kenan's Reply," 189–91.

39. Ibid., 190.

40. Miller, *Reading Narrative*, 222.

41. We should, however, avoid going to one extreme. It may be worth noting that in *Course in General Linguistics*, trans. Wade Baskin (London: Philosophical Library Inc., 1960), a collection of students' notes of lectures given by Ferdinand de Saussure nearly a century ago, there are two contending forces at work. One pays great attention to the relation between the signifier and the signified, defining language as "a system of signs in which the only essential thing is the union of meanings and sound-images, and in which both parts of the sign are psychological" (15). The other force views language only as a system of differences. "Even more important: a difference generally implies positive terms between which the difference is set up; but in language there are only differences *without positive terms*" (120). Indeed, a Western language consists of signs that are totally arbitrary, hence by no means positive terms. But we have to be aware that differences alone cannot generate signification. In English, "sun" (/ŝn/) can function as a sign not only because of its

difference from other signs in sound or "sound-image," but also, and more essentially, because of the conventional union between the sound-image "sun" and the signified concept. Given, for instance, the following sound-images "lun"(/l̂n/), "sul" (/ŝl/), and "qun" (/kŵn/), although each sound-image can be identified by its difference from the others, none of them can function as a sign in English, because there is no established conventional "union between meanings and sound-images." When commenting on Saussure's theory of language in *Positions*, trans. Alan Bass (University of Chicago Press, 1981) and other works, Jacques Derrida pays exclusive attention to Saussure's emphasis on language as a system of differences among the signifiers, to the neglect of Saussure's emphasis on the relation between the signifier and the signified. Consequently, language becomes a play of signifiers themselves, and meaning naturally becomes forever indeterminable.

42. Rimmon-Kenan, "Reply to J. Hillis Miller," 187.

43. Miller, "Reply to Shlomith Rimmon-Kenan's Reply," 190.

44. Miller, *Reading Narrative*, 48–49.

FINDING THE ZUMBAH: AN ANALYSIS OF INFELICITY IN
SPEECH ACTS IN LITERATURE
Glenn Odom

The author would like to thank Gail Davis, Bryan Reynolds, Carolyn Odom, Tom Hitchner, Dragan Kujundžić, Bond Love, and John Barton for their kind help with this article.

1. J. Hillis Miller, *Speech Acts in Literature* (Stanford, Calif.: Stanford University Press, 2001).

2. J. L. Austin, *How to Do Things with Words* (Oxford: Oxford University Press), 1980.

3. It would be rather easy to proceed in a programmatic style of critique. Austin has laid out a very specific set of definitions and also has noted exactly what the limits of such definitions are. As Stanley Fish points out in "How to Do Things with Austin and Searle," reprinted in *Is There a Text in This Class* (Cambridge, Mass.: Harvard University Press, 1980), theorists often slide "over from illocutionary acts to perlocutionary effects" and try to "include the latter in the felicity conditions of the former" (225). Austin is explicitly discussing illocutionary acts, acts that, by being said, are completed. Speech-act theory is not designed to reach beyond these acts, although Searle makes some beginning moves in this direction. Thus, in Miller's text, some of the events, labeled as performative are in fact, perlocutionary effects (i.e., the response to Derrida's utterance of "Je t'aime" (*Speech Acts in Literature*, 134–35).

Such finger wagging over precise definitions, however, is exactly what Derrida takes Searle to task for in *Limited Inc.* Not only does Austin himself recognize slippage between terms and the difficulty of distinguishing between certain cases, but Miller's aim is precisely to apply Austin's theory to a realm that Austin explicitly avoids. This project undoubtedly requires a certain flexibility of the initial terminology. Furthermore, while Fish maintains his precision, he does so at the expense of making a novel argument. His discussion of *Coriolanus* is interesting, but, as Fish himself confesses, not applicable to other literary works. Thus, the gains of such programmatic critique are doubtful, unless one's goal is simply to remain true to some ghostly Austinian system. I therefore accept, in my writing, the inevitability of certain slippages and beg the reader to do the same. I cannot, however, predict the perlocutionary effects of my illocutionary accepting and begging.

4. The idea of an inaugural performative is nascent in Austin's *How to Do Things with Words*. He declares that performatives can exist only if a set of constitutive rules has been established. As an example of such rules, he points out that we cannot be said to be playing football unless we are following a set of rules that constitute the game. Logically, however, there was a first game or perhaps several first games of football in which these rules were worked out and institutionalized. Derrida explicitly discusses such inaugural performatives in *Specters of Marx: The State of the Debt, the Work of Mourning, and the New International*, trans. Peggy Kamuf (New York: Routlege, 1994): "the originary performativity that does not conform to preexisting conventions, unlike all performatives analyzed by the theoreticians of speech acts, but whose force of *rupture* produces the institution or the constitution, the law itself, which is to say also the meaning" (31). Were I to have proceeded with the aforementioned programmatic critique of Miller's employment of Austin's terminology and theory, I would here reach a logical paradox. How can Austin have created a system of constitutive rules if all speech acts rely on a prior set of rules, or, if such rules are constitutive and not created, how could Miller break them and still be said to be speaking about speech acts?

5. Jacques Derrida, "Declarations of Independence," trans. Tom Keenan and Tom Pepper, *New Political Sciences* 15 (1986).

6. Ludwig Wittgenstein, *Philosophical Investigations*, trans. G. E. M. Anscomb, 3rd ed. (New York: Macmillan, 1958), section 257.

7. John R. Searle, *Speech Acts: An Essay in the Philosophy of Language* (1969; Cambridge: Cambridge University Press, 1988), 23.

8. As the final chapter on literature draws nigh, Miller abandons the laden term of "interrogation" of the Derridean chapter and chooses the milder "interpretation." His rationale for this becomes clear in the final chapter.

9. J. Hillis Miller, *On Literature* (London: Routlege, 2002).

10. When I presented this paper at the "J" conference, Hillis Miller suggested that I let the audience in on the joke of the title. Then my editor

pointed out that if those not in the know were to Google the term, they'd find a cartoon Website: My readers want the "Zumbah" to be explained up front and have been rather annoyed at my firm refusal to give in. The whole point of a performative utterance, however, is that the process creates the knowledge or the action. The "Zumbah" cannot be presented up front, it can come only after the performance of the contract of the paper has been fulfilled. The "Zumbah" is not in an additional definition, it is in the rhetoric itself.

11. Karin Barber, *I Could Speak until Tomorrow: Oriki, Women, and the Past in a Yoruba Town* (Edinburgh: Edinburgh University Press, 1991), 1.

BETWEEN "THE CUP AND THE LIP": RETROACTIVE CONSTRUCTIONS

OF INHERITANCE IN *OUR MUTUAL FRIEND*

Larisa Tokmakoff Castillo

1. See Jacques Derrida, *Limited Inc.*, ed. Gerald Graff, trans. Samuel Weber (Evanston: Northwestern University Press, 1988), 111–12. My notion of the term "violence" calls upon Jacques Derrida's use of the term in his afterword to *Limited Inc.*, where violence is bound not exclusively to physical acts, but also to nonphysical forms of violation.

2. Charles Dickens, *Our Mutual Friend*, ed. Adrian Poole (New York: Penguin, 1997), 24. Hereafter cited as *OMF*.

3. Dickens draws from this proverb in his title for the first book of the first volume of *Our Mutual Friend*, entitled "The Cup and the Lip." Adrian Poole tells us that this title refers to the saying that "there's many a slip 'twixt cup and lip."

4. J. L. Austin, *How to Do Things with Words*, ed. J. O. Urmson and Marina Sbisà (Cambridge, Mass.: Harvard University Press, 1962), 147. Hereafter cited as *HTW*.

5. See, for example, Anny Sadrin, *Parentage and Inheritance in the Novels of Charles Dickens* (Cambridge: Cambridge University Press, 1994), 130.

6. See critiques of such "inconsistency" with examinations of Dickens's "pious fraud": Philip Hobsbaum, "The Critics and *Our Mutual Friend*," *Essays in Criticism* 13 (1963): 231–40; Audrey Jaffe, *Vanishing Points: Dickens, Narrative, and the Subject of Omniscience* (Berkeley: University of California Press, 1991); Robert Newsom, " 'To Scatter Dust': Fancy and Authenticity in *Our Mutual Friend*," *Dickens Studies Annual* 8 (1980): 39–60; and Francis X. Shea, "No Change of Intention in *Our Mutual Friend*," *Dickensian* 63 (1967): 37–40.

7. J. Hillis Miller, *Speech Acts in Literature* (Stanford, Calif.: Stanford University Press, 2001), 11.

8. Austin, *HTW*, 47. An "entail" is an act of limiting inherited property by transmitting it to specified heirs.

9. For critics of Austin, see Miller, *Speech Acts*, 6–62, and Derrida, *Limited Inc.* Miller analyzes Austin's simultaneous dependence on and rejection of

"parasitic" literary language. Derrida undermines the possibility of developing a general theory of speech acts. Derrida exposes the fact that the attempt to control such utterances, or to categorize them, dooms itself to failure because iterability marks the very utterances that attempt to categorize language. In the same way that one cannot stand outside of gravity to illustrate its laws, an individual cannot transcend language for the sake of systematizing it, because the act of attempted systemization requires participation in language. Austin, whose intention may be to articulate a general theory of speech acts, performatively discloses that such an articulation is impossible because it is always infected by categories of language that he attempts to bracket. He displays this problem most tellingly in his attempt to eliminate literary speech acts—what he calls the "etiolations" of language—from his system of performative acts while at the same time using such literary language throughout his text to exemplify his postulates.

10. See Derrida, *Limited Inc.*, 148, for a discussion of "undecideability."

11. Ibid., 129.

12. Ibid., 42.

13. Ibid., 27.

14. Miller, *Speech Acts*, 12–13.

15. Nathaniel Hawthorne, *The House of the Seven Gables*, ed. Milton R. Stern (New York: Penguin, 1981), 182–83.

16. See Miller, *Speech Acts*, 215. With his closing words, Miller performatively "take[s] responsibility" for his utterance, his text.

17. J. Hillis Miller, *Charles Dickens: The World of His Novels* (Cambridge, Mass.: Harvard University Press, 1959), 282.

18. Dickens, *OMF*, 227.

19. On Eugene's rejection of the father, see Catherine Waters, *Dickens and the Politics of the Family* (Cambridge: Cambridge University Press, 1997), 200. Waters maintains that Eugene's marriage is a reversal of paternal authority.

20. Dickens, *OMF*, 797.

21. See Waters, *Politics of Family*. Waters argues that the symmetry of these two characters' conversions leads to a critique of gender difference, Bella's conversion functioning as a kind of imprisonment while Eugene's leaves him autonomous. Yet despite certain differences in their experiences, Bella and Eugene both deny the father's will and, in doing so, both reveal a degree of autonomy that facilitates their conversions.

22. Dickens, *OMF*, 585.

23. Miller, *Charles Dickens*, 306. Here, Miller characterizes John as a figure of speech.

24. See Carol Hanbery MacKay, "The Encapsulated Romantic: John Harmon and the Boundaries of Victorian Soliloquy," *Dickens Studies Annual* 18

(1989): 262, in which MacKay argues that Harmon, in this scene, has "neither a name or a spatial location."

25. Dickens, *OMF*, 360.

26. See MacKay, "Encapsulated Romantic." This scene carries with it a force that resonates throughout the text by dramatizing many of the text's central images and concerns. MacKay sees this scene as central to the novel as a whole and argues for the way in which the soliloquy encapsulates both Romantic and Victorian elements. She asserts that "Dickens invests Harmon and his soliloquy with the weight not only of the plotline but of the story's key imagery and its pattern of development. From its inception, the novel grew out of the Harmon character" (ibid., 269).

27. Dickens, *OMF*, 359.

28. Jan Gordon, "Dickens and the Transformation of Nineteenth-Century Narratives of 'Legitimacy,'" *Dickens Studies Annual* 19 (1990): 203–65. In considering Dickens's rejection of origins, Gordon discusses the historical move from a law based on precedent to one in which intentionality and interpretation was used. The latter, Gordon argues, is the one Dickens promotes. By rejecting the law of precedent, Dickens undermines traditional forms of legitimacy.

29. Sadrin, *Parentage and Inheritance*, 4.

30. See Richard Gaughan, "Prospecting for Meaning in *Our Mutual Friend*," *Dickens Studies Annual* 19 (1990): 231–46; Robert Keily, "Plotting and Scheming: The Design of Design in *Our Mutual Friend*," *Dickens Studies Annual* 12 (1983): 267–83. Gaughan argues that John must reintegrate himself among the living without submitting to his father's legacy, but that the only way to do so is for John to accept a suspended identity. In this way, he does not discover his ego, but merely adopts a substitute for that identity (Gaughan, 235). Keily notes that Dickens's characters run into danger when they fail to "put their own construction on things" (Keily, 272).

31. Dickens, *OMF*, 360.

32. See Miller, *Charles Dickens*, 324, where Miller accounts for the symbolism of baptism, which, in this scene, is especially difficult to ignore.

33. See Catherine Gallagher, "The Bioeconomics of *Our Mutual Friend*," in *Fragments for a History of the Human Body: Part Three*, ed. Michael Feher, Ramona Naddaff, and Nadia Tazi (New York: Zone, 1989), 355. See also, Waters, *Politics of Family* and Jaffe, *Vanishing Points*, which both point to John's role as omniscient narrator in this scene, as an authorial figure who controls the narrative.

34. See Keily, "Plotting and Scheming," 273. Keily recognizes that although the pseudonyms that John takes on might help him momentarily, they "do not completely extricate him from a scheme not of his own devising."

Keily would say that this "scheme" from which he cannot escape is the imposition of the "venerable parent" and the other characters in the text. However, it seems, instead, that John cannot escape from the performative effects of self-authorization. No matter which name he uses, a gap still exists between his name and his ontological status.

35. Dickens, *OMF*, 368.

36. We might note that John, symbolically, writes a will, when his namesake, little John Harmon, bequeaths his love to Bella. He wants to bequeath a "kiss for the boofer lady" (Dickens, *OMF*, 322). If we see the orphan as a symbol of John Harmon himself, then the will to "kiss the boofer lady" takes on greater significance. John's will for Bella is, after all, to relieve her from the "rust and tarnish" of the money so that she can develop the "warmth in her heart" (ibid., 357, 362). Thus it is that instead of money, John wills love upon Bella.

37. Jaffe, *Vanishing Points*, 150.

38. Ibid., 162–66.

39. Dickens, *OMF*, 800.

40. See Roland Barthes, "The Death of the Author," in *Image-Music-Text* (New York: Hill and Wang, 1977), 142–48. Here, Barthes speaks of the speech act as an empty process into which the author inserts himself. "The modern *scriptor* is born at the same time as his text" (ibid., 145). He does just what Dickens's author does—retroactively constructs an origin for himself in the act of writing or uttering a performative.

41. In linking his death to authority, Dickens discloses his preoccupation with his lack of absolute authorial control, a question that puzzled him throughout his career. One vestige of his concern with authority is his involvement in the International Copyright debate. In my larger project, I argue that Dickens's interest in copyright corresponds to his depiction of wills and inheritance. He uses the conveyance of real property to account for the problems that emerge in the transference of intellectual property.

42. Dickens, *OMF*, 798.

43. Gallagher, "Bioeconomics," 364.

44. Dickens, *OMF*, 801.

HILLIS'S CHARITY
Jennifer H. Williams

1. J. Hillis Miller, "Literature and Religion." In *Theory Now and Then* (Durham: Duke University Press, 1991). Hereafter, all references to this essay will appear parenthetically.

2. J. Hillis Miller, *The Disappearance of God* (Chicago: University of Illinois Press, 2000), ix. The full citation reads: "I believe that it is a severe limitation

of literary and cultural study today that a good bit of it tends not to interest itself much in what might be called the religious or ontological dimension of writers' and cultures' ideologies in favor of a more or less exclusive infatuation with the three mythological graces of contemporary humanistic study: Race, Class, and Gender. As Paul de Man, of all people, once said to me, 'Religious questions are the most important.' I see I said the same thing about my five authors in the original preface to this book."

3. For a more thorough reading of Augustine's hermeneutics of love, see Warren Charles Embree's "Ethics and Interpretation" (PhD diss., University of Nebraska–Lincoln, 1991). Embree writes, "Love, as Augustine understands, is involved in the hermeneutical enterprise from start to finish" (143).

4. Saint Augustine, *On Christian Teaching*, trans. R. P. H. Green (Oxford: Oxford University Press, 1997), 27. Hereafter, all references to this text will appear parenthetically.

5. I am aware that Derrida has made the notions of "proper," "propriety," and "property" problematic. One might argue that the possessive associations of the word "proper" contradict the kind of nontotalizing religious reading that I describe. However, I use "proper" here to mean fitting, proportional, or matching, in however an indirect and never wholly satisfactory way, the particularities of the text. That is to say, as opposed to a "proper reading" in the sense of a reading that is absolute or verifiably correct, or even that classifies the superficial properties of the text, "proper reading" describes a reading that attends to the text as other.

6. The dilemma of love's dual nature is also exemplified by the controversy surrounding William Tyndale's translation of the Vulgate word "caritas" as the English word "love" in the sixteenth century. When Tyndale translated "caritas" in 1 Corinthians 13:13 as "love" instead of "charity," Thomas More objected precisely because he thought "love" too vulgar a word and too apt to make readers think of all-too-human forms of love. More insisted that "charity" was the best translation because it avoided the problem of confusing divine love with eros. See Su Fang Ng's "Translation, Interpretation, and Heresy: The Wycliffite Bible, Tyndale's Bible, and the Contested Origin," *Studies in Philology* 98, no. 3 (Summer 2001): 315–38.

7. Hillis's books are literally love letters in at least one specific sense. As I look through the various dedications in his books, I find that they are dedicated to Dorothy, to Sarah, Michael, and Robin, and to other, presumably dear friends and colleagues. In fact, in *On Literature*, Miller seems to play his two loves against each other. After declaring that *On Literature* is "Another for Dorothy," he writes, "Finally, I thank the dedicatee of this book for suffering once more through my ordeals of composition. She had to endure my faraway look, my dreamy absentmindedness. I was dwelling again in imagina-

tion of the other side of Alice's looking-glass or on the deserted island where the Swiss Family Robinson made such an enchanting home." J. Hillis Miller, *On Literature* (London: Routledge, 2002), xii.

8. J. Hillis Miller, "The Ethics of Reading," in *Theory Now and Then* (Durham: Duke University Press, 1991), 338.

9. In the context of "Literature and Religion," it seems that one instance of what Miller has in mind here is the nonreligious critic who reads, for example, Milton and finds his theology distasteful, as well as the religious critic who seeks to turn every author into an unwitting believer. Neither critic wishes the text to be as it is.

10. Miller's most extensive work on the notion of the "wholly other" in literature is *Others*. Miller attempts to define the wholly other through a quote from Derrida's "Psyché: Invention de l'autre": "the other calls [something] to come and that does not happen except in multiple voices" (quoted in *Others*, 1, translated by Miller). Later Miller writes, "[t]he unseen remains just that: unseen. It is therefore unknown, submerged, obscure, invisible. It cannot be returned to the same. It remains heterogeneous to any act of understanding. It is 'wholly other.'" J. Hillis Miller, *Others* (Princeton, N.J.: Princeton University Press, 2001), 200.

11. Miller, "The Ethics of Reading," 339.

12. One example of this kind of reading that Miller gives in the same article is the response of William Empson to *Paradise Lost*. Miller reports that Empson found the theology and morality of *Paradise Lost* "appalling." Rather than dismissing *Paradise Lost* on those grounds or suspending the question of theology altogether, Miller writes that "we must dare to ask whether or not the theology of *Paradise Lost* is appalling" (ibid., 330, 337).

13. "If the preface as a genre is obligated to indicate some fundamental unity in the chapters that follow it, this is not a preface. Most of the essays gathered here are fairly recent, but the earliest goes back to 1952. They are brought together here by the accident that all are on twentieth-century works. . . . Each is the memorial record of a discrete event of reading, not a stage in some predetermined itinerary fulfilling a single 'research project.'" J. Hillis Miller, *Tropes, Parables, Performatives: Essays on Twentieth-Century Literature* (Durham: Duke University Press, 1991), vii.

14. Deconstruction "has questioned the assumption that literary history, or history as such, is a series of definable 'periods' that develop from one another according to some paradigm of organic growth. (Such metaphors are almost irresistible. I have used them myself here in my account of the 'development' of literary studies in America or in speaking of the 'flowering' of literary theory or in my suggestions that Kant begat Schiller begat Arnold begat Trilling. . . ." Miller, "The Ethics of Reading," 335.

15. "Moreover, every artist who crosses the frontier does so in his own way, a way to some degree unlike any other. I do not wish to minimize the differences between twentieth-century writers, but to suggest a context in which those differences may be fruitfully explored." J. Hillis Miller, *Poets of Reality*. (Cambridge: The Belknap Press of Harvard University Press, 1966), 10.

16. J. Hillis Miller, *Speech Acts in Literature* (Stanford, Calif.: Stanford University Press, 2001), ix.

17. Elsewhere Miller writes, "The effort of reading must be constantly renewed because no one reading suffices. None ever gets the reader where he or she would like to go. Each new reading discounts and disqualifies all that preceded, but each fails to satisfy. As Stevens puts it, the search for what suffices never reaches its goal. 'It can never be satisfied, the mind, never.' Neither poet nor critic ever reaches that palm at the end of the mind Stevens' last poem glimpses. The work of reading must always start again from the beginning, even in a rereading of a work already read. Close reading reaches its limit in the constantly renewed experience of its failure to take you where you think you want to go and ought to go." *Tropes, Parables, Performatives*, viii–ix.

18. For an excellent discussion of the danger of telling parables, see J. Hillis Miller, "Parable and Performatives in the Gospels and in Modern Literature," in ibid., 135–50.

19. Miller writes that "figures of speech turn aside the telling of a story" and that "'parable' is one name for this large-scale indirection characteristic of literary language, indeed of language generally." Ibid., ix.

20. Susan Stewart, *On Longing: Narrative of the Miniature, the Gigantic, the Souvenir, the Collection* (Durham: Duke University Press, 1993), ix.

21. Joseph Conrad, *Lord Jim*, ed. Thomas C. Moser (New York: W. W. Norton, 1996), 5. Hereafter, all references to *Lord Jim* will appear parenthetically.

22. Stewart, *On Longing*, 136.

23. Ibid., 151.

24. The way in which the context of the collection defines the specimen points to another feature of the collection in Stewart's book. Stewart argues that the work of the collection is to obliterate the past and replace it with the narrative of the collector. She writes, "The collection seeks a form of self-enclosure which is possible because of its ahistoricism. The collection replaces history with *classification*, with order beyond the realm of temporality. In the collection, time is not something to be restored to an origin; rather, all time is made simultaneous or synchronous within the collector's world." Ibid., 151.

25. Ibid., 144.

26. In contrast to the urban space of London, Stein will bequeath the butterfly to his "small native town."

27. Perhaps we cannot fault Stein entirely for turning the bronze butterfly's spots into text to be read. It seems that butterflies do this themselves. Entomologists have determined that butterflies choose mates by reading the markings on their wings. Individual marks not only tell the butterflies which ones belong to the same species of butterfly, but also help determine age, agility, and other desirable qualities in a prospective mate. See Ronald L. Rutowski, "Mating Strategies in Butterflies," *Scientific American*, July 1998, 64–69, and Paul Whalley, *Butterfly Watching* (London: Severn House Publishers, 1980), 21–22.

28. I am indebted to Hillis for pointing out that the Greek word for "butterfly" is *psyche*, or soul. When the butterfly flits past the dead men, it is as if their souls were flying out of their corpses, only to be caught and killed again by Stein. Stein, too, seems to lose his soul that day.

29. Walter Benjamin, "Unpacking My Library: A Talk about Book Collecting," in *Illuminations*, trans. Harry Zohn (New York: Schocken Books, 1968), 60. It is difficult to determine whether or not a collection is a use or a love. On the one hand, it seems that collectors love each object in their collection. That is, the individual objects become the occasion for the collection. On the other hand, because individual objects are used to make up a collection, their value to the collector is in their relationship to the whole. Once made part of the collection, individual objects seek to be individual. If they were removed from the collection, they would become dislocated parts.

30. Joseph Conrad, *Youth / Heart of Darkness / The End of the Tether*, ed. John Lyon (London: Penguin Books, 1995), 3.

31. Ibid., 4.

32. Ibid., 3.

33. J. Hillis Miller, "*Lord Jim*: Repetition as Subversion of Organic Form," in *Joseph Conrad's "Lord Jim,"* ed. Harold Bloom (New York: Chelsea House, 1987). First published in J. Hillis Miller, *Fiction and Repetition: Seven English Novels* (Cambridge, Mass.: Harvard University Press, 1982).

34. Ibid., 104.

35. Ibid., 105–6.

"J"; OR, HILLIS *LE MAL*
Tom Cohen

1. For a cunning biography of "the trickster zero," see Robert Kaplan, *The Nothing That Is—A Natural History of Zero* (New York: Oxford University Press, 1999), 132.

2. That might include the digitalized image that is today said to supplant analogical technologies when the numericism of digital calculus mimes, in turn, the nonsite where phenomenalization of the world, animation itself, arises from inscriptions.

3. If, as Brian Rotman suggests, the monotheistic era was introduced with alphabetism and stands to have been redistributed by the electronic accelerations of the video era and the redissolving of graphic-based epistemologies, then what letter would better return to accompany that passage and redistribution, say, than the "J"—resolved into a preletteral graphic, a slash or staff in which the digital and the *one* linger as virtual or incorporative tropes? See Brian Rotman, "The Alphabetic Body," in "Random Figures," a special issue pf *Parallax* 22 (January–March 2002): "The alphabet is an extraordinary simple, robust technology with a powerful viral capacity to disseminate and consolidate itself . . . across multiple linguistic platforms" (93). Its ability to morph into and inhabit the image, the "exogenesis of the psychic body," as in the link between marks and memory, is commented on: "philosophy's inability/refusal to countenance the presence of images in its texts, its unease in the face of the picture, is too thorough, unexamined, universal and deep-rooted not to suggest other—iconophobic or anti-visualist—forces at work" (100).

4. As Alain Badiou clumsily reminds us: "if the ethical 'consensus' is founded on the recognition of Evil, it follows that every effort to unite people around a positive idea of the Good, let alone identify Man with projects of this kind, becomes in fact the real source of evil itself." See Alain Badiou, *Manifesto for Philosophy* (Albany: SUNY Press, 1999), 13–14. For a critic to resort to invoking things like "black holes" and "fractals" is not a sign of communal trust. Fractal reading resembles an atomization and renetworking, a mushroom cloud impersonating time and tradition. Paul Grimstad has pointed out to me that, a propos the "J.," one would have to add to the *instance* of this initial the virtual father of military uses of atomic fission and "submolecular tearing," *J.* Robert Oppenheimer.

5. There would seem to be in Miller an oscillation between the good J and the bad J. And also between two Ds: the exponentially expanding fields of Derrida's writings, upon which Miller routinely dwells and comments, and the truncated oeuvre and self-engorging aporias of de Man, to which a separate band of commentaries are devoted—as if between two alternative experiences for what "justice" means. In the inside narratives of "American" deconstruction, Derrida might be called with ample reason "the good," as if in contrast to "the bad" de Man—whose posthumous implosion withdrew the afflatus of charisma or aura and left untimely scars or foreclosures never quite accounted for. This space is given refuge and incubated in Miller's work—as it is explicitly in the essay on the zero. Perhaps de Man's occlusion has yet to be narrated, or evaluated as the design of a certain "de Man," or assessed as an opportunity that was, generally, mishandled or missed. Miller has speculated how the structure of de Man's persona and thought, and not the campaign to assassinate his legibility, might be called "allergenic"—a chemistry,

say, before which others feel their powers of personification compromised. If there is an odd antitriad here, sided by two Js (J., Jacques) and two Ds (de Man, Derrida), or if the three devolves to a spectral pair (justice, *justesse*), Derrida's naming of "Hillis the Just" suggests a co-optation of Miller, an inscription and claim.

6. We hear the word "con" resonate, as it does in Melville's *Confidence-Man*, with cognates of cognition and rhetorical performance.

7. For tentative turns toward a void default term designed to escape the totalizations of the "global," see Gayatri Chakravorty Spivak, *Death of a Discipline* (New York: Columbia University Press, 2003), specifically the third chapter, "Planetarity," 71–102. Also see Wai Chee Dimock, "Literature for the Planet," *PMLA* 116, no. 1 (January 2001), and Masao Miyoshi, "Turn to the Planet: Literature, Diversity, and Totality," *Comparative Literature* (Winter 2002).

8. "Ocularcentrism" might be one broad example of this collusion between aesthetic ideology and historical epistemes, between the bodily sensorium and the course of political co-optations. Long naturalized, it occludes the interdependence of the seen with archival templates and mnemonics. Its prosthetic version of the *eye* still links knowing to seeing (extending the Platonic *eidein*) in a faux immediacy, and it is programmed, still, on a model of the chase and eating recurring to prehistorical needs. It is also a program that generates identification and mimesis or aura, upon which the facade of mediacratic "democracy" self-cancelingly depends—where the telegenic import of a leader's face presents a necessary trance.

9. It has been possible for some, mutating out of the figure of teletechnicity that Derrida generates and explores, to reframe this domain as a biopolitical "state of emergency"—where categories such as the human and "life" or facticities such as standing reserves or mediacratic democracy find themselves anaesthetized before *coming wars of reinscription*. One can relate the implications of Miller's trajectory to the sort of calls for conferences or responses one encounters today that are not quite formulated or formalized—addressing a perceived impasse or collective black hole, as when one turns to the categories of the "aesthetic" as the site for a reprogramming of the senses and mnemonics themselves. As one example among others, a recent conference initially titled "The Catastrophe of the *Sensible*," asks after the intervention, today, in a site where the "sensorium" is as if set: "If the sensible [has] always been the object of wars and combat, today, a kind of aesthetic war has become the heart of war period, on which consists what is designated more or less naively as 'globalization'. . . . [A]esthetics becomes (towards the end of the 20th century) the nerve of the economic war that ravages the planet." (The text comes from

a call for papers issued by Bernard Stiegler and Georges Collins outlining points of intervention for a May 2004 conference at Cerisy.) Aesthetic ideology becomes the determining site of a "war" for reinscribing the mnemotechnics of earth—if by "the aesthetic" is understood the site where programs in what may be called the archive, or inscriptions, are phenomenalized, accelerate or resist collective or mediatized blinds. In the present example, "the aesthetic" seems broadly reconceived as implanted *sensorial programming*—holdovers from hundreds of thousands of years of prehistorical conditioning inadequate to the teletechnic era. This combination of faux historicism and the identification of catastrophically inscribed programs of the senses and sense gives way, today, to positions as if beyond mourning. Yet this sort of project remains in ways proximate to where something in Miller's practice *points*, in particular in his incubation of the late de Man.

THE AFTERLIFE OF JUDAISM: THE ZOHAR, BENJAMIN, MILLER
Henry Sussman

1. The notion of three core Abrahamic religions, Judaism, Christianity, and Islam, is a conceptual matrix and platform that Derrida uses to culturally far-reaching effects in his writings on religion of the past three decades. This construct reminds us that the major Western religions, studied from a rigorous philosophical point of view, are in a far more intimate exchange and communication than the history of religious persecutions, expulsions, and genocide would allow us to suspect. For some of Derrida's major writings in this sphere, see his *Acts of Religion*, ed. Gil Anidjar (New York: Routledge, 2002); also, *On the Name*, trans. Thomas Dutoit (Stanford, Calif.: Stanford University Press, 1995). Also see Hent de Vries, *Philosophy and the Turn to Religion* (Baltimore: Johns Hopkins University Press, 1999).

2. A useful overview of Jewish positions on the afterlife is to be found in "The Domain of Heaven and the Domain of Hell," a chapter in Ben Zion Bokser, *Judaism: Profile of a Faith* (New York: Alfred A. Knopf, 1963), 131–60.

3. My own efforts to come to some productive terms with modernity are contained in *The Aesthetic Contract: Statutes of Art and Intellectual Work in Modernity* (Stanford, Calif.: Stanford University Press, 1997).

4. Among the many contributions furnished by Derrida's writings on Western religion is a full extrapolation of the otherworldly, spectral, abyssal, ghostly, and uncanny constructs and figures, including the revenant appearing in this very paragraph, upon which the edifice of the Abrahamic religions literally stands. Derrida places this sometimes downright flaky underside to our canonical faiths in full relief, and this in turn allows us to question their claim to have initiated an age of rationality, principle, and disinterest in religion and

the communities of Judeo-Christianity and Islam. Derrida's highly nuanced recognition of the spectral dimension of the core Western religions has helped me instrumentally in discerning the traits of the Jewish afterlife as it is staged in the Zohar. See Jacques Derrida, *Acts of Religion*, 62, 83–84, 87, 91–92, 100, 141, 151, 191, 198–203, 208, 210, 213–18, 222–23, 252–53, 258–59, 276–79, 296, 382, 384, 387, 399, 405, 413.

5. In sheer scholarly terms, Gershom Scholem's annotations and elucidations are indispensable to any approach to the Kabbalah. The fact that he was an intimate and lifelong friend of Benjamin's, having met him in 1912, at the age of seventeen, means that there is an important imaginary confluence of their views, even though their opinions diverged on many essential theological points. This citation, as well as the others that are so helpful to me in launching the present exploration, comes from Scholem's *Kabbalah* (New York: Meridian, 1978). The abbreviation *K* refers to this edition.

6. I have explored the Talmud's status as a multiregister text, above all in relation to Benjamin's *Arcades Project*, but also in conjunction with Derrida's *Glas*, in "Between the Registers: The Allegory of Space in Benjamin's Arcades Project," in *Benjamin Now: Critical Encounters with The Arcades Project*, *boundary 2* 30 (2003): 169–90.

7. J. Hillis Miller, "Border Crossings, Translating Theory: Ruth," in *Topographies* (Stanford, Calif.: Stanford University Press, 1995), 336.

8. I hope I can be forgiven for appropriating a highly suggestive term of Maurice Blanchot's, one that has intrigued me for a long time, and giving it a more crassly historical deployment than he would likely countenance. "The Limit-Experience" is the title of an extended essay taking up almost half of *The Infinite Conversation*, trans. Susan Hanson (Minneapolis: University of Minnesota Press, 1993). A limit-experience is both the borderline experience of verging on the systematic boundaries of Western thought and culture and a compositional process setting limits to the broader ideological pronouncements of precisely that tradition. In his proposal of the limit-experience, Blanchot weaves together a precisely ahistorical constellation of writers whose articulations resonate off of each other. These writers include Heraclitus, Pascal, Nietzsche, Hölderlin, Kafka, Weil, Camus, and Foucault. The limit-experience, like Derridean deconstruction, then seems to entail a performance proceeding through all memorable theaters and scenes of cultural production. But the term nevertheless seems most resonant to me in characterizing the broad retrofitting and refitting of Western concepts and intellectual operations that coincided with European Romanticism. Do we have a way of considering the ongoing constellation of philosophical and literary interests indicating, if nothing else, the exquisite refinement of Blanchot's taste? Do we have a way, in the interest of literary periodization in the broadest sense, of

classifying the major elements in Blanchot's literary network as Romantics before the fact, Romantics in and of themselves? I find this a worthwhile intellectual exercise. It may help when we grope for general formulations regarding Romanticism.

9. Michel Foucault, *The Order of Things*, trans. Richard Howard (New York: Vintage, 1973), 54–58, 71–76, 117, 130–31, 137–38, 167–68, 203–11, 316–19, 346–38.

10. This is, admittedly, a theoretically "over-the-top take" on *tikkun olam*, the Hebrew liturgical phrase for the reform or reconfiguration of the world on messianic lines.

11. For the notion of the dialectical image, see Walter Benjamin, *The Arcades Project*, ed. Howard Eiland and Kevin McLaughlin (Cambridge, Mass.: Harvard University Press, 1999), 13, 70, 150, 317, 388–89, 391–92, 396, 406, 417, 459–70, 473–76.

12. "The Talmud has been compared to the sea; you never enjoy swimming anywhere until you've gotten used to the water." Robert Goldenberg, "Talmud," in *Back to the Sources*, ed. Barry W. Holtz (New York: Simon and Schuster, 1984), 168.

13. Bruno Schulz, *Sanatorium under the Sign of the Hourglass*, trans. Celina Wieniewska (New York: Penguin, 1979), 117.

14. *Zohar: The Book of Splendor: Basic Readings from the Kabbalah*, ed. Gershom Scholem (New York: Schocken, 1963), 72–73. It makes all the difference to the present essay and intellectual exercise that Scholem selected and edited the slim compilation of Zoharic tales and elucidations, making my own extrapolations possible. The choice of texts in this slim volume is indeed selective: In English, it narrows the five-volume Soncino Edition down to less than a hundred pages. The folktales that Scholem included must have indeed enjoyed special resonance to the groundbreaking elucidator of Jewish mystical literature.

15. For a comprehensive and personally compelling account of this prayer, one entwining the pivotal aspects of the Judaic approach to death, see Leon Wieseltier, *Kaddish* (New York: Alfred A. Knopf, 1998), xiii, 4–11, 96–124, 264–95, 355–68.

16. The *Athenaeum Fragments* are a privileged site, one whose significance Benjamin fully recognized, for the theoretical working through of the poetic figurations of key philosophical issues explored, among different literatures, in Jewish mysticism. Benjamin's aspirations to an integration of Judaic images and narratives and German letters were not merely the stuff of wishes. They were founded on the hard data and solutions furnished by the likes of Fichte, the Schlegels, and their peers. See, above all, Friedrich Schlegel's *Lucinde and the Fragments*, trans. and intro. Peter Firchow (Minneapolis: University of Minnesota Press, 1971), 175–77, 191–98.

17. In *The Order of Things*, Michel Foucault earmarks analogical thought and imagery, capable of spanning vast distances of plane, realm, and category, a thinking not incompatible with the author(s) of the Zohar, with the *épistème* (or linguistically configured worldview) of the European Renaissance. This cultural moment is for him a domain saturated with radical similitudes. See Foucault, *The Order of Things*, 17–77.

18. See Gershom Scholem, *Major Trends in Jewish Mysticism* (New York: Schocken, 1961), 217–35; also, *On the Kabbalah and its Symbolism* (New York: Schocken, 1965), 130–53.

19. Given that Kafka did so much to dramatize and perform the twentieth-century cultural imaginary of texts and textually configured environments and institutions, it can be no accident that Deleuze and Guattari dedicated a book to his fiction and the philosophical notions that can be extracted from it. Two of Kafka's novels, *Amerika* and *The Trial*, and an extended late animal fable, "The Burrow," devote particular attention to the construction and performance of extended, interconnected, involuted, self-enclosing environments and architectures. Dedicated readers of Kafka, and of Deleuze and Guattari, owe much of their sense of a rhizomatic, schizo (that is, nonhierarchically) interconnected cultural landscape to Kafka's projections and imaginings. See Franz Kafka, *Amerika*, trans. Edwin Muir and Willa Muir (New York: Schocken, 1974), 4, 11, 41, 74–75, 108–10, 196–99; *The Trial*, trans. Edwin Muir and Willa Muir (New York: Schocken, 1974), 34–35, 63–67, 99, 116, 119–21, 142–45, 155, 213–14; "The Burrow," in *The Complete Stories*, ed. Nahum N. Glatzer (New York: Schocken, 1971), 326–28, 337, 339–40, 343–49. Deleuze and Guattari, above all in their "Capitalism and Schizophrenia" diptych, translate, in a Benjaminian sense, Kafka's images and tropings into a rhetoric of rhizomes and an architecture of "planes of consistency" and assemblages. For an introduction to this rhetoric, see Gilles Deleuze and Félix Guattari, *A Thousand Plateaus*, trans. Brian Massumi (Minneapolis: University of Minnesota Press, 1987), 3–18, 40–45, 49–57, 141–48, 208–27, 351–74.

20. For the Sefiroth, see Gershom Scholem, *Major Trends in Jewish Mysticism*, 204–15, 268–73; also, *On the Kabbalah and its Symbolism*, 94, 96–105.

21. Among many sites in Miller's discourse at which he eventuates at and lavishes careful attention on irony, see, for example, his *Versions of Pygmalion* (Cambridge, Mass.: Harvard University Press, 1990), 43–46, 59, 75–76, 90–93, 157–60. Miller's own intuitions of the privileged, if nuanced affinity between reading, writing, interpretation, and death—as negotiated by an elaborated rhetorical figure of prosopopoeia—reaches an apotheosis in this volume.

22. In the present sentence, I revert back to the "J" conference, which took place at the University of California, Irvine on April 18 and 19, 2003.

The senior scholars at the colloquium, which in this passage I reinvent as a Talmudic conference, were J. Hillis Miller, whose work the occasion celebrated and extended, and Jacques Derrida. It is in this sense that I figure Miller as Rabbi Yose and Derrida as Rabbi Eliyahu or Eli. (Derrida elaborates on this play on his name in "Ulysses Gramophone," in *Acts of Literature*, ed. Derek Attridge [New York: Routledge, 1992], 277). In a separate current project, *The Task of the Critic*, I explore the effect of occasionality on literary and cultural criticism over and against the commitments to a conceptual operating system and to particular texts, shaping, respectively, philosophical discourse and what has constituted itself as "close reading."

23. I refer here of course to the character of the Angelus Novus, culled from Klee's drawings (and once owned by Benjamin), a figure for the cultural redemption attainable only through the "tasks" of close exegesis, translation, collecting, dedicated archival work, and even urban cruising. This image, as its possibility, rises to its full aura and eloquence in section IX of the "On the Concept of History," in *Selected Writings*, vol. 4, ed. Howard Eiland and Michael W. Jennings (Cambridge, Mass.: Harvard University Press, 2003), 392–93.

24. Rochelle Tobias's recent work on the figure of the stars in the work of Paul Celan is highly suggestive as to the culmination of this "line of imagery." See her forthcoming *Stars, Stones, and Bodies in the Poetry of Paul Celan* (Baltimore: Johns Hopkins University Press, 2005).

25. Georg Büchner, *Complete Works and Letters*, trans. Henry J. Schmidt, The German Library 23 (New York, Continuum, 1986), 161.

26. This is my translation of a passage from Paul Celan, "Gespräch im Gebirg," in *Gesammelte Werke*, vol. 3 (Frankfurt am Main: Suhrkamp, 1983), 169.

27. Benjamin, *The Arcades Project*, 25–26, 64–65, 112–19, 337, 339–40, 343, 347–49, 357, 462–64, 466, 470, 475, 540.

28. Walter Benjamin, "Goethe's *Die Wahlverwandschaften*," in *Selected Writings*, vol. 1, ed. Marcus Bullock and Michael W. Jennings (Cambridge, Mass.: Harvard University Press, 1997), 354–56, 357n.

29. Benjamin, *Selected Writings*, 4:397.

30. Ibid., 4:331.

31. Ibid.

32. Ibid.

ON THE LINE

Alexander Gelley

1. J. Hillis Miller, *Ariadne's Thread: Story Lines* (New Haven: Yale University Press, 1992).

2. The others are *Illustration* (Cambridge, Mass.: Harvard University Press, 1992), *Topographies* (Stanford, Calif.: Stanford University Press, 1995), and *Reading Narrative* (Norman: University of Oklahoma Press, 1998).

3. Gérard Genette, *Narrative Discourse: An Essay in Method*, trans. Jane E. Lewin (Ithaca, N.Y.: Cornell University Press, 1980).

4. Northrop Frye, *Anatomy of Criticism* (Princeton, N.J.: Princeton University Press, 1957), 16.

5. Jacques Derrida, "La Loi du genre/The Law of Genre," *Glyph: Textual Studies* 7 (1980). Also in *Acts of Literature*, ed. Derek Attridge (New York: Routledge, 1992).

6. Originally published as part of *Figures III* (Paris: Seuil, 1972). The French title underscores not only that discourse is a component of narrative, but also that a certain discourse is generated by narrative.

7. See *Ariadne's Thread*, 14. The confusion and fusion of the names and myths of Ariadne and Arachne are further developed by Miller in a chapter of *Reading Narrative*, "Ariachne's Broken Woof," 129–45.

8. "The Storyteller: Reflections on the Works of Nikolai Leskov," in Walter Benjamin, *Illuminations*, trans. Harry Zohn (New York: Schocken, 1969). I am aware that the German title "Der Erzähler" supports Benjamin's focus on the narrating instance. While *Erzählung* can be translated as both (a) "narrative" and (a) "story," none of the forms of the German word exactly correspond to the conceptual sense of the English "narrative."

9. *Aristotle on Poetics*, trans. Seth Benardete and Michael Davis (South Bend, Ind.: St. Augustine's Press, 2002), 24.

10. See also the discussion of entanglement (*desis*) and unraveling (*lusis*) in chapter 18 of the *Poetics*. Of these Michael Davis comments, "Now there is no question that in some sense Aristotle means us to take this account linearly or temporally. There is a part of any tragedy in which things are put together and a part in which they are taken apart. At the same time, the key terms of the account all allow for an alternative interpretation. . . . Now, if *lusis* meant analysis or interpretation here, Aristotle would be saying that tragedies ought to supply their own analyses." *Aristotle on Poetics*, xxvii.

11. Yuri Lotman cites Tomashevsky on this: "We use the word *fabula* to describe the sum total of interconnected events communicated by the work. . . . In opposition to the *fabula* stands the *sujet*, i.e. the same events, but in the form of their *exposition*, the order in which they are communicated in the work, the system of connections through which we are informed of the events in the work." *The Structure of the Artistic Text*, Michigan Slavic Contributions no. 7 (Ann Arbor: The University of Michigan Press, 1977), 232.

12. Bernard Dupriez, *A Dictionary of Literary Devices, Gradus, A–Z*, trans. Albert W. Halsall (Toronto: University of Toronto Press, 1991), 93.

13. Jacques Derrida, "White Mythology: Metaphor in the Text of Philosophy," in *Margins of Philosophy*, trans. Alan Bass (Chicago: University of Chicago Press, 1982), 252.

14. Paul de Man, *The Resistance to Theory* (Minneapolis: University of Minnesota Press, 1986), 15.

15. I realize this question cannot be easily settled. De Man's tenet, "any narrative is primarily the allegory of its own reading" (*Allegories of Reading* [New Haven: Yale University Press, 1979], 76), may be taken either as a blanket rejection of any metatheory or as a challenge to invent new ones.

16. De Man discusses *S/Z* in an essay on Barthes written in the early 1970s, but does not consider its contribution to narrative theory to be as important as that of Greimas, Genette, or Todorov, "though it is only fair to point out," de Man comments, "its avowed indebtedness to him." "Roland Barthes and the Limits of Structuralism," in *Romanticism and Contemporary Criticism*, ed. E. S. Burt et al. (Baltimore: Johns Hopkins University Press, 1993), 165.

17. Neil Hertz, *George Eliot's Pulse* (Stanford, Calif.: Stanford University Press, 2003).

18. Neil Hertz, *The End of the Line: Essays on Psychoanalysis and the Sublime* (New York: Columbia University Press, 1985), 218.

19. Claudia Brodsky Lacour, *Lines of Thought: Discourse, Architectonics, and the Origin of Modern Philosophy* (Durham: Duke University Press, 1996).

20. The act of architectural drawing that Descartes develops in the *Discours* is, as Brodsky Lacour puts it, a "hybrid 'thought' of the act of nonfigural delineation . . . a structure in which conception is . . . identical with manifestation" (ibid., 36–37).

21. "The Second Meditation will pose the question, 'but how much time' is the temporality of the certainty, the intuition of 'je'? . . . and answer that question in the terms of the temporality of thought given in the *Discours*: 'as long as I think'" (ibid., 97).

22. Miller, *Reading Narrative*, 149.

WAR ON TERROR
Marc Redfield

1. Bob Woodward, *Bush at War* (New York: Simon and Schuster, 2002), 46.

2. Bush's first words to Dick Cheney on the morning of September 11, according to Woodward, were "We're at war" (ibid., 17). Sentences about being at war were drafted for Bush for his evening statement on September 11. Wanting a more reassuing message, the president ordered them struck out, even though the phrase "reflected what Bush had been saying all day to the NSC [National Security Council] and his staff" (ibid., 30). A day later, however, in his 11 A.M. news briefing on September 12, Bush resurrected the

elided sentences: "The deliberate and deadly attacks which were carried out yesterday against our country were more than acts of terror. They were acts of war." Cited in ibid., 45.

3. Jean-Luc Nancy, "War, Law, Sovereignty—Techné," in *Rethinking Technologies*, ed. Verena Andermatt Conley (Minneapolis: University of Minnesota Press, 1993), 29, italics in the original.

4. Walter Benjamin, "Kritik der Gewalt," *Gesammelte Schriften*, ed. Rolf Tiedemann and Hermann Schweppenhäuser (Frankfurt: Suhrkamp, 1977), vol. 2.1, 179–203. For the English translation see "Critique of Violence," in *Reflections: Essays, Aphorisms, Autobiographical Writings*, trans. Edmund Jephcott (New York: Schocken Books, 1978), 277–300.

5. The quotation is attributed to a suspect in the Bali bombing of October 2002, as reported by the *New York Times*: "At least one suspect has said that the Bali attacks were meant to hurt 'America and its allies because they are international terrorists'" ("Indonesia Bombing Kills At Least 10 in Midday Attack," *New York Times*, Wednesday, August 6, 2003, A1). Although I don't pretend to have conducted a proper empirical survey of contemporary usage, my sense is that one almost never encounters the words "terrorism" or "terrorist" being used as affirmative labels by contributors to the mainstream media.

6. The allusion here of course is to Carl Schmitt's epigrammatic definition of sovereignty in the opening sentence of *Politische Theologie*: "Sovereign is he who decides on the exception." *Politische Theologie: Vier Kapitel zur Lehre von der Souveränität* (1922; Munich: Duncker and Humbolt, 1996). For the English translation, see *Political Theology: Four Chapters on the Concept of Sovereignty*, trans. George Schwab (Cambridge, Mass.: MIT Press, 1985).

7. Immanuel Kant, "Zum ewigen Frieden. Ein philosophischer Entwurf" (1795), in *Schriften zur Anthropologie, Geschichtsphilosophie, Politik, und Pädagogik* 1, vol. 11 of *Werkausgabe*, ed. Wilhelm Weischedel (Frankfurt: Suhrkamp, 1977), 191–251.

8. Bush's statement comes from a speech on September 20, 2001, as cited in Woodward, *Bush at War*, 108. For the remarks by Cheney and Rumsfeld, my source is "After the Attacks: The White House; Bush Warns of a Wrathful, Shadowy and Inventive War," *New York Times*, Monday, September 17, 2001, A2. Bush's characterization of the war on terror as a "crusade" (a pseudogaffe that was, of course, also a message to his religious base) dates from September 12. "Operation Infinite Justice" was the original title of the Pentagon's Afghanistan operation, later retitled "Operation Enduring Freedom." The phrase "axis of evil," describing North Korea, Iraq, and Iran, was launched over the course of a presidential address on January 29, 2002.

9. See Walter Benjamin, "Die Waffen von Morgen: Schlagen mit Chlorazetophenol, Diphenylaminchlorasin und Dichloräthylsulfid" (1925), in *Ges-*

ammelte Schriften 4, 1.2, 473–76. Benjamin's speculations concern the intangible notion of a "front" in the case of sophisticated chemical warfare.

10. The War Powers Act of 1973 affirms the president's sovereignty insofar as he decides—at least to some extent—on the exception: "The constitutional powers of the President as Commander-in-Chief to introduce United States Armed Forces into hostilities, or into situations where imminent involvement in hostilities is clearly indicated by the circumstances, are exercised only pursuant to 1) a declaration of war, 2) specific statutory authorization, or 3) a national emergency created by attack upon the United States, its territories or possessions, or its armed forces" (War Powers Act, sec. 2. [c]). Bush had the right to respond in sovereign (although limited and local) fashion to the "national emergency" of September 11. The Bush administration subsequently, under the provisos of the War Powers Act, sought and obtained statutory authorizations for military action against Afghanistan (or more precisely against "those nations, organizations, or persons [the president] determines planned, authorized, committed, or aided the terrorist attacks that occurred on September 11, 2001, or harbored such organizations or persons") in 2001 and against Iraq in 2002.

11. The earliest appearance in the United States of the specific phrase "war on terrorism" that my research assistant, Mary Powell, and I have been able to find is in the title of a *Newsweek* article from October, 1977, "The New War on Terrorism." But the notion of war overlaps with that of terror in much Vietnam-era war reporting (the Viet Cong are terrorists, purveyors of terror, etc.), while the first governmental agency focused on the "terrorist" threat per se and created in the wake of the Munich Olympics of 1972 was the Cabinet Committee to *Combat* Terrorism (my italics). There are many studies of the history of (the notion of) terrorism and of terrorism's link to mass mediatization. For a long-range perspective, see Jeffory A. Clymer, *America's Culture of Terrorism: Violence, Capitalism, and the Written Word* (Chapel Hill: University of North Carolina Press, 2003). For a study more focused on the 1970s to the present, see Melani McAlister, "A Cultural History of the War without End," in *History and September 11th*, ed. Joanne Meyerowitz (Philadelphia: Temple University Press, 2003), 94–116.

12. Brief of amicus curiae, American Center for Law and Justice, in support of petitioners in the matter of *Donald H. Rumsfeld, et al., Petitioners, v. José Padilla, et al., Respondents*, Supreme Court case no. 03–1027, 8.

13. The present essay is not set up to weigh this question—for my purposes here it suffices simply to ask it, as a way of suggesting the nonobviousness of the shape and extent of the "war on terror." The question obviously turns on the problem of what differences ought to be regarded as "fundamental" ones. That the Bush administration has indulged in more violent displays

of sovereignty than its precursors—withdrawing from the Anti-Ballistic Missile Treaty and the Kyoto Protocol; rejecting and undermining the International Criminal Court; unilaterally launching what a different U.S. leadership probably would have judged, on pragmatic grounds, an unnecessary invasion of Iraq; and so on—has certainly resulted in the temporary alienation of First World allies and has probably resulted in more death and destruction than previous post-Vietnam U.S. administrations can claim to have accomplished directly. Small ideological differences can have considerable impact on the world when so much power is wielded by a single government. The question remains, however, whether the Bush administration's unilateralism and bellicosity adds up to a "fundamental" shift in U.S. foreign policy. For arguments to the contrary, see the many books and other writings of Noam Chomsky, especially *Rogue States: The Rule of Force in World Affairs* (Cambridge, Mass.: South End Press, 2000). Jacques Derrida reminds us that "as early as 1993, Clinton, after coming to power, in effect inaugurated the politics of retaliation and sanction against rogue states by declaring in an address to the United Nations that his country would make use whenever it deemed it appropriate of article 51, that is, of the article of exception, and that the United States would act 'multilaterally when possible, but unilaterally when necessary.'" *Rogues: Two Essays on Reason*, trans. Pascale-Anne Brault and Michael Naas (Stanford: Stanford University Press, 2005), 103. (Article 51 recognizes a state's right to defend itself if attacked.)

14. J. L. Austin, *How to Do Things With Words*, 2d ed., ed. J. O. Urmson and Marina Sbisà (Oxford: Oxford University Press, 1980), 21.

15. I cannot, of course, even begin to suggest in a footnote the ramifications of the Bush administration's actions (to remain only within that context) over the last couple of years. Perhaps it may be noted that the legal consequences of Bush's pronouncements are of particular interest for present purposes, since one is able to observe first-hand the transformation of an ambiguous figure (the "declaration" of war on terror) and a complex political process (the Congress's granting of the president's right to perform certain military actions, etc.) into a literal affirmation of presidential "wartime powers" in the courts. (For one relatively restrained example among many, see the arguments before the Supreme Court in *Rasul et al. v. Bush, President of the United States, et al.* [no. 03–334; argued April 20, 2004; decided June 28, 2004], particularly Justice Scalia's dissent. For more full-throated affirmations of the president's near-infinite wartime powers, see the American Center for Law and Justice's brief of amicus curiae, cited earlier, for the Supreme Court case *Donald H. Rumsfeld et al., Petitioners, v. José Padilla, et al., Respondents* [no. 03–1027].) One might also recall here the notorious legal brief drawn up for President Bush by administration lawyers in March 2003, which argued that "in

order to respect the president's inherent constitutional authority to manage a military campaign," prohibition against torture "must be construed as inapplicable to interrogation undertaken pursuant to his commander-in-chief authority" (as cited in "Lawyers Decided Bans on Torture Didn't Bind Bush," *New York Times*, June 8, 2004). (The full document, which may be had on-line at various locations, is titled "Working Group Report on Detainee Interrogations in the Global War on Terrorism: Assessment of Legal, Historical, Policy, and Operational Considerations," March 6, 2003.)

16. J. Hillis Miller, *Speech Acts in Literature* (Stanford, Calif.: Stanford University Press, 2001), 28.

17. Miller's wonderful summary reads in part: "In Austin's examples Murphy's law is abundantly obeyed. What can go wrong does go wrong. People marry monkeys. Horses are appointed consul. British warships are christened the *Generalissimo Stalin* by some 'low type' who happens to come by. Someone is tempted not to eat an apple, as Adam was tempted by Eve to do, but to have another whack of ice cream, perhaps even more unhealthy than the Edenic apple. Patients in lunatic asylums are boiled alive. The purser rather than the captain tries to marry people on shipboard. Someone in a football game breaks the rules by picking up the ball and running with it, thereby inventing rugby. Monkeys utter the command 'Go!' Donkeys are shot. Cats are drowned in butter. Dogs or penguins are baptized. The command is given 'Shoot her!' A ferocious bull paws the field, ready to charge, or a thunderstorm threatens, and all you can do is shout 'Bull!' or 'Thunder!' People bequeath objects they do not own" (50).

18. Giorgio Agamben, *Homo Sacer: Sovereign Power and Bare Life*, trans. Daniel Heller-Roazen (Stanford, Calif.: Stanford University Press, 1998), 174.

19. Much of Agamben's thinking in this section of *Homo Sacer* bears the imprint of Arendt's incisive meditations on statelessness in *The Origins of Totalitarianism* (1951; New York: Harvest, 1994); see especially 266–302, where Arendt takes up the paradox that "a man who is nothing but a man has lost the very qualities which make it possible for other people to treat him as a man" (300). What Agamben will call "bare life" Arendt calls "natural givenness" (302), "the abstract nakedness of being nothing but human" (300). Agamben's claim to have discovered a difference between Aristotle's use of the words *zoē* and *bios* also bears some resemblance to some of Arendt's reflections in *The Human Condition* (1958; Chicago: University of Chicago Press, 1998); see especially 12–15.

20. Derrida, *Rogues*, 101.

21. The charade of the United States granting "sovereignty" to Iraq in the early summer of 2004 offers a good example of the way in which sovereignty exploits its own nominal self-curtailing—and also a good example of the wider

ambiguities and contingencies within which even a superpower is forced to operate (it being obvious both that the United States intended to continue to control Iraq as thoroughly as possible through military means and that the United States was not sufficiently in control of Iraq to make good political theater out of the "handover" of sovereignty). We may take time out for an anecdote. As reported by media (my source is the *Los Angeles Times*, June 29, 2004, A10, "A Brief Note Upends NATO Summit in Istanbul"), Bush was passed a note by Condoleezza Rice: "Mr President, Iraq is sovereign. Letter was passed from Bremer at 10:26 A.M. Iraq time—Condi." Bush scrawled on the note: "Let Freedom Reign!" The idea of freedom reigning rather than ringing is a nice touch, utterly unintended by the president, one imagines, but appropriate to the fictionality and ambiguity of Iraqi "sovereignty."

22. See *Rasul et al. v. Bush*, 5 (per the pagination of the case at the FindLaw Web site). The concurring opinion of Justice Kennedy specifies that "Guantanamo Bay is in every practical respect a United States territory" and that "this lease is no ordinary lease" (9). Justice Scalia's dissent insists, on the contrary, that "Guantanamo Bay is not a sovereign domain, and even if it were, jurisdiction would be limited to subjects" (14).

23. At times this excessive character of sovereignty comes through in Agamben's analysis, as in his discussion of Benjamin's notion (in "Kritik der Gewalt") of "divine violence" as a more than sovereign violence "situated in a zone in which it is no longer possible to distinguish between exception and rule" (*Homo Sacer*, 65), but even here, Agamben fails to emphasize the uncertain status of sovereign violence (which maintains "the link between violence and law even at the point of their indistinction," as opposed to divine violence, which is "the dissolution of the link between violence and law" [ibid.]). Throughout his study, Agamben can be said to downplay or repress the fundamental contamination afflicting concepts such as "sovereignty" or "bare life." His ungenerous remarks about Jacques Derrida's work and his misrepresentation of "deconstruction" (ibid., 54) are no doubt in this respect symptomatic.

24. Doyne Dawson, *The Origins of Western Warfare: Militarism and Morality in the Ancient World* (Boulder, Colo.: Westview Press, 1996), 13.

25. Paul Virilio, *Pure War* (New York: Semiotext(e), 1983), 26. Like so many voices within the modern Western tradition, Virilio places war at the origin of politics, although he does not make clear whether the city constitutes itself in war or whether war constitutes itself in the city: On the one hand, "the city is the result of war" (3); on the other hand, "when the State was constituted, it developed war as an organization, as territorial economy, as economy of capitalization, of technology" (4). Ever since World War I, Virilio suggests, we have been living in a permanent wartime economy, and ever since

the development of the possibility of nuclear war, we have been living in what Virilio paradoxically calls "pure war": an endless deferral of war by way of an endless militarization of life, all conducted under the shadow of a pure war that would be fought by machines ("Pure War no longer needs men, and that's why it's pure" [171]).

26. John Arquilla and David Ronfeldt, *Networks and Netwars* (Santa Monica, Calif.: RAND, 2001), 2, as cited and discussed in Samuel Weber, *Targets of Opportunity* (New York: Fordham University Press, 2005). Weber is interested in the complexities of "netwar" (a mode of conflict in which the combatants are organized into nets of horizontal relationships, without "heads" that can be targeted easily), but he points out that as long as *targeting* persists, an effort to limit and control indeterminacy still remains. Targeting is binary (you hit or you miss). Thus, Weber concludes, RAND-type speculations remain driven by a doomed effort to control the future and strip death of its terrors.

27. George Orwell, *Nineteen Eighty-Four* (New York: Harcourt, Brace, 1949), 5. "War is Peace" is one of the three slogans of the Party (the other two are "Freedom is Slavery" and "Ignorance is Strength").

28. "Even in a fully civilized society there remains this superior esteem for the warrior. . . . Hence, no matter how much people may dispute, when they compare the statesman with the general, as to which one deserves the superior respect, an aesthetic judgement decides in favor of the general. Even war has something sublime about it if it is carried out in an orderly way and with respect for the sanctity of the citizens' rights." Immanuel Kant, *Kritik der Urteilskraft*, par. 28, in *Werkausgabe*, 10, 187; *Critique of Judgment*, trans. Werner S. Pluhar (Indianapolis: Hackett, 1987), 121–22. The affects or themes of sublimity and glory can easily be granted pathetic or existential dimensions. Cormac McCarthy gives fine voice to a nihilistic, pseudo-Nietzschean version of war's sublimity in *Blood Meridian* in one of the terrible Judge Holden's speeches: "This is the nature of war, whose stake is at once the game and the authority and the justification. Seen so, war is the truest form of divination. It is the testing of one's will and the will of another within that larger will which because it binds them is therefore forced to select. War is the ultimate game because war is at last a forcing of the unity of existence. War is god." Cormac McCarthy, *Blood Meridian, or The Evening Redness in the West* (1985; New York, Vintage, 1992), 249.

29. I have studied the figure of "the body" at some length in *The Politics of Aesthetics: Nationalism, Gender, Romanticism* (Stanford, Calif.: Stanford University Press, 2003), 74–94.

30. Samuel Weber, "Wartime," in *Violence, Identity, and Self-Determination*, ed. Hent de Vries and Samuel Weber (Stanford, Calif.: Stanford University Press, 1997), 99. This very rich essay makes necessary reading for anyone

interested in the rhetorical and epistemological complexity of the notion of "war." The fact that, in an essay originally written in 1994, Weber was able to predict that "the isolated act of terrorism becomes the pretext for a war against it, in which cause and perpetrator tend to converge in the shadowy figure of the elusive enemy" (102) is a tribute both to Weber's keen-sightedness and to the overdetermination of the "war on terror" as a notion and figure.

31. See, for example, the speech of the Spartan king Archidamus in Thucydides' *Peloponnesian War*: A pragmatic soldier, Archidamus stresses that in war, no calculation can predict what will happen because "it is impossible to calculate accurately [beforehand] events that are determined by chance [*tas prospiptousas tuchas ou logo diairetas*]" (1.84).

32. The German *Krieg*, meanwhile, according to the *Kluge Etymologisches Wörterbuch* (Berlin: de Gruyter, 1989), derives from words meaning variously "stubbornness," "persistence," "exertion," or "striving." Definitions of war typically shuttle between invocations of form, order, and institution, on the one hand, and chaos and randomness, on the other. On the one hand, the confusion of war is often returned to the turbulent mystery of human nature: "Warfare is almost as old as man himself, and reaches into the most secret places of the human heart, places where self dissolves rational purpose, where pride reigns, where emotion is paramount, where instinct is king." John Keegan, *A History of Warfare* (New York: Knopf, 1993), 3. On the other hand, stressing the difference between war and other sorts of violence, scholars will stress the fundamental role of some degree of organization and goal-directedness: "At the risk of grotesque simplification let me suggest that 'organized warfare' can best be defined with one word. That word is *formation*." Arthur Ferrill, *The Origins of War From the Stone Age to Alexander the Great*, rev. ed. (Boulder, Colo.: Westview Press, 1997), 11.

33. Daniel Pick, *The War Machine: The Rationalization of Slaughter in the Modern Age* (New Haven: Yale University Press, 1993), 106.

34. Pick's reference is to Clausewitz's notion of friction (a complementary trope to the more famous Clausewitzian "fog of war"): "The conduct of war resembles the workings of an intricate machine with tremendous friction, so that combinations which are easily planned on paper can be executed only with great effort." Carl von Clausewitz, *Principles of War*, trans. Hans W. Gaske (Harrisburg, Pa.: The Stackpole Co., 1942), 50.

35. Jacqueline Rose, *Why War?—Psychoanalysis, Politics, and the Return to Melanie Klein* (Oxford: Blackwell, 1993), 16.

36. "The fog of war is quite literally noise, war's resistance to language, to objectification, to the code: both its problematic and its seductiveness, the limit of its intelligibility and the depth of its sublimity." Paul Mann, *Masocriticism* (Albany: State University of New York Press, 1999), 119. For a shrewdly

self-reflexive meditation on the figure of war in academic writing, see Mann's chapter "The Nine Grounds of Intellectual Warfare," 91–126.

37. Michel Foucault, *"Society Must Be Defended"*: *Lectures at the Collège de France*, 1975–76, ed. Mauro Bertani and Allesandro Fontana (New York: Picador, 2003), 46.

38. Michel Foucault, "L'oeil de pouvoir," *Dits et écrits*, vol. 3 (Paris: Gallimard, 1994), 206, cited in Allesandro Fontana and Mauro Bertani, "Situating the Lectures," in Foucault, *"Society,"* 282.

39. Geoffrey Nunberg, "The -Ism Schism; How Much Wallop Can a Simple Word Pack?" *New York Times*, Sunday, July 11, 2004, Week in Review, 7. I cannot vouch for the accuracy of Nunberg's claim about the relative frequency of use of these words in the media, but he is by profession a linguist and claims to have done some loosely empirical research: "In his speech of [September 11, 2001], Mr. Bush said, 'We stand together to win the war against terrorism,' and over the following year the White House described the enemy as terrorism twice as often as terror. But in White House speeches over the past year, those proportions have been reversed. And the shift from 'terrorism' to 'terror' has been equally dramatic in major newspapers, according to the search of several databases."

40. Edmund Burke, *A Philosophical Enquiry into the Origin of our Ideas of the Sublime and the Beautiful*, ed. James T. Boulton (Notre Dame, Ind.: University of Notre Dame Press, 1968), 40.

41. Edmund Burke, *Four Letters on the Proposals for Peace with the Regicide Directory of France*, ed. E. J. Payne (Oxford: Clarendon Press, 1926), Letter I, 87. Subsequent references to this text will be indicated by short title *Regicide Peace*, plus letter and page number. It should be noted that Letter IV (referred to by the *Oxford English Dictionary* as containing the first use of the word "terrorist" in English, as noted above) was in fact the first composed, in December 1795, acquiring its misleading Roman numeral because it remained unpublished until 1812. Burke published I and II together in 1796; III appeared posthumously in 1797.

42. The more rigidly political label "terrorist," as noted earlier, rapidly became a pejorative as it drifted away from its Jacobin meaning to signify, in the nineteenth and twentieth centuries, groups wielding "illegitimate" violence in opposition to standing governments. A few such groups have accepted and affirmed the terrorist label (the Russian anarchist movement of the 1880s, portions of the Zionist movement of the 1940s), but most have sought recognition under other names.

43. Maximilien Robespierre, "Séance du 17 Pluviose An II (5 février 1794)," *Oeuvres de Maximilien Robespierre*, ed. Marc Bouloiseau and Albert Soboul, 10 vols. (Paris: Presses Universitaires de France, 1912–67), 10:357. Here

and elsewhere, unless otherwise noted, translations are mine. In the original: "La terreur n'est autre chose que la justice prompte, sévère, inflexible; elle est donc une émanation de la vertu; elle est moins un principe particulaire, qu'une conséquence du principe général de la démocratie, appliqué aux plus pressans besoins de la patrie."

44. Xenophon, *Hiero or Tyrannicus*, 4, 5, quoted in the translation provided in Leo Strauss, *On Tyranny* (1963; Ithaca, N.Y.: Cornell University Press, 1975). Fear is the fabric of tyranny: The tyrant sees and fears enemies everywhere precisely because everyone fears the tyrant. (And thus, "as if there were a perpetual war on, [tyrants] are compelled to support an army or perish" [4, 11].)

45. Brian Massumi, preface to *The Politics of Everyday Fear*, ed. Brian Massumi (Minneapolis: University of Minnesota Press, 1993), vii.

46. "If we speak of the fear of emancipation from the fear-regime, we put the whole situation into a single phrase" (James as cited in Pick, *The War Machine*, 16). Pick explains: "A world of peaceful pleasure with no external conflict would be terrifying indeed," since there would be no distractions from internal conflict (16).

47. In the postmodern biomapping of the body, fear's locus of manufacture is now in paths between nerve cells in the amygdala. "Chemically speaking fear is close to curiosity" according to Paul Newman, *A History of Terror: Fear and Dread Through the Ages* (Phoenix Mill, U.K.: Sutton Publishing, 2000), xiv.

48. Sigmund Freud, *Massenpsychologie und Ich-Analyse*, in *Gesammelte Werke*, vol. 13 (London: Replika, 1940), 104–5; *Group Pyschology and the Analysis of the Ego*, in *The Standard Edition of the Complete Psychological Works of Sigmund Freud*, trans. James Strachey, vol. 18 (London: The Hogarth Press, 1955), 95–96.

49. On the irreducibility of affect to individual identity, see, in the field of literary criticism, Adela Pinch, *Strange Fits of Passion: Epistemologies of Emotion, Hume to Austen* (Stanford, Calif.: Stanford University Press, 1996), and Rei Terada, *Feeling in Theory: Emotion after the "Death of the Subject"* (Cambridge: Harvard University Press, 2001).

50. Martin Heidegger, *Grundbegriffe der Metaphysik: Welt—Endlichkeit—Einsamkeit*. In *Gesamtausgabe, II Abteilung* (Frankfurt am Main: Vittorio Klostermann, 1983), vol. 29/30; *The Fundamental Concepts of Metaphysics: World, Finitude, Solitude*, trans. William McNeill and Nicholas Walker (Bloomington: Indiana University Press, 1995), 66. The seminar is that of the winter semester, 1929–30.

51. I will have to defer an analysis of Heidegger's *The Fundamental Concepts of Metaphysics* to another occasion, but it may be remarked here that in this

important text, which substitutes a focus on boredom for *Being and Time*'s focus on anxiety, Heidegger repeatedly calls for terror as the antidote required by a degenerate society (a disturbing emphasis, in 1929–30): "The mystery [*Geheimnis*] is lacking in our Dasein, and thereby the inner terror [*innere Schrecken*] that every mystery carries with it and that gives Dasein its greatness remains absent. The absence of oppressiveness is what fundamentally oppresses and leaves us profoundly empty, i.e., the *fundamental emptiness that bores us*" (English, 164; German, 244, italics in original); "We must first call for someone capable of instilling terror [*Schrecken*] into our Dasein again. For how do things stand with our Dasein, when an event like the Great War can to all extents and purposes pass us by without leaving a trace?" (English, 172; German 255–56). Philosophy, for Heidegger, is an encounter with terror: "This is merely idle talk that talks in a direction leading away from philosophy. We must rather uphold and hold out in this terror [*Schrecken*]. For in it there becomes manifest something essential about all philosophical comprehension, namely, that in the philosophical concept, man and indeed man as a whole, is in the grip of an attack—driven out of everydayness and driven back into the ground of things. Yet the attacker is not man, the dubious subject of the everyday and of the bliss of knowledge. Rather, *in philosophizing the Dasein in man launches the attack upon man*" (21/31, italics in original). A close reading of the seminar would, I believe, show that, although Heidegger of course understands attunement as prior to subjectivity, a creeping voluntarism in his text weakens his analysis in ways that both map onto the temptation that National Socialism was to pose for his thought and vitiate the analysis of attunement precisely to the extent that the notion of "terror" in sentences like those cited above remains unexamined. Extreme boredom, in this text, reveals being (and is therefore the privilege of the human: the animal, poor in world [*weltarm*] cannot truly be bored). Does terror? Heidegger suggests that extreme boredom *is* terror, but perhaps it would become necessary to discover in terror an excess beyond the possibility of disclosure—to understand terror as both *Stimmung*'s condition of possibility and, in a certain sense, its ruin.

51. Søren Kierkegaard, *The Concept of Irony, with Continual Reference to Socrates*, ed. and trans. Howard V. Hong and Edna H. Hong (Princeton, N.J.: Princeton University Press, 1989). In Heidegger's *Fundamental Concepts of Metaphysics*, one must qualify, the animal is *not* capable of experiencing terror, insofar as terror is aligned with the extreme boredom that reveals being and with the wonder that is the life of true philosophy: "And only because he is thus mistaken and transposed can [man] be *seized by terror*. And only where there is the perilousness of being seized by terror do we find the bliss of astonishment—being torn away in that wakeful manner that is the breath of all philosophizing, and which the greats among the philosophers called *enthousi-*

asmos" (366); "Und nur weil so versehen und versetzt, kann er sich *entsetzen*. Und nur, wo die Gefährlichkeit des Entsetzens, da die Seligkeit des Staunens—jene wache Hingerissenheit, die der Odem alles Philosophierens ist, und was die Grössten der Philosophen den *enthousiasmos* nannten" (531). Heidegger's play on words is hard to translate: *entsetzen* means "to frighten," while the reflexive *sich entsetzen* means "to get a fright": one is human because one can *give oneself terror*, which is also to say, hold oneself open to terror.

53. For brilliant discussions of trauma as "the inability fully to witness the event as it occurs, or the ability to witness the event fully only at the cost of witnessing oneself," see the work of Cathy Caruth. I quote here from her introduction to *Trauma: Explorations in Memory*, ed. Cathy Caruth (Baltimore: Johns Hopkins University Press, 1995), 7. See also her *Unclaimed Experience: Trauma, Narrative, and History* (Baltimore: Johns Hopkins University Press, 1996).

54. Jacques Derrida, *The Politics of Friendship* (London: Verso, 1997), 173–74.

55. Jacques Derrida, "Autoimmunity," interview with Giovanna Borradori in *Philosophy in a Time of Terror: Dialogues with Jürgen Habermas and Jacques Derrida*, ed. Giovanna Borradori (Chicago: University of Chicago Press, 2003), 97. This observation is a common one in intelligent writing about the September 11 attacks. Slavoj Žižek writes, for instance, that "the true long-term threat is further acts of mass terror in comparison with which the memory of the WTC collapse will pale—acts that are less spectacular, but much more horrifying. . . . We are entering a new era of paranoiac warfare in which the greatest task will be to identify the enemy and his weapons." *Welcome to the Desert of the Real! Five Essays on September 11 and Related Dates* (London: Verso, 2002), 36–37.

56. Primo Levi, *Survival in Auschwitz*, trans. Stuart Woolf (1959; New York: Collier, 1986), 62.

57. W. G. Sebald, *On the Natural History of Destruction*, trans. Anthea Bell (New York: Random House, 2003), 53. The first two-thirds of this book is obtainable in the original German as *Luftkrieg und Literatur, Mit einem Essay zu Alfred Andersch* (Munich: Carl Hanser Verlag, 1999).

58. Jean Paulhan, *Les fleurs de Tarbes, ou, La terreur dans les letters* (Paris: Gallimard, 1941), 53.

59. Maurice Blanchot, "Comment la littérature est-elle possible?" in *Faux pas* (Paris: Gallimard, 1943), 97.

60. Perhaps a thumbnail sketch of Kojève's anthropomorphic reading of Hegel's master-slave dialectic is in order. In this narrative, the two subjects who are to become master and slave enter into a deadly fight for recognition. The subject who risks his life utterly becomes the master, and the subject who

doesn't becomes the slave. The master thus, as master, personifies terror—more specifically, the fear of death—for the slave. He forces the slave to work; working causes the slave to attain genuine, technical, mediate mastery of the world, as opposed to the master's immediate mastery; thus, ultimately, the slave becomes the master's master, the master of the world. Mapping this mythico-theoretical narrative onto history, Kojève claims that the modern state emerges in and as the Terror of the French Revolution. See Alexandre Kojève, *Introduction to the Reading of Hegel*, trans. James H. Nichols, Jr. (Ithaca, N.Y.: Cornell University Press, 1969), 3–30, 69.

61. Maurice Blanchot, "Literature and the Right to Death," trans. Lydia Davis, in *The Work of Fire*, trans. Charlotte Mandell (Stanford, Calif.: Stanford University Press, 1995), 313. I quote from Davis's translation. For the original, see *La part du feu* (Paris: Gallimard, 1949), 293–331.

62. Although Blanchot is certainly not offering a sociological account here, his and Paulhan's rendering of Jacobin ideology has historical purchase. On the importance of a certain ideal of communicational and representational transparency in Jacobin rhetoric, see Lynn Hunt, *Politics, Culture, and Class in the French Revolution* (Berkeley: University of California Press, 1984), especially 19–51. The effort to break absolutely with the past, Hunt suggests, invested language with "sacred authority" (26). Meanwhile, the effort to make democracy as immediate as possible in Jacobin circles was of a piece with the presumptive transparency of charged words ("patriot," "virtue," etc.), and a Rousseauist emphasis on sentiment and conscience. As Hunt emphasizes throughout her fine study, the Jacobin stress on transparency was equally an obsession with conspiracy. The Terror, she goes so far as to suggest, "followed logically from the presuppositions of revolutionary language" (46)—from the double fealty to, on the one hand, rhetoric and the power of the spoken word, and, on the other hand, the abolition of all rhetoric and mediation in the name of transparency.

63. William Wordsworth, *The Prelude: 1799, 1805, 1850*, ed. Jonathan Wordsworth, M. H. Abrams, and Stephen Gill (New York: W. W. Norton, 1979), 1850 version, 7, 527–30. Wordsworth probably drafted these lines between 1820 and 1828. For discussion, see James K. Chandler, *Wordsworth's Second Nature: A Study of the Poetry and Politics* (Chicago: University of Chicago Press, 1984), especially 15–16.

64. Edmund Burke, "Thoughts on French Affairs" (1791), in *Further Reflections on the Revolution in France*, ed. Daniel E. Ritchie (Indianapolis: Liberty Fund, 1993), 208; see also 213–15. In the final section of the present essay, a number of texts by Burke will be cited from Ritchie's collection: "Letter to Philip Francis" (1790), "An Appeal from the New to the Old Whigs" (1791), "A Letter to a Member of the National Assembly" (1791), "Letter to William

Elliot" (1795), and "A Letter to a Noble Lord" (1796). These essays will be cited by full title, with pagination to Ritchie. See previous endnotes for bibliographical references for two other Burke texts that are playing a role in this essay: the *Enquiry* (1757) and the *Regicide Peace* (1795–97). My references to Burke's *Reflections on the Revolution in France* (1790) will be short-titled *Reflections* and are to the edition edited by Conor Cruise O'Brien (New York: Penguin, 1986).

65. David Simpson, *Romanticism, Nationalism, and the Revolt against Theory* (Chicago: University of Chicago Press, 1993) 173. See also Neil Hertz, *The End of the Line: Essays on Psychoanalysis and the Sublime* (New York: Columbia University Press, 1985), for a trenchant analysis of the "resistance to theory" from the Romantic era to the present. Simpson, for his part, usefully associates the American academy's resistance to Paul de Man with a nationalist resistance to "radical cosmopolitanism" (180), which resonates with the Burkean resistance to the Jacobin threat. He also sees theory as associated with a dangerous leveling tendency in the form of a rationalist assault on custom and habit (see Simpson's discussion, 38–39). I provide an extensive analysis of de Man's role as the embodiment of "theory" in *The Politics of Aesthetics*, especially 1–42 and 95–124.

66. See my *Politics of Aesthetics*, especially 5–29 and 95–124, for a more extensive account of these issues.

67. Paul de Man, *Allegories of Reading: Figural Language in Rousseau, Nietzsche, Rilke, and Proust* (New Haven: Yale University Press, 1979), 151. See Terada's *Feeling in Theory* for a fine reading of this chapter and of de Man's work generally that emphasizes the degree to which de Man's work theorizes and thematizes emotion.

68. As Terada nicely puts it, "If we have emotions because we can't know what to believe (what texts and people are up to) as de Man suggests, then we have emotions even though we can't know which emotions we ought to have. If we truly *knew* which emotions we should have, we would no longer feel like having any" (*Feeling in Theory*, 89). The (self-defacing) name of that nonknowing for de Man, I think, is "fear" or "terror." De Man's work not infrequently returns to the theme of terror's uncertain ontology, which is also that of reading. In "Hypogram and Inscription," de Man characterizes Saussure's uncertain perception of anagrammatic pattern in Latin poetry as "a terror glimpsed": See *The Resistance to Theory*, 37. Improvising in "Kant and Schiller," de Man develops an extended riff on the sort of "terror" Kant might have felt when approaching the materiality of the letter—but again, the point is that this terror is not something we can claim to know anything about: "I don't think that Kant, when he wrote about the heavens and the sea there, that he was shuddering in mind. Any literalism there would not be called for.

It is terrifying in a way we don't know." *Aesthetic Ideology* (Minneapolis: University of Minnesota Press, 1996), 134.

The present essay is seeking to suggest that it is critically useful to think of terror as essentially linked to uncertainty. Hannah Arendt's version of the Rousseauist parable in *Origins of Totalitarianism* offers a cautionary instance: "the Boers," she claims, seeking an etiology for racism in South Africa, "were never able to forget their first horrible fright before a species of men whom human pride and the sense of human dignity could not allow them to accept as fellow men" (192; cf. 195, 197). This is a reductive moment in Arendt's brilliant book. It would be more critically useful, I think, to thematize racism (in this fictional scenario) as a further freezing whereby the "giant" of Rousseau is resurrected as the literal, and abjected, body of the other.

69. John Searle, "The Word Turned Upside Down," *New York Review of Books*, October 27, 1983, 77.

70. See Martin Heidegger, "Die Frage nach der Technik," in *Vorträge und Aufsätze* (Tübingen: Verlag Günther Neske, 1954), 13–44: "Steuerung und Sicherung werden sogar die Hauptzüge des herausfordernden Entbergens" (24). For the English, see "The Question concerning Technology," in *The Question concerning Technology and Other Essays*, trans. William Lovitt (New York: Harper Torchbooks, 1977), 3–35: "Regulating and securing even become the chief characteristics of the challenging revealing" (16).

71. Such is the thesis of, among others, Conor Cruise O'Brien, who in his intelligent introduction to the Penguin edition of the *Reflections* teases out links between Burke's conservatism and the complexities of Anglo-Irish identity: "his power to penetrate the processes of the revolution derives from a suppressed sympathy with revolution, combined with an intuitive grasp of the subversive possibilities of *counter*-revolutionary propaganda, as affecting the established order in the land of his birth" (81). As so often, one can go to Novalis for a rich epigram: "Many antirevolutionary books have been written for the Revolution. Burke, however, has written a revolutionary book against the Revolution."

72. Burke frequently claims that his principles are grounded in religion, and more specifically Christianity: "religion is the basis of civil society"; "man is by his constitution a religious animal" (*Reflections*, 186, 187). That latter formulation shades into the Burkean anthropological-pragmatic claim about religion: whether or not religion is true, it is natural and good that we have it. Religion like all else is both affirmed and rendered fictional.

73. Thus, because Burke's conservatism is all about mediation, in opposition to the immediacy of revolution and terror, his "aesthetic ideology" can take Coleridgean form as a celebration of the symbol: See, for example, Richie's neo-Burkean claim that Burke "symboliz[es] the Constitution as Cole-

ridge defines 'symbol' "—as the "translucence of the Eternal through and in the Temporal." Thus, Richie says, "the individual elements of the nation (King, Lords, Commons) participate in the unity of the Constitution without losing their identity" (xx), producing "a union of the spirit and the flesh" (xxi). For a more rigorous discussion of the similarities and congruences between Coleridge's organicist aesthetic of the symbol and Burke's political writing, see Tom Furniss, *Edmund Burke's Aesthetic Ideology: Language, Gender, and Political Economy in Revolution* (Cambridge: Cambridge University Press, 1993), 228.

74. One encounters the charged figure of the potentially self-erasing line throughout Burke's writings on the Revolution: for example, "duties, at their extreme bounds, are drawn very fine, so as to become almost evanescent" ("An Appeal from the New to the Old Whigs," 162). Sometimes anti-Semitism marks the threat of a dissolving border; see, for example, "A Letter to a Member of the National Assembly," in which the Jew is linked to pollution across borders and to forgery, housebreaking, and stolen goods (39). Mahomet is also mentioned as a prototype of the revolutionary (40–41).

AMERICAN LITERARY STUDIES AND AMERICAN CULTURAL STUDIES IN THE
TIMES OF THE NATIONAL EMERGENCY: J'S PARADOXES
Donald Pease

1. J. Hillis Miller delivered a series of lectures at Dartmouth College over a four-week period (from October 28 to November 18, 2004) on the topic "Literature as Models of Community." The lectures were entitled: "'We Were as Danes in Denmark': Wallace Stevens' Idea of Community," "Community.Alt: Jean-Luc Nancy's Congregation of Singularities," "Under the Glass Case: Anthony Trollope's Knowable Communities," and "The Vanishing Community: What's Awkward about Henry James' *The Awkward Age*?"

2. Virginia Carmichael has supplied the following elaboration of Kenneth Burke's notion of a justifying myth: "An explanatory narrative that achieves the status of perfecting myth serves to reconcile discrepancies and irrationalities while appearing to obviate public or official scrutiny of actual circumstances. Such a narrative becomes effectively monolithic and saturating, demonizing its opposite and canceling or absorbing all mediatory and intermediate terms and kinds of activity." *Framing History: The Rosenberg Story and the Cold War* (Minneapolis: University of Minnesota Press, 1993), 7.

3. I have drawn this formulation from the essay "New Americanists: Revisionist Interventions into the Canon," where I elaborate the importance of these works to the formation of the field imaginary of American Studies.

4. Robyn Wiegman and I have elaborated upon the myth-symbol school as an aesthetic ideology of the centralizing postwar state in the introduction

to *Futures of American Studies* (Durham: Duke University Press, 2002). Although I have replicated some of the major claims of that essay, a more nuanced discussion of this dynamic can be found there (16–21).

5. Ironically, the role that the national metanarrative played as a regulatory intertext for state policy makers was noticed most vividly after the Vietnam War had resulted in the debunking of its grounding mythemes. In "The Care and Repair in Public Myth," the lead article in a 1981 issue of the journal *Foreign Affairs*, the historian William McNeill recommended that revisionist historians reconsider their policies of demythologization because "[a] people without a full quiver of relevant agreed upon statements, accepted in advance through education or less formalized acculturation, soon finds itself in deep trouble, for, in the absence of believable myths, coherent public action becomes very difficult to improvise or sustain," *Foreign Affairs* 61 (1981): 1–13. Joseph Campbell pronounced a comparable complaint in an interview in *U.S. News and World Report* under the scare headline "Our Mythology Has Been Wiped Out by Rapid Change," April 16, 1984, 72.

6. John Hellmann, *American Myth and the Legacy of Vietnam* (New York: Columbia University Press, 1986), x.

7. These remarks condense the discussion of the role that poststructuralist theory played in the transformation of the field of American Studies that is more fully laid out in the essay "The Place of Theory in American Cultural Studies" in the 2003 volume of *REAL: Yearbook of Research in English and American Studies*, ed. Winfried Fluck and Thomas Claviez, 19–37.

8. In their introduction to *What's Left of Theory: New Work on the Politics of Literary Theory* (New York: Routledge, 2000), the editors, Judith Butler, John Guillory, and Kendall Thomas have described the conditions of this rift with considerable clarity: "this . . . leftist skepticism toward theory has sought to historicize the reading of literature, reintroduce the importance of context and intention, and interrogate the conditions of literary reception and influence. Whereas some argue that literature should remain cordoned off from social science and social theory, others are relieved that literary studies has moved toward a more active engagement with social issues, with race studies, practices of gender and sexuality, colonial space and its aftermath, with the interstitial spaces of globalization." *What's Left of Theory*, xi.

9. Eric Cheyfitz asserts that "in order to energize itself American literary study must take the form of American cultural studies that breaks decisively with the American exceptionalism that has constituted in one way or another the dominant form." "What Work Is There for Us to Do? American Literary Studies or American Cultural Studies," *American Literature* 67, no. 4 (December 1995): 843.

10. This paragraph initially appeared in an essay entitled "The Other Victorian at Yale," in *The Yale Critics: Deconstruction in America*, ed. Jonathan Arac,

Wlad Godzich, and Terrence Martin (Minneapolis: University of Minnesota Press, 1993), 68. Given my revaluation of the significance of Miller's intervention, I should probably now change the title of that essay to read "The 'Other' of the Other Victorian at Yale."

11. The first of these essays, "The Work of Cultural Criticism in the Age of Digital Reproduction" was published in *Illustration* (Cambridge, Mass.: Harvard University Press, 1992), 9–60. Hereafter the page numbers from this essay will be included in the body of the text. The second essay, "Literary and Cultural Studies in the Transnational University," was published in *"Culture" and the Problem of the Disciplines*, ed. John Carlos Rowe (New York: Columbia University Press, 1998), 45–69. A more recent and extended version appears as "Literary Study in the Transnational University" in *Black Holes* (Stanford, Calif.: Stanford University Press, 1999).

12. Miller cited the tendency of cultural studies scholars rapidly to scan the evident features of a cultural artifact in order to represent it as an exemplary case of the culture it manifested as evidence of their having become extensions of these new technologies.

13. Lisa Lowe has stated this paradox with characteristic brilliance: "on the one hand, institutionalization (of fields like Ethnic Studies) provides a material base within the university for a transformative critique of traditional disciplines and their traditional separations; yet, on the other hand, the institutionalization of any field or curriculum that establishes orthodox objects and methods submits in part to the demands of the university and its educative function of socializing subjects into the state." Lisa Lowe, "Canon, Institutionalization, Identity: Contradictions for Asian American Studies," in *The Ethnic Canon: Histories, Institutions and Interventions*, ed. David Palumbo-Liu (Minneapolis: University of Minnesota Press, 1995), 51.

14. In articulating the paradoxical logic that underwrites Miller's aporetic praxis, I have drawn inspiration from Thomas Keenan's wonderful discussion of paradoxical propositions: "Because one wants so much to say 'either-or,' to hold to the *doxa* that one must be true and the other false, the experience of the truth of the paradox forces the acceptance of the 'both-and,' the transcendence of the exclusion." In Thomas Keenan, *Fables of Responsibility: Aberrations and Predicaments in Ethics and Politics* (Stanford, Calif.: Stanford University Press, 1997), 144.

15. "How," Miller wondered apropos of such complicities, "can the culture of the Palestinians, the Kurds, the Croats, the Quebecois of Canada or the Catholics of Northern Ireland be preserved and productively transformed as long as they do not have territorial and national sovereignty?" "The Work of Cultural Criticism," 50.

16. "In the case of resistance to the dangers of nationalism, the aporia lies in the fact that all vocabulary for naming and bringing about such new, non-nationalistic kinds of group formation must be drawn from the nationalistic terminology that is being contested. The terms must be twisted to new uses and to new performative ends. That, as they say, takes some doing, since nothing is easier than falling back into essentialist or nationalist thinking." Ibid.

17. "But the work of cultural criticism," Miller explains, "can transform and then reinscribe these terms ["justice," "democratic equity"] in a founding gesture that is without precedent or ground." Ibid., 57.

18. Throughout this discussion of sovereign performatives, I have drawn from Judith Butler's *Excitable Speech: A Politics of the Performative* (New York: Routledge, 1997), especially the chapter entitled "Sovereign Performatives," 71–103.

19. Claude Lefort, "Human Rights and the Welfare State," in *Democracy and Political Theory*, 37–38, 51.

20. Miller, "Literary Study in the Transnational University," 33, 35.

21. See William Readings, *The University in Ruins* (Cambridge, Mass.: Harvard University Press, 1996).

22. The following remarks draw upon formulations from my essay "The Global Homeland State: Bush's Biopolitical Settlement," *boundary 2* 30, no. 3 (Fall 2003).

23. My understanding of the fantasy structure of war draws upon Renata Salecl's discussion of this topic in *Spoils of Freedom: Psychoanalysis and Feminism after the Fall of Socialism* (New York: Routledge, 1994), especially 15–19.

24. My discussion of the biopolitical settlement as well as my understanding of the state of emergency and the space of the exception is indebted to Giorgio Agamben's remarkable discussion of the relationship between forms of life and biopolitics, the internally antagonized concept of the "people and the Concentration Camp as the *nomos* of modern life." *Means without End: Notes on Politics* (Minneapolis: University of Minnesota Press, 2000). Agamben examines the transformation of politics into biopolitics through a reconsideration of Foucault's account of this mutation in *Means Without End*. Ibid., 3–14.

25. Agamben has proposed that the modern nation-state was organized out of a nexus that correlated a determinate localization (the land) with a determinate order (the state) as these are mediated by the state's rules for the inscription of bare life. But the state's localizations necessarily produce dislocated peoples whose disorderly movements exceed the political that would order these errant forms of life in a determinate space by way of juridical rules. Ibid., 19–20.

26. Jacques Rancière elaborates upon the importance of the phrase "the part of no part" to political contestations in *Disagreement: Politics and Philosophy* (Minneapolis: University of Minnesota Press, 1999), 1–60.

J IS FOR JUST A MINUTE: IT'S MILLER TIME WHEN IT SHIMMERS
Peggy Kamuf

1. J. Hillis Miller, *"Mrs. Dalloway*: Repetition as the Raising of the Dead," in *Fiction and Repetition: Seven English Novels* (Cambridge, Mass.: Harvard University Press, 1982), 177.

2. Paul de Man, *The Resistance to Theory* (Minneapolis: University of Minnesota Press, 1986), 11.

3. Miller, *Fiction and Repetition*, 187.

4. Virginia Woolf, *Mrs. Dalloway* (San Diego: Harcourt Brace, 1981), 3.

5. Miller, *Fiction and Repetition*, 187.

6. "And what is more let [the reader] try to imagine the hand that is writing [these pages]; if he saw it, then perhaps reading would become a serious task for him." Cited in "Death Mask: Blanchot's *L'arrêt de mort*," in J. Hillis Miller, *Versions of Pygmalion* (Cambridge, Mass.: Harvard University Press, 1990), 185. This is the last sentence of the 1948 edition of Blanchot's text.

7. But can one or should one even speak of a narrator, still less of a narrator who is a "she," in a fiction that proceeds, as Nicholas Royle has observed, as "a writing of distant minds, apprehensions of feeling and suffering in and of the distance, phantom communications, unconscious, absent or ghostly emotions, without any return to stabilized identities"? Royle asserts that it is "misleading, in the context of Woolf's work, even to talk about a narrator: it is not so much a matter of a telepathic narrator . . . but rather any identity that one might assign to a narrator would be inseparable from the movements it enacts. It would be more accurate to speak of a fictional narrative like *Mrs. Dalloway* in terms of its telepathic narration (as distinct from a narrato*r*). The novel is a telepathic network or tunnel-work." "The Telepathy Effect," in Nicholas Royle, *The Uncanny* (Manchester: Manchester University Press, 2003), 268–69. Curiously, this essay embeds, in a final note (n. 43, 276), its own uncanny and "telepathic" relation to Hillis Miller.

8. See J. Hillis Miller, *The Disappearance of God: Five Nineteenth-Century Writers* (Cambridge, Mass.: Harvard University Press, 1963).

9. As cited in Miller, "Fractal Proust" in J. Hillis Miller, *Black Holes*, and Manuel Asensi, *J. Hillis Miller; or, Boustrephedonic Reading* (Stanford, Calif.: Stanford University Press, 1999), 355.

10. On Miller's ethics of choosing and treating examples, see, in this volume, Jacques Derrida, "Justices": "Miller's exemplary justice consists of paying essential attention to the irreplaceability of the example" (p. 234 of this volume.).

11. Miller, *Black Holes*, 353.

12. J. Hillis Miller, "Who Is He? Melville's 'Bartleby the Scrivener,'" in *Versions of Pygmalion*, 177.

13. Elsewhere, Miller similarly insists on the compulsion that a fiction can induce in its commentators and likewise takes up the diversity of critical response as a key to the work: "The literature on *Wuthering Heights* is abundant and its incoherence is striking. Even more than some other works of great literature this novel seems to have an inexhaustible power to call forth commentary and more commentary. . . . The criticism of *Wuthering Heights* is characterized by the unusual degree of incoherence among the various explanations and by the way each takes some one element of the novel and extrapolates it toward a total explanation." J. Hillis Miller, "Wuthering Heights: Repetition and the 'Uncanny,' " in *Fiction and Repetition*, 50.

14. Herman Melville, "Bartleby, the Scrivener: A Story of Wall-Street" in *The Writings of Herman Melville*, vol. 9, ed. Harrison Hayford et al. (Evanston: Northwestern University Press and the Newberry Library, 1987), 13.

15. Jacques Derrida, "As If It Were Possible, 'Within Such Limits' . . ." in *Negotiations: Interventions and Interviews 1971–2001*, ed. and trans. Elizabeth Rottenberg (Stanford, Calif.: Stanford University Press, 2002), 357; "Comme si c'était possible, 'within such limits' . . ." in Derrida, *Papier machine* (Paris: Galilée, 2002), 303. This deconstructive analysis of the concept of decision is carried out at greater length in Derrida, *Politics of Friendship*, trans. George Collins (London: Verso, 1997).

16. For just two examples, see Gilles Deleuze, "Bartleby; or, the Formula," in Deleuze, *Essays Critical and Clinical*, trans. Daniel W. Smith and Michael A. Greco (Minneapolis: University of Minnesota Press, 1997), 75, and Philippe Jaworski, *Melville: Le désert et l'empire* (Paris: Presses de L'École Normale Supérieure, 1986), 271.

17. Miller, *Black Holes*, 479.

THREE LITERARY THEORISTS IN SEARCH OF O
J. Hillis Miller

1. Wolfgang Iser, "Auktorialität: Die Nullstelle des Diskurses," in *Spielräume des Auktorialen Diskurses*, ed. Klaus Städtke and Ralph Kray (Berlin: Akademie Verlag), 220; Wolfgang Iser, "Authoriality: The Zero Point of Discourse," partial trans. of "Auktorialität" by Ingo Berensmeyer, unpublished manuscript, 2. Henceforth identified as G (for German) or E (for English). I am grateful to Dr. Berensmeyer for providing me with this partial translation. Page numbers are those in my computer-file version, but these are of course arbitrary, depending on the format.

2. The section of this essay on Paul de Man is drawn from my "Zero," in *Glossalalia: An Alphabet of Critical Keywords*, ed. Julian Wolfreys (Edinburgh: Edinburgh University Press, 2003), 369–90. The other two sections have been published in slightly different form, with another essay, as part of *Zero plus*

One by the Biblioteca Javier Coy d'estudis nord-americans of the Departament de Filologia Anglesa i Alemanya Universitat de València. I am grateful for permission to reuse material from these other versions of my essay. I am also grateful for the opportunity to have tried out my ideas about zero at the "J" conference, as well as for the great intellectual and personal generosity shown to me by the participants in that conference, by the organizers, Dragan Kujundžić, Barbara Cohen, and by the wonderfully kind and hardworking student committee.

3. See Brian Rotman, *Signifying Nothing: The Semiotics of Zero* (Stanford, Calif.: Stanford University Press, 1993), and Robert Kaplan, *The Nothing That Is: A Natural History of Zero* (Oxford: Oxford University Press, 1999). Another helpful book on zero, not cited by Iser, is Charles Seife, *Zero: The Biography of a Dangerous Idea* (Harmondsworth, UK: Penguin, 2000).

4. Maurice Blanchot, "The Song of the Sirens: Encountering the Imaginary," in *The Gaze of Orpheus and other Literary Essays*, trans. Lydia Davis (Barrytown, N.Y.: Station Hill Press, 1981), 105–13.

5. Maurice Blanchot, "L'homme au point zero," in *L'Amitié* (Paris: Gallimard, 1971), 88; "Man at Point Zero," in *Friendship*, trans. Elizabeth Rottenberg (Stanford, Calif.: Stanford University Press, 1997), 74. Further references will be to page numbers only, indicated F (for French) and E (for English).

6. Wallace Stevens, *The Collected Poems* (New York: Knopf, 1954), 440, 443, 388.

7. Maurice Blanchot, *The Book to Come*, trans. Charlotte Mandell (Stanford, Calif.: Stanford University Press, 2003), ix. This note is not given in the French original, *Le livre à venir* (Paris: Gallimard, 1959). Further references to these volumes will be by page numbers only, E (for English) and F (for French).

8. See Roland Barthes, *Le degree zero de l'écriture* (Paris: Seuil, 1953); *Writing Degree Zero and Elements of Semiology*, trans. Annette Lavers and Colin Smith (Boston: Beacon Press, 1970).

9. Paul de Man, "Pascal's Allegory of Persuasion," in *Aesthetic Ideology*, ed. Andrzej Warminski (Minneapolis: University of Minnesota Press, 1996), 69, henceforth indicated by page numbers only.

JUSTICES
Jacques Derrida

1. Quoted by J. Hillis Miller in *The Disappearance of God: Five Nineteenth-Century Writers* (Cambridge, Mass.: Harvard University Press, 1963), 271. Further page references to this work will be given in the main body of the text following the abbreviation *DG*.

2. John 17:25.

3. Gerard Manley Hopkins, *De l'origine de la beauté, suivi de Poèmes et d'E-crits* (bilingual edition), trans. J. P. Audigier and R. Gallet (Seyssel: Editions Comp'Act, 1989), 116.

4. J. Hillis Miller, *The Ethics of Reading: Kant, de Man, Eliot, Trollope, James, and Benjamin* (New York: Columbia University Press, 1987), 2.

5. René Descartes, *Meditations on First Philosophy*, vol. 2 of *The Philosophical Writings of Descartes*, trans. John Cottingham et al. (Cambridge: Cambridge University Press, 1984), 19.

6. J. Hillis Miller, *Victorian Subjects* (Durham: Duke University Press, 1991), 95.

7. J. Hillis Miller, *Fiction and Repetition: Seven English Novels* (Cambridge, Mass.: Harvard University Press, 1982), 71.

8. J. Hillis Miller, "Border Crossings, Translating Theory: Ruth," in *The Translatability of Cultures: Figurations of the Space Between*, ed. Sanford Budick and Wolfgang Iser (Stanford, Calif.: Stanford University Press, 1996), 219–20. Also in *Topographies* (Stanford, Calif.: Stanford University Press, 1995), 323, 330

9. Miller, *The Ethics of Reading*, 2–3.

10. Miller, *Fiction and Repetition*, 72.

11. Miller, *The Ethics of Reading*, 102.

12. J. Hillis Miller, *Trope, Parables, Performatives: Essays on Twentieth-Century Literature* (Durham: Duke University Press, 1991), 29–30.

13. Ibid.

14. J. Hillis Miller, *Black Holes*, and Manuel Asensi, *J. Hillis Miller; or, Boustrophedonic Reading* (Stanford, Calif.: Stanford University Press, 1999), 139.

15. Miller, *The Ethics of Reading*, 43.

16. J. Hillis Miller, *Hawthorne and History: Defacing It* (Cambridge, Mass.: Basil Blackwell, 1991), 121.

Agamben, Giorgio, 135, 137–38, 142, 144–45, 147–48, 291n18, 292n22, 305n25, 306n26
Arendt, Hannah, 135, 145, 148, 291n18, 300–301n67
Aristotle, 15–16, 120–21, 147, 286n10
Arnold, Matthew, xvi
Augustine, Saint, 12, 65–74, 76–77, 275n3
Austin, J. L., 4, 30–41, 43, 45–50, 62–63, 133, 264n9, 269–70n3, 270n4, 271–72n9

Badiou, Alain, 11, 279n5
Bakhtin, Mikhail, 23
Barthes, Roland, 118, 123–24, 215, 218–20, 274n40
Baudrillard, Jean, 133
Beckett, Samuel, 212–13, 219
Benjamin, Walter, xvii, 77, 91, 103–104, 106, 112, 115–16, 120, 130–31, 168–69, 179–80, 283n16
Berensmeyer, Ingo, 211
Blanchot, Maurice, xix, 149–51, 199, 210, 215–21, 282–83n8
Bloom, Harold, 164–66, 175–76, 263–64n7
Brodsky Lacour, Claudia, 125–26, 287n19
Brontë, Emily, xvi
Browning, Robert, xvi
Büchner, Georg, 112–15
Burke, Edmund, 142–43, 152–58, 295n40, 301nn69, 71, 301–302n72, 302n73
Burke, Kenneth, 124, 160, 167
Bush, George H. W., 177, 182
Bush, George W., 129–32, 140, 160, 185, 188–92, 287–88n2, 288n8, 290–91n14

Carmichael, Virginia, 302n2
Castillo, Larisa Tokmakoff, 263n2
Celan, Paul, 112, 114–15
Cheyfitz, Eric, 167, 303n9
Clausewitz, Carl von, 141, 294n33
Cohen, Tom, xvi, xxi
Conrad, Joseph, 68, 71–72, 77–78, 252–53
Culler, Jonathan, 153

Deleuze, Gilles, 11, 265n9, 284n19
de Man, Paul, xix, 4–5, 8, 13, 84, 86–87, 90–94, 123–24, 152, 164, 198–99, 202–203, 210, 221–27, 263–64n7, 264n9 (Kujundžić), 264n4 (MacCannell), 279–80n6, 300nn64, 66, 300–301n67
de Quincey, Thomas, xvi
Derrida, Jacques, xv–xviii, xx, 4, 6–8, 30, 34–41, 43, 48–51, 68, 85–86, 96, 119, 122, 136, 147, 153, 164, 167, 204–205, 263nn1, 4, 263–64n7, 264n9, 269–70n3, 270n4, 271n1, 271–72n9, 276n10, 279–80n6, 281–82n4, 284–85n22
Descartes, René, 125–26, 238
Dickens, Charles, xvi, 21, 43–46, 48, 51–54, 60–63, 127, 263n2, 273n28, 274n41
Dupriez, Bernard, 121

Faulkner, William, 89–90
Ferrill, Arthur, 294n31
Fish, Stanley, 269–70n3
Foucault, Michel, 138, 141–42, 145, 153, 213, 284n17
Freud, Sigmund, 8–9, 12, 141, 146, 265–66n13
Friedrich, Caspar David, 112–13
Frye, Northrup, 118–19

Gallagher, Catherine, 56, 62
Gaskell, Elizabeth, 20–21, 27, 117, 127

Gaughan, Richard, 273n30
Gelley, Alexander, xvi
Genette, Gerard, 15–16, 118–19, 123–24
Goethe, Johann Wolfgang von, 112, 115
Gordon, Jan, 273n28
Greimas, A. J., 123
Guattari, Félix, 265n9, 284n19

Hardy, Thomas, 68
Hartman, Geoffrey, 164, 263–64n7
Hawthorne, Nathaniel, 260–61
Heidegger, Martin, xvii, 8, 146–47, 154,
    249, 296–97n50, 297–98n51
Hellmann, John, 163
Hertz, Neil, 124
Hitchcock, Alfred, 87, 89
Hopkins, Gerard Manley, xvi, 229–30,
    232–37, 239–45, 249, 257–60, 263n4
Hunt, Lynn, 299n61

Iser, Wolfgang, xix, 210–15

Jaffe, Audrey, 60
James, Henry, 25, 27–28, 70, 256–57
James, William, 146
Jameson, Fredric, 10
Joubert, Joseph, 116

Kafka, Franz, xvii, 68, 109, 219, 255, 257–
    59, 284n19
Kamuf, Peggy, xv–xvi, xx–xxi
Kant, Immanuel, 8–9, 12–13, 131, 139–
    40, 158, 257, 293n27, 300–301n67
Kaplan, Robert, 84, 211
Keats, John, 101, 123–24
Keegan, John, 294n31
Keenan, Thomas, 304n13
Keily, Robert, 273n30, 273–74n34
Kermode, Frank, 118, 123
Kierkegaard, Søren, 147, 212–13
Kojève, Alexandre, 298–99n59
Kristeva, Julia, 123
Kujundžić, Dragan, 263n1

Lacan, Jacques, 8–9, 12, 264n4, 265n8,
    265–66n13
Lefort, Claude, 305n21
Lenz, Jakob Michael Reinhold, 112–15
Levi, Primo, 148
Lévinas, Emmanuel, 245, 249
Lévi-Strauss, Claude, 215–16

Lotman, Yuri, 286n11
Lowe, Lisa, 304n13

MacCannell, Juliet Flower, xv–xvi
MacKay, Carol Hanbery, 272–73n24,
    273n26
Mallarmé, Stéphane, 215, 219
Mann, Paul, 294–95n35
Marin, Louis, 123
Marx, Karl, 217
Massumi, Brian, 145–46
McCarthy, Cormac, 293n27
McNeill, William, 302–303n4
Melville, Herman, 203–205
Miller, James Edwin, Jr., 159–60, 167,
    186, 189
Montaigne, Michel de, 212–14
Moore, Michael, 129–30
More, Thomas, 275n6

Nancy, Jean-Luc, 130
Nietzsche, Friedrich, 8, 122, 212–14
Nunberg, Geoffrey, 142, 295n38

Oberlin, Johann Friedrich, 112–14
Odom, Glenn, xvi, 264n9
Orwell, George, 140

Pascal, Blaise, 221–22, 224, 226–27, 233,
    259
Paulhan, Jean, 149, 151
Pease, Donald, xvi, xix–xx
Pick, Daniel, 141
Plato, 87
Poulet, Georges, 167
Propp, Vladimir, 15
Proust, Marcel, 6, 39, 68, 198–99, 202–
    203, 208–209, 215, 220, 251, 264n9

Readings, Bill, 188
Redfield, Marc, xvi, xxi
Ricoeur, Paul, 118
Rimmon-Kenan, Shlomith, 14, 23, 25–28
Robespierre, Maximilien, 143–44, 150,
    152–53, 158
Rose, Jacqueline, 141
Rotman, Brian, 211, 279n4
Rousseau, Jean-Jacques, 8, 12, 152–53,
    265n10
Royle, Nicholas, 306n7

Sadrin, Amy, 56
Saint-Just, Louis, 150
Saussure, Ferdinand de, 268–69n41
Schlegel, Friedrich, 106, 127, 223, 226
Schmitt, Carl, 288n6
Scholem, Gershom, 96–97, 102–104,
    106–11, 116, 282n5, 283n14
Schopenhauer, Arthur, 212–13
Schulz, Bruno, 104
Scotus, Duns, 240–43
Searle, John, 36, 153, 269–70n3
Sebald, W. G., 148–49, 151
Shen, Dan, xvi
Simpson, David, 152, 300n64
Sophocles, 16–17
Stevens, Wallace, 217–18
Stewart, Susan, 70–71, 73–74, 277n24
Sussman, Henry, xvi–xvii

Terada, Rei, 300n66, 300–301n67
Thoreau, Henry David, 168–69
Todorov, Tzvetan, 123–24

Torgovnick, Marianna, 19
Trollope, Anthony, 17–18, 21, 127
Tydale, William, 275n6

Virilio, Paul, 139, 292–93n24

Wagner, Richard, 212–13
Warminski, Andrzej, 221
Waters, Catherine, 272nn19, 21
Weber, Samuel, 140, 293n25, 293–94n29
Williams, Jennifer H., xvii, xx
Williams, William Carlos, 68
Wittgenstein, Ludwig, 4, 35–38, 41,
    264n9
Wolfreys, Julian, 263n1
Woodward, Bob, 129–30
Woolf, Virginia, 17, 199–200, 203–204
Wordsworth, William, 152–53

Xenophon, 144

Zarathustra, 212–13